A collection of masterful, sensual stories by Kou Yoneda!

NightS

Story & Art by Kou YONEDA

In the title story, Masato Karashima is a "transporter," a man paid to smuggle anything from guns to drugs to people. When he's hired by yakuza gang member Masaki Hozumi, he finds himself attracted to the older man, and what starts out as a business transaction quickly spirals into a cat-and-mouse game of lust and deception. In "Emotion Spectrum," a high-school student tries to be a good wingman for a classmate, with an unexpected result, while "Reply" is told from the alternating perspectives of an emotionally reserved salesman and the shy mechanic who's in love with him.

SUBLIME

Downloading is as easy as:

1

Login/Email
Password

LOGIN
REGISTER NOW
Forgot Password

2

PAY with **PayPal**

— or —

Pay Now with **amazon**
The Simple, Trusted Way to Pay

Digital Edition includes **BOTH**
Download-to-own PDF and
online viewing option.

3

View your purchase as:

DOWNLOAD-TO-OWN PDF

The World's Greatest First Love:
The Case of Ritsu Onodera
Volume 3
SuBLime Manga Edition

Story and Art by **Shungiku Nakamura**

Translation—**Adrienne Beck**
Touch-up Art and Lettering—**NRP Studios**
Cover and Graphic Design—**Fawn Lau**
Editor—**Jennifer LeBlanc**

SEKAIICHI HATSUKOI ~ONODERA RITSU NO BAAI~ Volume 3
© Shungiku NAKAMURA 2009
Edited by KADOKAWA SHOTEN
First published in Japan in 2009 by KADOKAWA CORPORATION, Tokyo.
English translation rights arranged with KADOKAWA CORPORATION,
Tokyo.

ASUKA
COMICS
CL^D_X

Printed in the U.S.A.

Published by SuBLime Manga
P.O. Box 77010
San Francisco, CA 94107

10 9 8 7 6 5 4 3
First printing, October 2015
Third printing, October 2020

 PARENTAL ADVISORY
THE WORLD'S GREATEST FIRST LOVE is rated M for Mature and is
recommended for mature readers. This volume contains graphic
MATURE imagery and mature themes.

www.SuBLimeManga.com

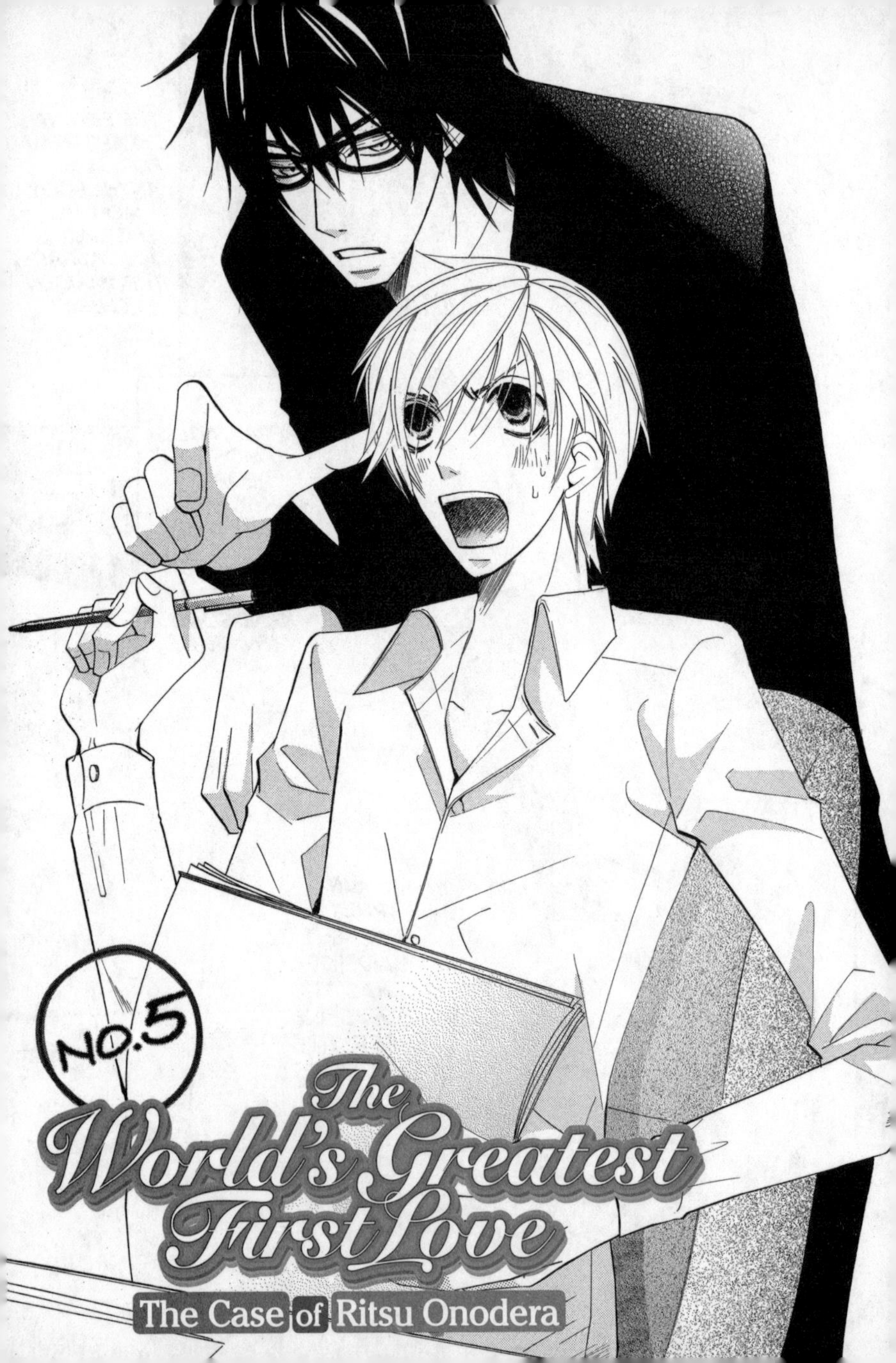
No.5
The World's Greatest First Love
The Case of Ritsu Onodera

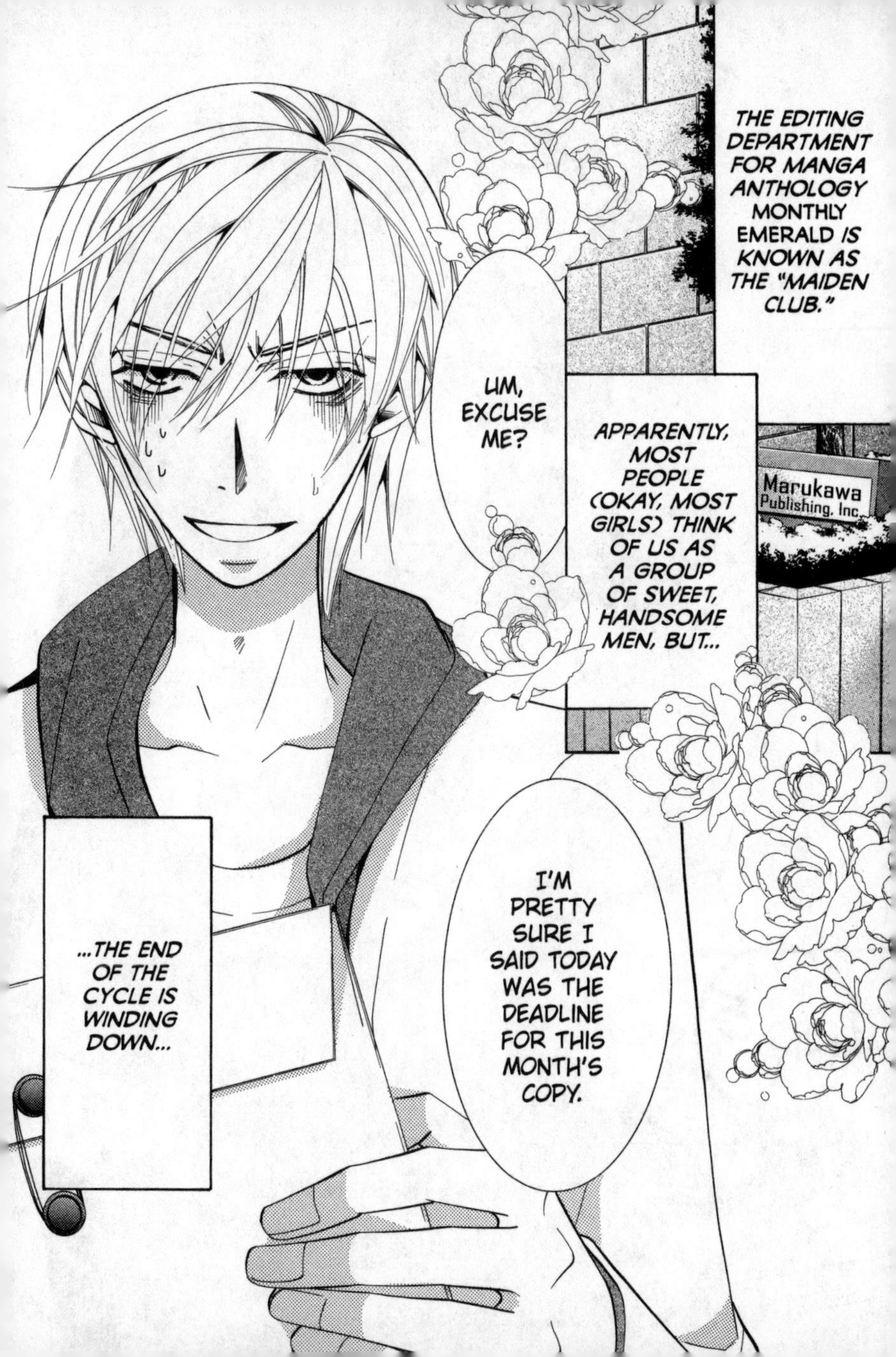

THE EDITING DEPARTMENT FOR MANGA ANTHOLOGY MONTHLY EMERALD *IS* KNOWN AS THE "MAIDEN CLUB."
Marukawa Publishing, Inc.
APPARENTLY, MOST PEOPLE (OKAY, MOST GIRLS) THINK OF US AS A GROUP OF SWEET, HANDSOME MEN, BUT...
UM, EXCUSE ME?
I'M PRETTY SURE I SAID TODAY WAS THE DEADLINE FOR THIS MONTH'S COPY.
...THE END OF THE CYCLE IS WINDING DOWN...

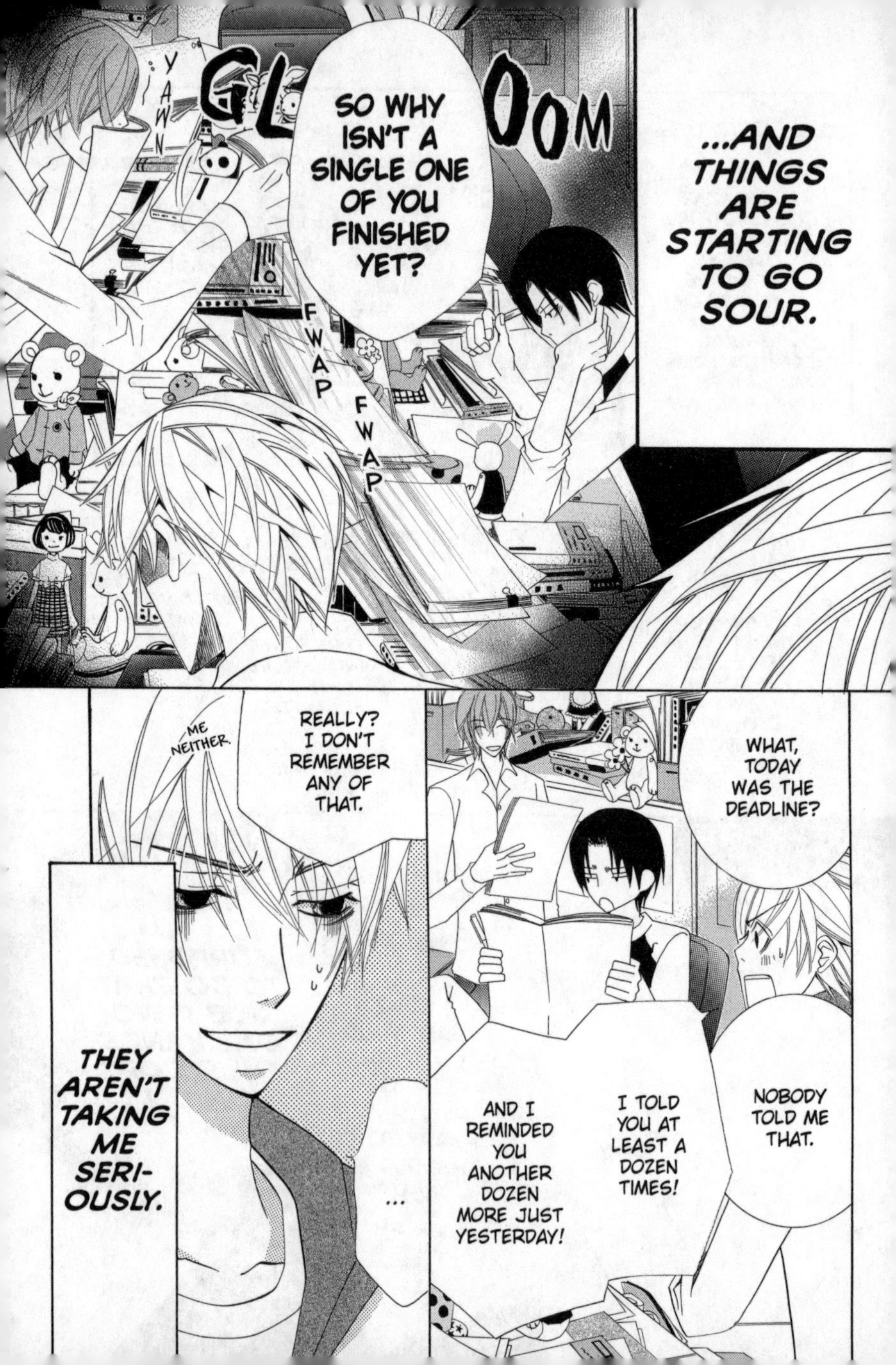
...AND THINGS ARE STARTING TO GO SOUR.
GLOOOM
SO WHY ISN'T A SINGLE ONE OF YOU FINISHED YET?
YAWN
FWAP
FWAP
WHAT, TODAY WAS THE DEADLINE?
NOBODY TOLD ME THAT.
I TOLD YOU AT LEAST A DOZEN TIMES!
AND I REMINDED YOU ANOTHER DOZEN MORE JUST YESTERDAY!
...
REALLY? I DON'T REMEMBER ANY OF THAT.
ME NEITHER.
THEY AREN'T TAKING ME SERI-OUSLY.

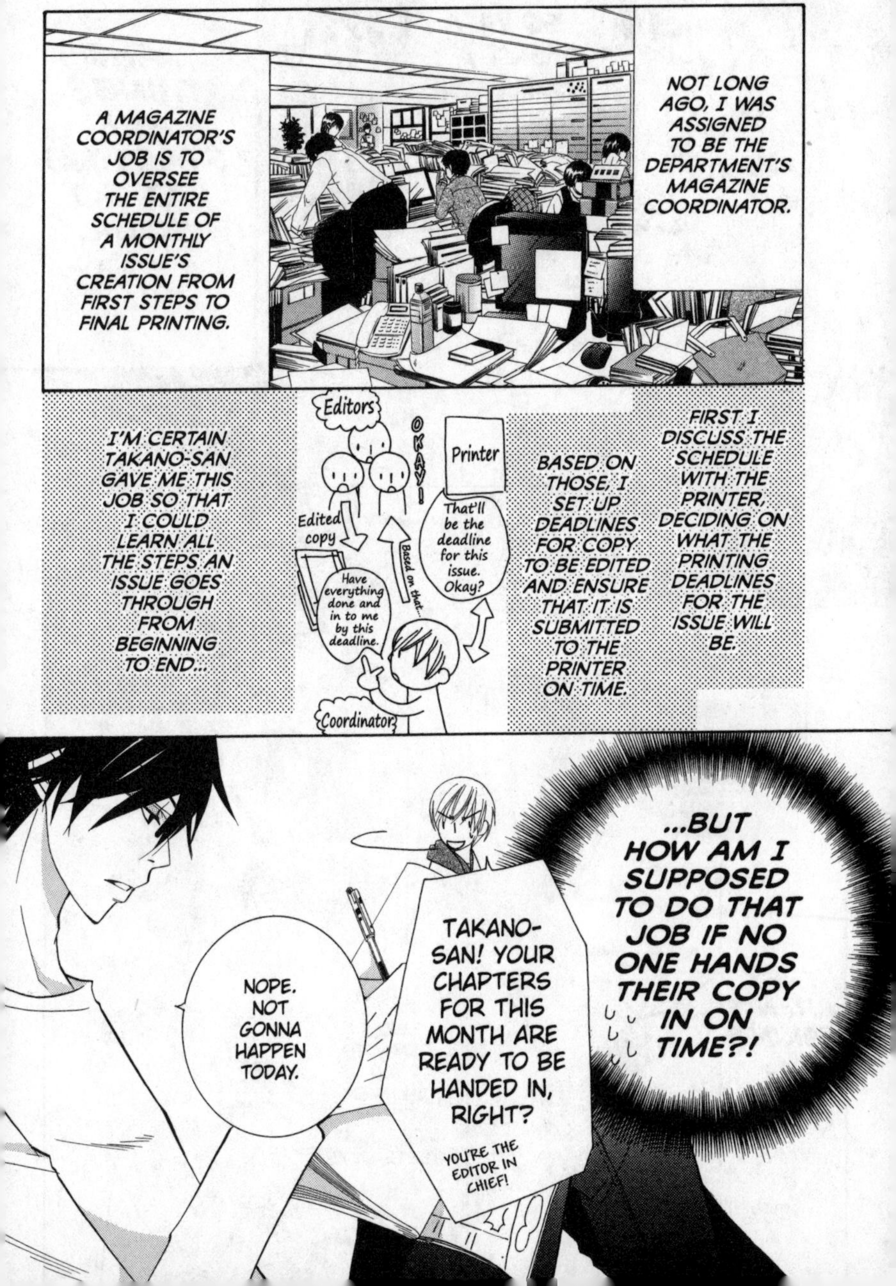
NOT LONG AGO, I WAS ASSIGNED TO BE THE DEPARTMENT'S MAGAZINE COORDINATOR.
A MAGAZINE COORDINATOR'S JOB IS TO OVERSEE THE ENTIRE SCHEDULE OF A MONTHLY ISSUE'S CREATION FROM FIRST STEPS TO FINAL PRINTING.
FIRST I DISCUSS THE SCHEDULE WITH THE PRINTER, DECIDING ON WHAT THE PRINTING DEADLINES FOR THE ISSUE WILL BE.
BASED ON THOSE, I SET UP DEADLINES FOR COPY TO BE EDITED AND ENSURE THAT IT IS SUBMITTED TO THE PRINTER ON TIME.
Printer
That'll be the deadline for this issue. Okay?
OKAY!
Editors
Based on that...
Have everything done and in to me by this deadline.
Edited copy
Coordinator
I'M CERTAIN TAKANO-SAN GAVE ME THIS JOB SO THAT I COULD LEARN ALL THE STEPS AN ISSUE GOES THROUGH FROM BEGINNING TO END...
...BUT HOW AM I SUPPOSED TO DO THAT JOB IF NO ONE HANDS THEIR COPY IN ON TIME?!
TAKANO-SAN! YOUR CHAPTERS FOR THIS MONTH ARE READY TO BE HANDED IN, RIGHT?
YOU'RE THE EDITOR IN CHIEF!
NOPE. NOT GONNA HAPPEN TODAY.

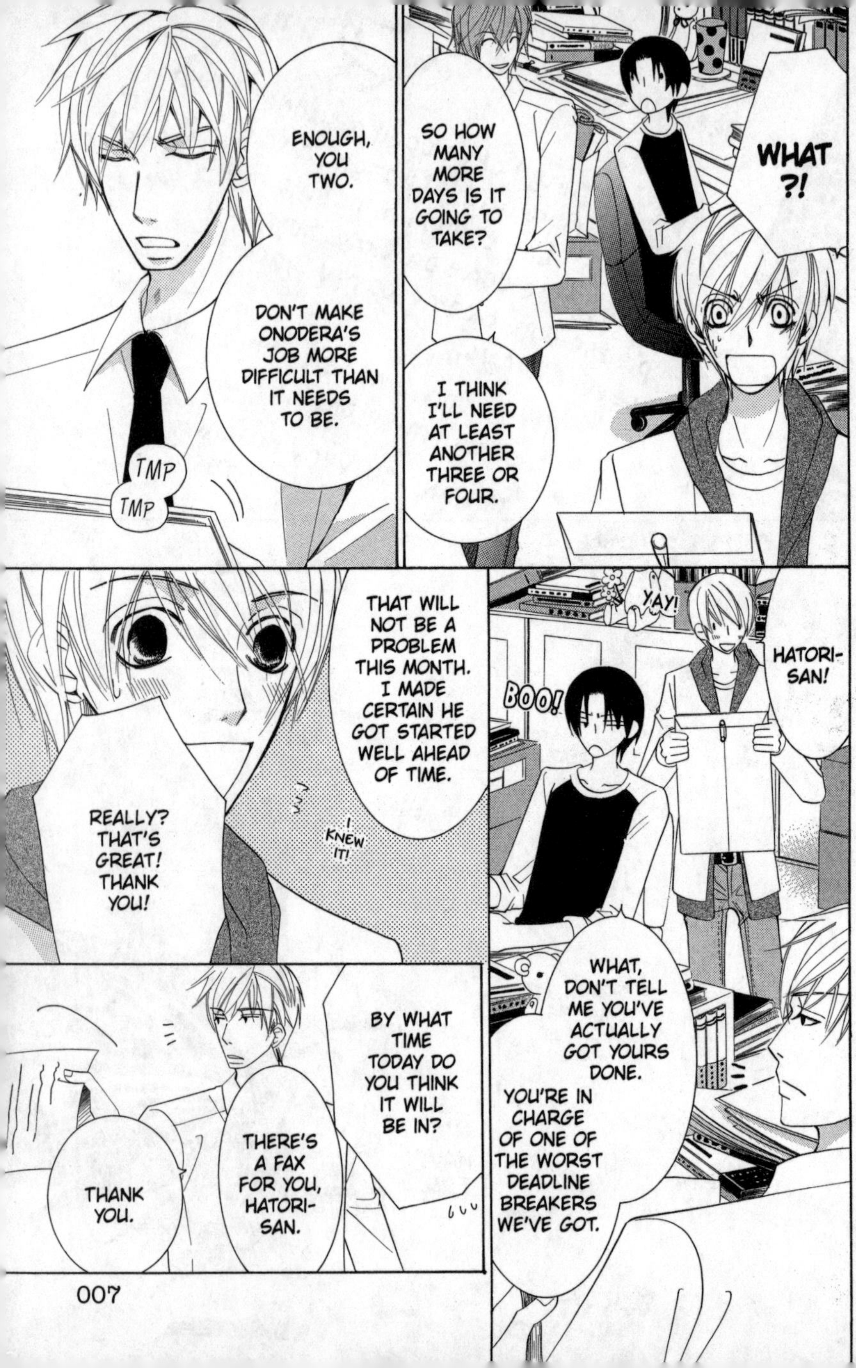
SO HOW MANY MORE DAYS IS IT GOING TO TAKE?
I THINK I'LL NEED AT LEAST ANOTHER THREE OR FOUR.
WHAT ?!
ENOUGH, YOU TWO.
DON'T MAKE ONODERA'S JOB MORE DIFFICULT THAN IT NEEDS TO BE.
TMP
TMP
HATORI-SAN!
YAY!
BOO!
WHAT, DON'T TELL ME YOU'VE ACTUALLY GOT YOURS DONE.
YOU'RE IN CHARGE OF ONE OF THE WORST DEADLINE BREAKERS WE'VE GOT.
THAT WILL NOT BE A PROBLEM THIS MONTH. I MADE CERTAIN HE GOT STARTED WELL AHEAD OF TIME.
I KNEW IT!
REALLY? THAT'S GREAT! THANK YOU!
BY WHAT TIME TODAY DO YOU THINK IT WILL BE IN?
THERE'S A FAX FOR YOU, HATORI-SAN.
THANK YOU.

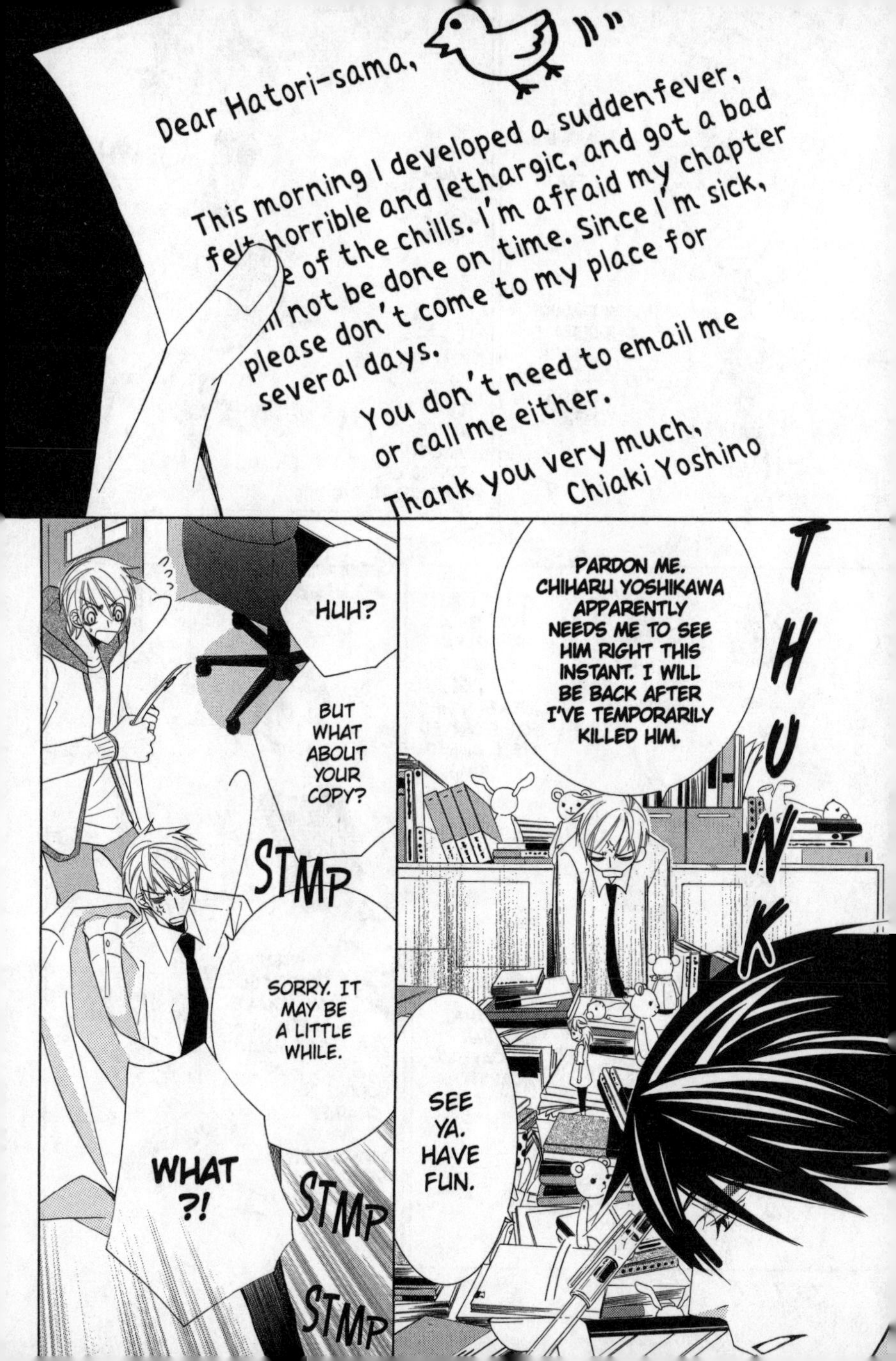
Dear Hatori-sama,
This morning I developed a suddenfever, felt horrible and lethargic, and got a bad e of the chills. I'm afraid my chapter ll not be done on time. Since I'm sick, please don't come to my place for several days.
You don't need to email me or call me either.
Thank you very much,
Chiaki Yoshino
THUNK
PARDON ME. CHIHARU YOSHIKAWA APPARENTLY NEEDS ME TO SEE HIM RIGHT THIS INSTANT. I WILL BE BACK AFTER I'VE TEMPORARILY KILLED HIM.
SEE YA. HAVE FUN.
HUH?
BUT WHAT ABOUT YOUR COPY?
STMP
SORRY. IT MAY BE A LITTLE WHILE.
WHAT ?!
STMP
STMP

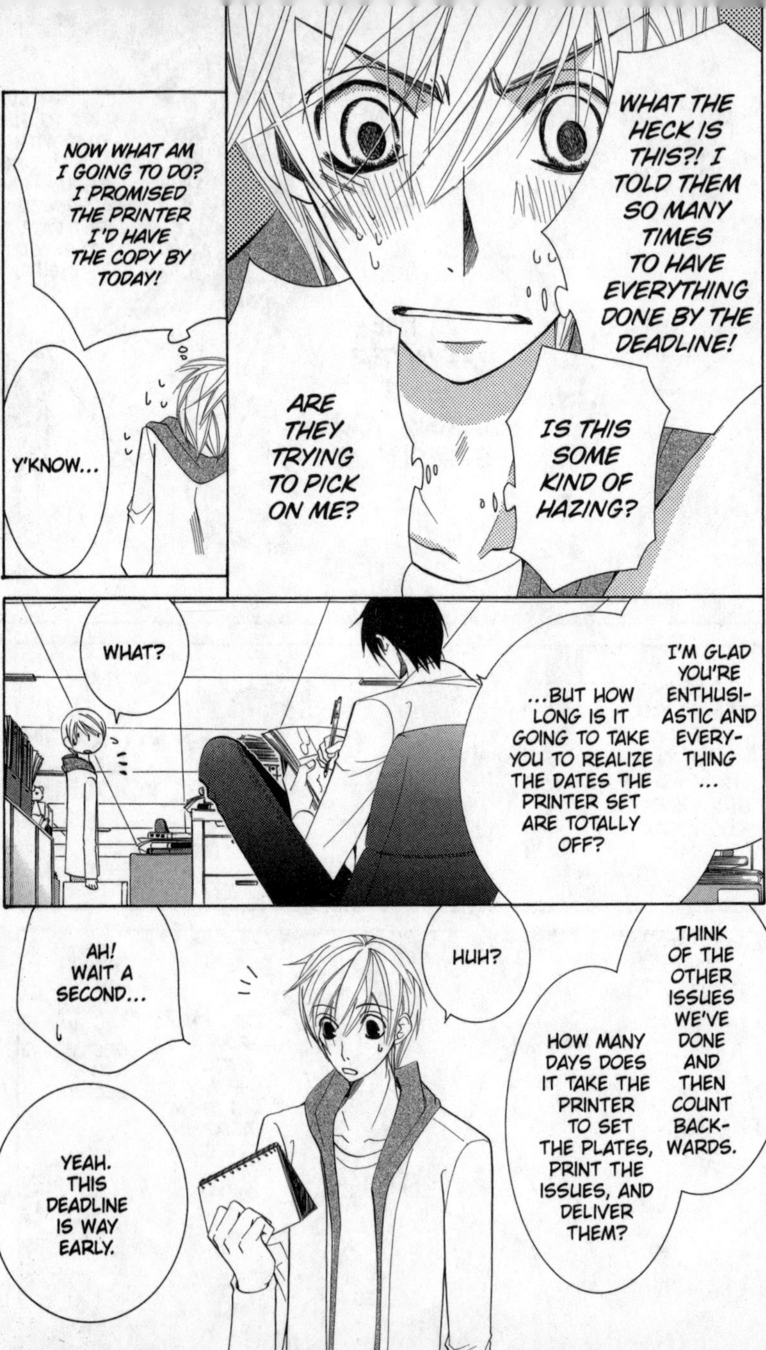
WHAT THE HECK IS THIS?! I TOLD THEM SO MANY TIMES TO HAVE EVERYTHING DONE BY THE DEADLINE!
IS THIS SOME KIND OF HAZING?
ARE THEY TRYING TO PICK ON ME?
NOW WHAT AM I GOING TO DO? I PROMISED THE PRINTER I'D HAVE THE COPY BY TODAY!
Y'KNOW...
I'M GLAD YOU'RE ENTHUSI-ASTIC AND EVERY-THING...
...BUT HOW LONG IS IT GOING TO TAKE YOU TO REALIZE THE DATES THE PRINTER SET ARE TOTALLY OFF?
WHAT?
THINK OF THE OTHER ISSUES WE'VE DONE AND THEN COUNT BACK-WARDS.
HOW MANY DAYS DOES IT TAKE THE PRINTER TO SET THE PLATES, PRINT THE ISSUES, AND DELIVER THEM?
HUH?
AH! WAIT A SECOND...
YEAH. THIS DEADLINE IS WAY EARLY.

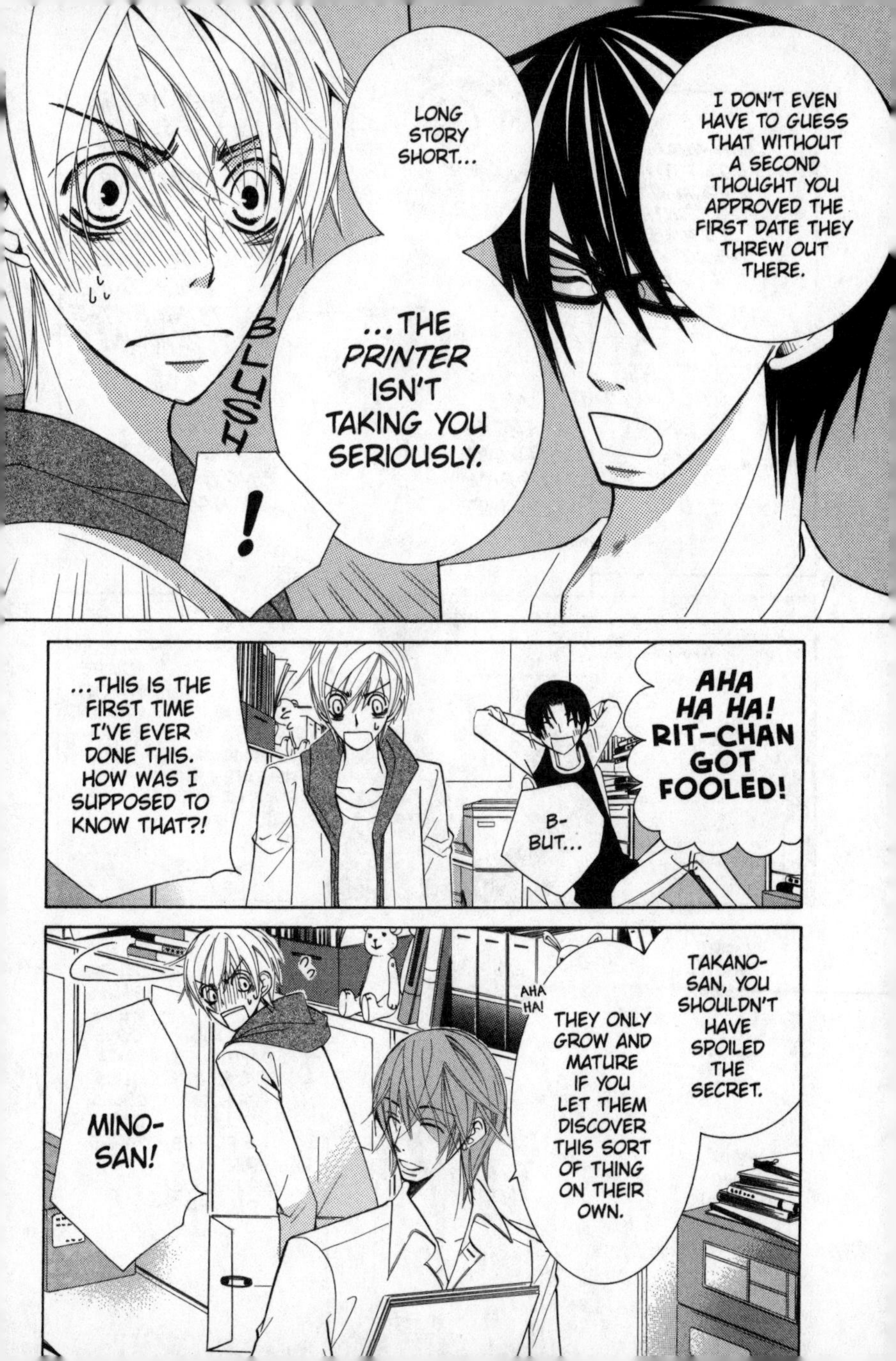
I DON'T EVEN HAVE TO GUESS THAT WITHOUT A SECOND THOUGHT YOU APPROVED THE FIRST DATE THEY THREW OUT THERE.
LONG STORY SHORT...
...THE *PRINTER* ISN'T TAKING YOU SERIOUSLY.
BLUSH
!
AHA HA HA! RIT-CHAN GOT FOOLED!
B-BUT...
...THIS IS THE FIRST TIME I'VE EVER DONE THIS. HOW WAS I SUPPOSED TO KNOW THAT?!
TAKANO-SAN, YOU SHOULDN'T HAVE SPOILED THE SECRET.
AHA HA!
THEY ONLY GROW AND MATURE IF YOU LET THEM DISCOVER THIS SORT OF THING ON THEIR OWN.
MINO-SAN!

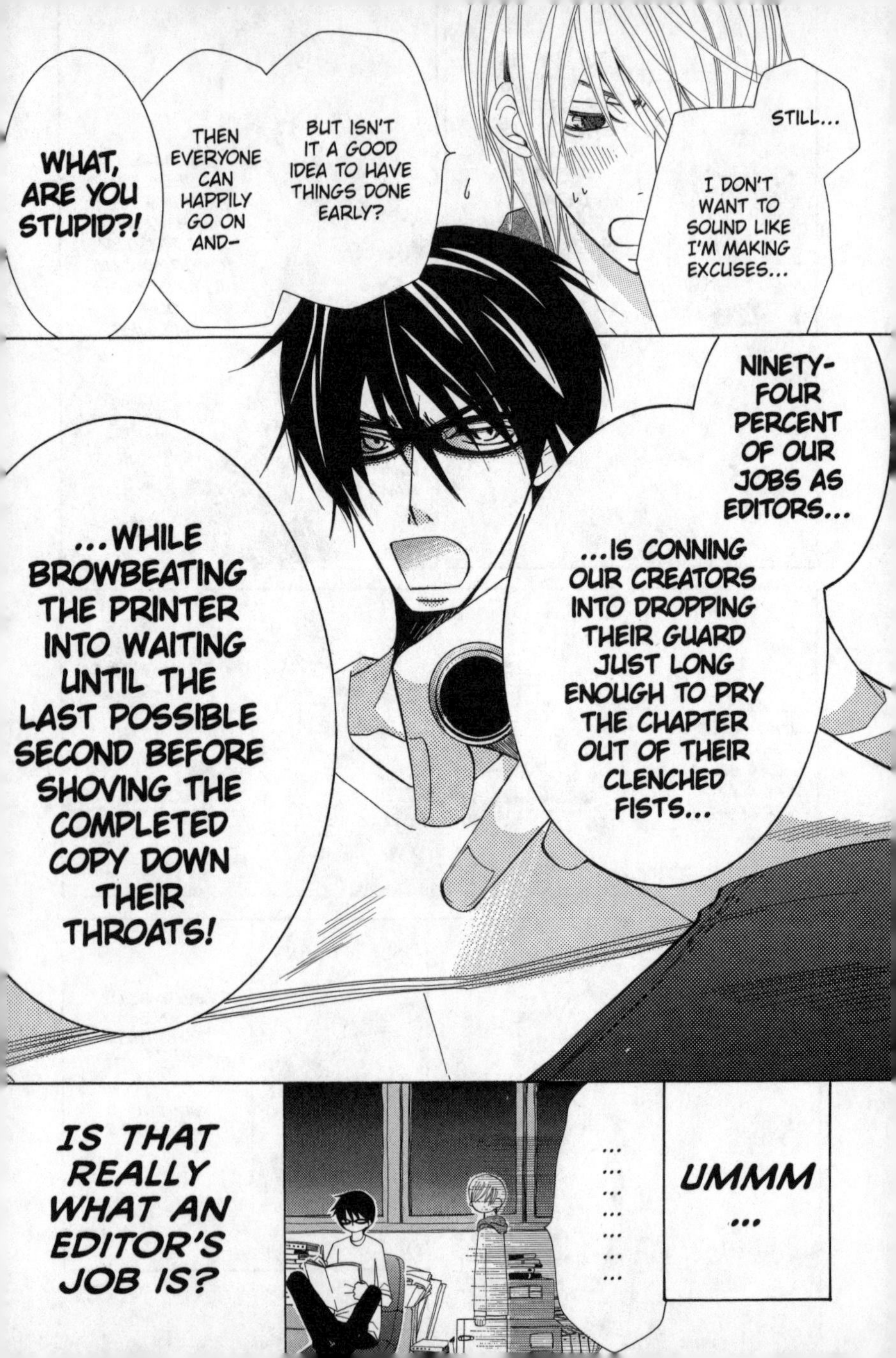
STILL...
I DON'T WANT TO SOUND LIKE I'M MAKING EXCUSES...
BUT ISN'T IT A GOOD IDEA TO HAVE THINGS DONE EARLY?
THEN EVERYONE CAN HAPPILY GO ON AND-
WHAT, ARE YOU STUPID?!
NINETY-FOUR PERCENT OF OUR JOBS AS EDITORS...
...IS CONNING OUR CREATORS INTO DROPPING THEIR GUARD JUST LONG ENOUGH TO PRY THE CHAPTER OUT OF THEIR CLENCHED FISTS...
...WHILE BROWBEATING THE PRINTER INTO WAITING UNTIL THE LAST POSSIBLE SECOND BEFORE SHOVING THE COMPLETED COPY DOWN THEIR THROATS!
UMMM ...
....
IS THAT REALLY WHAT AN EDITOR'S JOB IS?

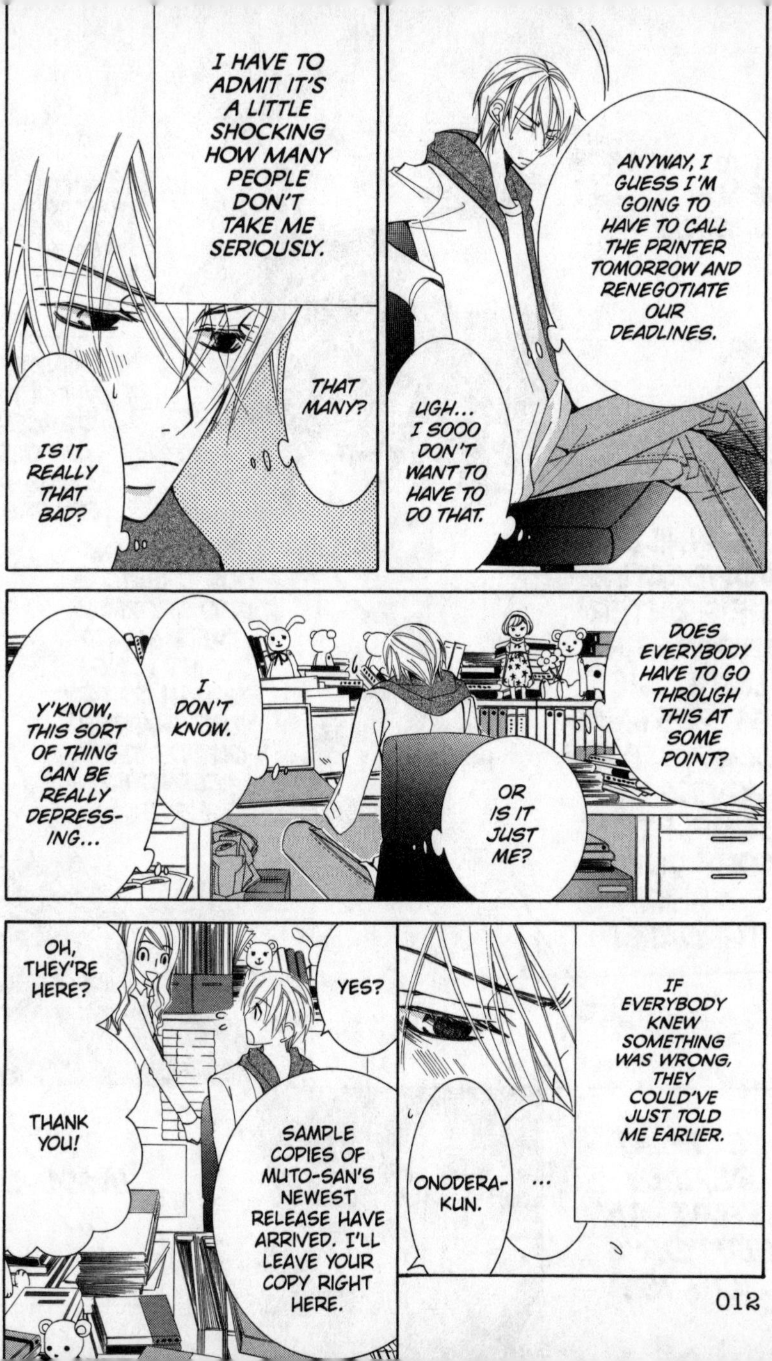
ANYWAY, I GUESS I'M GOING TO HAVE TO CALL THE PRINTER TOMORROW AND RENEGOTIATE OUR DEADLINES.
UGH... I SOOO DON'T WANT TO HAVE TO DO THAT.
I HAVE TO ADMIT IT'S A LITTLE SHOCKING HOW MANY PEOPLE DON'T TAKE ME SERIOUSLY.
THAT MANY?
IS IT REALLY THAT BAD?
DOES EVERYBODY HAVE TO GO THROUGH THIS AT SOME POINT?
OR IS IT JUST ME?
I DON'T KNOW.
Y'KNOW, THIS SORT OF THING CAN BE REALLY DEPRESS-ING...
IF EVERYBODY KNEW SOMETHING WAS WRONG, THEY COULD'VE JUST TOLD ME EARLIER.
...
ONODERA-KUN.
YES?
SAMPLE COPIES OF MUTO-SAN'S NEWEST RELEASE HAVE ARRIVED. I'LL LEAVE YOUR COPY RIGHT HERE.
OH, THEY'RE HERE?
THANK YOU!

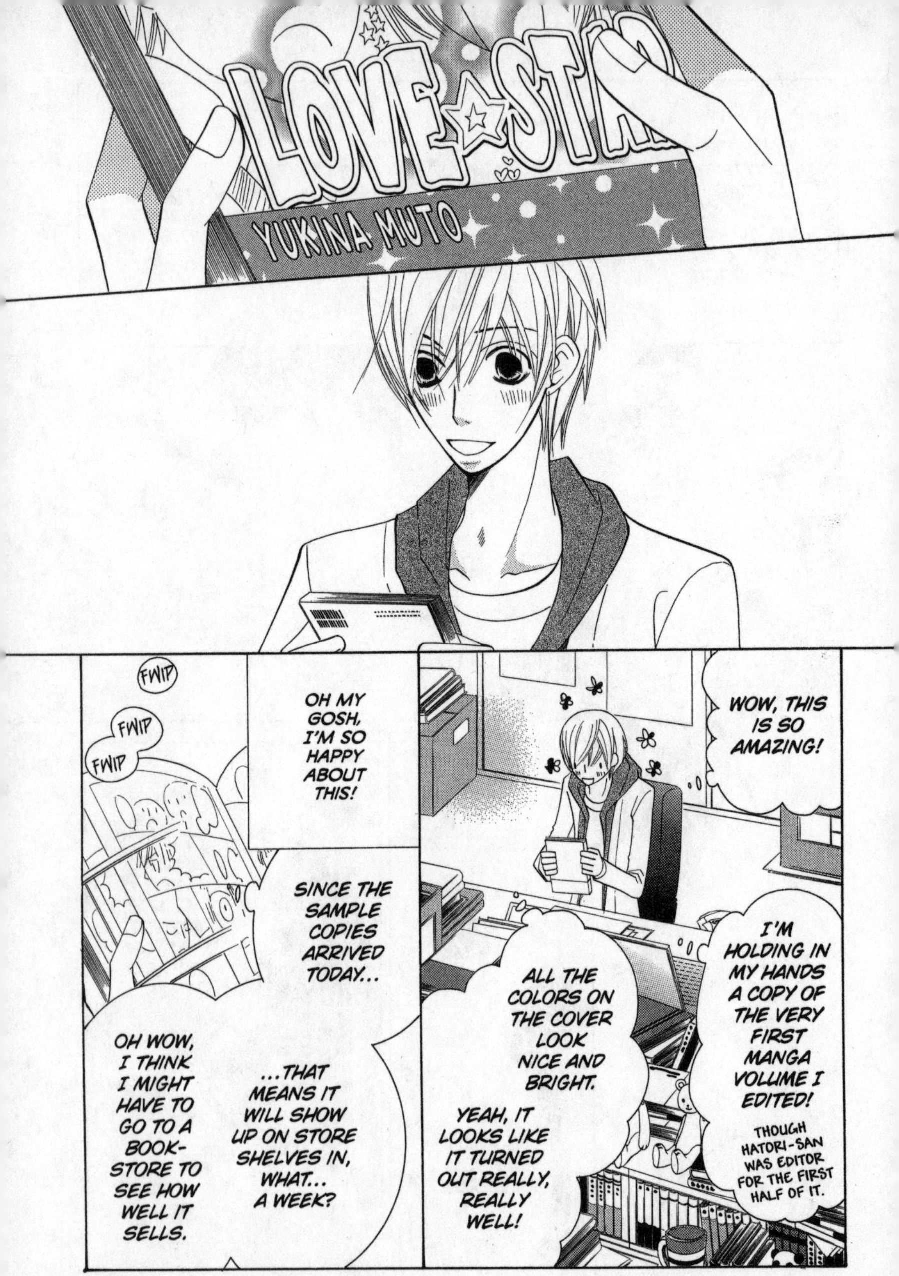
LOVE☆STA
YUKINA MUTO
WOW, THIS IS SO AMAZING!
I'M HOLDING IN MY HANDS A COPY OF THE VERY FIRST MANGA VOLUME I EDITED!
THOUGH HATORI-SAN WAS EDITOR FOR THE FIRST HALF OF IT.
ALL THE COLORS ON THE COVER LOOK NICE AND BRIGHT.
YEAH, IT LOOKS LIKE IT TURNED OUT REALLY, REALLY WELL!
OH MY GOSH, I'M SO HAPPY ABOUT THIS!
FWIP
FWIP
FWIP
SINCE THE SAMPLE COPIES ARRIVED TODAY...
...THAT MEANS IT WILL SHOW UP ON STORE SHELVES IN, WHAT... A WEEK?
OH WOW, I THINK I MIGHT HAVE TO GO TO A BOOK-STORE TO SEE HOW WELL IT SELLS.

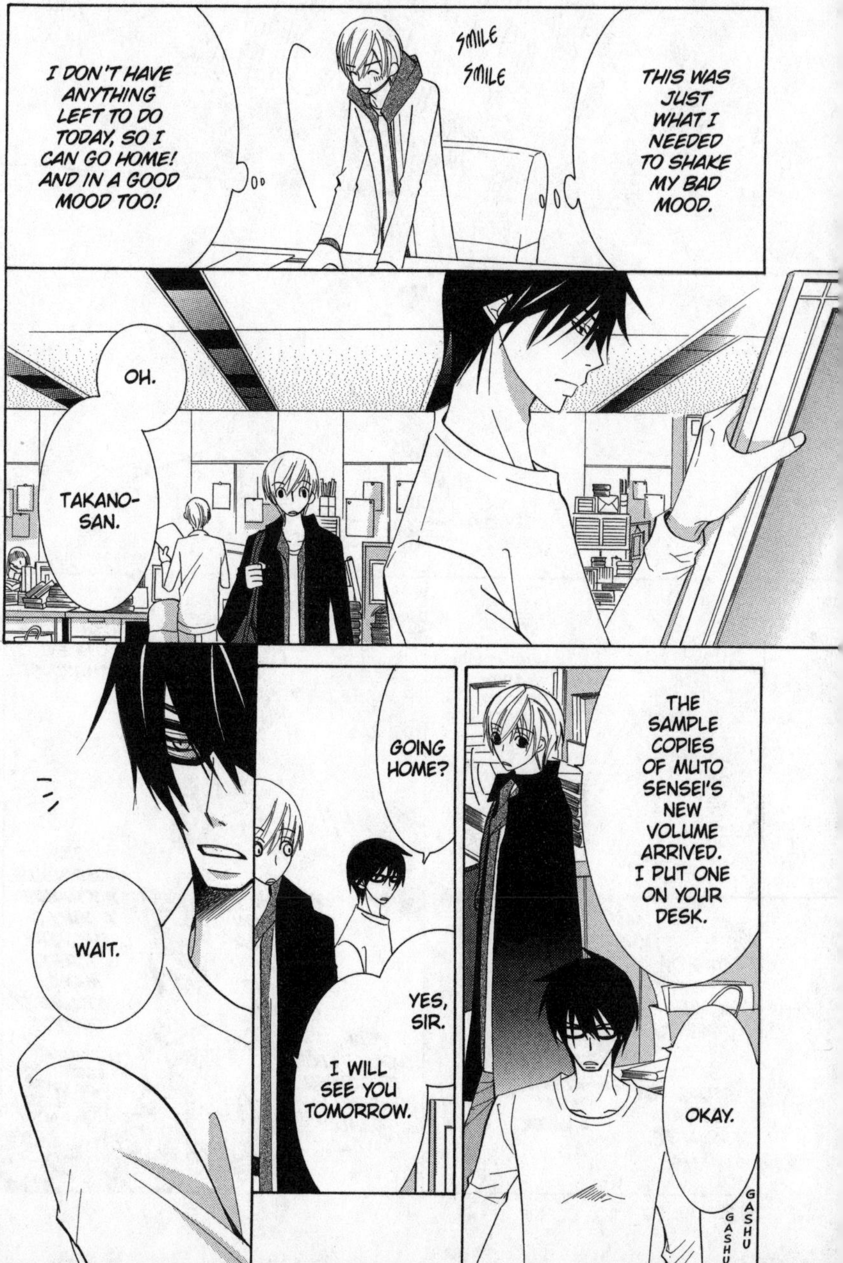
THIS WAS JUST WHAT I NEEDED TO SHAKE MY BAD MOOD.
SMILE
SMILE
I DON'T HAVE ANYTHING LEFT TO DO TODAY, SO I CAN GO HOME! AND IN A GOOD MOOD TOO!
OH.
TAKANO-SAN.
THE SAMPLE COPIES OF MUTO SENSEI'S NEW VOLUME ARRIVED. I PUT ONE ON YOUR DESK.
OKAY.
GASHU
GASHU
GOING HOME?
YES, SIR.
I WILL SEE YOU TOMORROW.
WAIT.

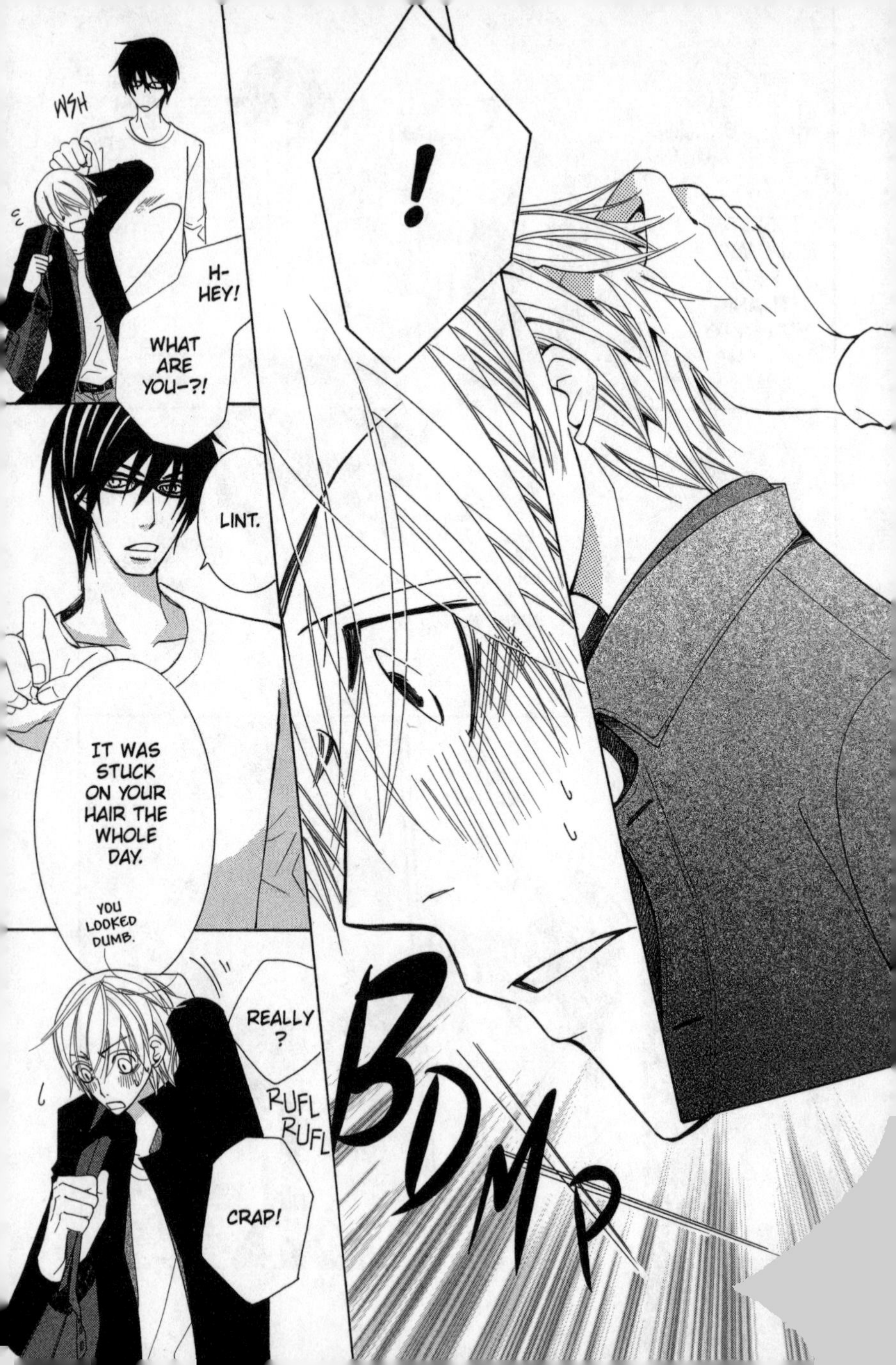
!
BDMP
WSH
H-HEY!
WHAT ARE YOU-?!
LINT.
IT WAS STUCK ON YOUR HAIR THE WHOLE DAY.
YOU LOOKED DUMB.
REALLY?
RUFL RUFL
CRAP!

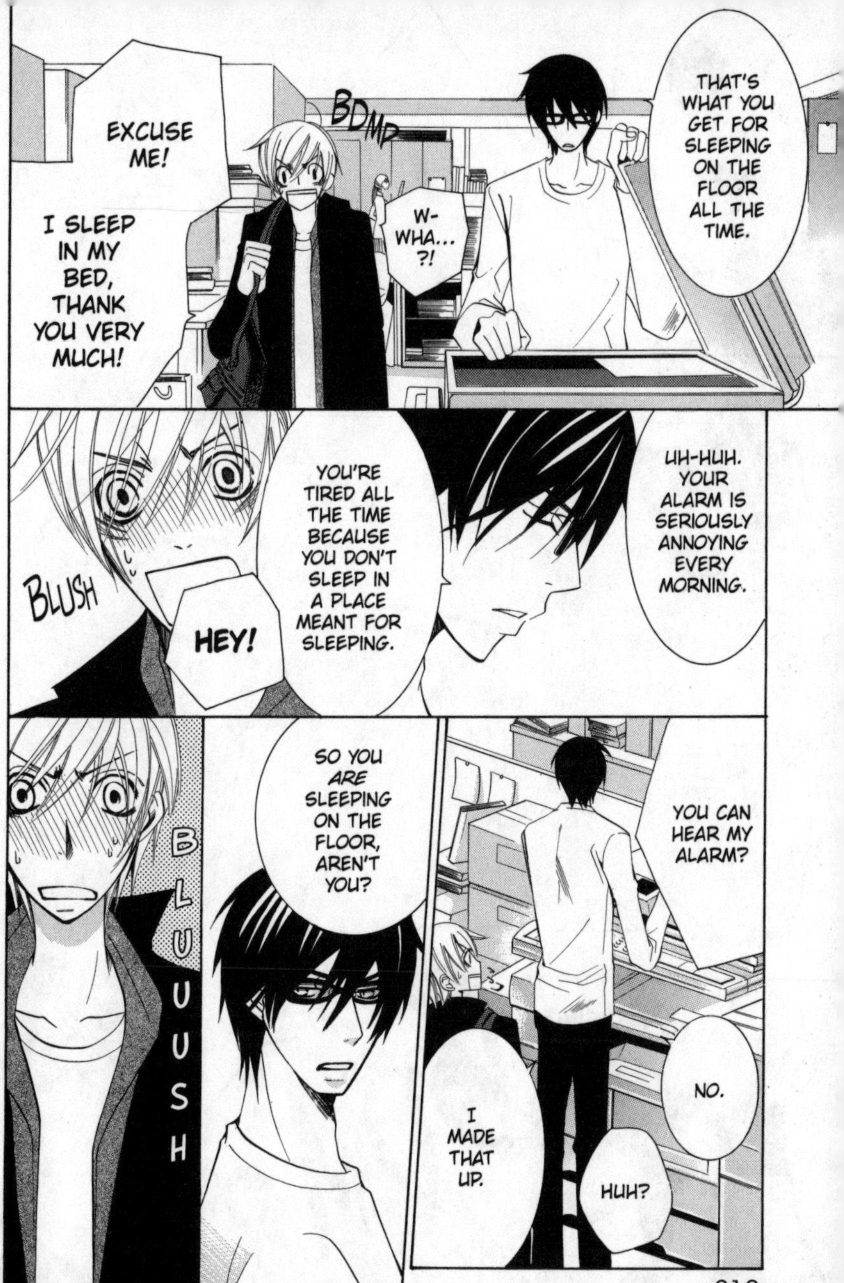
THAT'S WHAT YOU GET FOR SLEEPING ON THE FLOOR ALL THE TIME.
BDMP
W-WHA...?!
EXCUSE ME!
I SLEEP IN MY BED, THANK YOU VERY MUCH!
UH-HUH. YOUR ALARM IS SERIOUSLY ANNOYING EVERY MORNING.
YOU'RE TIRED ALL THE TIME BECAUSE YOU DON'T SLEEP IN A PLACE MEANT FOR SLEEPING.
HEY!
BLUSH
YOU CAN HEAR MY ALARM?
NO.
HUH?
I MADE THAT UP.
SO YOU *ARE* SLEEPING ON THE FLOOR, AREN'T YOU?
BLUUUSH

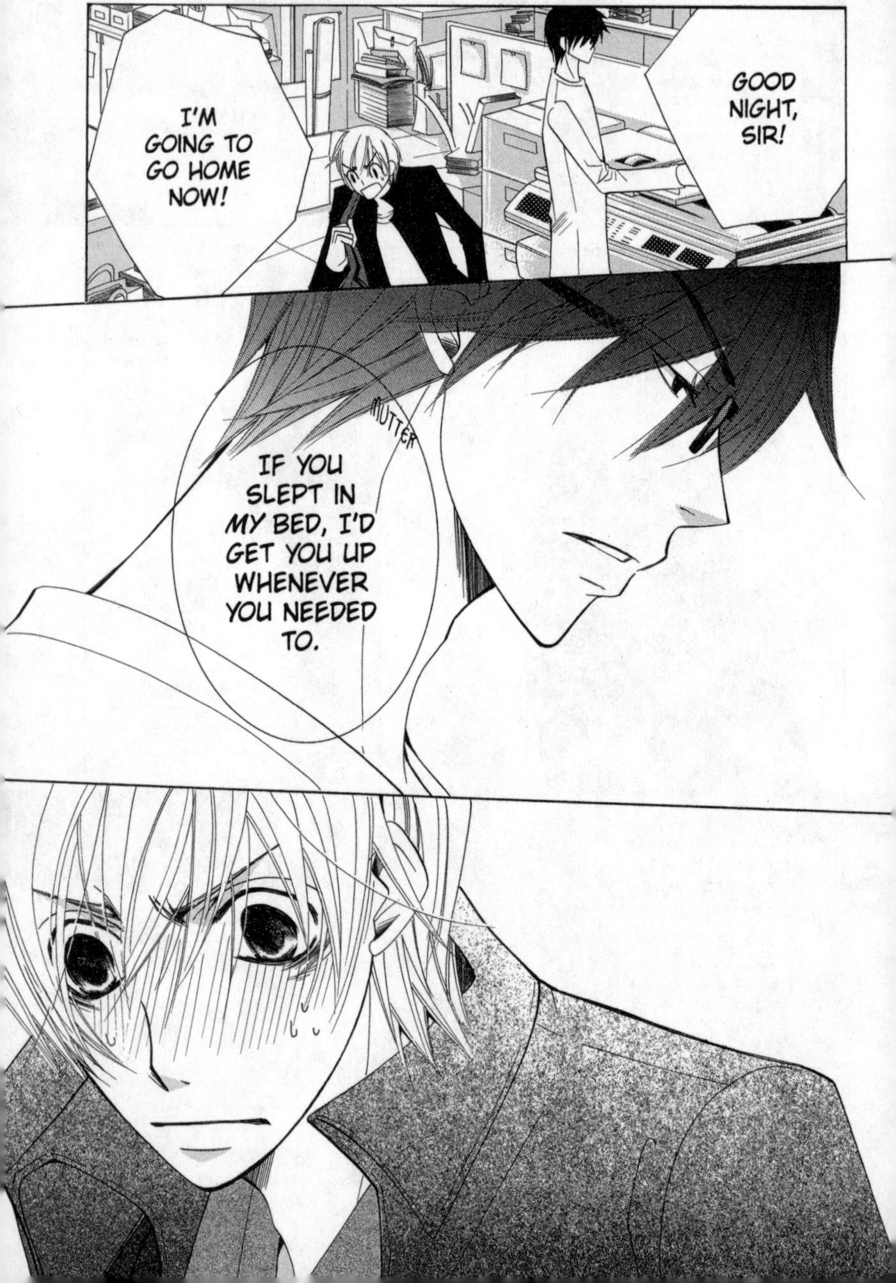
GOOD NIGHT, SIR!
I'M GOING TO GO HOME NOW!
MUTTER
IF YOU SLEPT IN MY BED, I'D GET YOU UP WHENEVER YOU NEEDED TO.

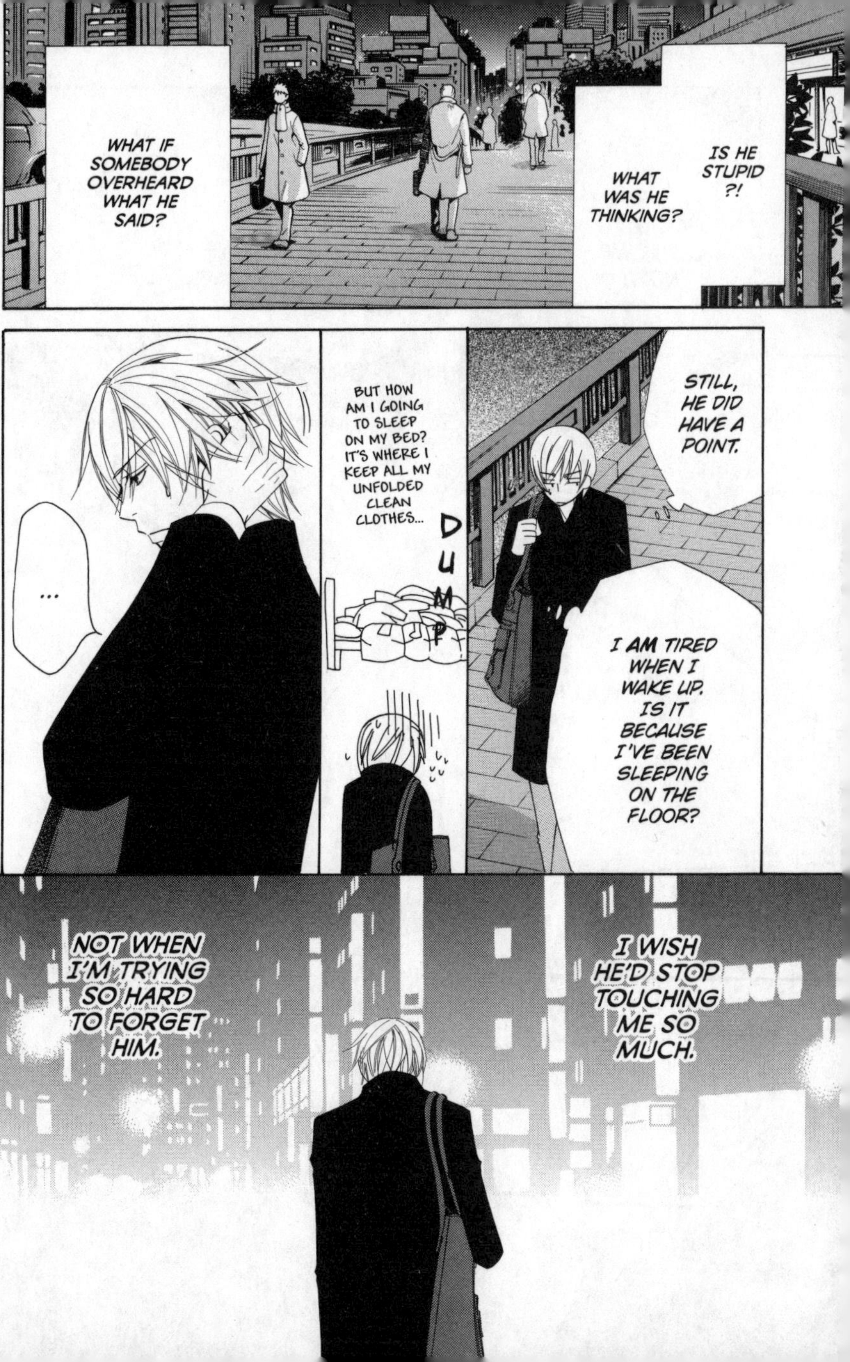
IS HE STUPID?!
WHAT WAS HE THINKING?
WHAT IF SOMEBODY OVERHEARD WHAT HE SAID?
STILL, HE DID HAVE A POINT.
I AM TIRED WHEN I WAKE UP. IS IT BECAUSE I'VE BEEN SLEEPING ON THE FLOOR?
BUT HOW AM I GOING TO SLEEP ON MY BED? IT'S WHERE I KEEP ALL MY UNFOLDED CLEAN CLOTHES...
DUMP
...
I WISH HE'D STOP TOUCHING ME SO MUCH.
NOT WHEN I'M TRYING SO HARD TO FORGET HIM.

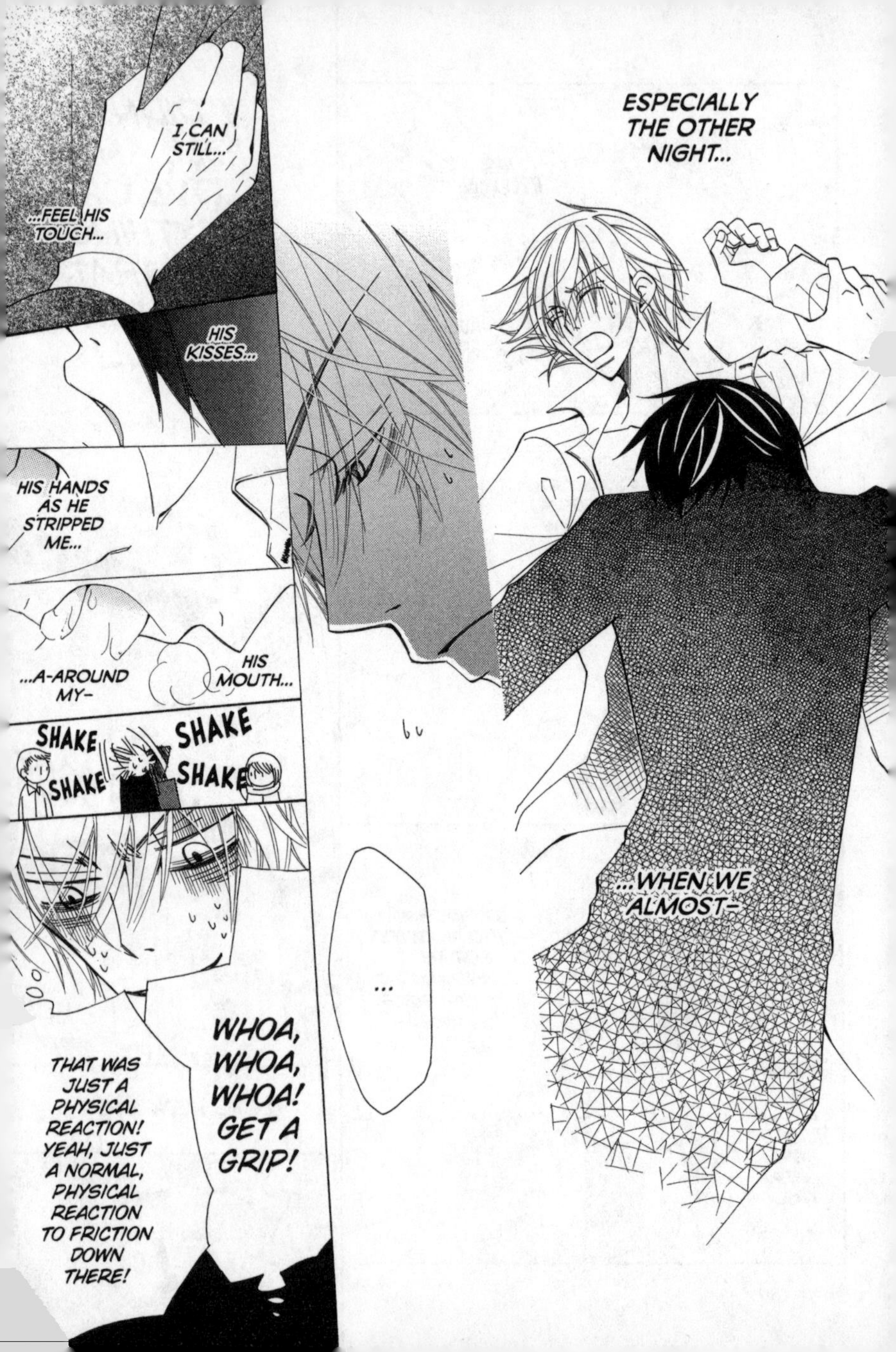
ESPECIALLY THE OTHER NIGHT...
...WHEN WE ALMOST-
...
I CAN STILL...
...FEEL HIS TOUCH...
HIS KISSES...
HIS HANDS AS HE STRIPPED ME...
HIS MOUTH...
...A-AROUND MY-
SHAKE SHAKE
SHAKE SHAKE
WHOA, WHOA, WHOA! GET A GRIP!
THAT WAS JUST A PHYSICAL REACTION! YEAH, JUST A NORMAL, PHYSICAL REACTION TO FRICTION DOWN THERE!

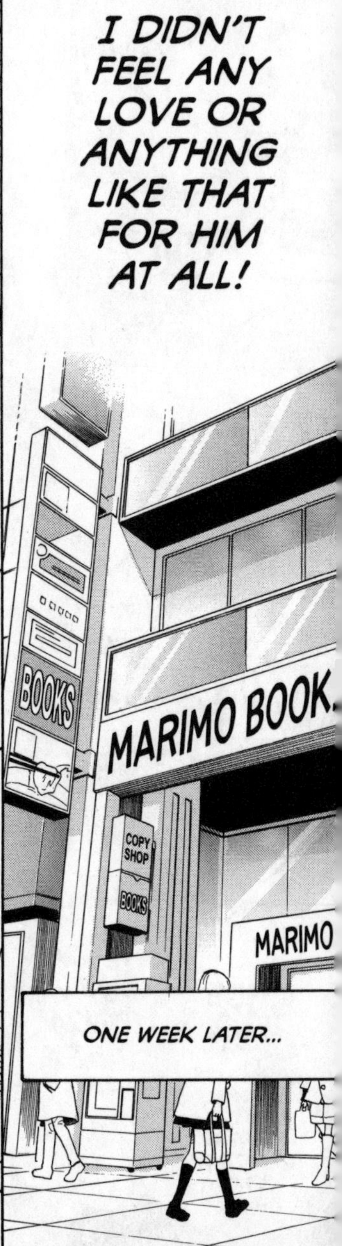
I DIDN'T FEEL ANY LOVE OR ANYTHING LIKE THAT FOR HIM AT ALL!
BOOKS
MARIMO BOOK
COPY SHOP
BOOKS
MARIMO
ONE WEEK LATER...

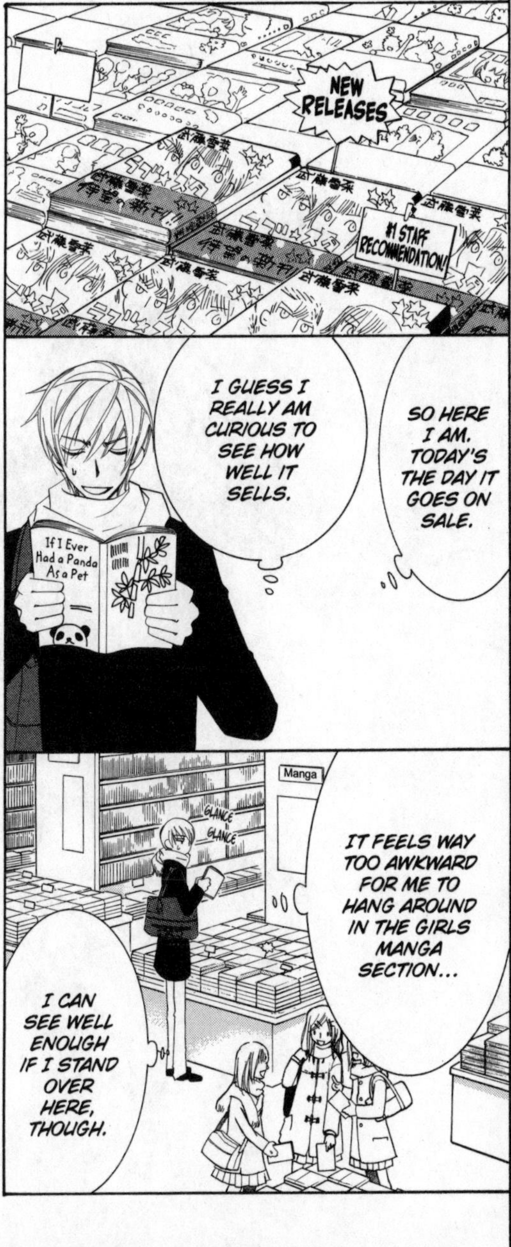
NEW RELEASES
#1 STAFF RECOMMENDATION!
SO HERE I AM. TODAY'S THE DAY IT GOES ON SALE.
I GUESS I REALLY AM CURIOUS TO SEE HOW WELL IT SELLS.
If I Ever Had a Panda As a Pet
Manga
GLANCE
GLANCE
IT FEELS WAY TOO AWKWARD FOR ME TO HANG AROUND IN THE GIRLS MANGA SECTION...
I CAN SEE WELL ENOUGH IF I STAND OVER HERE, THOUGH.

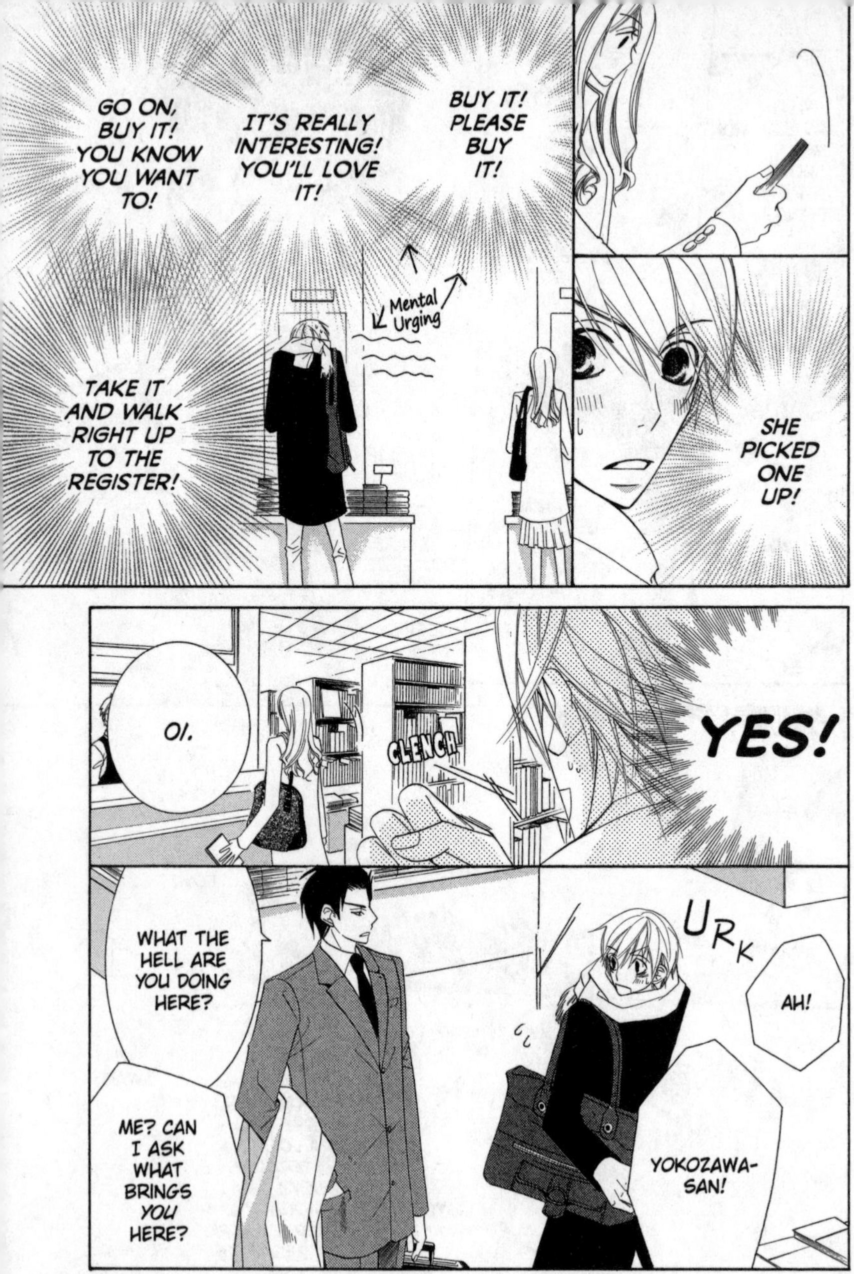

SHE PICKED ONE UP!
BUY IT! PLEASE BUY IT!
IT'S REALLY INTERESTING! YOU'LL LOVE IT!
GO ON, BUY IT! YOU KNOW YOU WANT TO!
Mental Urging
TAKE IT AND WALK RIGHT UP TO THE REGISTER!
YES!
CLENCH
OI.
URK
AH!
YOKOZAWA-SAN!
WHAT THE HELL ARE YOU DOING HERE?
ME? CAN I ASK WHAT BRINGS YOU HERE?

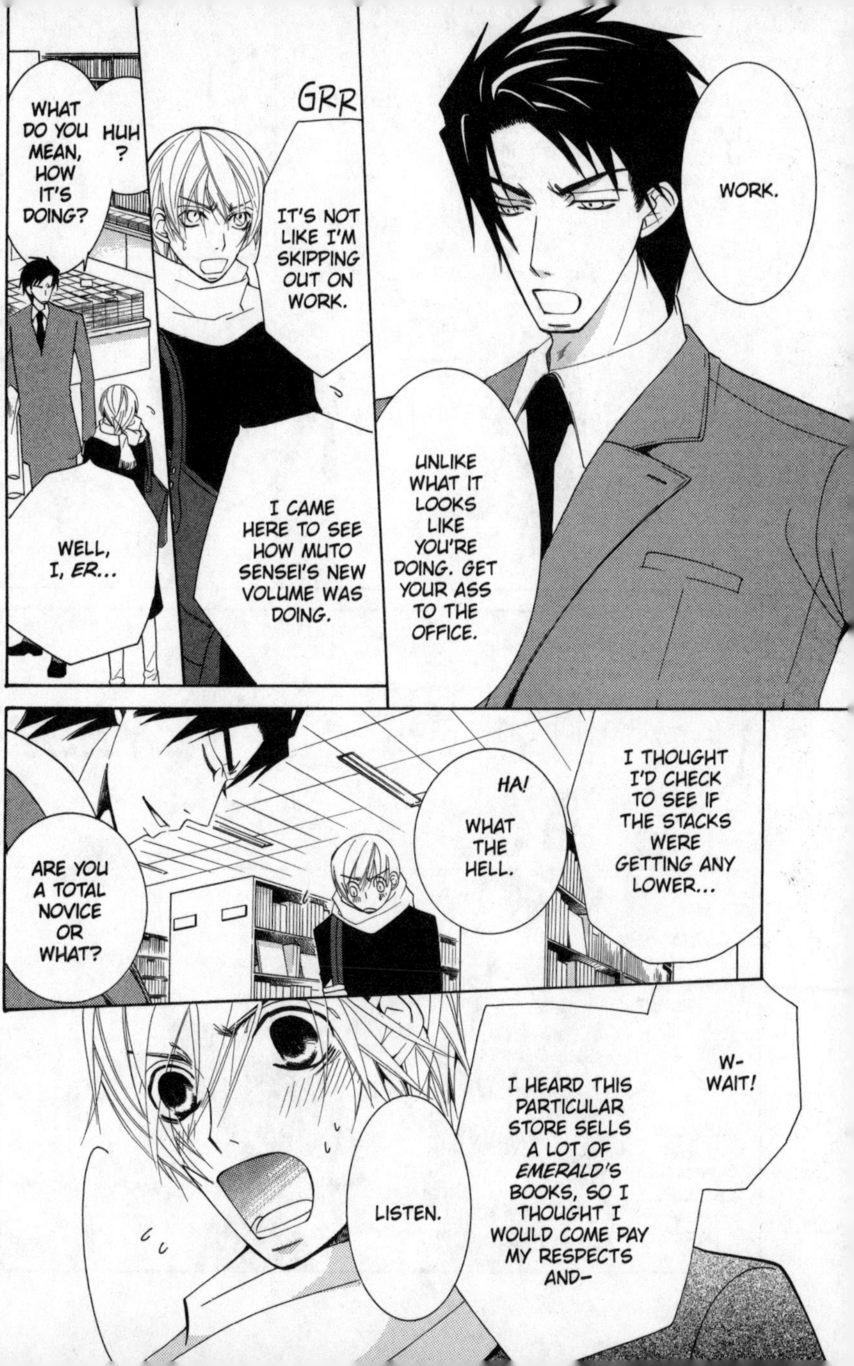
WORK.
UNLIKE WHAT IT LOOKS LIKE YOU'RE DOING. GET YOUR ASS TO THE OFFICE.
GRR
IT'S NOT LIKE I'M SKIPPING OUT ON WORK.
I CAME HERE TO SEE HOW MUTO SENSEI'S NEW VOLUME WAS DOING.
HUH?
WHAT DO YOU MEAN, HOW IT'S DOING?
WELL, I, *ER*...
I THOUGHT I'D CHECK TO SEE IF THE STACKS WERE GETTING ANY LOWER...
HA! WHAT THE HELL.
ARE YOU A TOTAL NOVICE OR WHAT?
W-WAIT!
I HEARD THIS PARTICULAR STORE SELLS A LOT OF *EMERALD'S* BOOKS, SO I THOUGHT I WOULD COME PAY MY RESPECTS AND–
LISTEN.

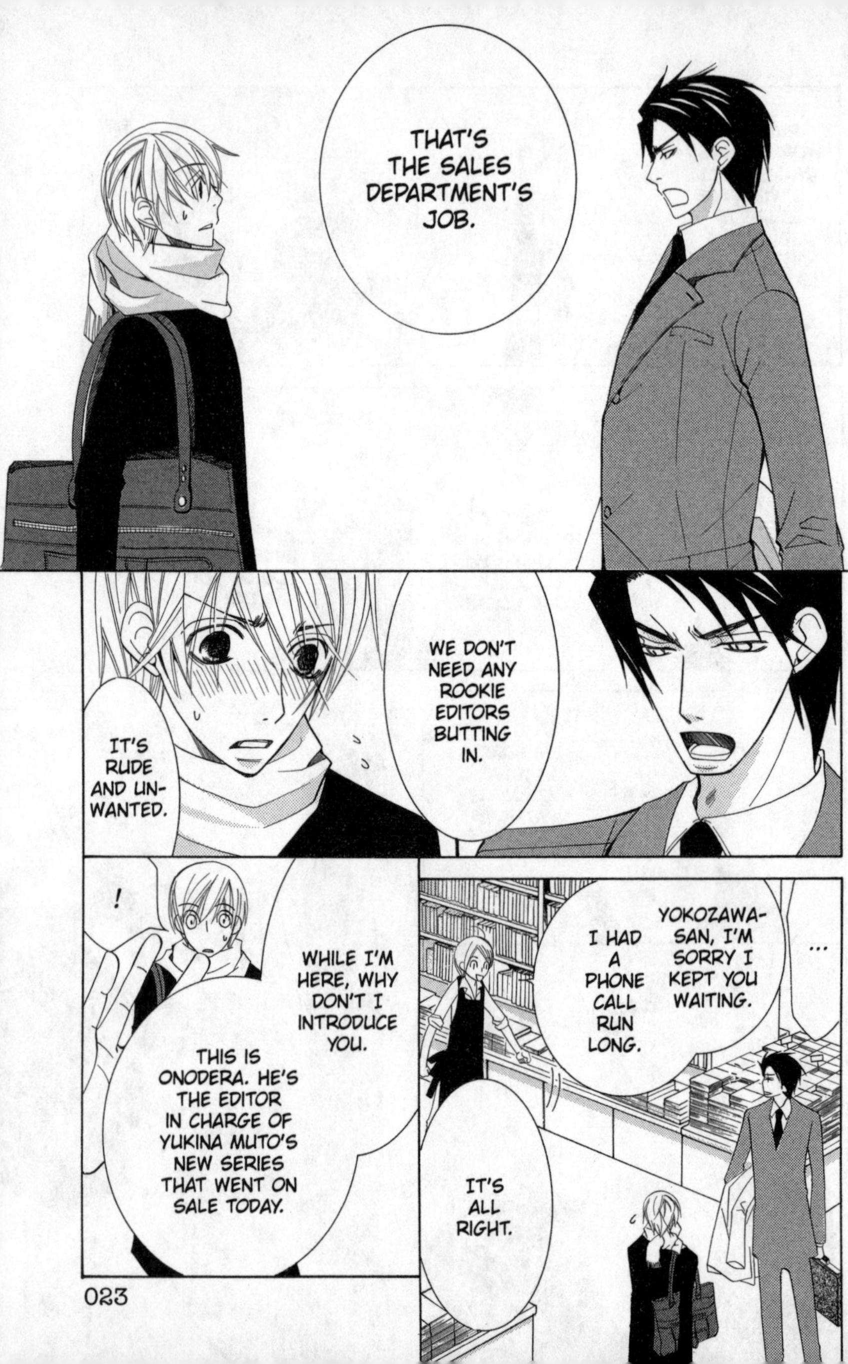
THAT'S THE SALES DEPARTMENT'S JOB.
WE DON'T NEED ANY ROOKIE EDITORS BUTTING IN.
IT'S RUDE AND UN-WANTED.
YOKOZAWA-SAN, I'M SORRY I KEPT YOU WAITING.
I HAD A PHONE CALL RUN LONG.
...
IT'S ALL RIGHT.
WHILE I'M HERE, WHY DON'T I INTRODUCE YOU.
!
THIS IS ONODERA. HE'S THE EDITOR IN CHARGE OF YUKINA MUTO'S NEW SERIES THAT WENT ON SALE TODAY.

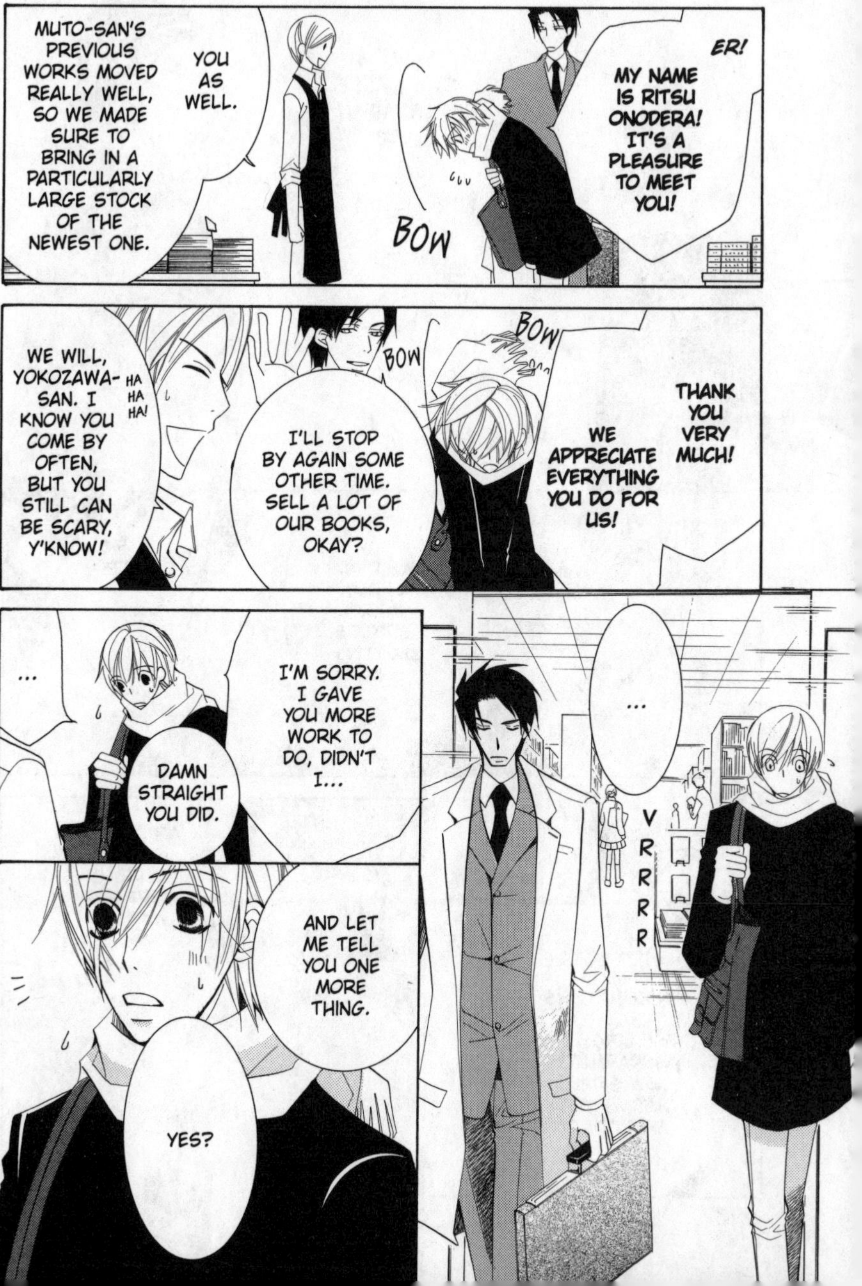
ER!
MY NAME IS RITSU ONODERA! IT'S A PLEASURE TO MEET YOU!
BOW
YOU AS WELL.
MUTO-SAN'S PREVIOUS WORKS MOVED REALLY WELL, SO WE MADE SURE TO BRING IN A PARTICULARLY LARGE STOCK OF THE NEWEST ONE.
THANK YOU VERY MUCH!
WE APPRECIATE EVERYTHING YOU DO FOR US!
BOW
BOW
I'LL STOP BY AGAIN SOME OTHER TIME. SELL A LOT OF OUR BOOKS, OKAY?
HA HA HA!
WE WILL, YOKOZAWA-SAN. I KNOW YOU COME BY OFTEN, BUT YOU STILL CAN BE SCARY, Y'KNOW!
...
VRRRR
I'M SORRY. I GAVE YOU MORE WORK TO DO, DIDN'T I...
DAMN STRAIGHT YOU DID.
...
AND LET ME TELL YOU ONE MORE THING.
YES?

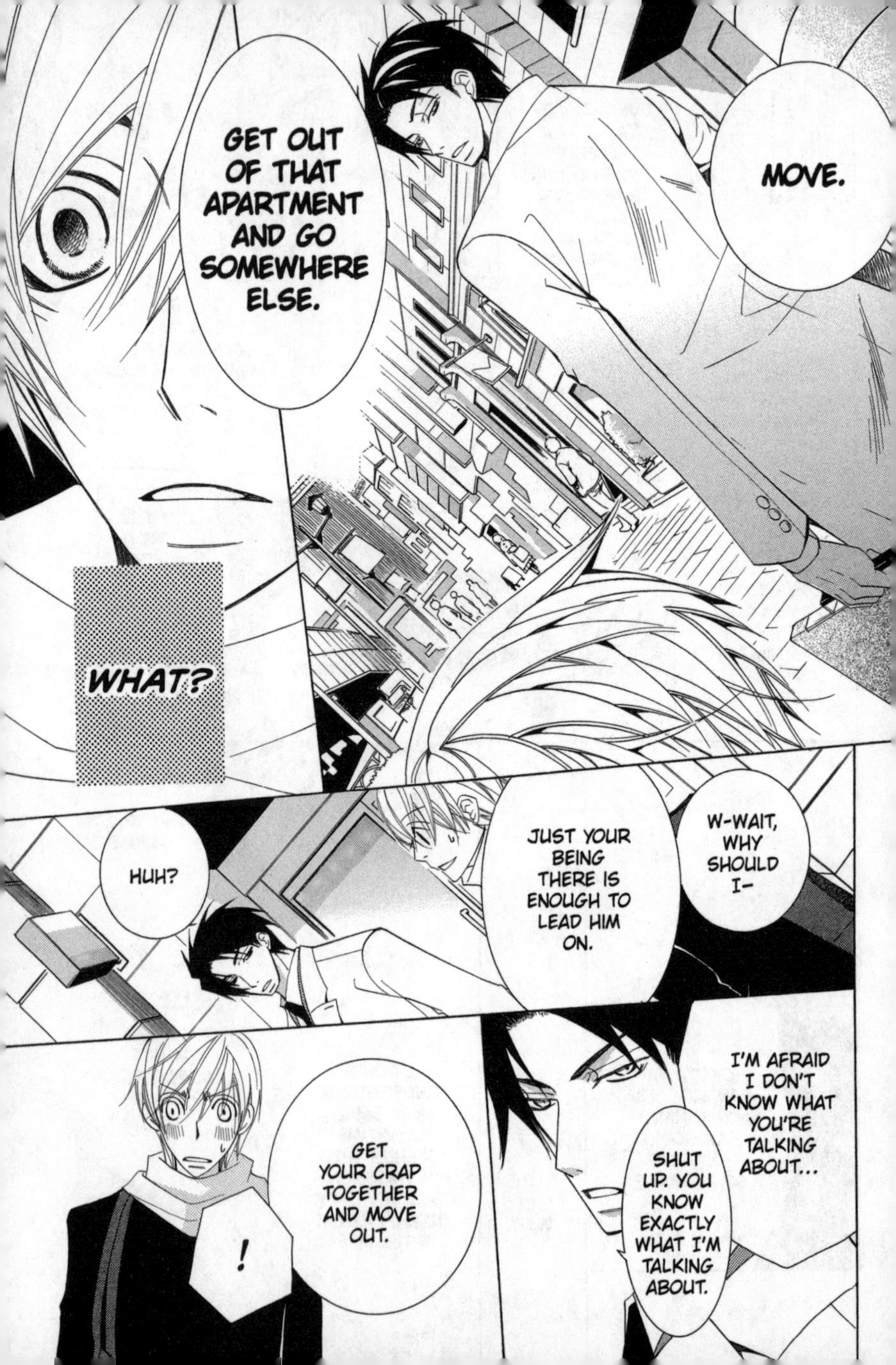
MOVE.
GET OUT OF THAT APARTMENT AND GO SOMEWHERE ELSE.
WHAT?
W-WAIT, WHY SHOULD I-
JUST YOUR BEING THERE IS ENOUGH TO LEAD HIM ON.
HUH?
I'M AFRAID I DON'T KNOW WHAT YOU'RE TALKING ABOUT...
SHUT UP. YOU KNOW EXACTLY WHAT I'M TALKING ABOUT.
GET YOUR CRAP TOGETHER AND MOVE OUT.
!

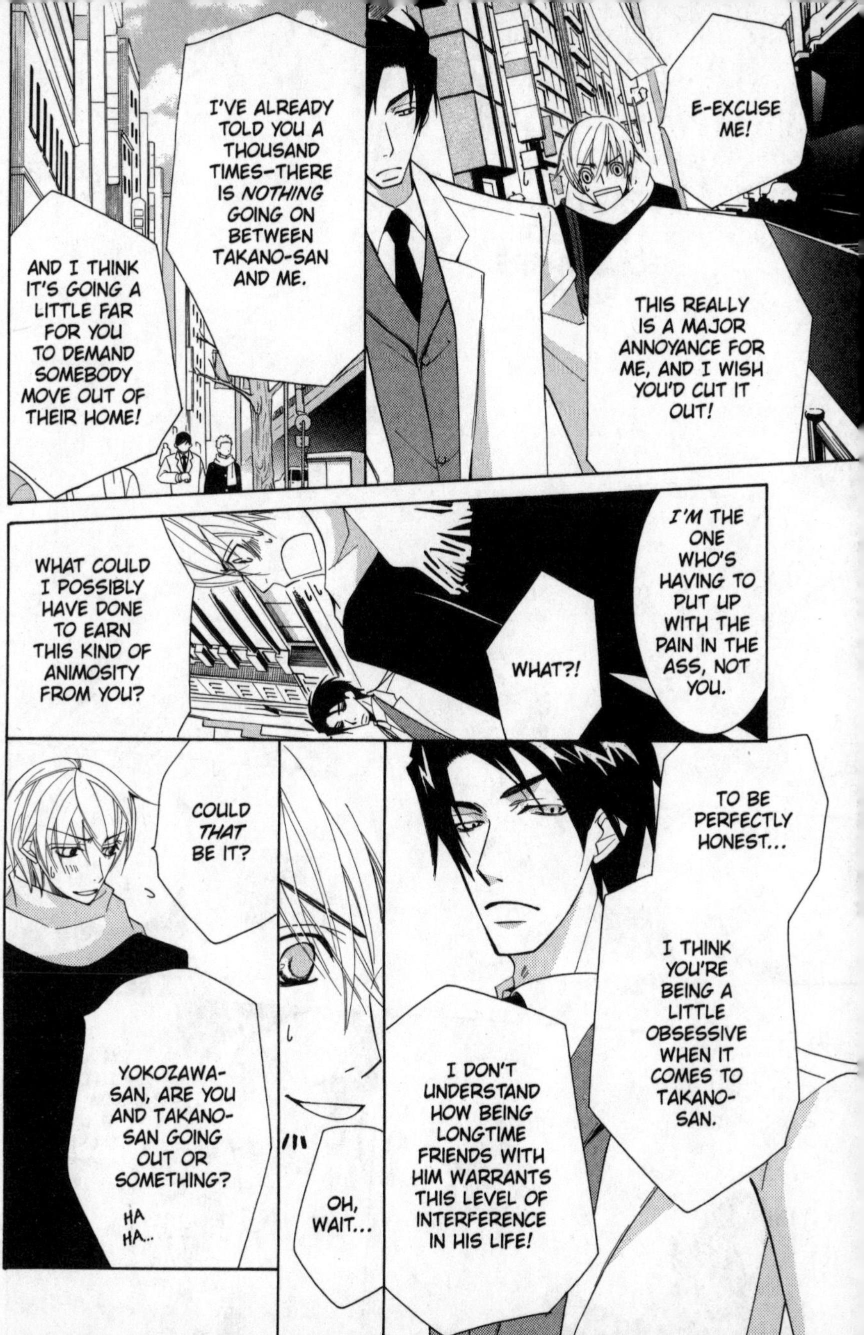
E-EXCUSE ME!
THIS REALLY IS A MAJOR ANNOYANCE FOR ME, AND I WISH YOU'D CUT IT OUT!
I'VE ALREADY TOLD YOU A THOUSAND TIMES—THERE IS *NOTHING* GOING ON BETWEEN TAKANO-SAN AND ME.
AND I THINK IT'S GOING A LITTLE FAR FOR YOU TO DEMAND SOMEBODY MOVE OUT OF THEIR HOME!
I'M THE ONE WHO'S HAVING TO PUT UP WITH THE PAIN IN THE ASS, NOT YOU.
WHAT?!
WHAT COULD I POSSIBLY HAVE DONE TO EARN THIS KIND OF ANIMOSITY FROM YOU?
TO BE PERFECTLY HONEST...
I THINK YOU'RE BEING A LITTLE OBSESSIVE WHEN IT COMES TO TAKANO-SAN.
I DON'T UNDERSTAND HOW BEING LONGTIME FRIENDS WITH HIM WARRANTS THIS LEVEL OF INTERFERENCE IN HIS LIFE!
OH, WAIT...
COULD *THAT* BE IT?
YOKOZAWA-SAN, ARE YOU AND TAKANO-SAN GOING OUT OR SOMETHING?
HA HA...

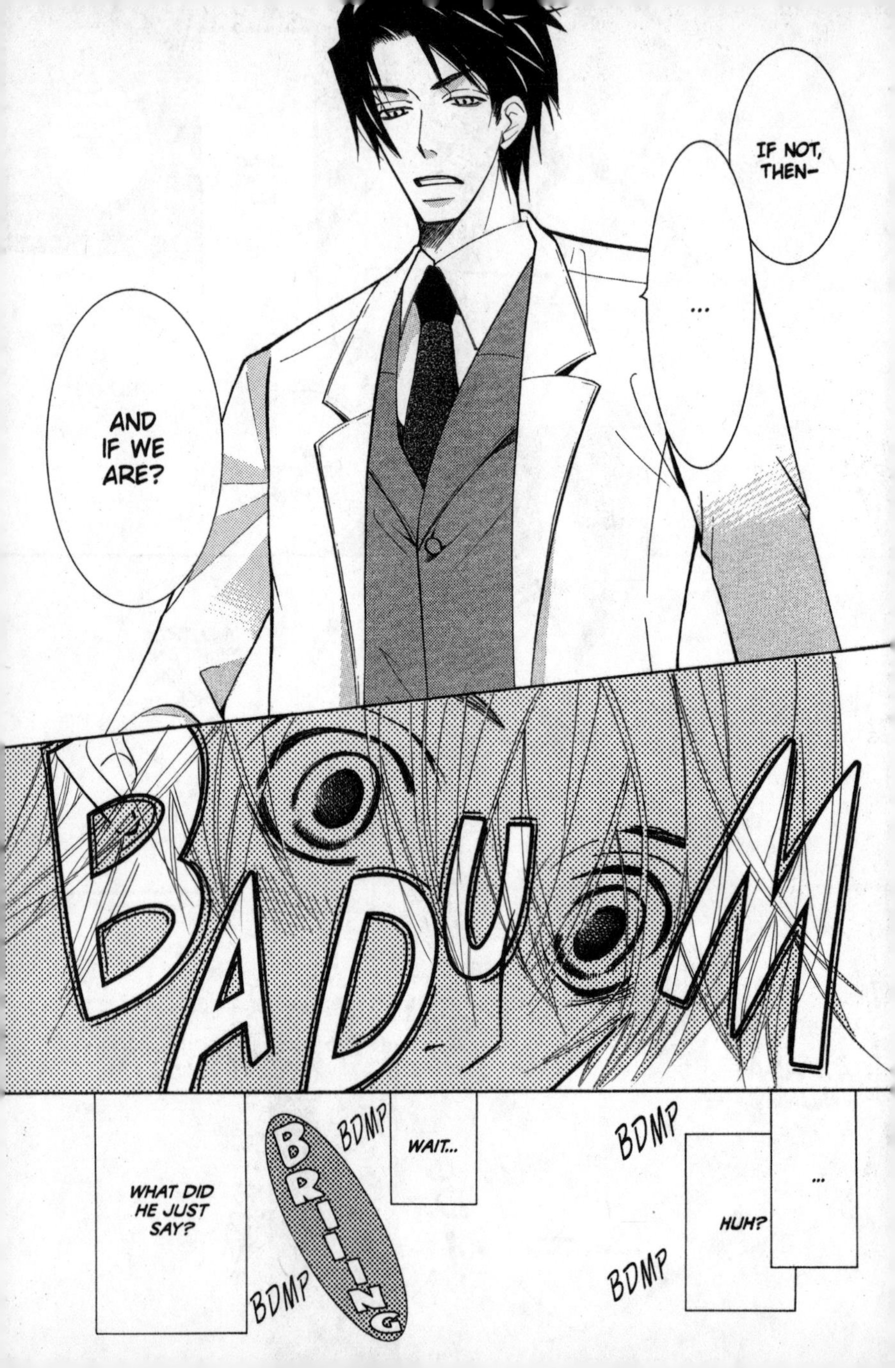
IF NOT, THEN–
...
AND IF WE ARE?
BADUM
...
HUH?
BDMP
BDMP
WAIT...
BDMP
BRIIING
WHAT DID HE JUST SAY?
BDMP

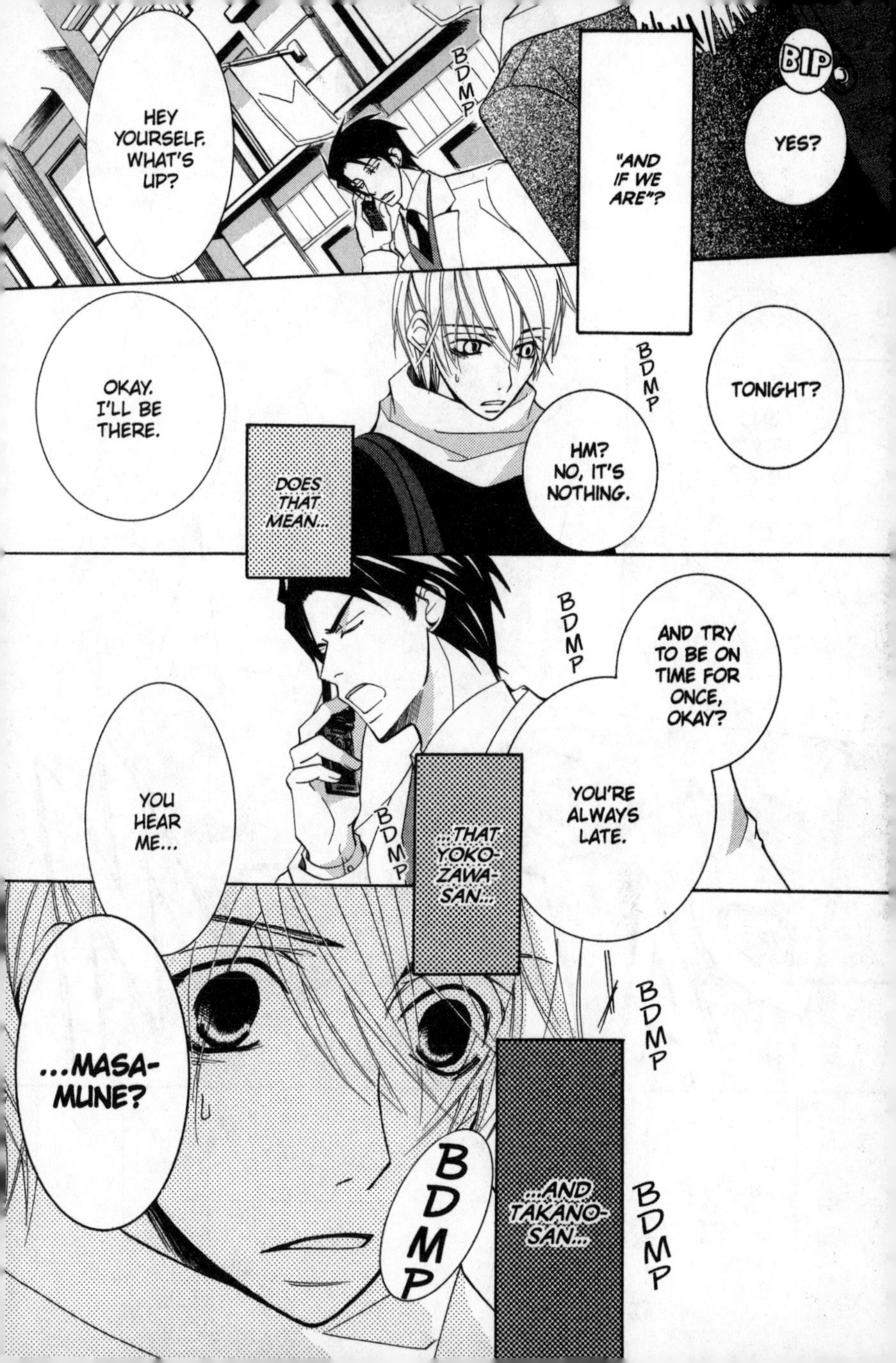
BIP
YES?
"AND IF WE ARE"?
BDMP
HEY YOURSELF. WHAT'S UP?
TONIGHT?
BDMP
HM? NO, IT'S NOTHING.
DOES THAT MEAN...
OKAY. I'LL BE THERE.
BDMP
AND TRY TO BE ON TIME FOR ONCE, OKAY?
YOU'RE ALWAYS LATE.
...THAT YOKO-ZAWA-SAN...
BDMP
YOU HEAR ME...
BDMP
BDMP
...AND TAKANO-SAN...
BDMP
...MASA-MUNE?

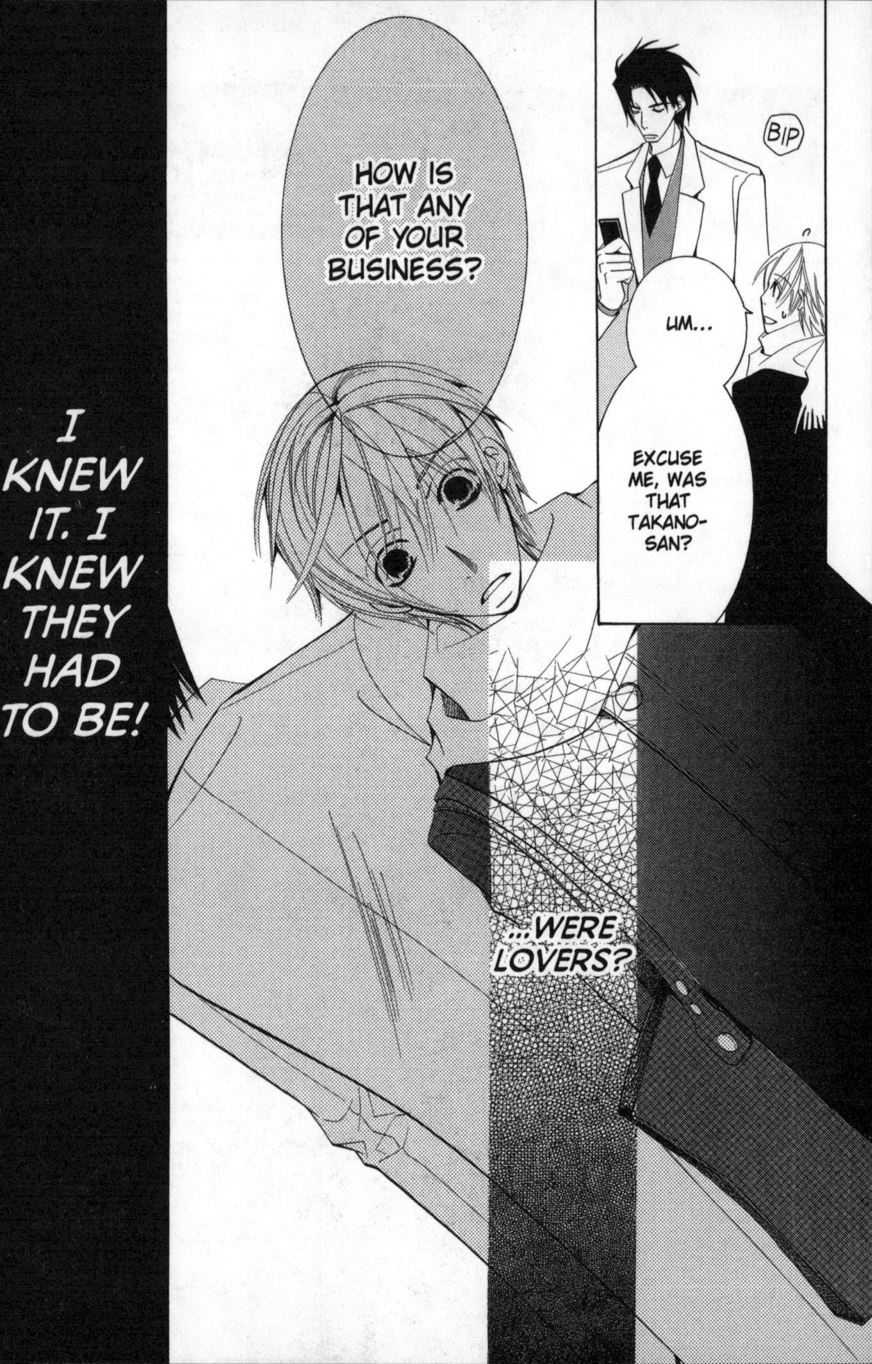
BIP
UM...
EXCUSE ME, WAS THAT TAKANO-SAN?
HOW IS THAT ANY OF YOUR BUSINESS?
...WERE LOVERS?
I KNEW IT. I KNEW THEY HAD TO BE!

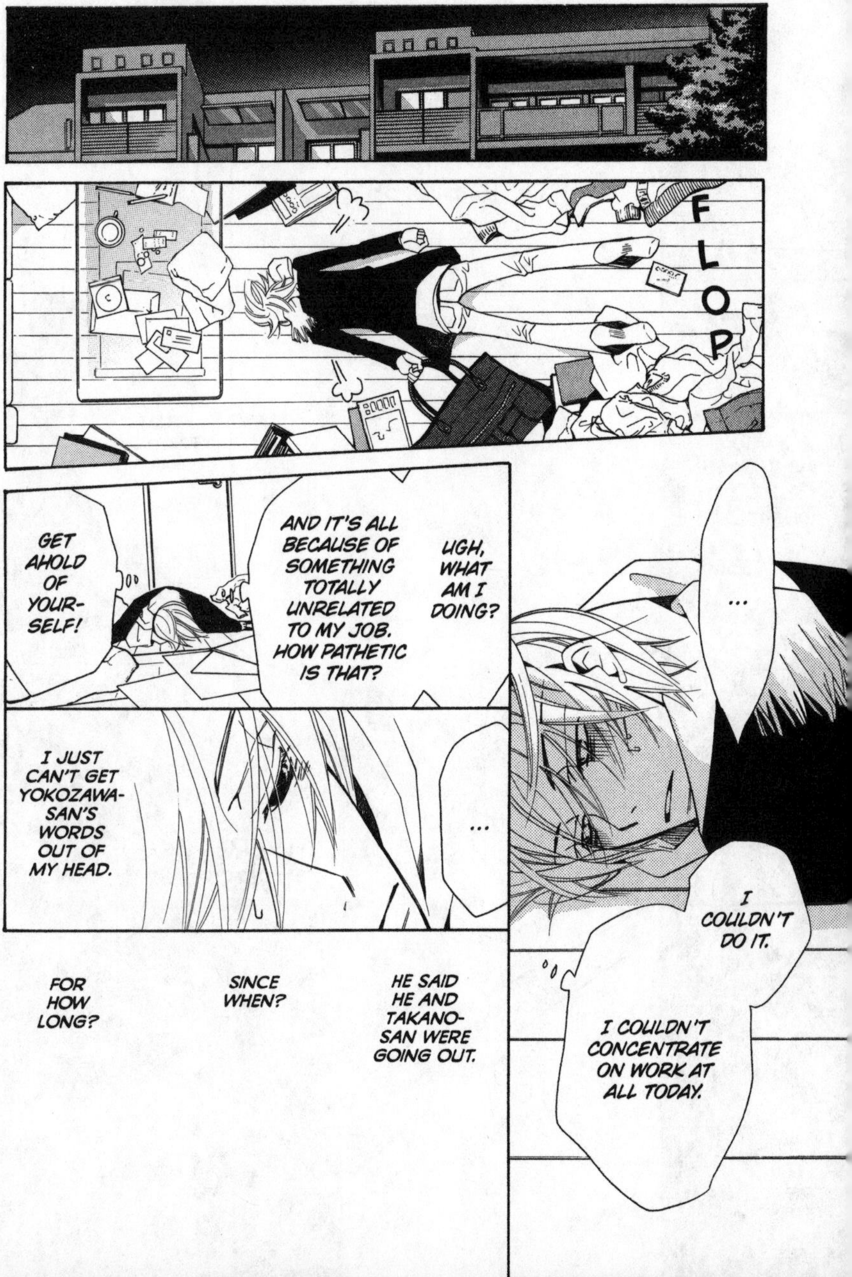
FLOP
...
I COULDN'T DO IT.
I COULDN'T CONCENTRATE ON WORK AT ALL TODAY.
UGH, WHAT AM I DOING?
AND IT'S ALL BECAUSE OF SOMETHING TOTALLY UNRELATED TO MY JOB. HOW PATHETIC IS THAT?
GET AHOLD OF YOUR-SELF!
...
I JUST CAN'T GET YOKOZAWA-SAN'S WORDS OUT OF MY HEAD.
HE SAID HE AND TAKANO-SAN WERE GOING OUT.
SINCE WHEN?
FOR HOW LONG?

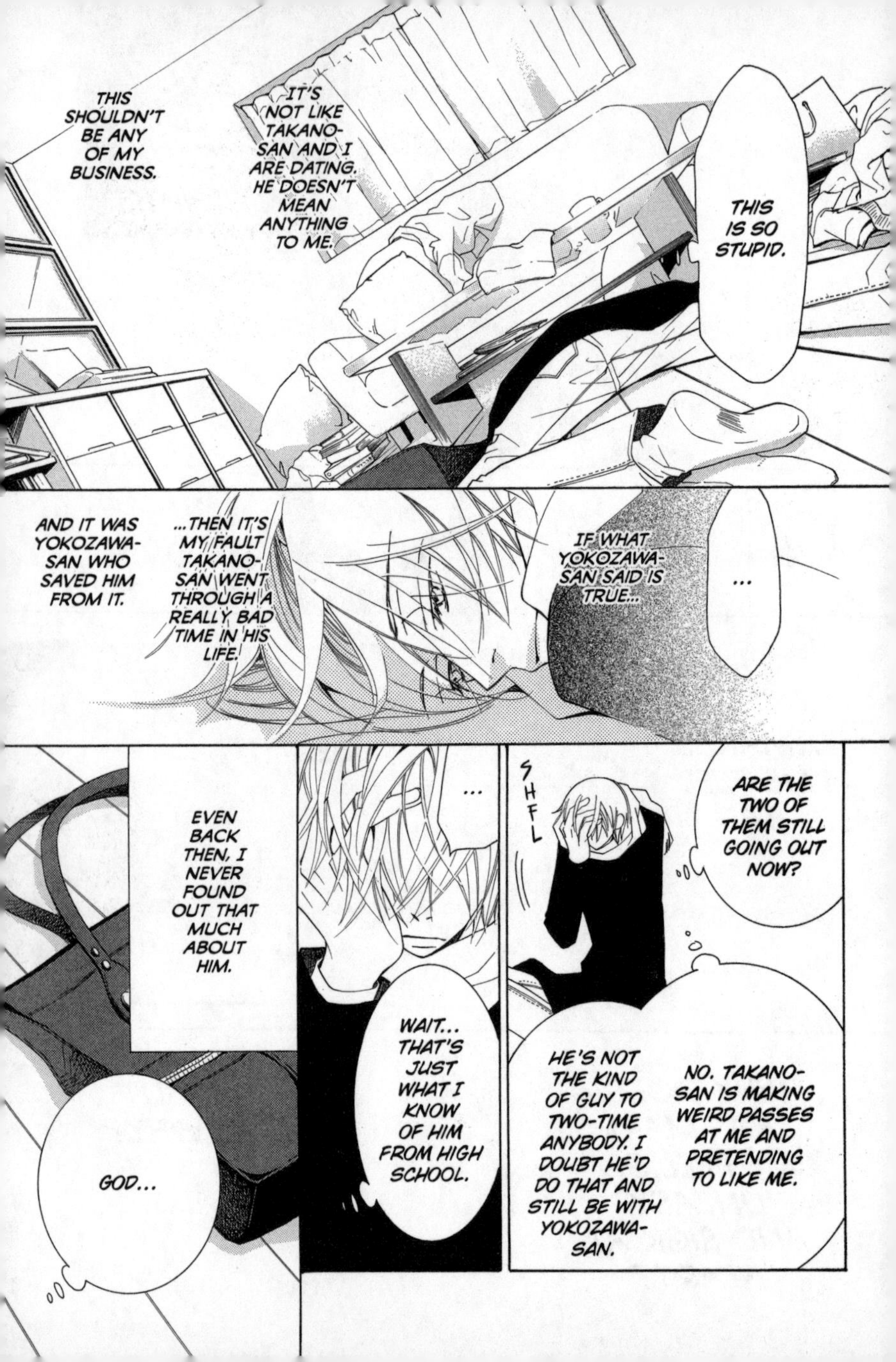
THIS IS SO STUPID.
IT'S NOT LIKE TAKANO-SAN AND I ARE DATING. HE DOESN'T MEAN ANYTHING TO ME.
THIS SHOULDN'T BE ANY OF MY BUSINESS.
...
IF WHAT YOKOZAWA-SAN SAID IS TRUE...
...THEN IT'S MY FAULT TAKANO-SAN WENT THROUGH A REALLY BAD TIME IN HIS LIFE.
AND IT WAS YOKOZAWA-SAN WHO SAVED HIM FROM IT.
ARE THE TWO OF THEM STILL GOING OUT NOW?
SHFL
NO. TAKANO-SAN IS MAKING WEIRD PASSES AT ME AND PRETENDING TO LIKE ME.
HE'S NOT THE KIND OF GUY TO TWO-TIME ANYBODY. I DOUBT HE'D DO THAT AND STILL BE WITH YOKOZAWA-SAN.
...
WAIT... THAT'S JUST WHAT I KNOW OF HIM FROM HIGH SCHOOL.
EVEN BACK THEN, I NEVER FOUND OUT THAT MUCH ABOUT HIM.
GOD...

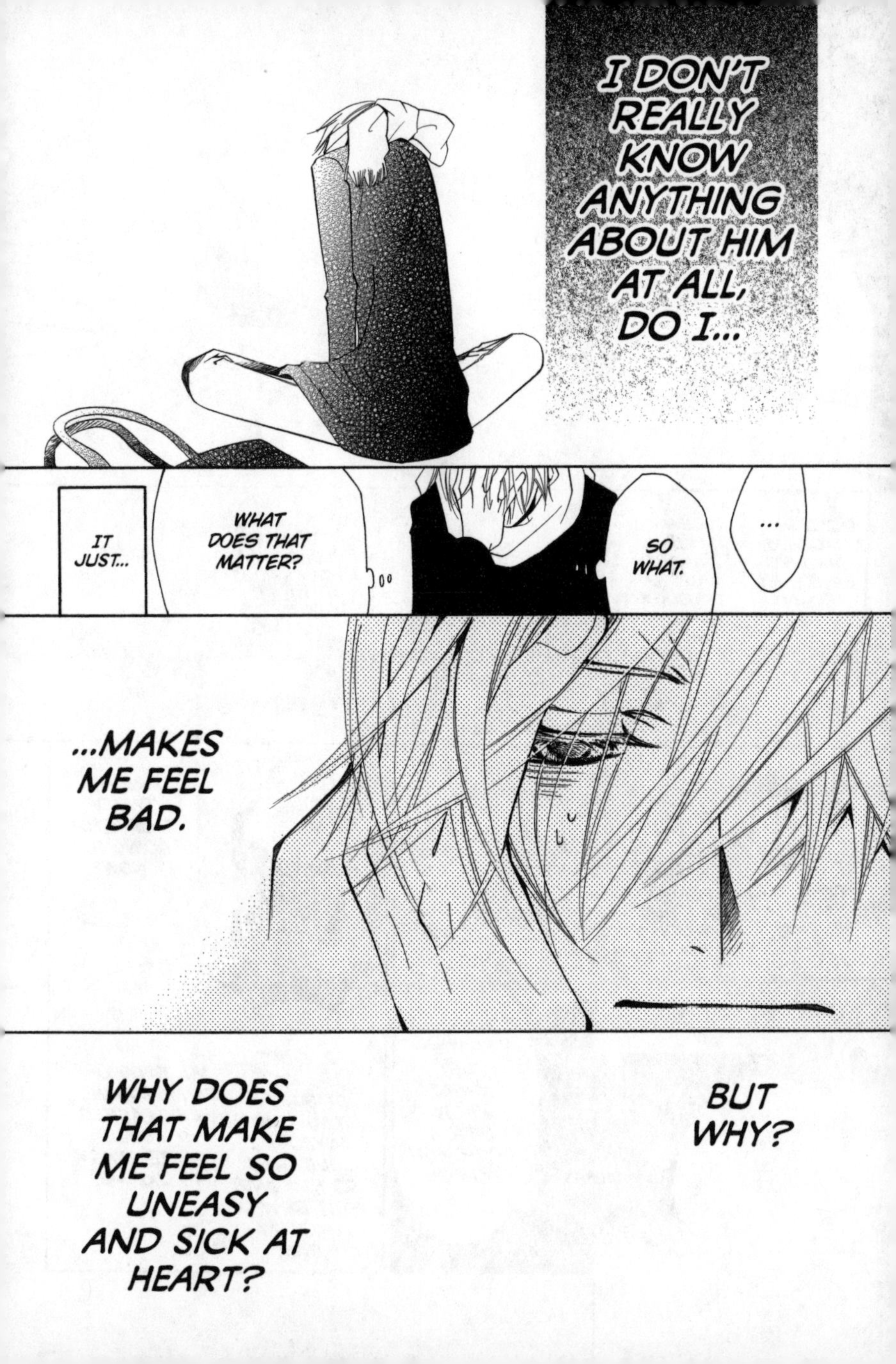
I DON'T REALLY KNOW ANYTHING ABOUT HIM AT ALL, DO I...
...
SO WHAT.
WHAT DOES THAT MATTER?
IT JUST...
...MAKES ME FEEL BAD.
BUT WHY?
WHY DOES THAT MAKE ME FEEL SO UNEASY AND SICK AT HEART?

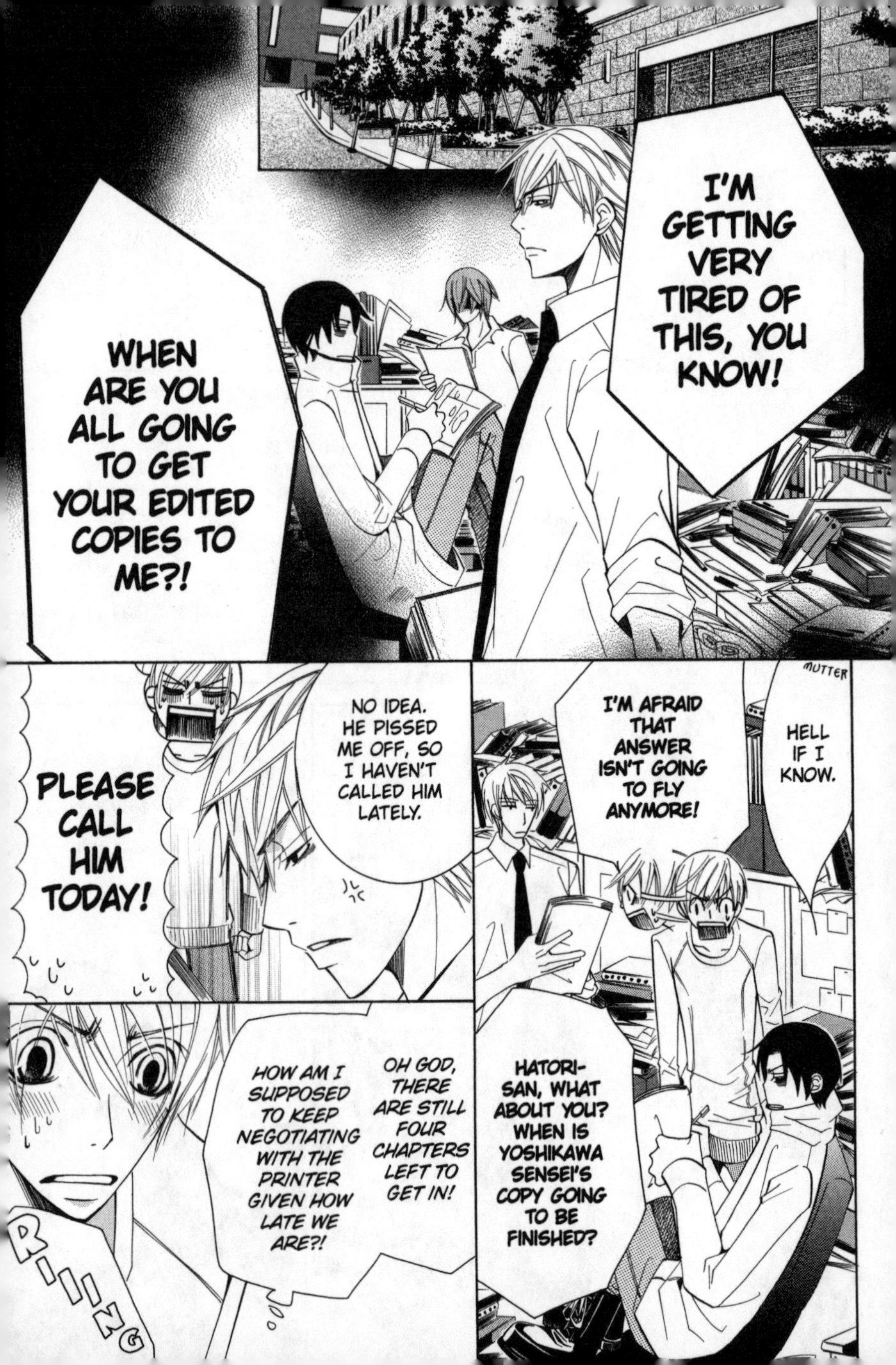
I'M GETTING VERY TIRED OF THIS, YOU KNOW!
WHEN ARE YOU ALL GOING TO GET YOUR EDITED COPIES TO ME?!
MUTTER
HELL IF I KNOW.
I'M AFRAID THAT ANSWER ISN'T GOING TO FLY ANYMORE!
HATORI-SAN, WHAT ABOUT YOU? WHEN IS YOSHIKAWA SENSEI'S COPY GOING TO BE FINISHED?
NO IDEA. HE PISSED ME OFF, SO I HAVEN'T CALLED HIM LATELY.
PLEASE CALL HIM TODAY!
OH GOD, THERE ARE STILL FOUR CHAPTERS LEFT TO GET IN!
HOW AM I SUPPOSED TO KEEP NEGOTIATING WITH THE PRINTER GIVEN HOW LATE WE ARE?!
RIIING

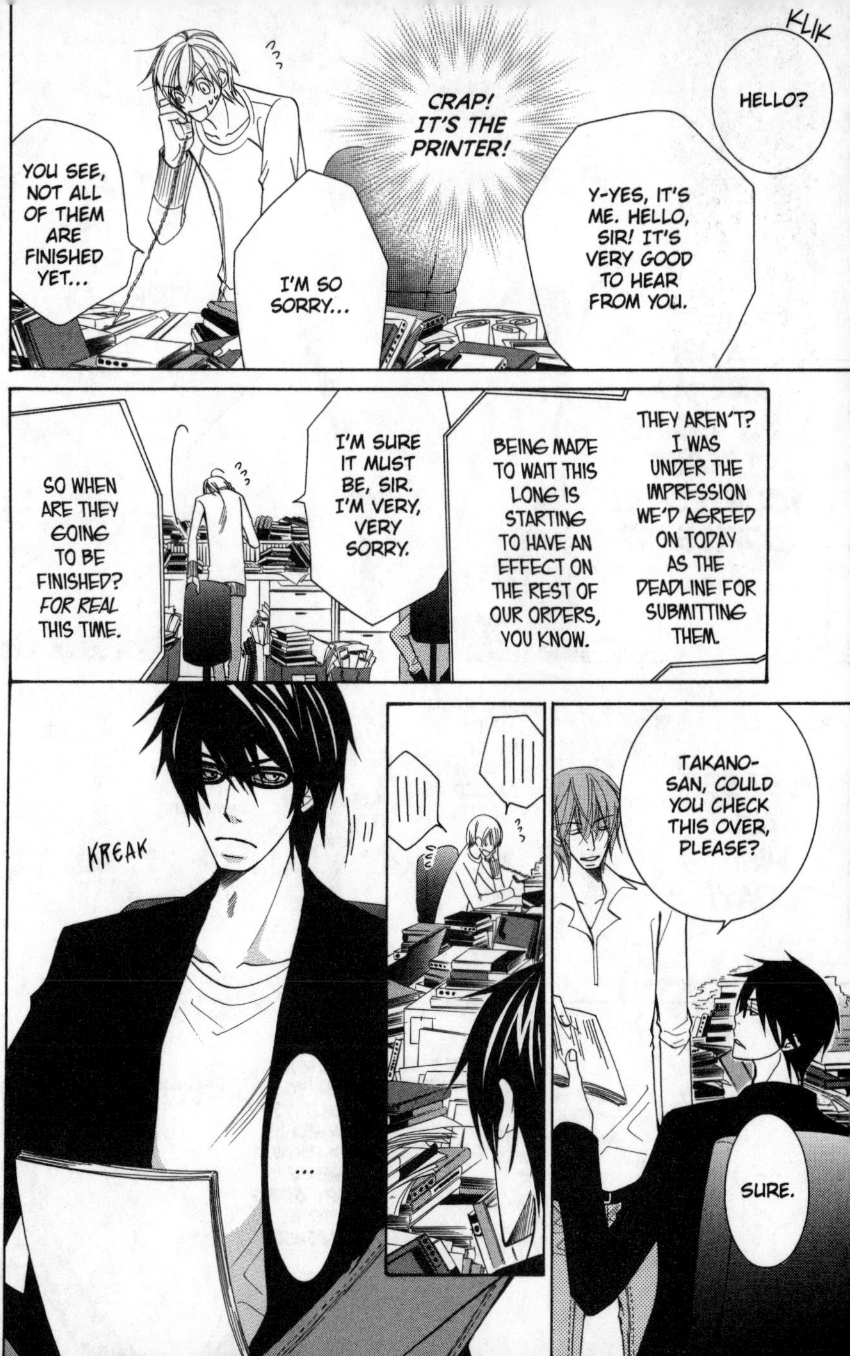
KLIK
HELLO?
Y-YES, IT'S ME. HELLO, SIR! IT'S VERY GOOD TO HEAR FROM YOU.
CRAP! IT'S THE PRINTER!
I'M SO SORRY...
YOU SEE, NOT ALL OF THEM ARE FINISHED YET...
THEY AREN'T? I WAS UNDER THE IMPRESSION WE'D AGREED ON TODAY AS THE DEADLINE FOR SUBMITTING THEM.
BEING MADE TO WAIT THIS LONG IS STARTING TO HAVE AN EFFECT ON THE REST OF OUR ORDERS, YOU KNOW.
I'M SURE IT MUST BE, SIR. I'M VERY, VERY SORRY.
SO WHEN ARE THEY GOING TO BE FINISHED? FOR REAL THIS TIME.
TAKANO-SAN, COULD YOU CHECK THIS OVER, PLEASE?
SURE.
KREAK
...

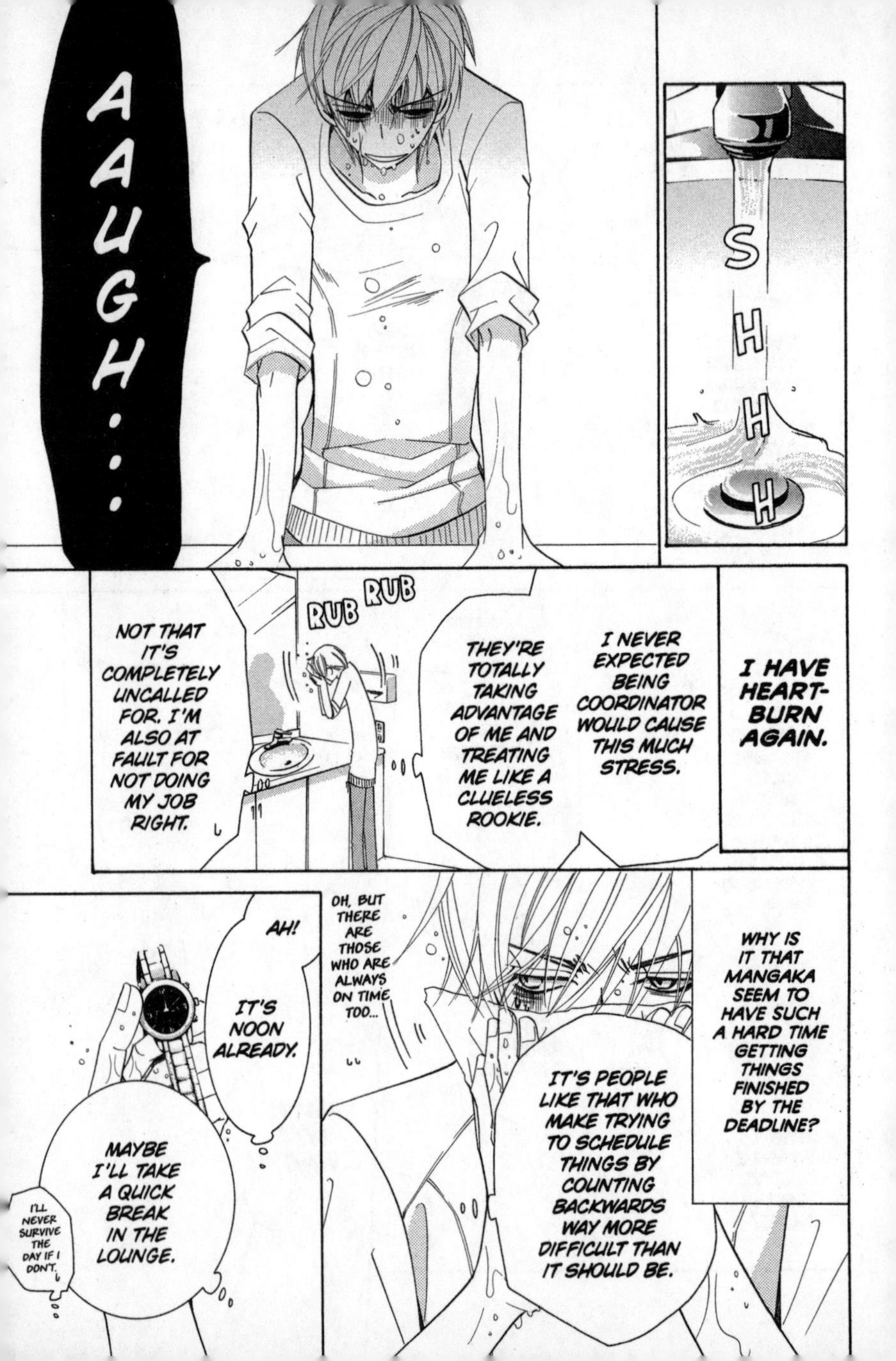
SHHHH
AAUGH...
I HAVE HEARTBURN AGAIN.
I NEVER EXPECTED BEING COORDINATOR WOULD CAUSE THIS MUCH STRESS.
THEY'RE TOTALLY TAKING ADVANTAGE OF ME AND TREATING ME LIKE A CLUELESS ROOKIE.
RUB RUB
NOT THAT IT'S COMPLETELY UNCALLED FOR. I'M ALSO AT FAULT FOR NOT DOING MY JOB RIGHT.
WHY IS IT THAT MANGAKA SEEM TO HAVE SUCH A HARD TIME GETTING THINGS FINISHED BY THE DEADLINE?
IT'S PEOPLE LIKE THAT WHO MAKE TRYING TO SCHEDULE THINGS BY COUNTING BACKWARDS WAY MORE DIFFICULT THAN IT SHOULD BE.
OH, BUT THERE ARE THOSE WHO ARE ALWAYS ON TIME TOO...
AH!
IT'S NOON ALREADY.
MAYBE I'LL TAKE A QUICK BREAK IN THE LOUNGE.
I'LL NEVER SURVIVE THE DAY IF I DON'T.

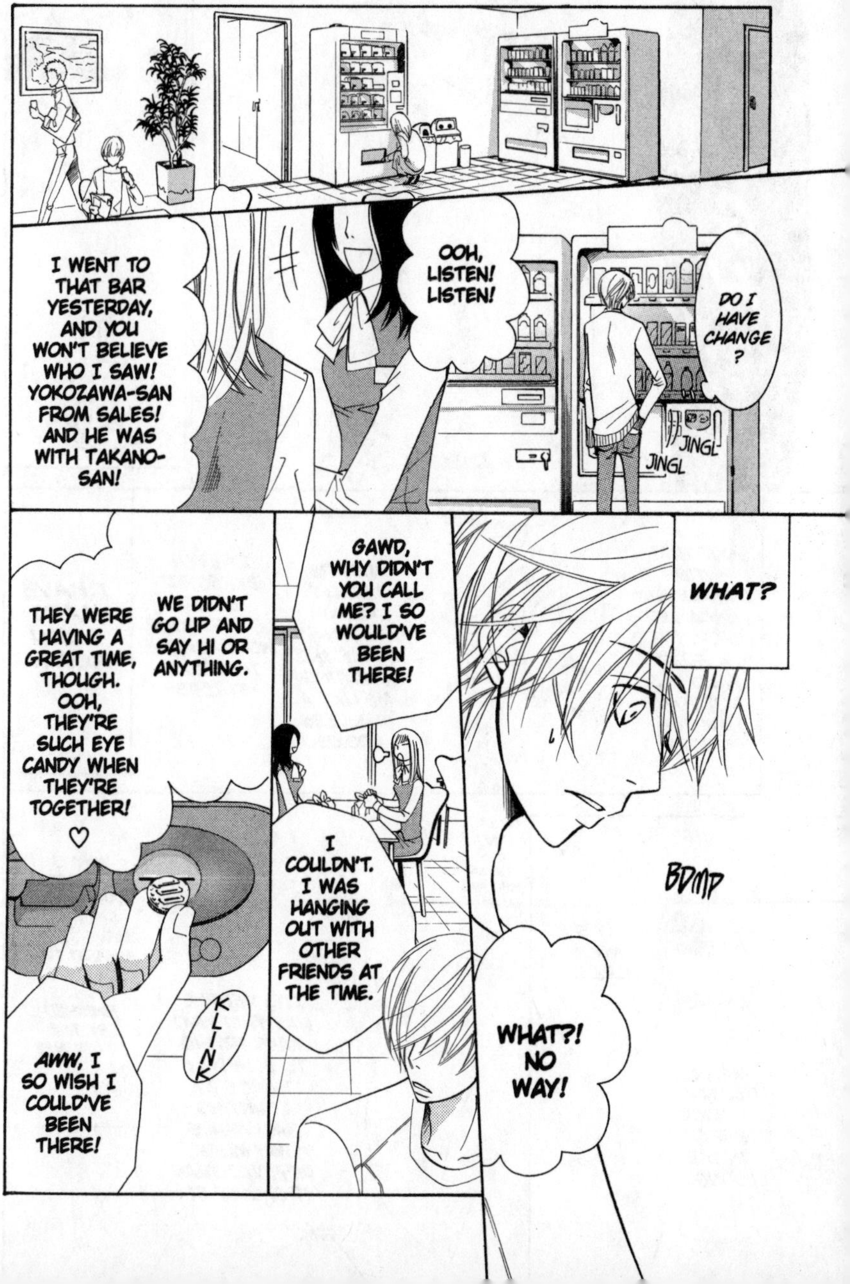
DO I HAVE CHANGE?
JINGL
JINGL
OOH, LISTEN! LISTEN!
I WENT TO THAT BAR YESTERDAY, AND YOU WON'T BELIEVE WHO I SAW! YOKOZAWA-SAN FROM SALES! AND HE WAS WITH TAKANO-SAN!
WHAT?
BDMP
WHAT?! NO WAY!
GAWD, WHY DIDN'T YOU CALL ME? I SO WOULD'VE BEEN THERE!
I COULDN'T. I WAS HANGING OUT WITH OTHER FRIENDS AT THE TIME.
WE DIDN'T GO UP AND SAY HI OR ANYTHING.
THEY WERE HAVING A GREAT TIME, THOUGH. OOH, THEY'RE SUCH EYE CANDY WHEN THEY'RE TOGETHER! ♡
KLINK
AWW, I SO WISH I COULD'VE BEEN THERE!

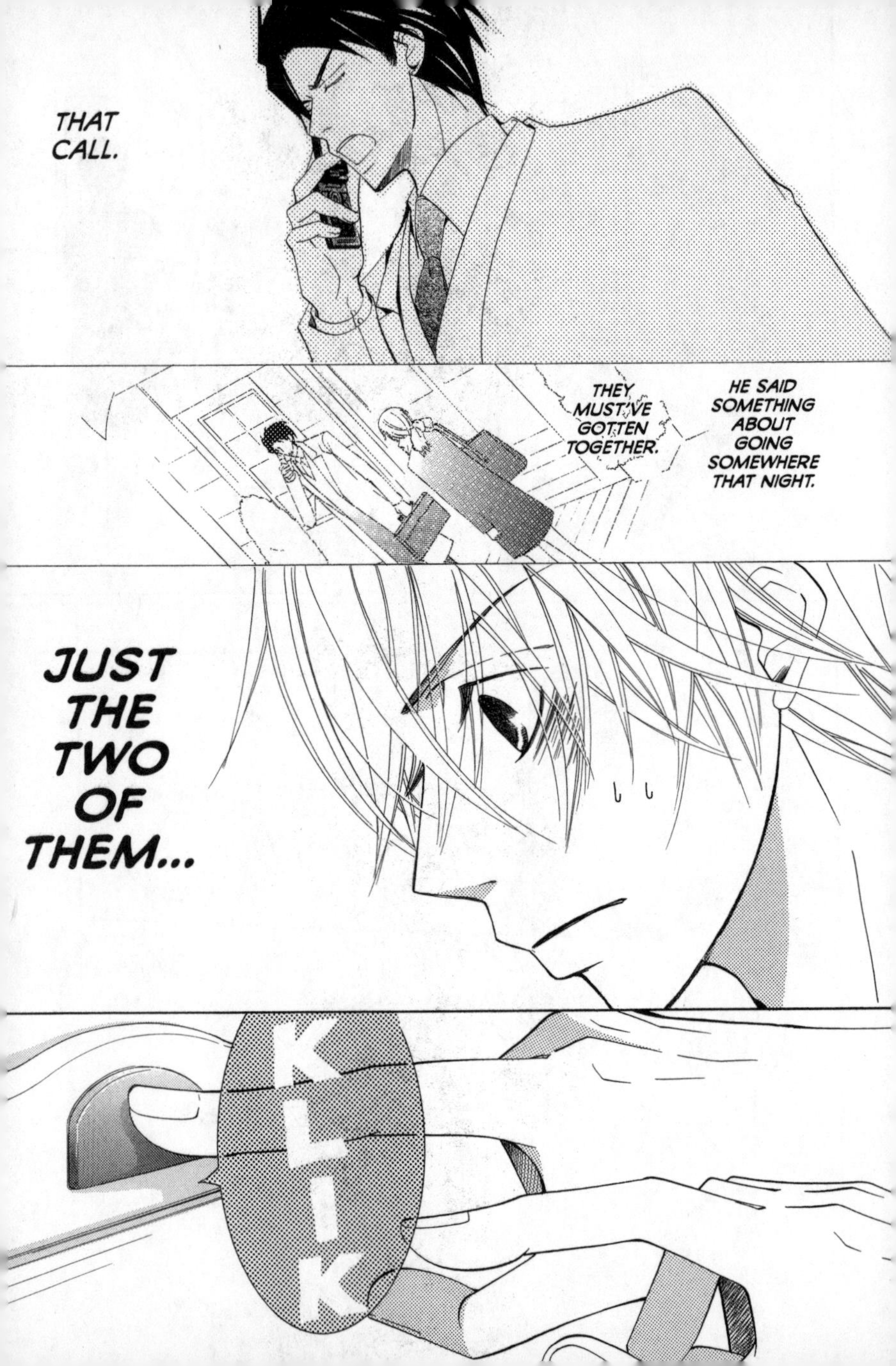
THAT CALL.
HE SAID SOMETHING ABOUT GOING SOMEWHERE THAT NIGHT.
THEY MUST'VE GOTTEN TOGETHER.
JUST THE TWO OF THEM...
KLIK

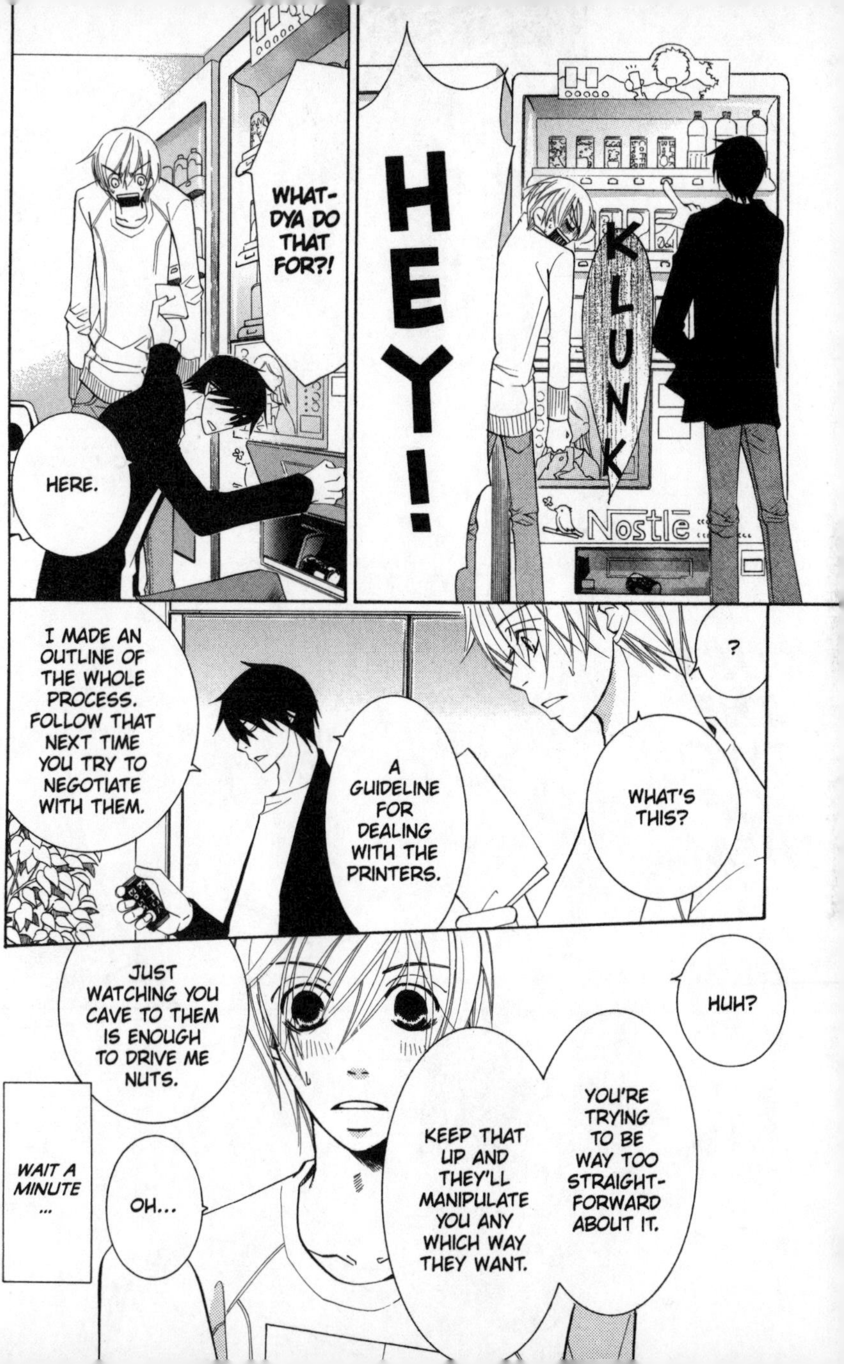
HEY!
KLUNK
WHAT-DYA DO THAT FOR?!
HERE.
?
WHAT'S THIS?
A GUIDELINE FOR DEALING WITH THE PRINTERS.
I MADE AN OUTLINE OF THE WHOLE PROCESS. FOLLOW THAT NEXT TIME YOU TRY TO NEGOTIATE WITH THEM.
HUH?
JUST WATCHING YOU CAVE TO THEM IS ENOUGH TO DRIVE ME NUTS.
YOU'RE TRYING TO BE WAY TOO STRAIGHT-FORWARD ABOUT IT.
KEEP THAT UP AND THEY'LL MANIPULATE YOU ANY WHICH WAY THEY WANT.
OH...
WAIT A MINUTE ...

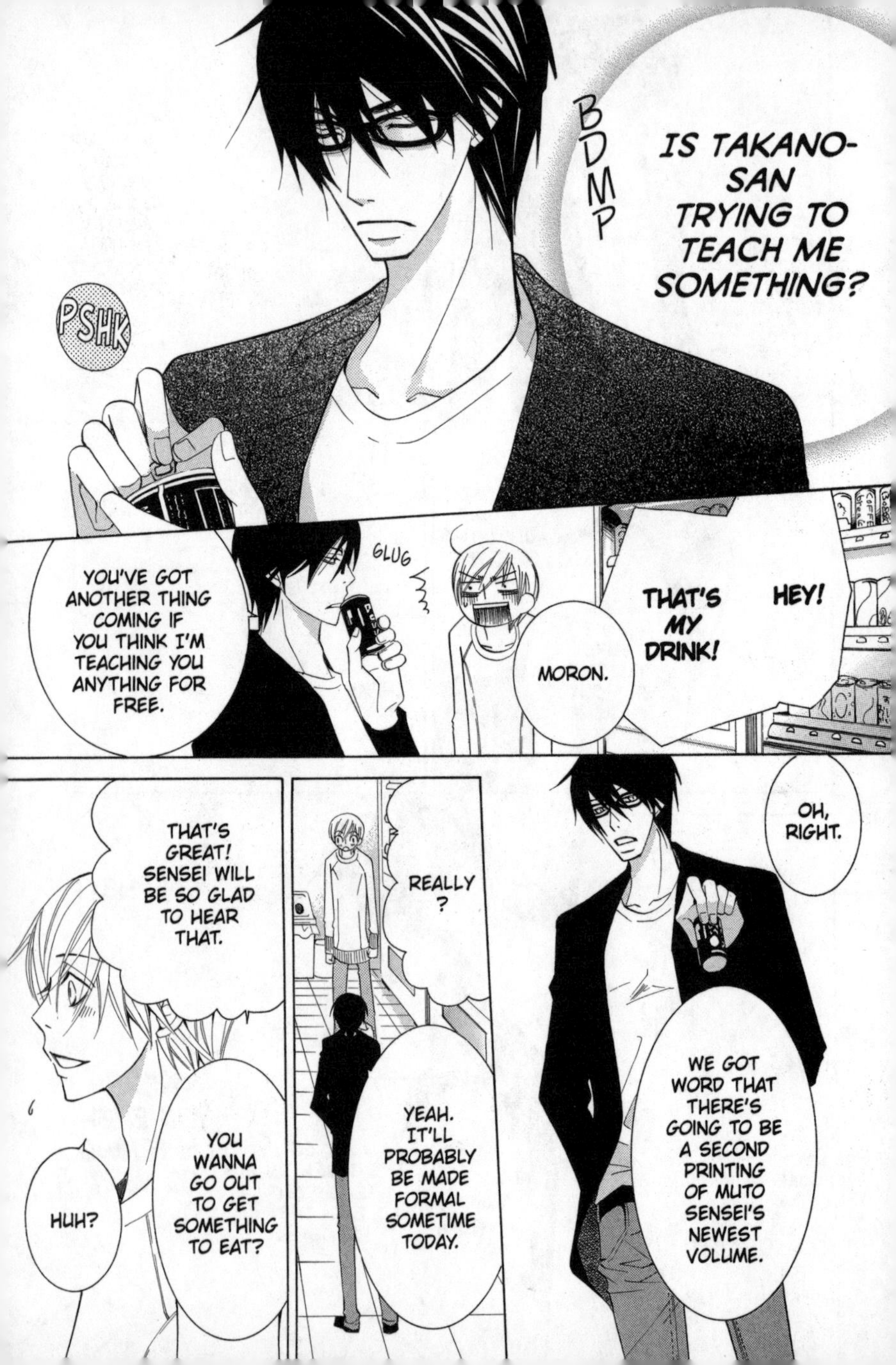
BDMP
IS TAKANO-SAN TRYING TO TEACH ME SOMETHING?
PSHK
HEY!
THAT'S MY DRINK!
MORON.
GLUG
YOU'VE GOT ANOTHER THING COMING IF YOU THINK I'M TEACHING YOU ANYTHING FOR FREE.
OH, RIGHT.
WE GOT WORD THAT THERE'S GOING TO BE A SECOND PRINTING OF MUTO SENSEI'S NEWEST VOLUME.
REALLY?
YEAH. IT'LL PROBABLY BE MADE FORMAL SOMETIME TODAY.
THAT'S GREAT! SENSEI WILL BE SO GLAD TO HEAR THAT.
YOU WANNA GO OUT TO GET SOMETHING TO EAT?
HUH?

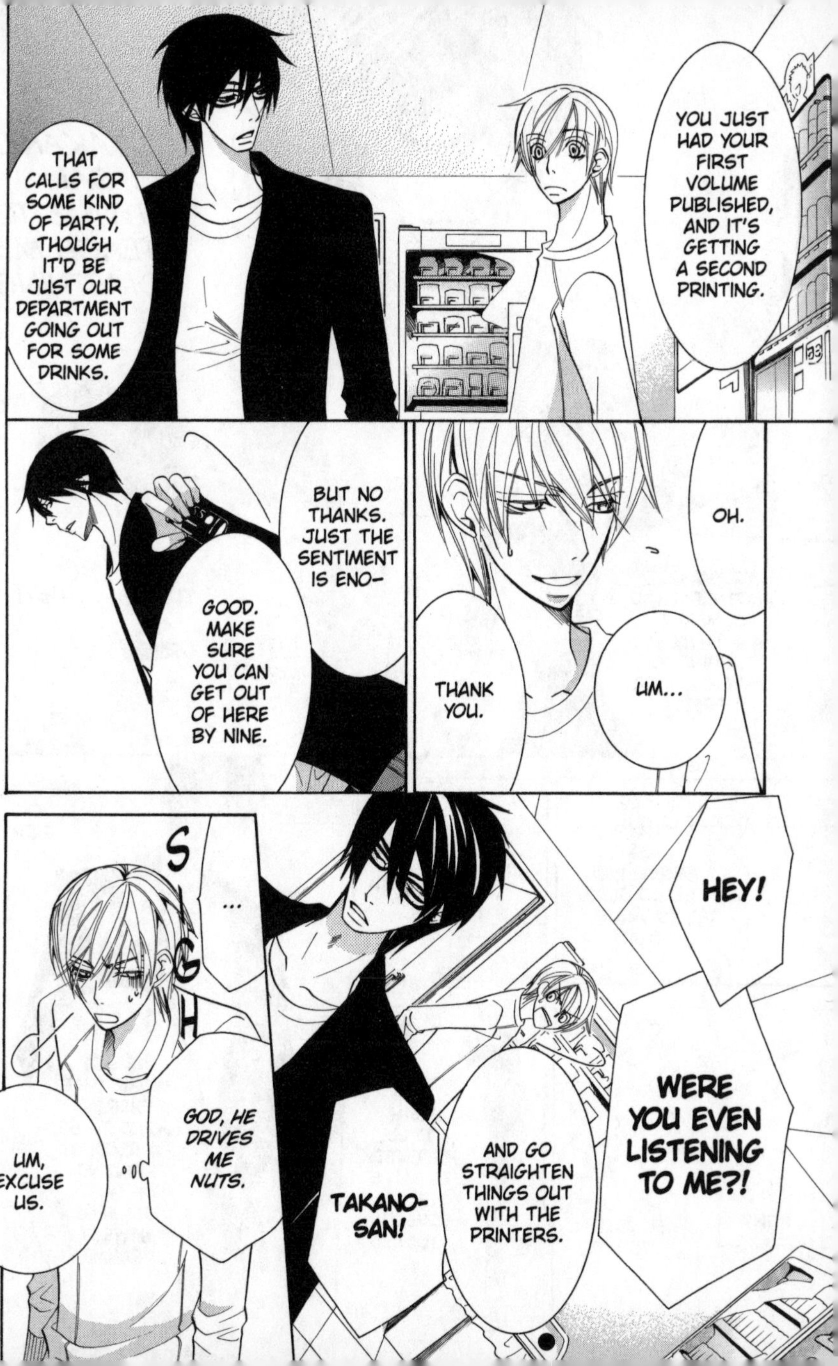
YOU JUST HAD YOUR FIRST VOLUME PUBLISHED, AND IT'S GETTING A SECOND PRINTING.
THAT CALLS FOR SOME KIND OF PARTY, THOUGH IT'D BE JUST OUR DEPARTMENT GOING OUT FOR SOME DRINKS.
OH.
UM...
THANK YOU.
BUT NO THANKS. JUST THE SENTIMENT IS ENO-
GOOD. MAKE SURE YOU CAN GET OUT OF HERE BY NINE.
HEY!
WERE YOU EVEN LISTENING TO ME?!
...
AND GO STRAIGHTEN THINGS OUT WITH THE PRINTERS.
TAKANO-SAN!
GOD, HE DRIVES ME NUTS.
SIGH
UM, EXCUSE US.

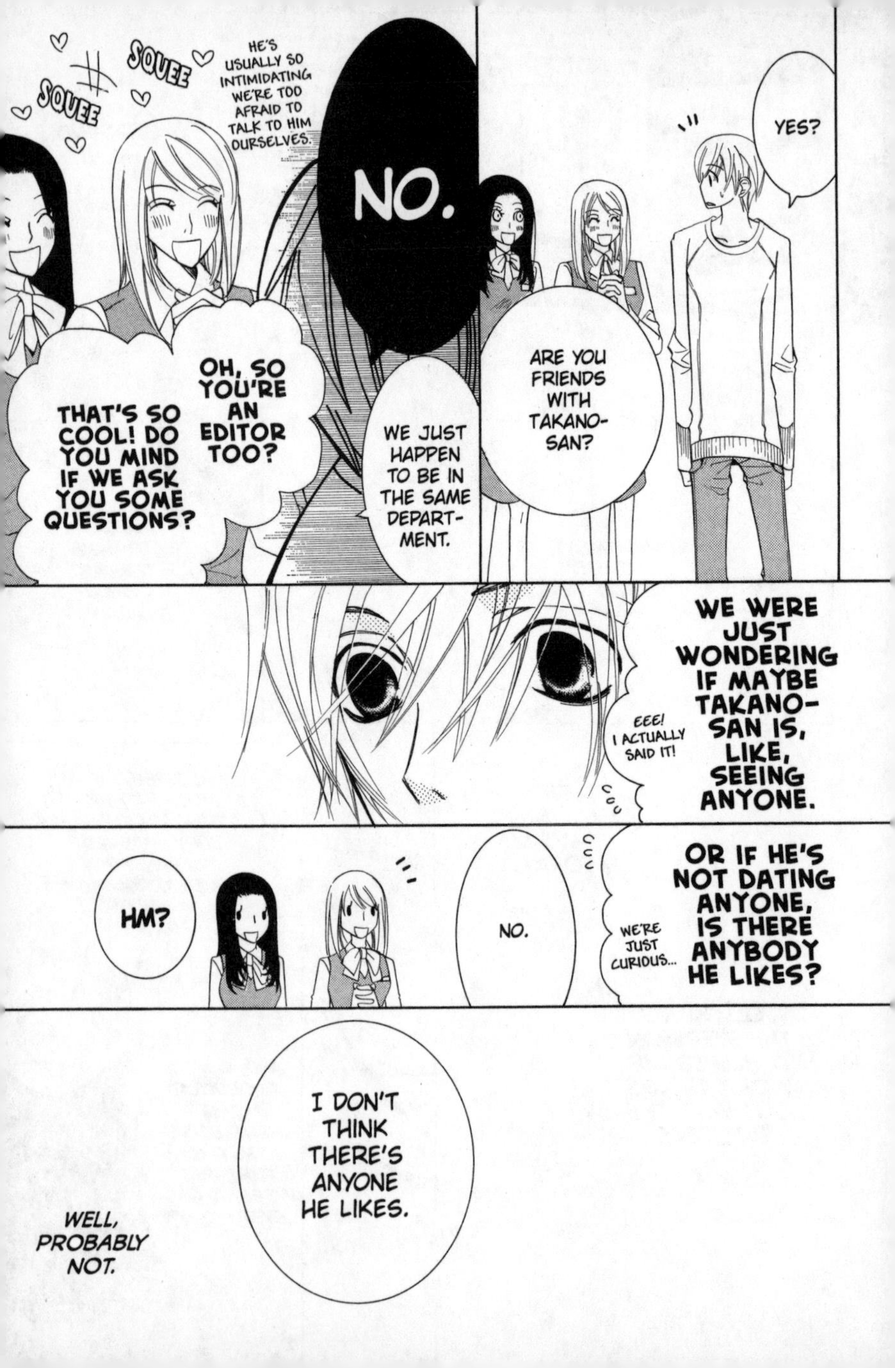

YES?
ARE YOU FRIENDS WITH TAKANO-SAN?
NO.
WE JUST HAPPEN TO BE IN THE SAME DEPART-MENT.
OH, SO YOU'RE AN EDITOR TOO?
THAT'S SO COOL! DO YOU MIND IF WE ASK YOU SOME QUESTIONS?
HE'S USUALLY SO INTIMIDATING WE'RE TOO AFRAID TO TALK TO HIM OURSELVES.
SQUEE
SQUEE
WE WERE JUST WONDERING IF MAYBE TAKANO-SAN IS, LIKE, SEEING ANYONE.
EEE! I ACTUALLY SAID IT!
OR IF HE'S NOT DATING ANYONE, IS THERE ANYBODY HE LIKES?
WE'RE JUST CURIOUS...
NO.
HM?
I DON'T THINK THERE'S ANYONE HE LIKES.
WELL, PROBABLY NOT.

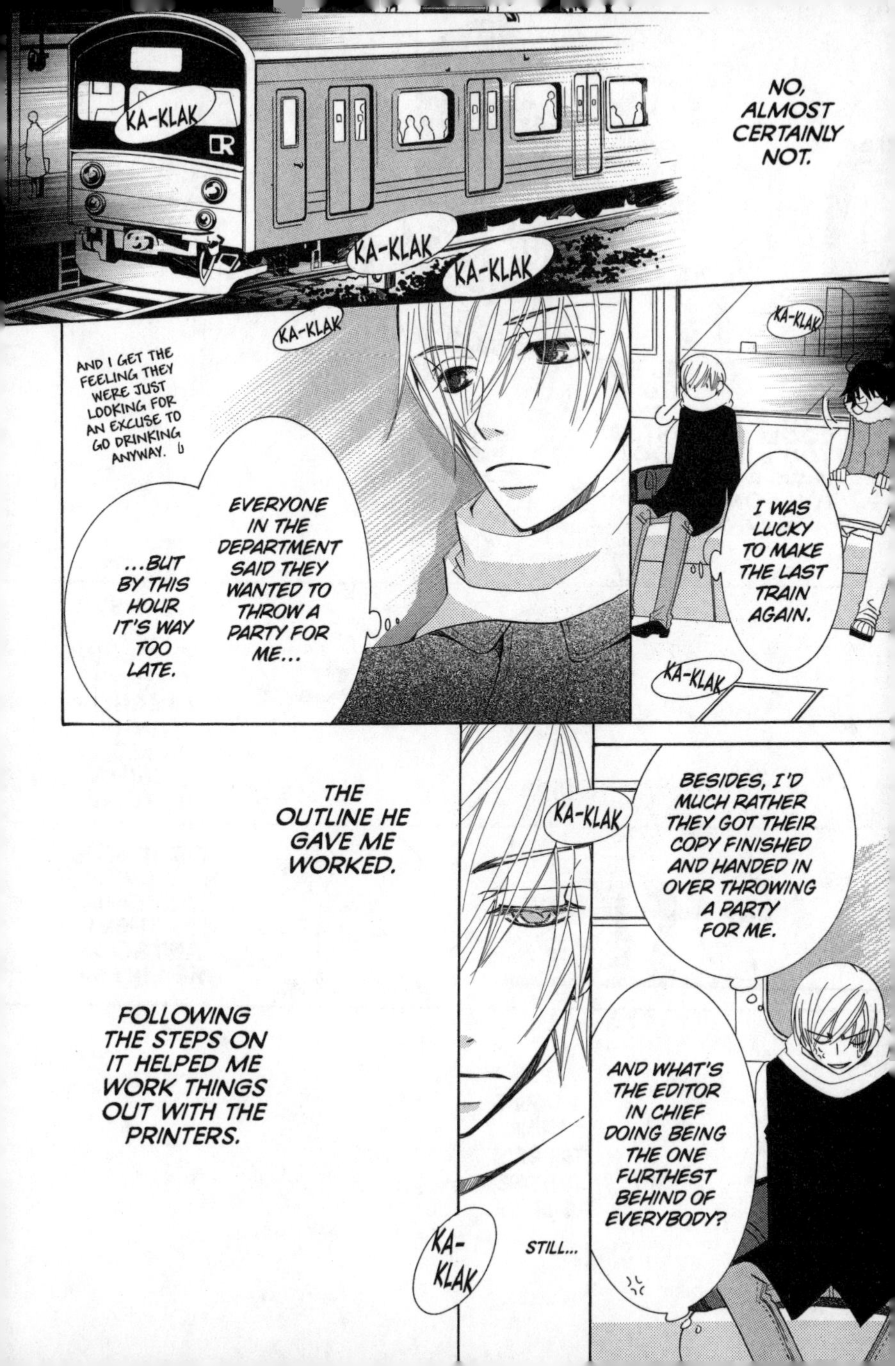
NO, ALMOST CERTAINLY NOT.
KA-KLAK
KA-KLAK
KA-KLAK
KA-KLAK
I WAS LUCKY TO MAKE THE LAST TRAIN AGAIN.
KA-KLAK
KA-KLAK
EVERYONE IN THE DEPARTMENT SAID THEY WANTED TO THROW A PARTY FOR ME...
...BUT BY THIS HOUR IT'S WAY TOO LATE.
AND I GET THE FEELING THEY WERE JUST LOOKING FOR AN EXCUSE TO GO DRINKING ANYWAY.
BESIDES, I'D MUCH RATHER THEY GOT THEIR COPY FINISHED AND HANDED IN OVER THROWING A PARTY FOR ME.
AND WHAT'S THE EDITOR IN CHIEF DOING BEING THE ONE FURTHEST BEHIND OF EVERYBODY?
KA-KLAK
STILL...
KA-KLAK
THE OUTLINE HE GAVE ME WORKED.
FOLLOWING THE STEPS ON IT HELPED ME WORK THINGS OUT WITH THE PRINTERS.

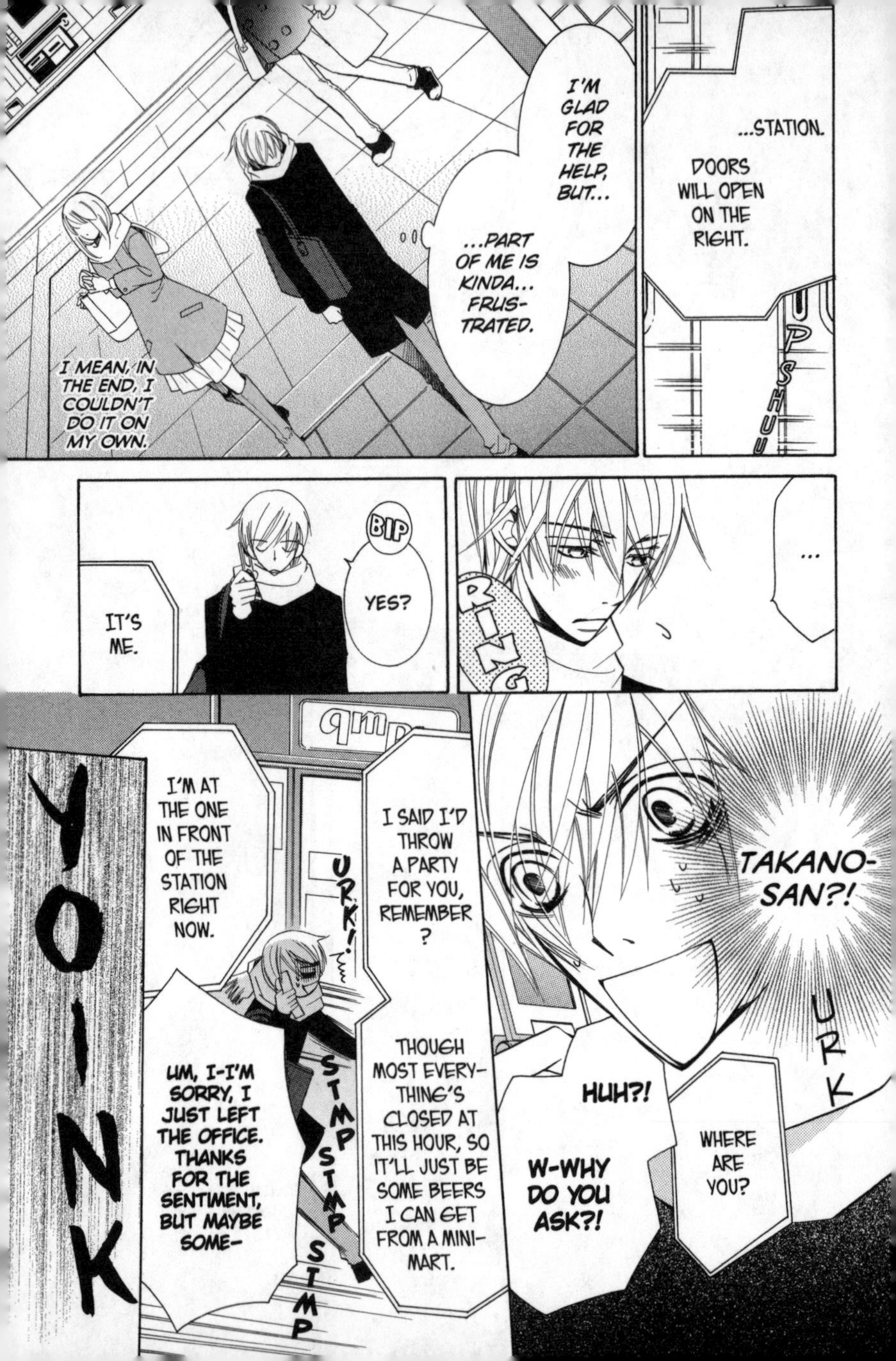
...STATION.
DOORS WILL OPEN ON THE RIGHT.
PSHUU
I'M GLAD FOR THE HELP, BUT...
...PART OF ME IS KINDA... FRUS-TRATED.
I MEAN, IN THE END, I COULDN'T DO IT ON MY OWN.
RING
...
BIP
YES?
IT'S ME.
TAKANO-SAN?!
URK
WHERE ARE YOU?
HUH?!
W-WHY DO YOU ASK?!
I SAID I'D THROW A PARTY FOR YOU, REMEMBER?
I'M AT THE ONE IN FRONT OF THE STATION RIGHT NOW.
URK!
THOUGH MOST EVERY-THING'S CLOSED AT THIS HOUR, SO IT'LL JUST BE SOME BEERS I CAN GET FROM A MINI-MART.
UM, I-I'M SORRY, I JUST LEFT THE OFFICE. THANKS FOR THE SENTIMENT, BUT MAYBE SOME-
STMP
STMP
STMP
STMP
YOINK

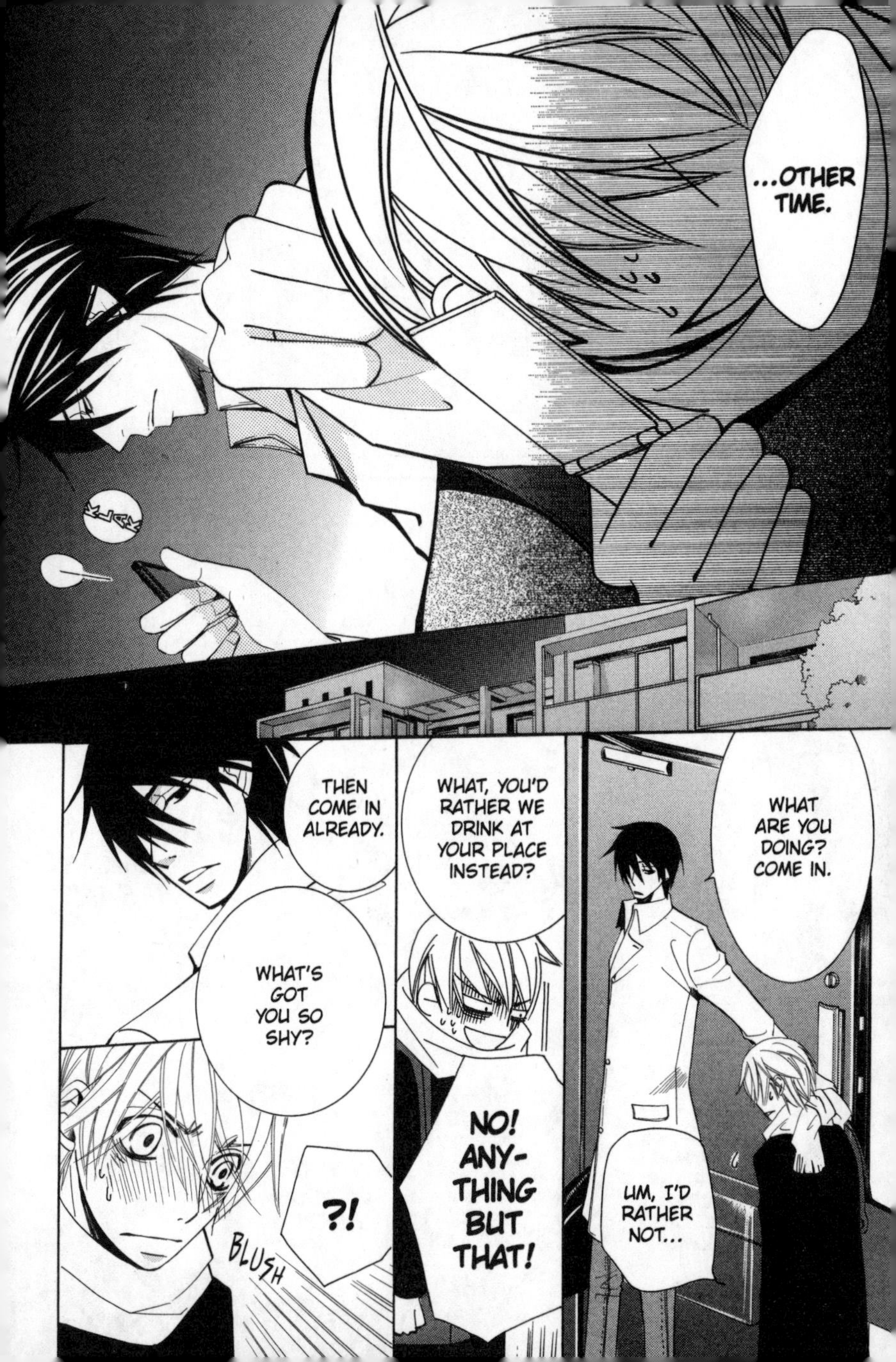
...OTHER TIME.
WHAT ARE YOU DOING? COME IN.
UM, I'D RATHER NOT...
WHAT, YOU'D RATHER WE DRINK AT YOUR PLACE INSTEAD?
NO! ANYTHING BUT THAT!
THEN COME IN ALREADY.
WHAT'S GOT YOU SO SHY?
?!
BLUSH

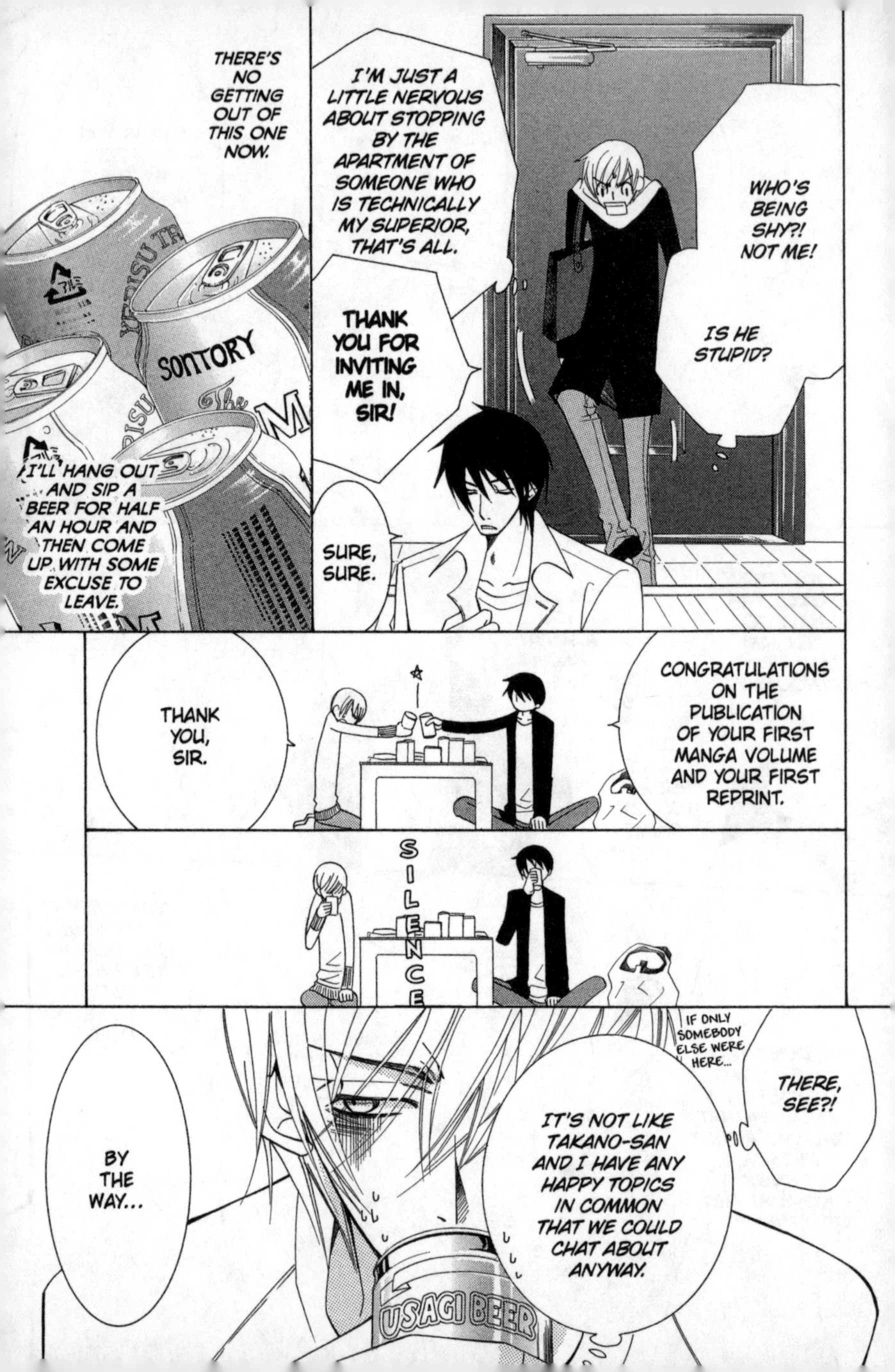
WHO'S BEING SHY?! NOT ME!
I'M JUST A LITTLE NERVOUS ABOUT STOPPING BY THE APARTMENT OF SOMEONE WHO IS TECHNICALLY MY SUPERIOR, THAT'S ALL.
IS HE STUPID?
THANK YOU FOR INVITING ME IN, SIR!
SURE, SURE.
THERE'S NO GETTING OUT OF THIS ONE NOW.
SONTORY
I'LL HANG OUT AND SIP A BEER FOR HALF AN HOUR AND THEN COME UP WITH SOME EXCUSE TO LEAVE.
CONGRATULATIONS ON THE PUBLICATION OF YOUR FIRST MANGA VOLUME AND YOUR FIRST REPRINT.
THANK YOU, SIR.
SILENCE
THERE, SEE?!
IF ONLY SOMEBODY ELSE WERE HERE...
IT'S NOT LIKE TAKANO-SAN AND I HAVE ANY HAPPY TOPICS IN COMMON THAT WE COULD CHAT ABOUT ANYWAY.
USAGI BEER
BY THE WAY...

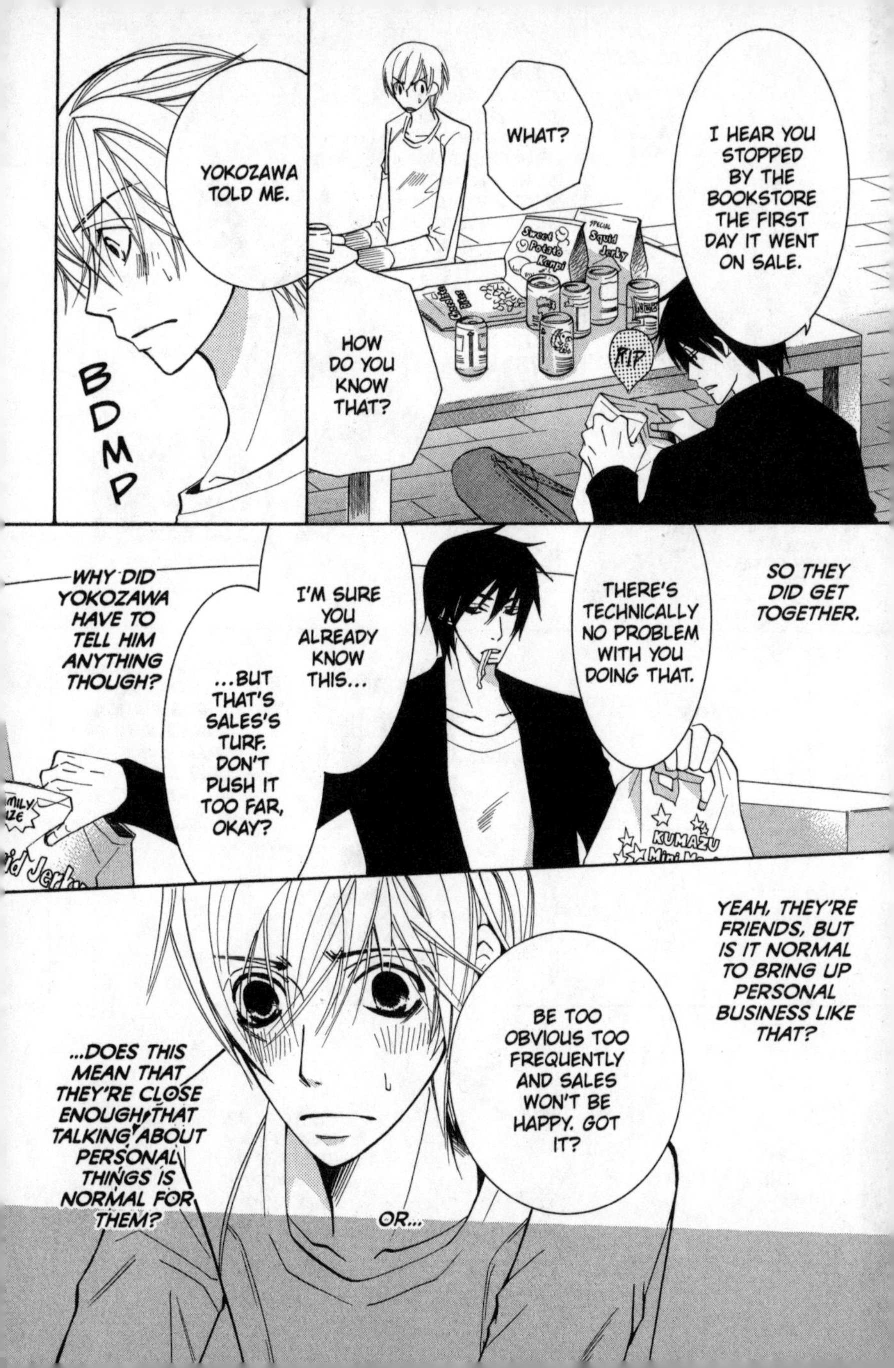
I HEAR YOU STOPPED BY THE BOOKSTORE THE FIRST DAY IT WENT ON SALE.
WHAT?
Special Squid Jerky
Sweet Potato Kenpi
RIP
HOW DO YOU KNOW THAT?
YOKOZAWA TOLD ME.
BDMP
SO THEY DID GET TOGETHER.
THERE'S TECHNICALLY NO PROBLEM WITH YOU DOING THAT.
I'M SURE YOU ALREADY KNOW THIS...
...BUT THAT'S SALES'S TURF. DON'T PUSH IT TOO FAR, OKAY?
WHY DID YOKOZAWA HAVE TO TELL HIM ANYTHING THOUGH?
YEAH, THEY'RE FRIENDS, BUT IS IT NORMAL TO BRING UP PERSONAL BUSINESS LIKE THAT?
BE TOO OBVIOUS TOO FREQUENTLY AND SALES WON'T BE HAPPY. GOT IT?
...DOES THIS MEAN THAT THEY'RE CLOSE ENOUGH THAT TALKING ABOUT PERSONAL THINGS IS NORMAL FOR THEM?
OR...

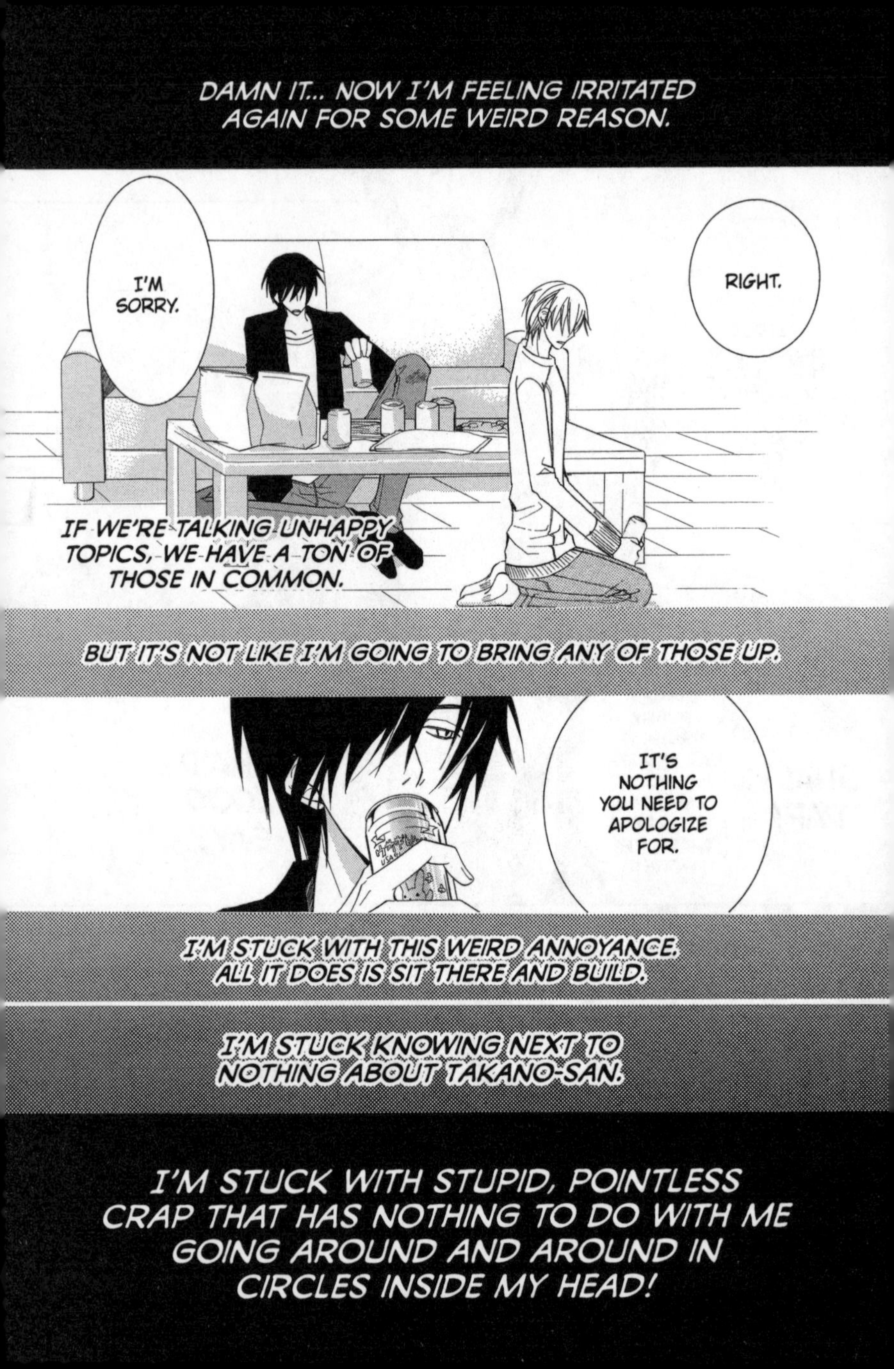
DAMN IT... NOW I'M FEELING IRRITATED AGAIN FOR SOME WEIRD REASON.
RIGHT.
I'M SORRY.
IF WE'RE TALKING UNHAPPY TOPICS, WE HAVE A TON OF THOSE IN COMMON.
BUT IT'S NOT LIKE I'M GOING TO BRING ANY OF THOSE UP.
IT'S NOTHING YOU NEED TO APOLOGIZE FOR.
I'M STUCK WITH THIS WEIRD ANNOYANCE. ALL IT DOES IS SIT THERE AND BUILD.
I'M STUCK KNOWING NEXT TO NOTHING ABOUT TAKANO-SAN.
I'M STUCK WITH STUPID, POINTLESS CRAP THAT HAS NOTHING TO DO WITH ME GOING AROUND AND AROUND IN CIRCLES INSIDE MY HEAD!

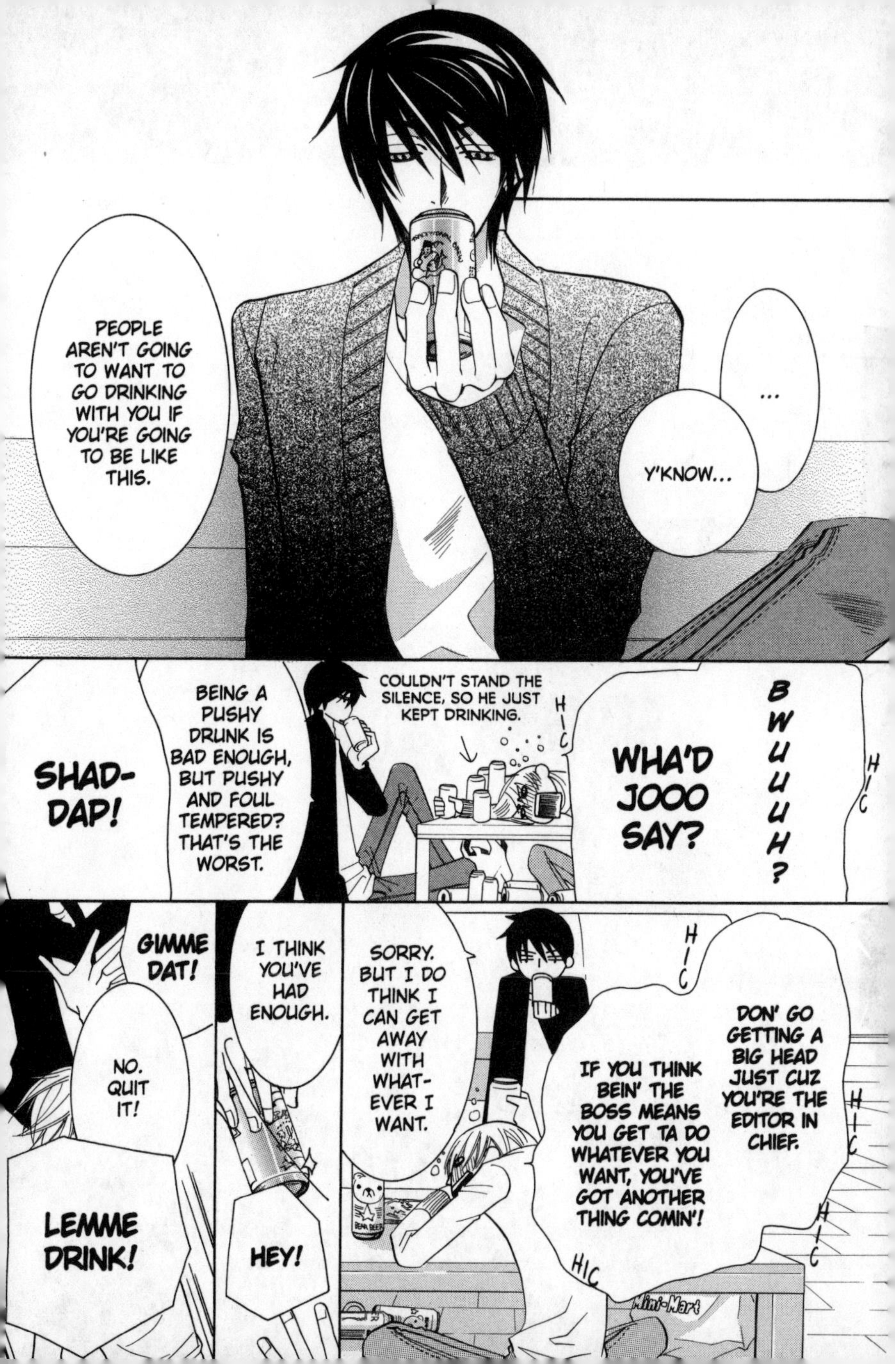
...
Y'KNOW...
PEOPLE AREN'T GOING TO WANT TO GO DRINKING WITH YOU IF YOU'RE GOING TO BE LIKE THIS.
BWUUUH?
HIC
WHA'D JOOO SAY?
HIC
COULDN'T STAND THE SILENCE, SO HE JUST KEPT DRINKING.
BEING A PUSHY DRUNK IS BAD ENOUGH, BUT PUSHY AND FOUL TEMPERED? THAT'S THE WORST.
SHAD-DAP!
HIC
DON' GO GETTING A BIG HEAD JUST CUZ YOU'RE THE EDITOR IN CHIEF.
HIC
IF YOU THINK BEIN' THE BOSS MEANS YOU GET TA DO WHATEVER YOU WANT, YOU'VE GOT ANOTHER THING COMIN'!
HIC
HIC
Mini-Mart
BEAR BEER
SORRY. BUT I DO THINK I CAN GET AWAY WITH WHAT-EVER I WANT.
I THINK YOU'VE HAD ENOUGH.
HEY!
GIMME DAT!
NO. QUIT IT!
LEMME DRINK!

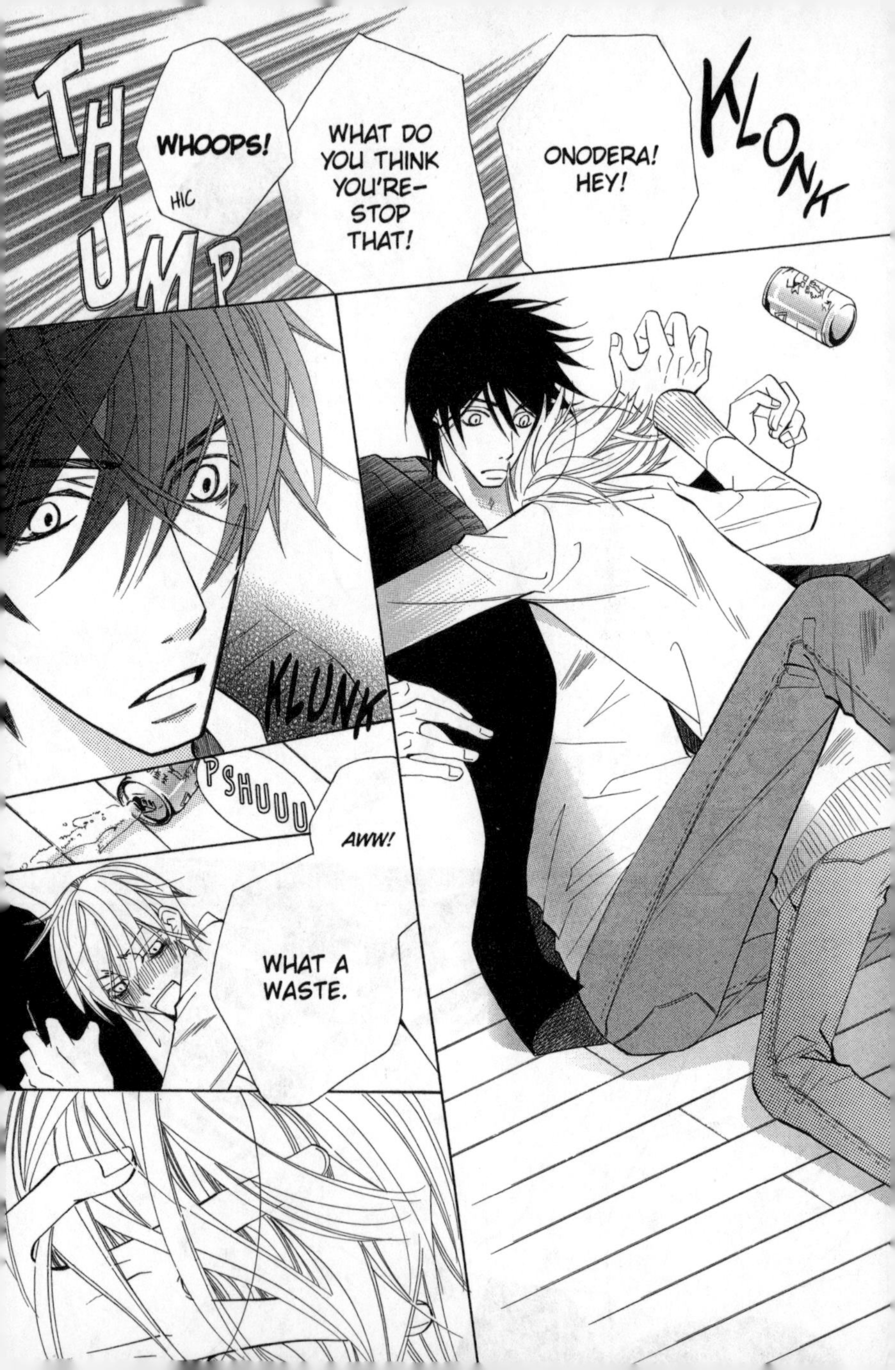
KLONK
ONODERA! HEY!
WHAT DO YOU THINK YOU'RE- STOP THAT!
WHOOPS!
HIC
THUMP
KLUNK
PSHUUU
AWW!
WHAT A WASTE.

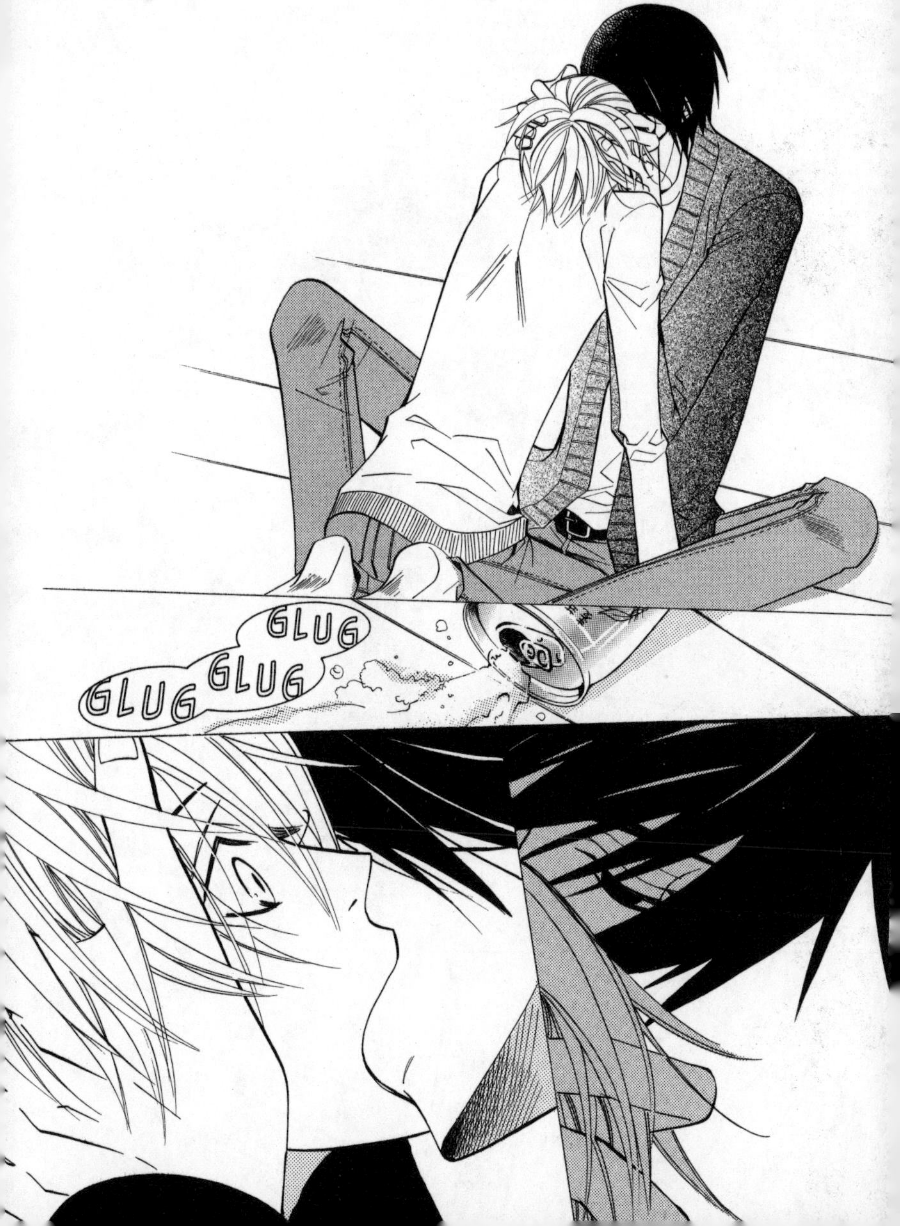
GLUG GLUG GLUG

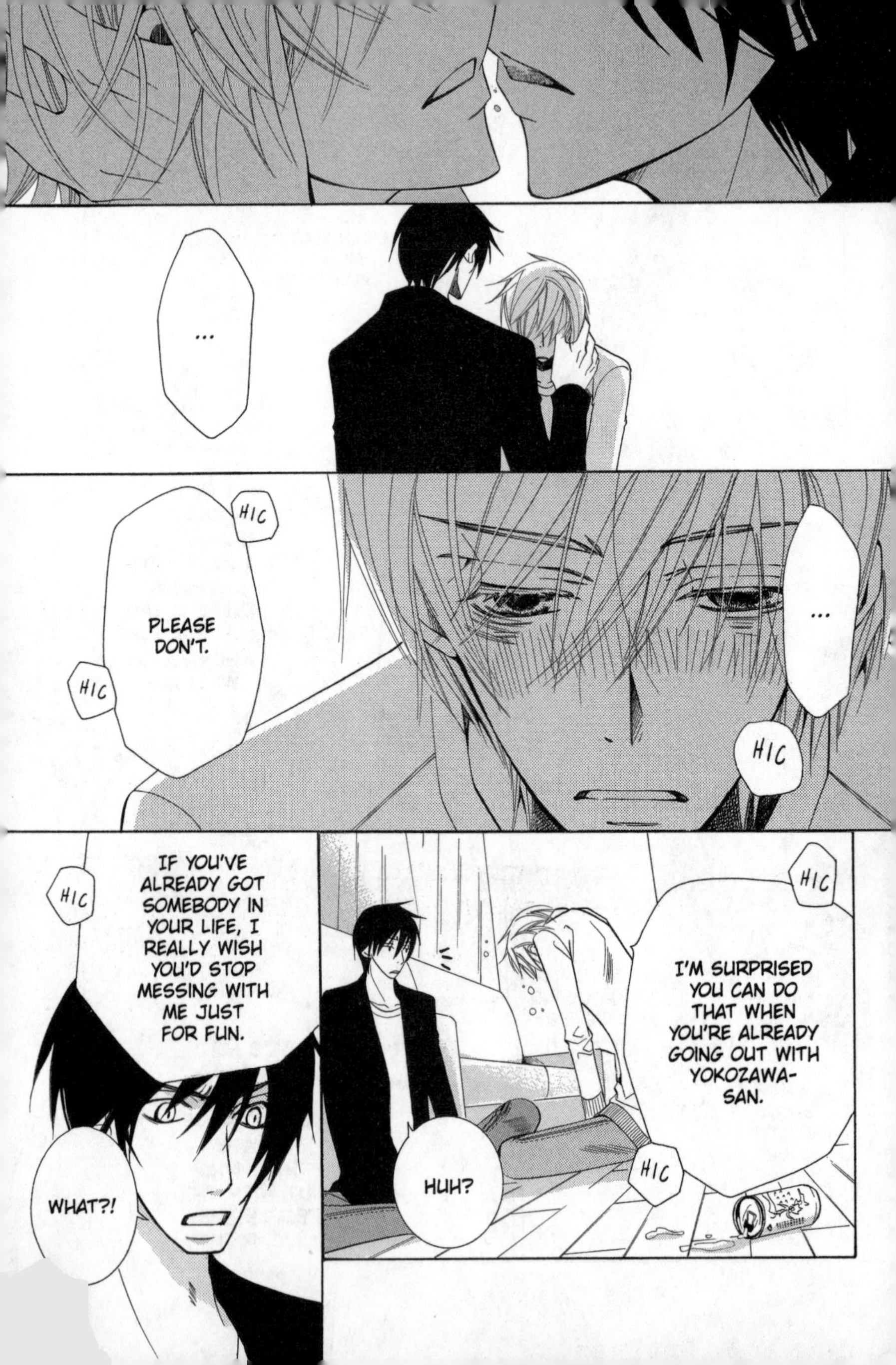
...
...
HIC
HIC
PLEASE DON'T.
HIC
HIC
I'M SURPRISED YOU CAN DO THAT WHEN YOU'RE ALREADY GOING OUT WITH YOKOZAWA-SAN.
HIC
HUH?
IF YOU'VE ALREADY GOT SOMEBODY IN YOUR LIFE, I REALLY WISH YOU'D STOP MESSING WITH ME JUST FOR FUN.
HIC
WHAT?!

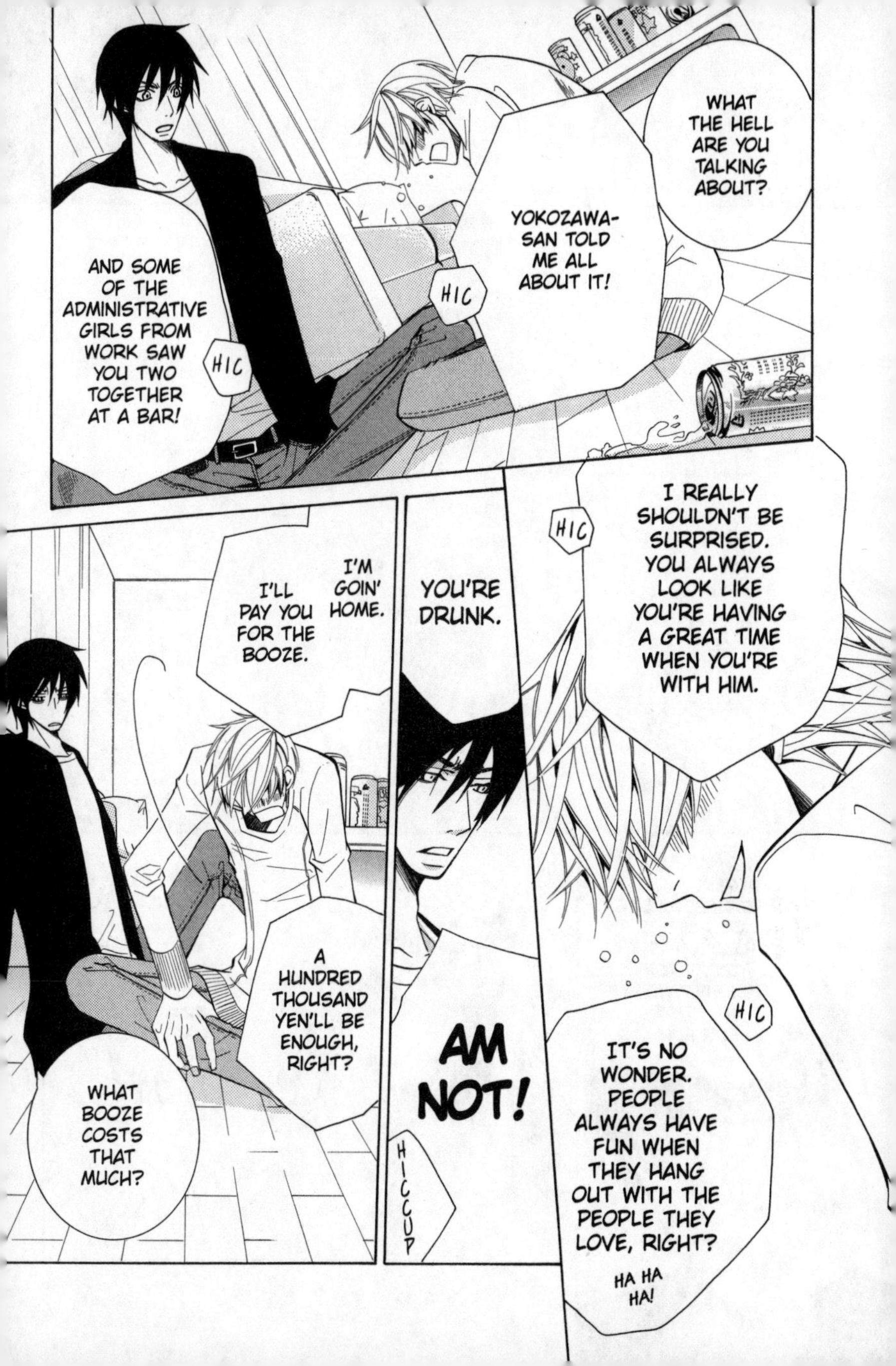
WHAT THE HELL ARE YOU TALKING ABOUT?
YOKOZAWA-SAN TOLD ME ALL ABOUT IT!
HIC
AND SOME OF THE ADMINISTRATIVE GIRLS FROM WORK SAW YOU TWO TOGETHER AT A BAR!
HIC
HIC
I REALLY SHOULDN'T BE SURPRISED. YOU ALWAYS LOOK LIKE YOU'RE HAVING A GREAT TIME WHEN YOU'RE WITH HIM.
HIC
IT'S NO WONDER. PEOPLE ALWAYS HAVE FUN WHEN THEY HANG OUT WITH THE PEOPLE THEY LOVE, RIGHT?
HA HA HA!
YOU'RE DRUNK.
AM NOT!
HICCUP
I'M GOIN' HOME.
I'LL PAY YOU FOR THE BOOZE.
A HUNDRED THOUSAND YEN'LL BE ENOUGH, RIGHT?
WHAT BOOZE COSTS THAT MUCH?

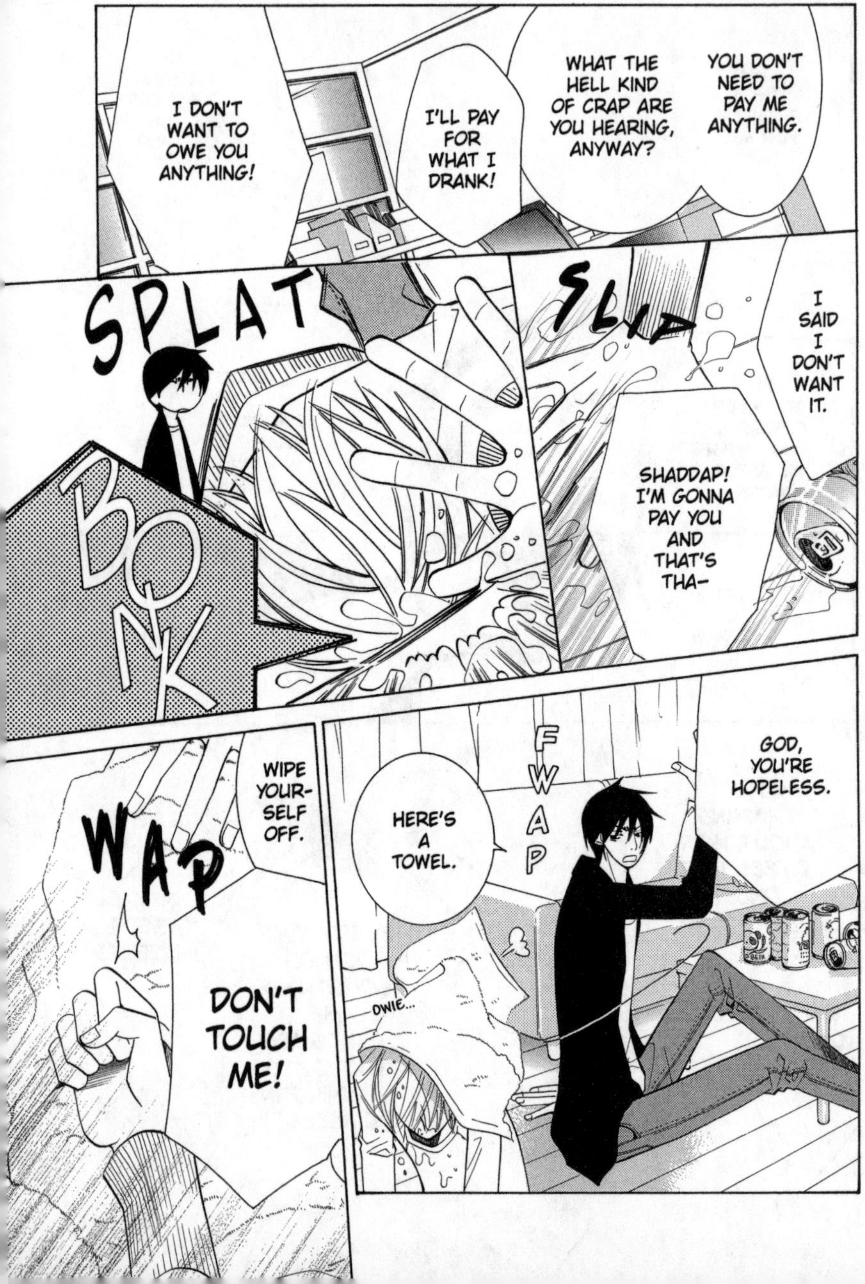
YOU DON'T NEED TO PAY ME ANYTHING.
WHAT THE HELL KIND OF CRAP ARE YOU HEARING, ANYWAY?
I'LL PAY FOR WHAT I DRANK!
I DON'T WANT TO OWE YOU ANYTHING!
I SAID I DON'T WANT IT.
SLID
SHADDAP! I'M GONNA PAY YOU AND THAT'S THA-
SPLAT
BONK
GOD, YOU'RE HOPELESS.
FWAP
HERE'S A TOWEL.
OWIE...
WIPE YOUR-SELF OFF.
WAP
DON'T TOUCH ME!

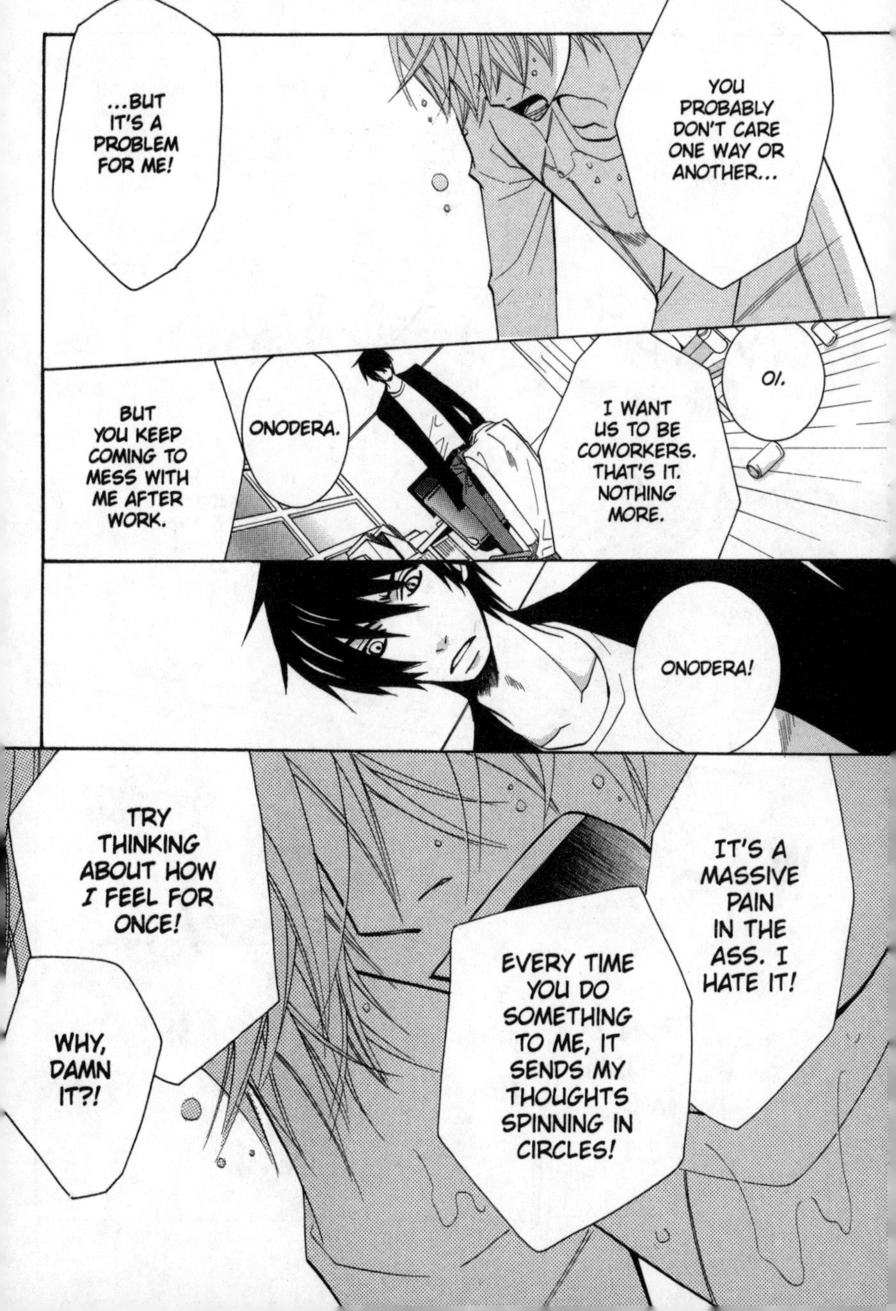
YOU PROBABLY DON'T CARE ONE WAY OR ANOTHER...
...BUT IT'S A PROBLEM FOR ME!
OI.
I WANT US TO BE COWORKERS. THAT'S IT. NOTHING MORE.
ONODERA.
BUT YOU KEEP COMING TO MESS WITH ME AFTER WORK.
ONODERA!
IT'S A MASSIVE PAIN IN THE ASS. I HATE IT!
EVERY TIME YOU DO SOMETHING TO ME, IT SENDS MY THOUGHTS SPINNING IN CIRCLES!
TRY THINKING ABOUT HOW *I* FEEL FOR ONCE!
WHY, DAMN IT?!

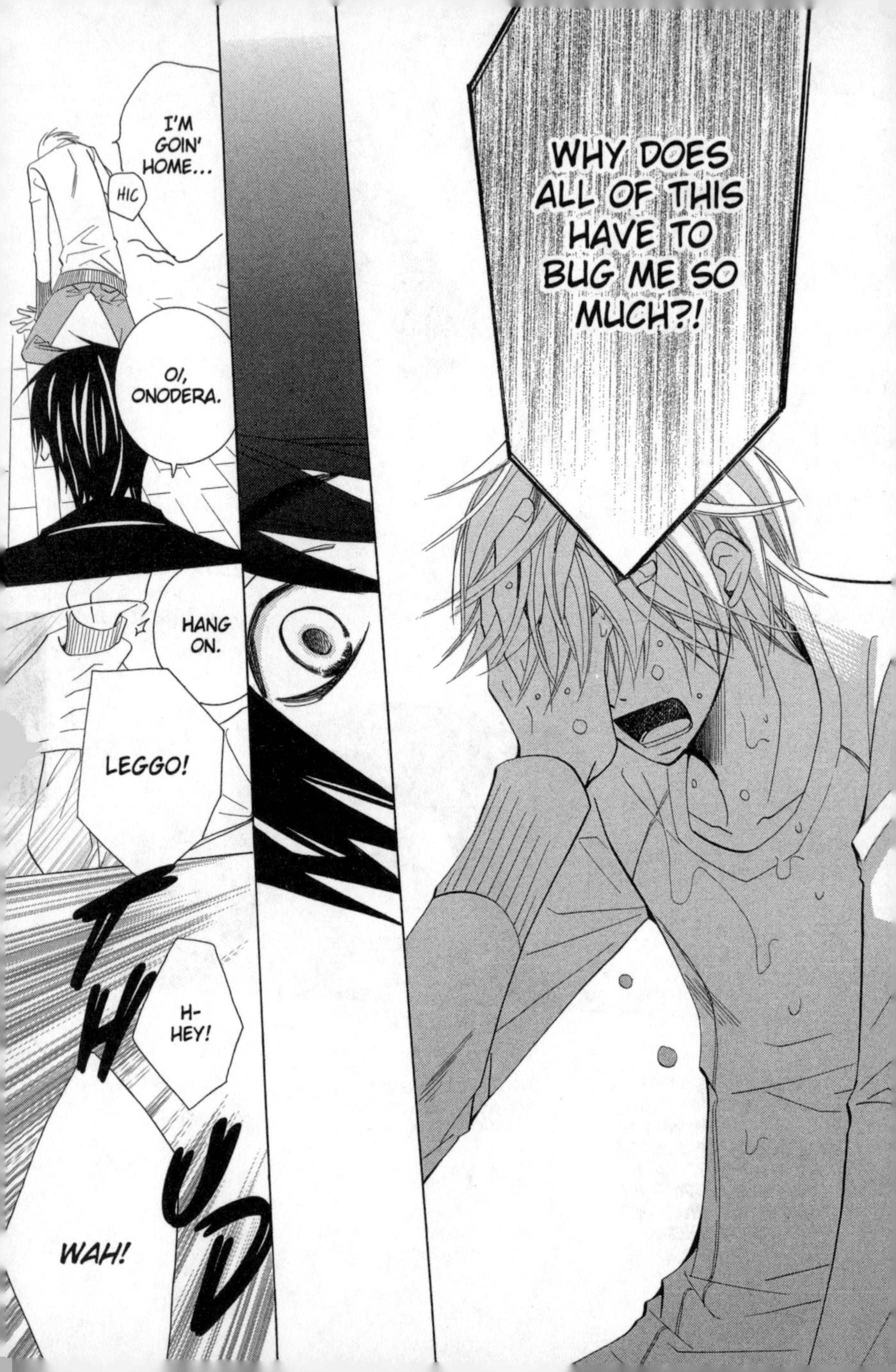
WHY DOES ALL OF THIS HAVE TO BUG ME SO MUCH?!
I'M GOIN' HOME...
HIC
OI, ONODERA.
HANG ON.
LEGGO!
H-HEY!
THUD
WAH!

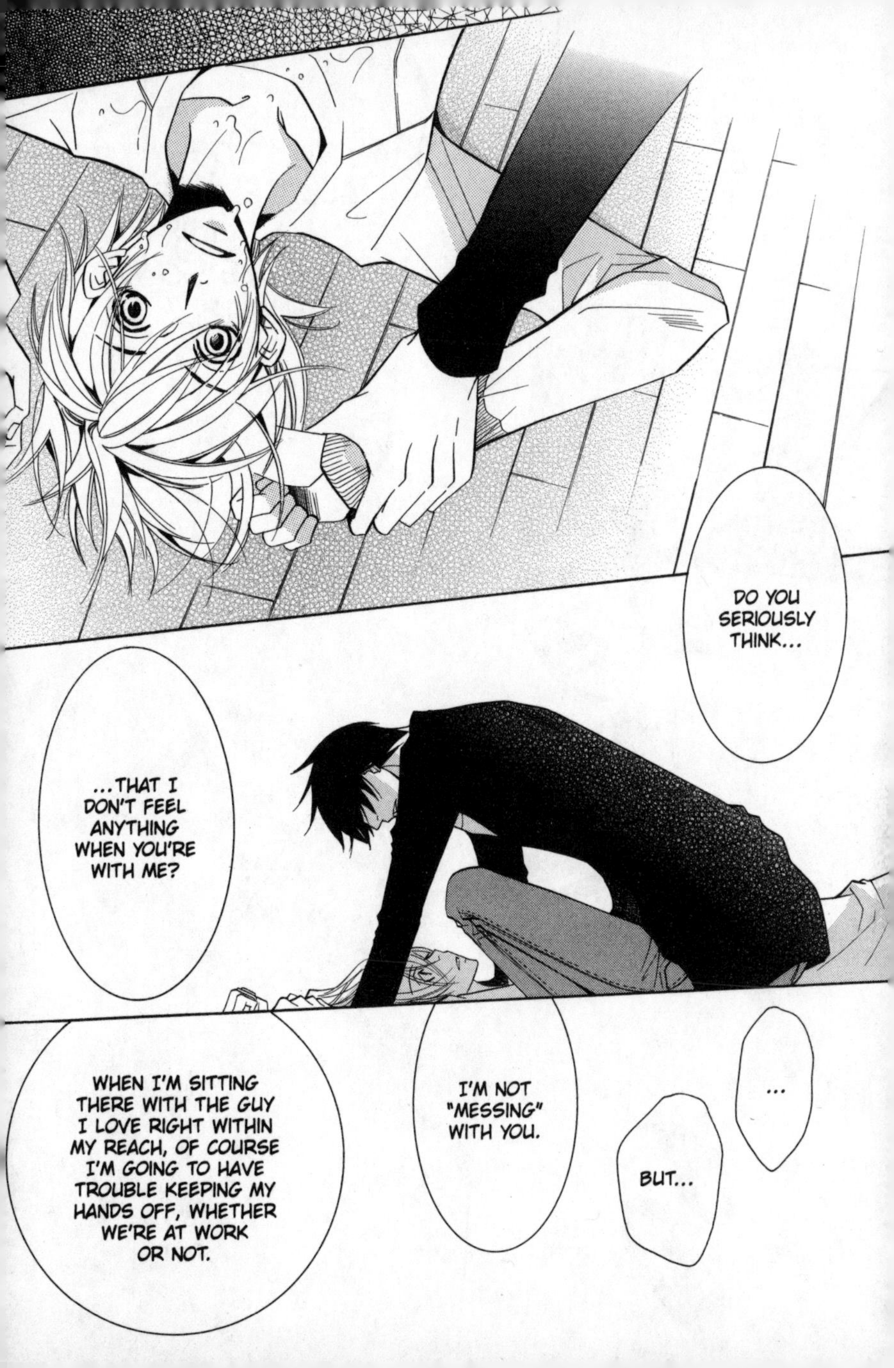
DO YOU SERIOUSLY THINK...
...THAT I DON'T FEEL ANYTHING WHEN YOU'RE WITH ME?
...
BUT...
I'M NOT "MESSING" WITH YOU.
WHEN I'M SITTING THERE WITH THE GUY I LOVE RIGHT WITHIN MY REACH, OF COURSE I'M GOING TO HAVE TROUBLE KEEPING MY HANDS OFF, WHETHER WE'RE AT WORK OR NOT.

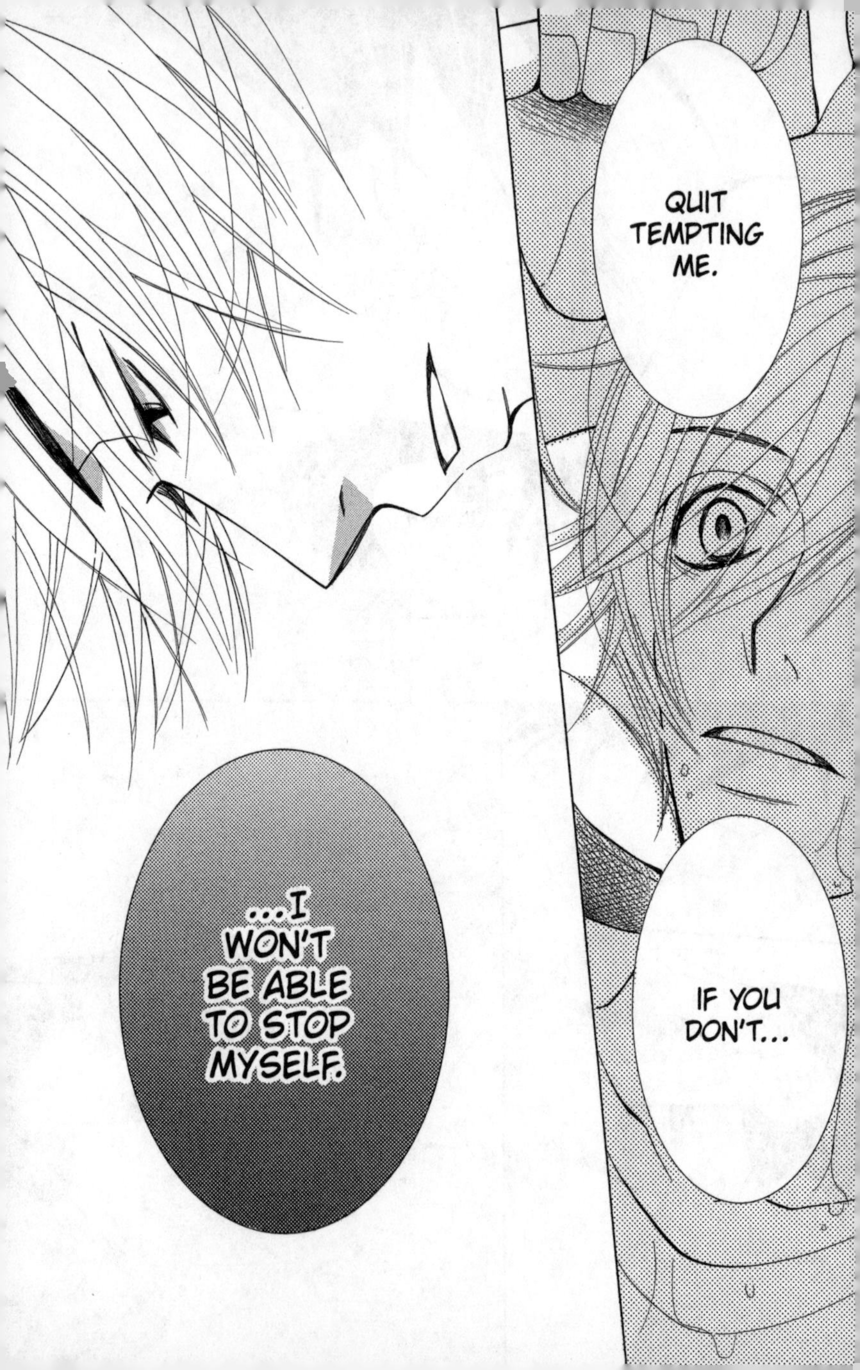
QUIT TEMPTING ME.
IF YOU DON'T...
...I WON'T BE ABLE TO STOP MYSELF.

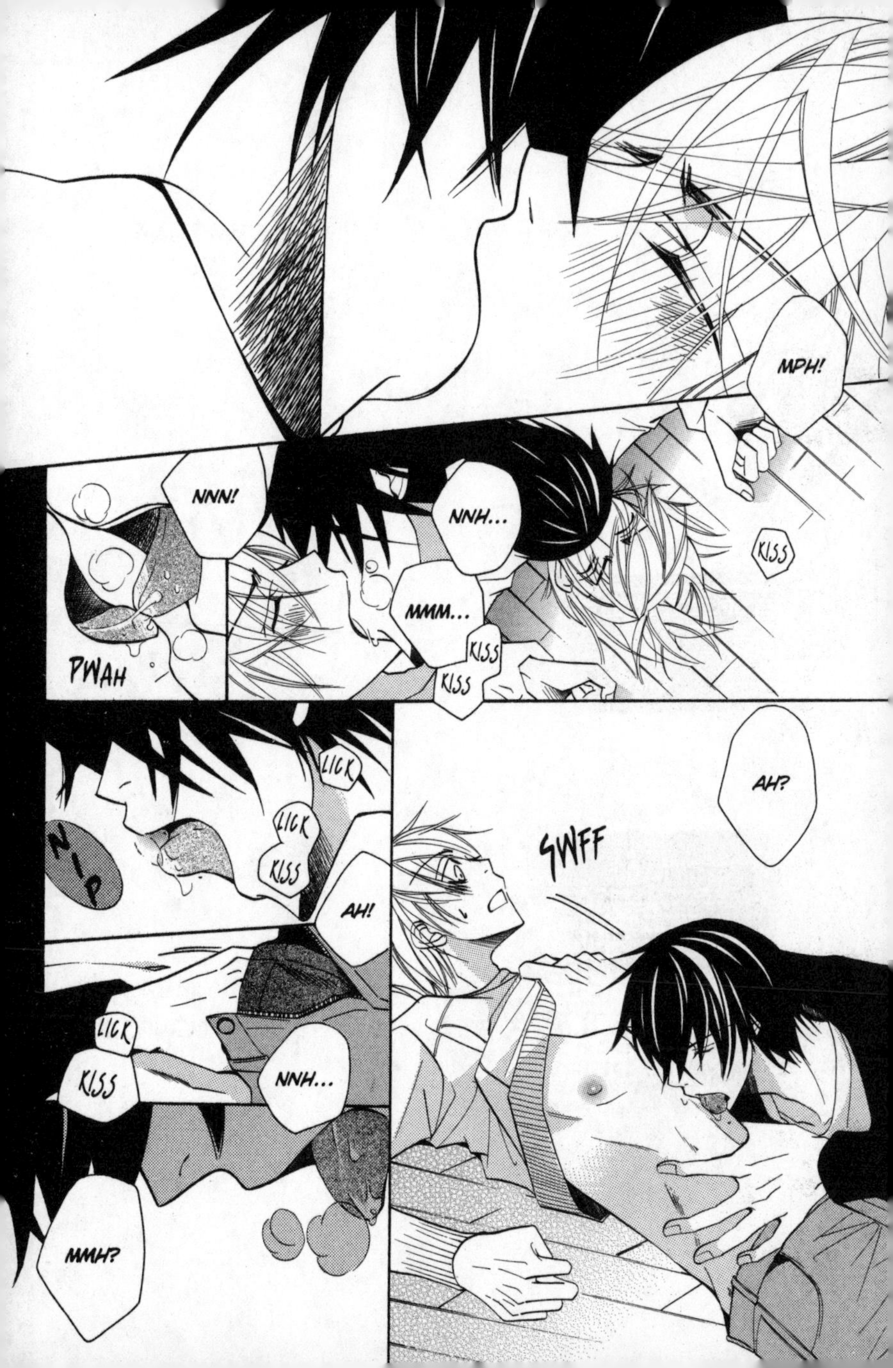
MPH!
NNH...
KISS
MMM...
KISS
KISS
NNN!
PWAH
AH?
SWFF
LICK
LICK
KISS
ZIP
AH!
LICK
KISS
NNH...
MMH?

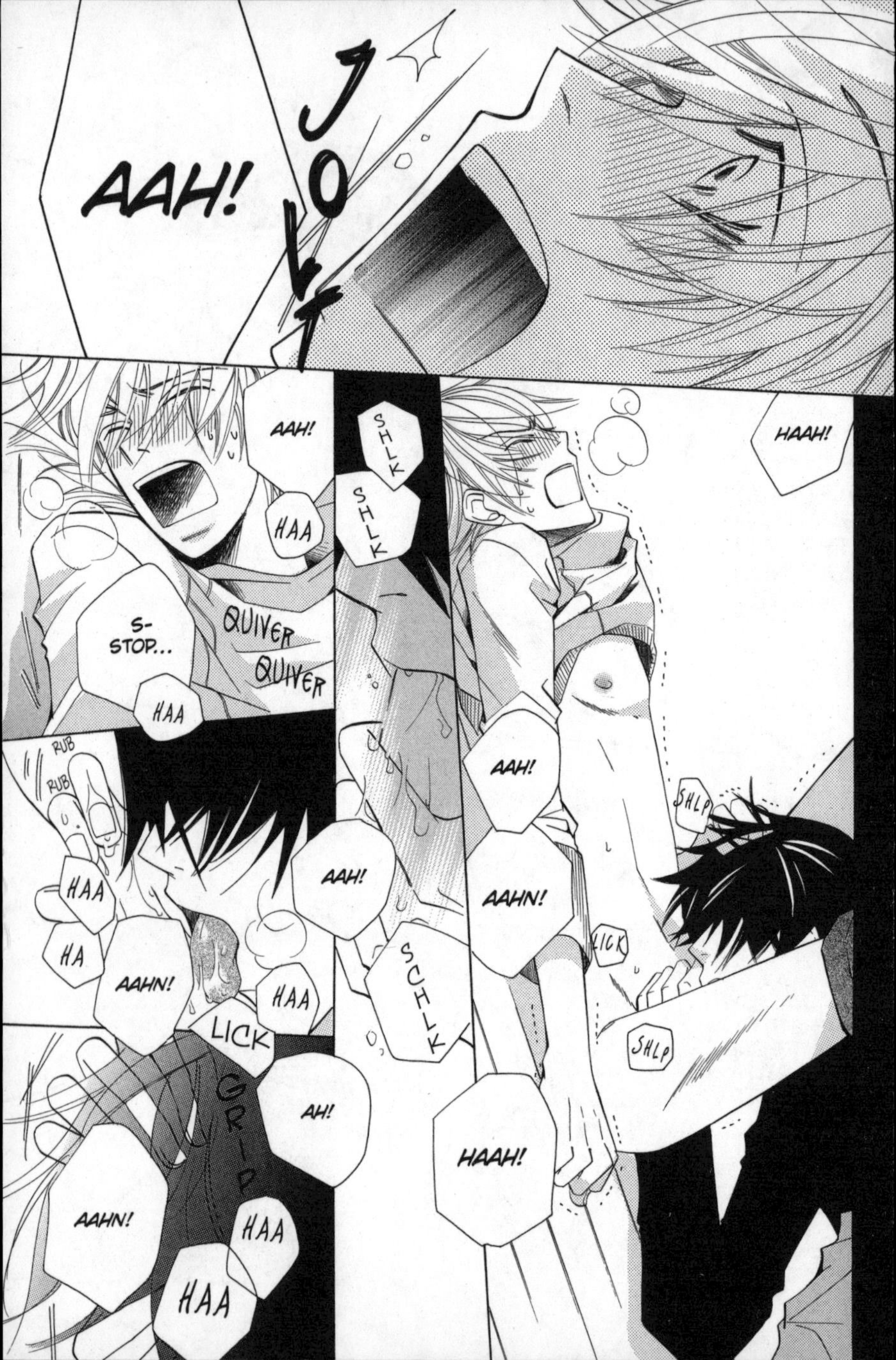
JOLT
AAH!
HAAH!
AAH!
SHLP
AAHN!
LICK
SHLP
HAAH!
SHLK
SHLK
SCHLK
AAH!
HAA
S-STOP...
QUIVER
QUIVER
HAA
RUB
RUB
AAH!
HAA
HA
AAHN!
HAA
LICK
GRIP
AH!
AAHN!
HAA
HAA

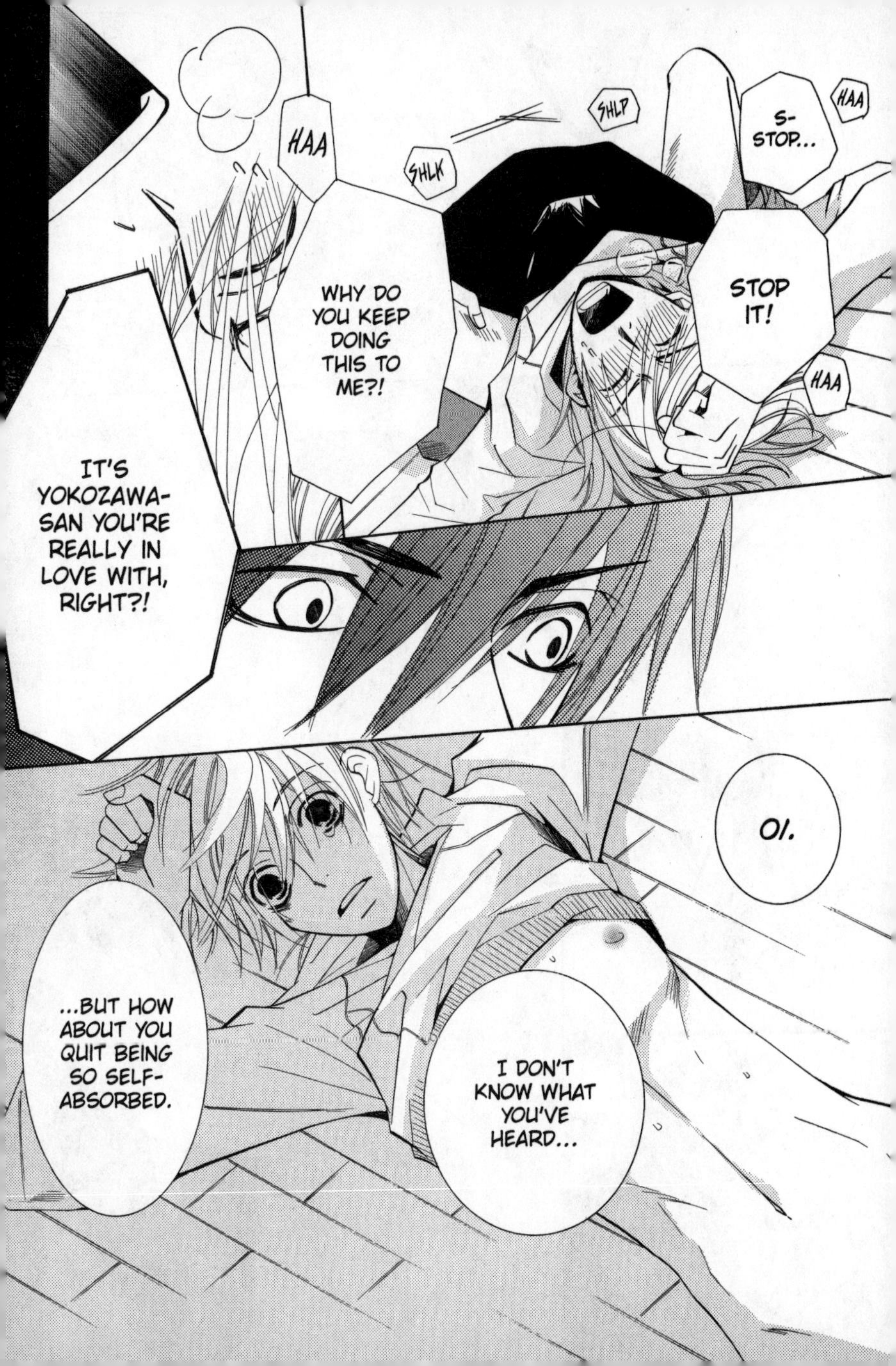
HAA
S-STOP...
SHLP
STOP IT!
HAA
SHLK
HAA
WHY DO YOU KEEP DOING THIS TO ME?!
IT'S YOKOZAWA-SAN YOU'RE REALLY IN LOVE WITH, RIGHT?!
OI.
I DON'T KNOW WHAT YOU'VE HEARD...
...BUT HOW ABOUT YOU QUIT BEING SO SELF-ABSORBED.

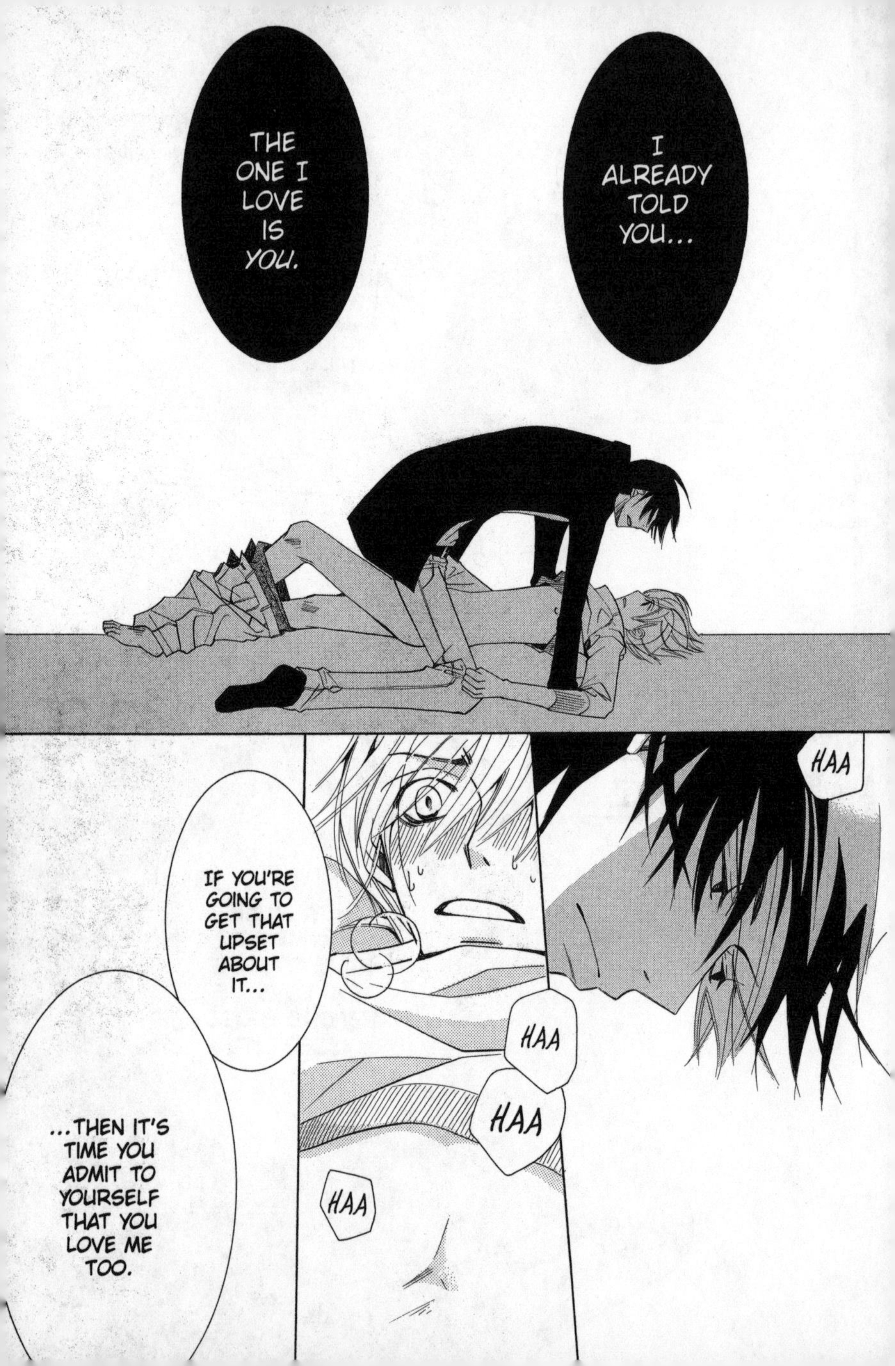
I ALREADY TOLD YOU...
THE ONE I LOVE IS *YOU.*
HAA
HAA
HAA
HAA
IF YOU'RE GOING TO GET THAT UPSET ABOUT IT...
...THEN IT'S TIME YOU ADMIT TO YOURSELF THAT YOU LOVE ME TOO.

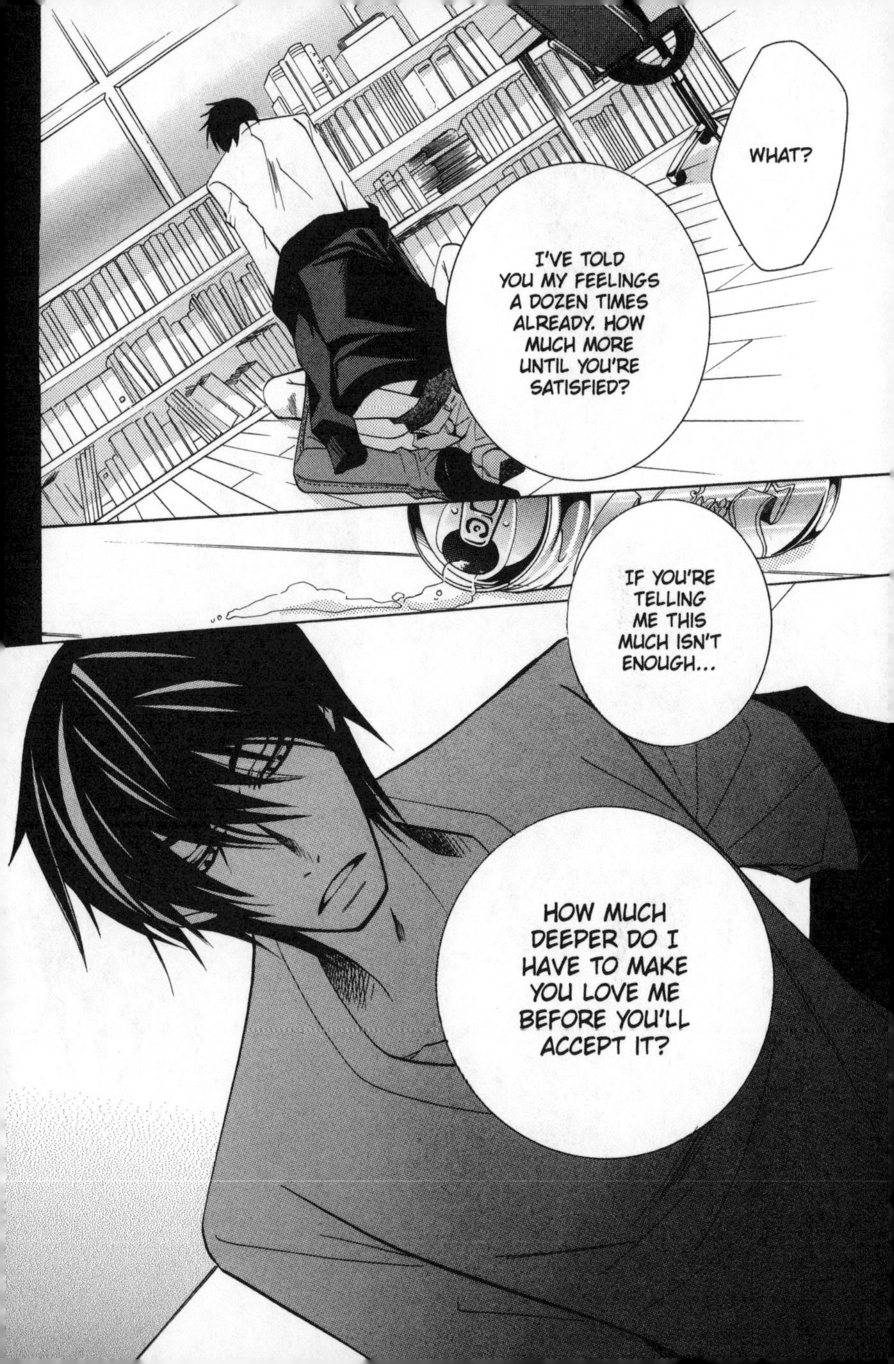
WHAT?
I'VE TOLD YOU MY FEELINGS A DOZEN TIMES ALREADY. HOW MUCH MORE UNTIL YOU'RE SATISFIED?
IF YOU'RE TELLING ME THIS MUCH ISN'T ENOUGH...
HOW MUCH DEEPER DO I HAVE TO MAKE YOU LOVE ME BEFORE YOU'LL ACCEPT IT?

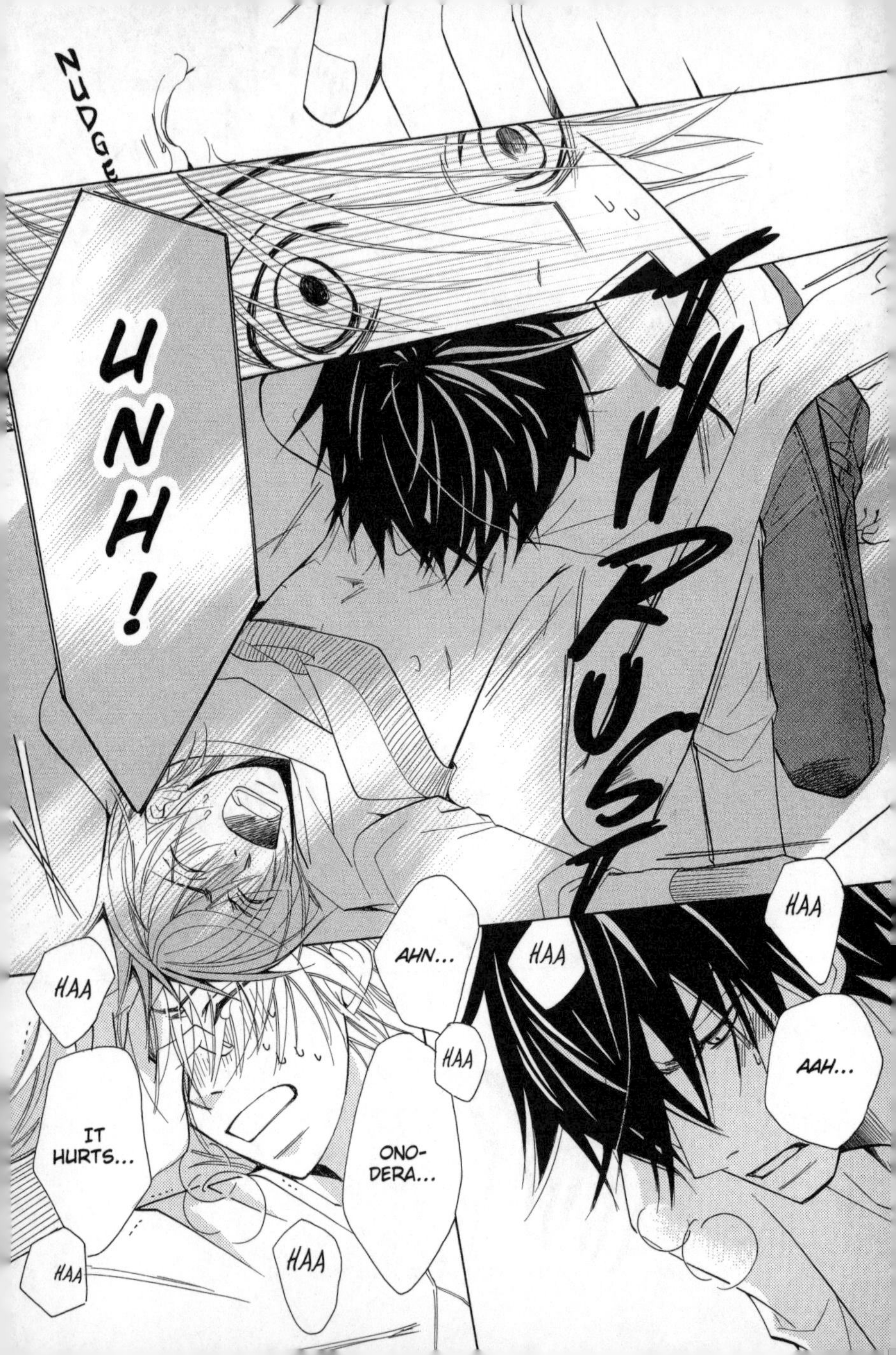
NUDGE
THRUST
UNH!
HAA
AAH...
HAA
AHN...
HAA
ONO-DERA...
HAA
HAA
IT HURTS...
HAA

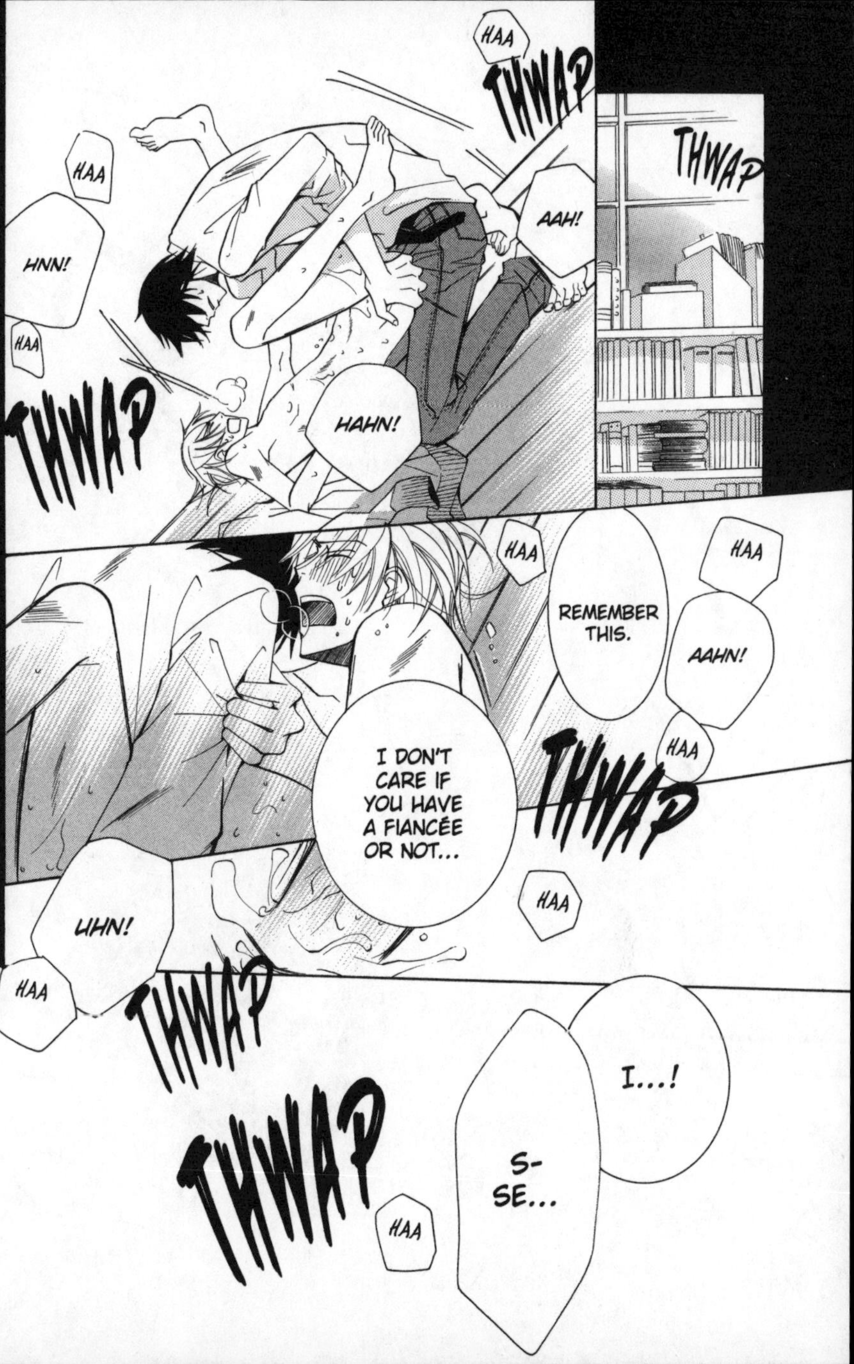
THWAP
HAA
THWAP
AAH!
HAA
HNN!
HAA
THWAP
HAHN!
HAA
REMEMBER THIS.
HAA
AAHN!
HAA
THWAP
I DON'T CARE IF YOU HAVE A FIANCÉE OR NOT...
HAA
UHN!
HAA
I...!
S- SE...
THWAP
HAA
THWAP

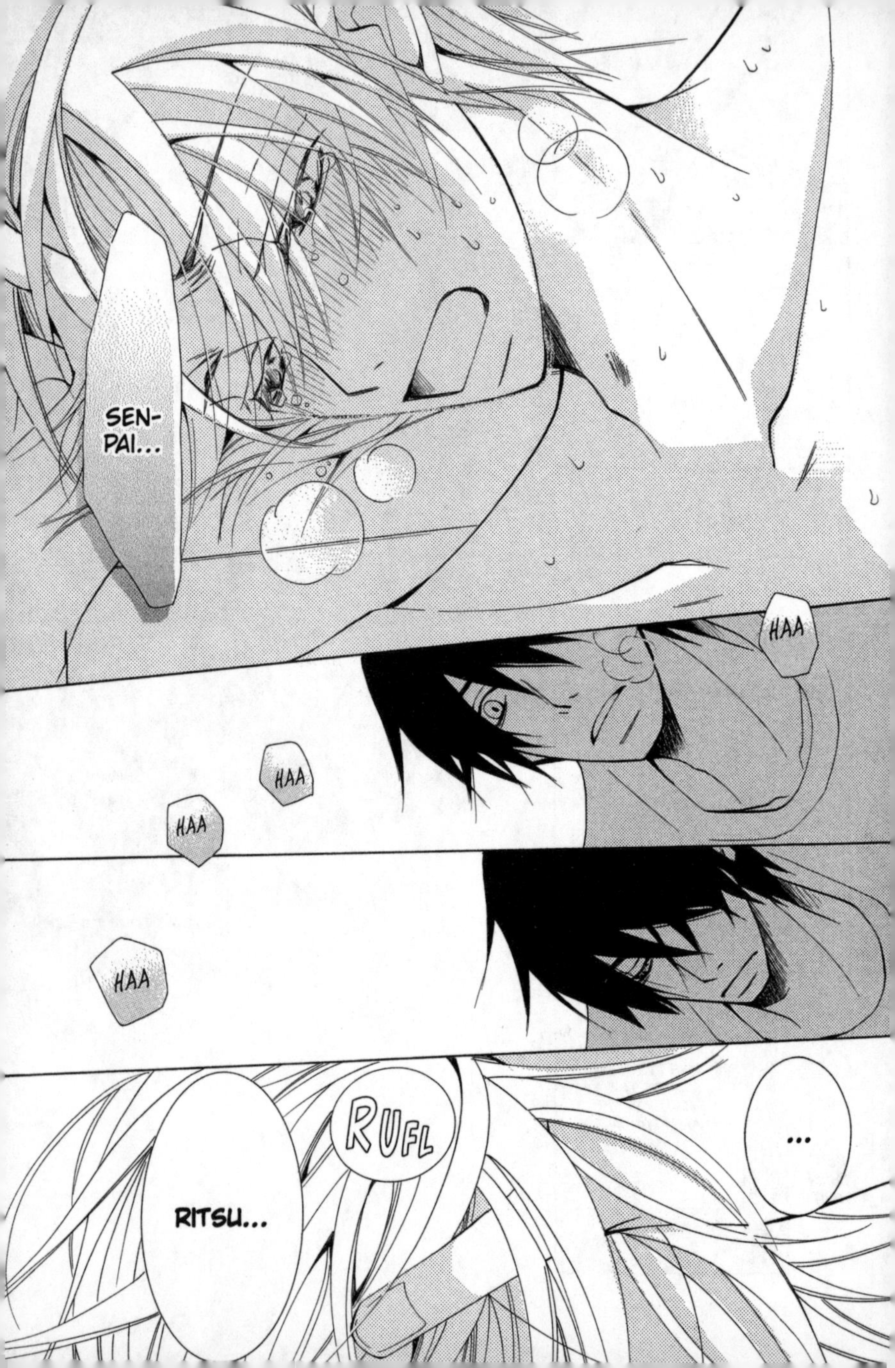
SEN-PAI...
HAA
HAA
HAA
HAA
...
RUFL
RITSU...

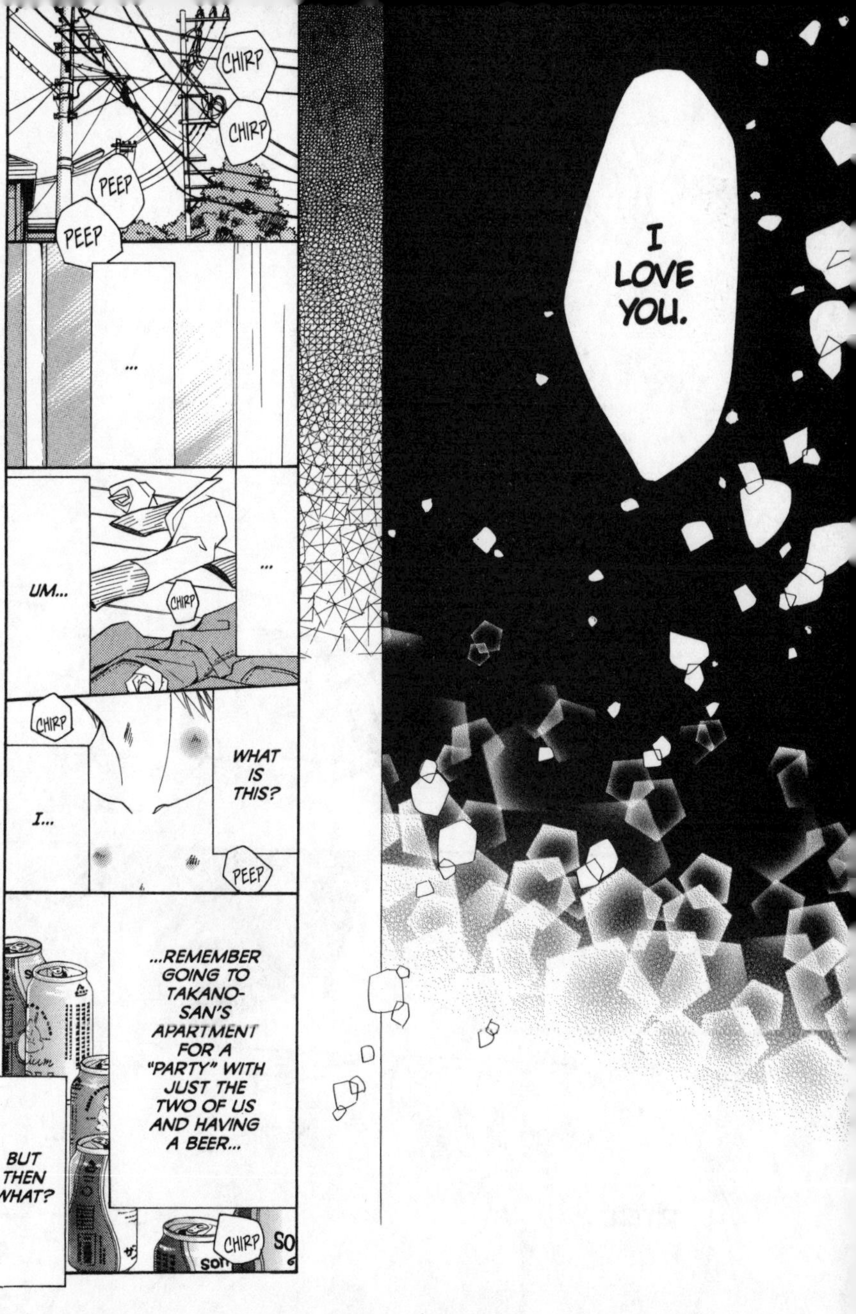
I LOVE YOU.
CHIRP
CHIRP
PEEP
PEEP
...
...
CHIRP
UM...
CHIRP
WHAT IS THIS?
I...
PEEP
...REMEMBER GOING TO TAKANO-SAN'S APARTMENT FOR A "PARTY" WITH JUST THE TWO OF US AND HAVING A BEER...
BUT THEN WHAT?
CHIRP

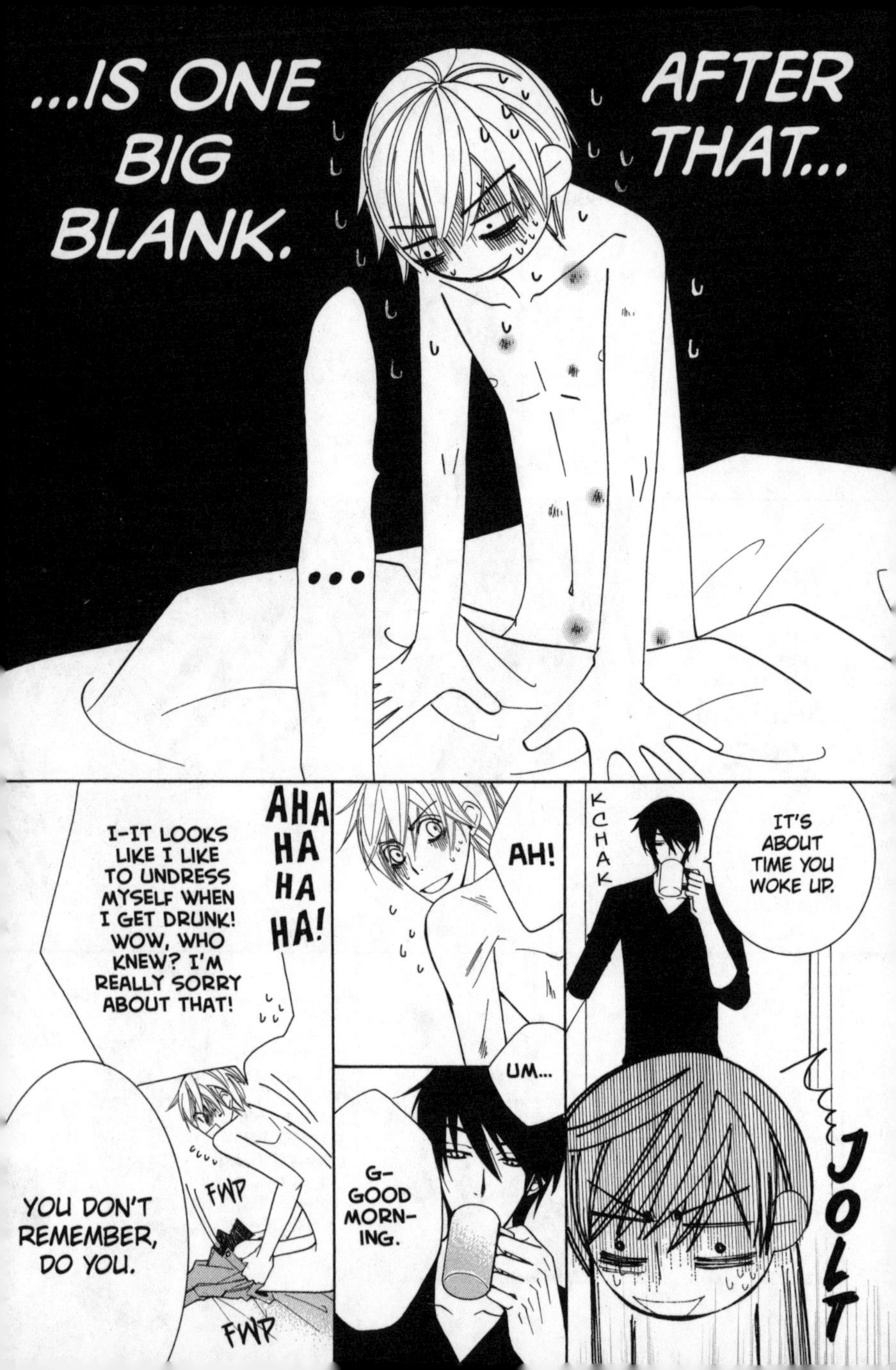

AFTER THAT...
...IS ONE BIG BLANK.
...
KCHAK
IT'S ABOUT TIME YOU WOKE UP.
AH!
JOLT
UM...
G-GOOD MORNING.
AHAHAHAHA!
I-IT LOOKS LIKE I LIKE TO UNDRESS MYSELF WHEN I GET DRUNK! WOW, WHO KNEW? I'M REALLY SORRY ABOUT THAT!
FWP
FWP
YOU DON'T REMEMBER, DO YOU.

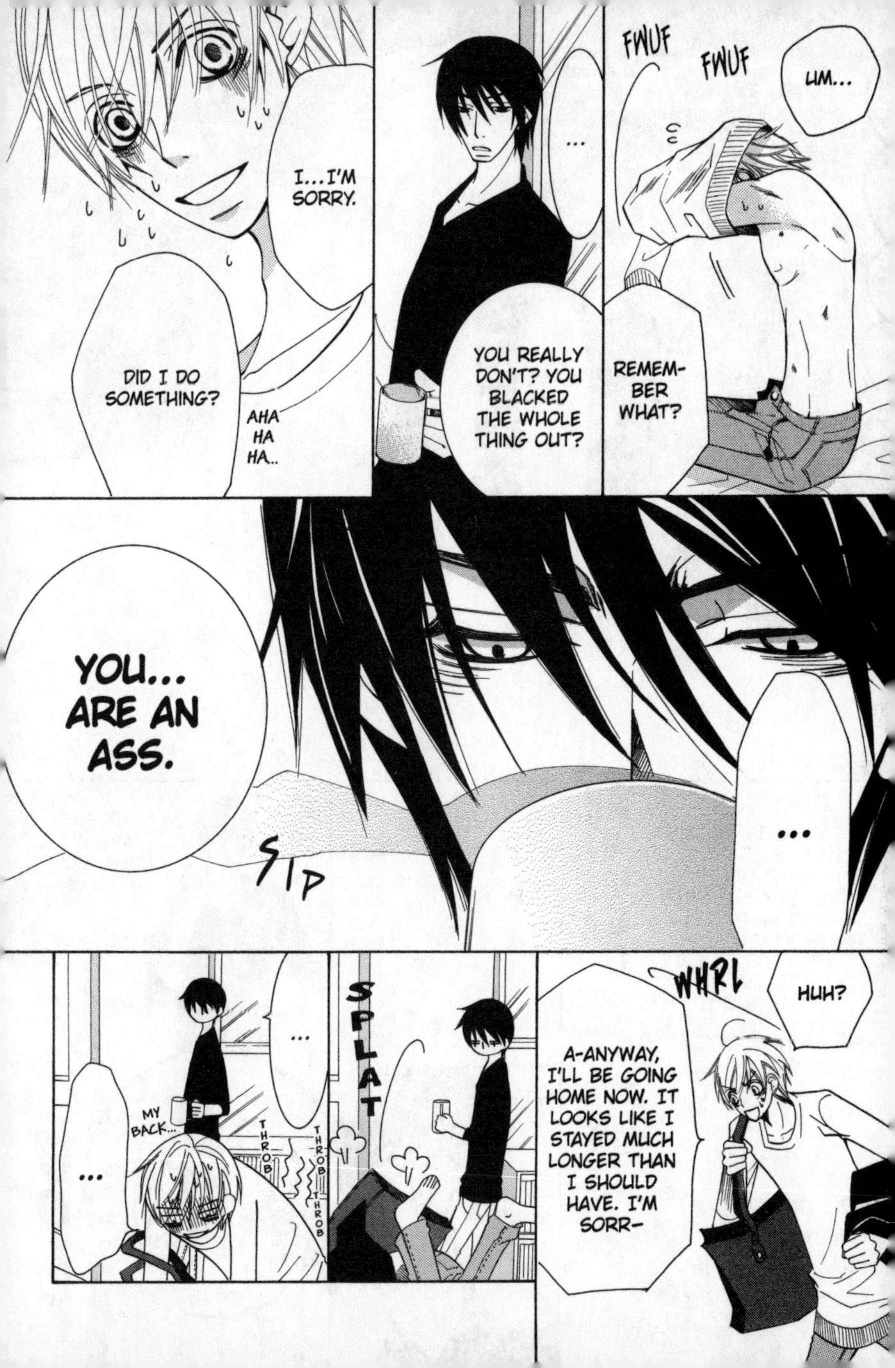
UM...
FWUF
FWUF
REMEM-BER WHAT?
...
YOU REALLY DON'T? YOU BLACKED THE WHOLE THING OUT?
I...I'M SORRY.
AHA HA HA..
DID I DO SOMETHING?
...
SIP
YOU... ARE AN ASS.
HUH?
WHRL
A-ANYWAY, I'LL BE GOING HOME NOW. IT LOOKS LIKE I STAYED MUCH LONGER THAN I SHOULD HAVE. I'M SORR-
SPLAT
...
THROB
THROB
THROB
MY BACK...
...

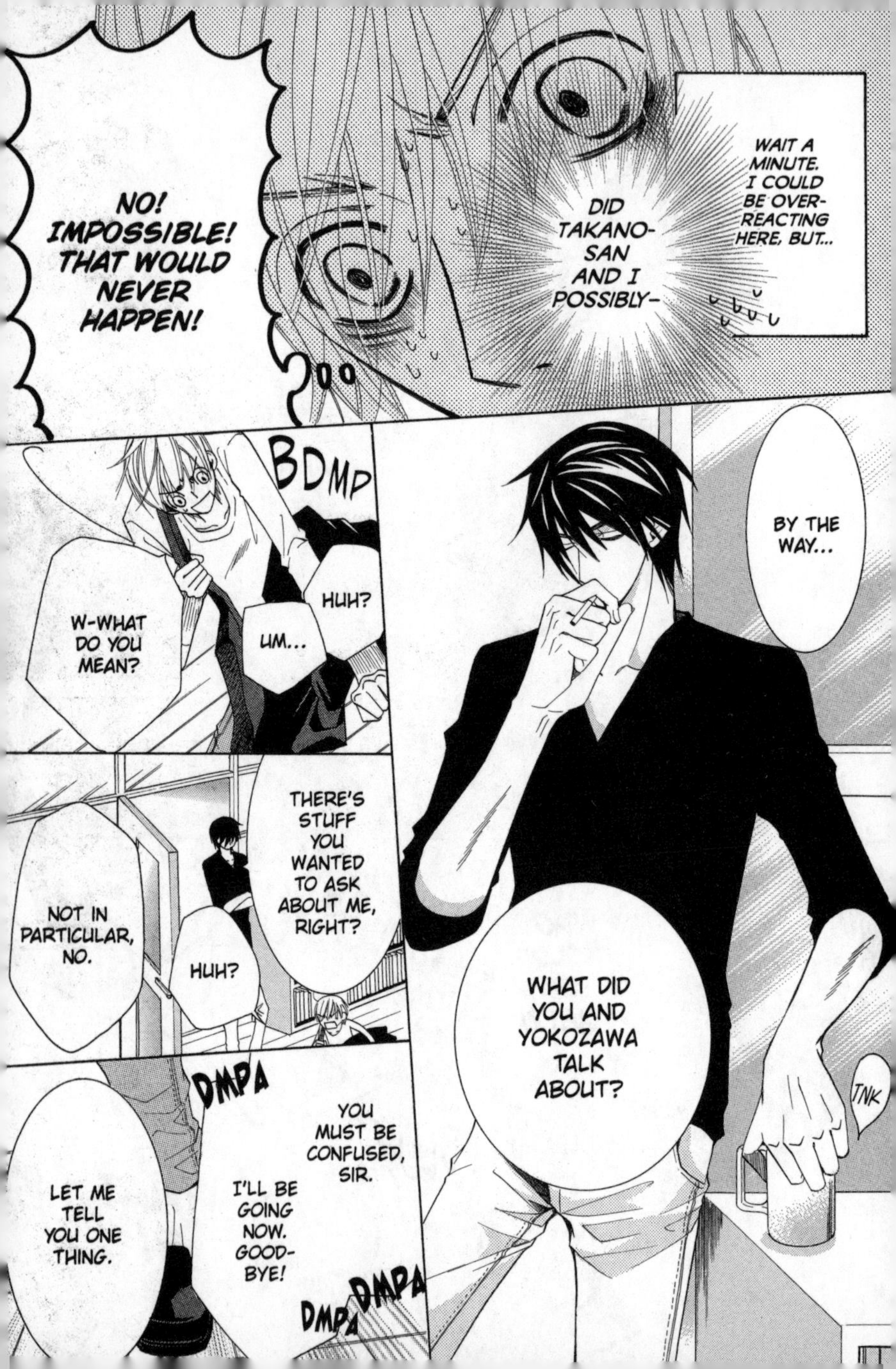
WAIT A MINUTE. I COULD BE OVER-REACTING HERE, BUT...
DID TAKANO-SAN AND I POSSIBLY-
NO! IMPOSSIBLE! THAT WOULD NEVER HAPPEN!
BY THE WAY...
WHAT DID YOU AND YOKOZAWA TALK ABOUT?
TNK
BDMP
HUH?
UM...
W-WHAT DO YOU MEAN?
THERE'S STUFF YOU WANTED TO ASK ABOUT ME, RIGHT?
HUH?
NOT IN PARTICULAR, NO.
DMPA
YOU MUST BE CONFUSED, SIR.
I'LL BE GOING NOW. GOOD-BYE!
LET ME TELL YOU ONE THING.
DMPA
DMPA

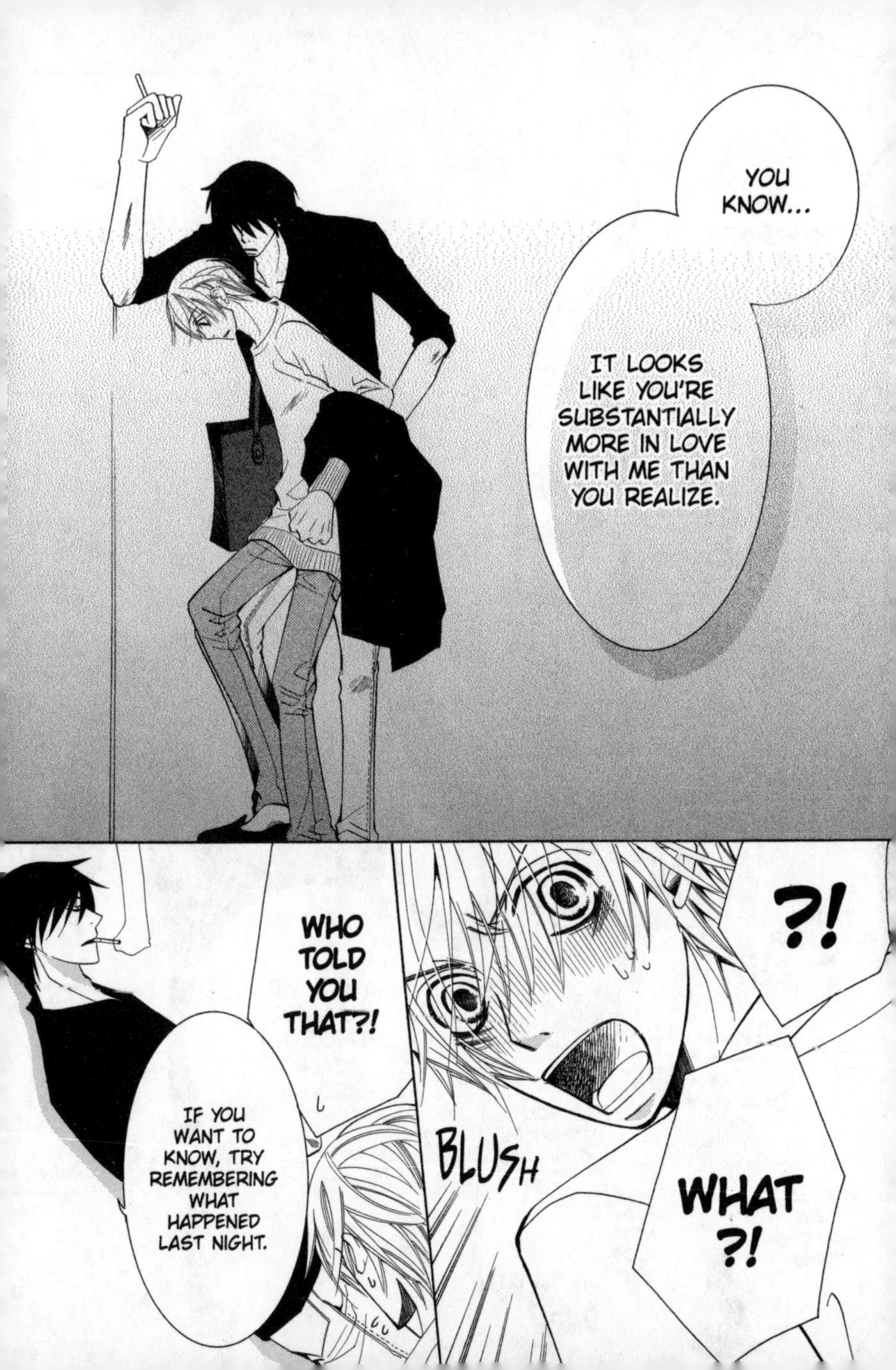
YOU KNOW...
IT LOOKS LIKE YOU'RE SUBSTANTIALLY MORE IN LOVE WITH ME THAN YOU REALIZE.
?!
WHAT ?!
WHO TOLD YOU THAT?!
BLUSH
IF YOU WANT TO KNOW, TRY REMEMBERING WHAT HAPPENED LAST NIGHT.

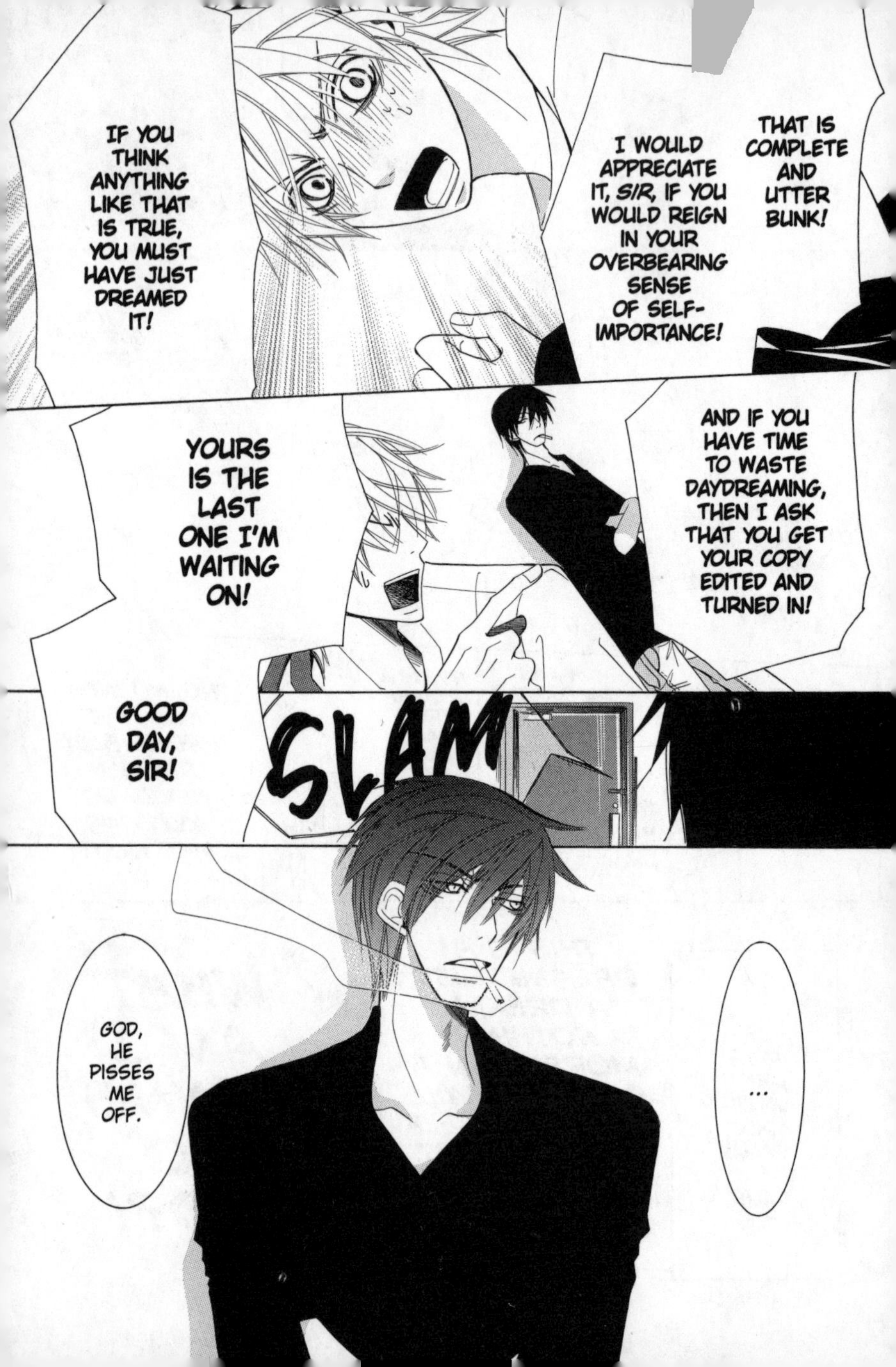
THAT IS COMPLETE AND UTTER BUNK!
I WOULD APPRECIATE IT, *SIR*, IF YOU WOULD REIGN IN YOUR OVERBEARING SENSE OF SELF-IMPORTANCE!
IF YOU THINK ANYTHING LIKE THAT IS TRUE, YOU MUST HAVE JUST DREAMED IT!
AND IF YOU HAVE TIME TO WASTE DAYDREAMING, THEN I ASK THAT YOU GET YOUR COPY EDITED AND TURNED IN!
YOURS IS THE LAST ONE I'M WAITING ON!
SLAM
GOOD DAY, SIR!
...
GOD, HE PISSES ME OFF.

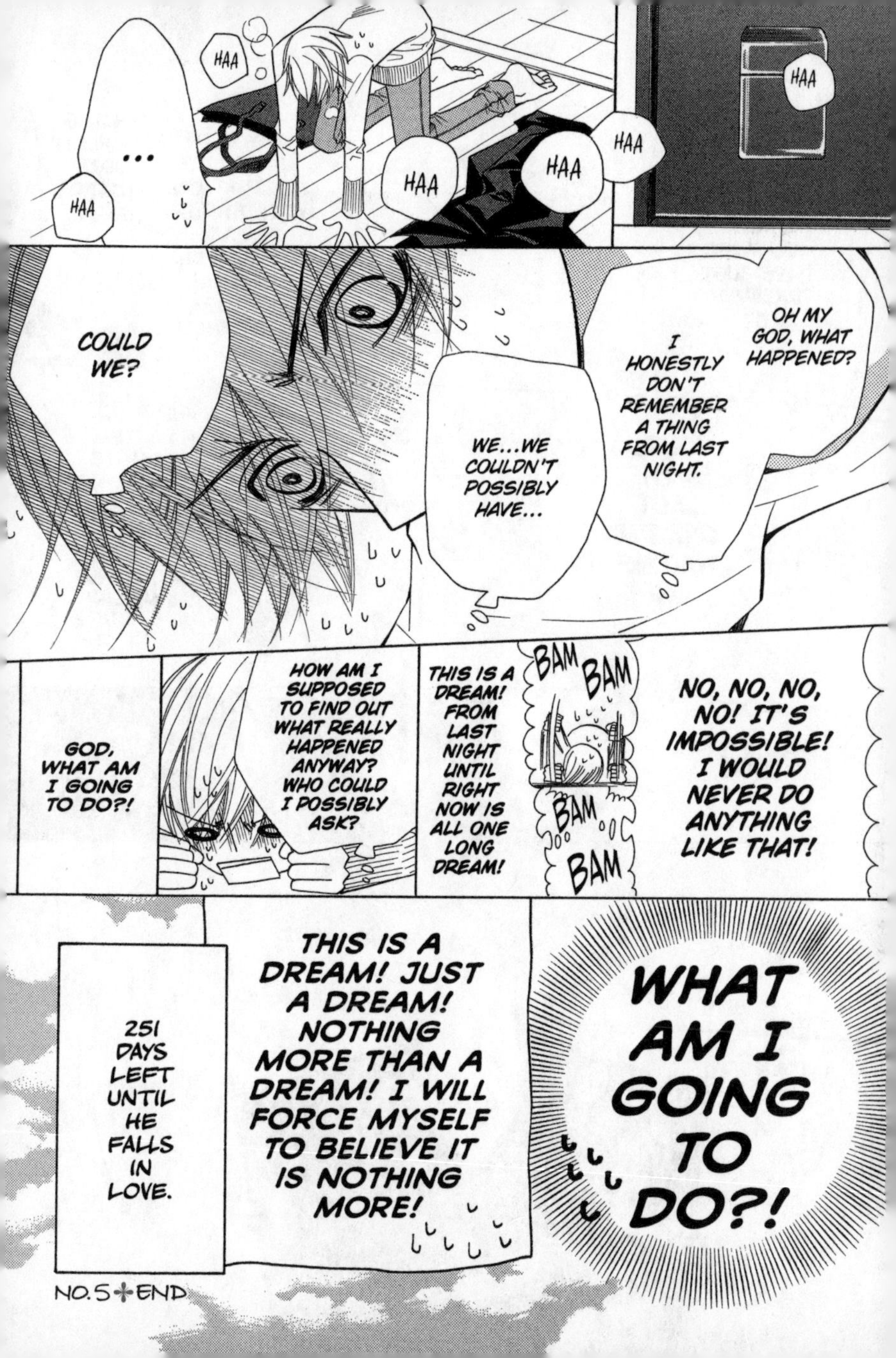
HAA
HAA
HAA
HAA
HAA
...
HAA
OH MY GOD, WHAT HAPPENED?
I HONESTLY DON'T REMEMBER A THING FROM LAST NIGHT.
WE...WE COULDN'T POSSIBLY HAVE...
COULD WE?
NO, NO, NO, NO! IT'S IMPOSSIBLE! I WOULD NEVER DO ANYTHING LIKE THAT!
BAM BAM
BAM BAM
THIS IS A DREAM! FROM LAST NIGHT UNTIL RIGHT NOW IS ALL ONE LONG DREAM!
HOW AM I SUPPOSED TO FIND OUT WHAT REALLY HAPPENED ANYWAY? WHO COULD I POSSIBLY ASK?
GOD, WHAT AM I GOING TO DO?!
WHAT AM I GOING TO DO?!
THIS IS A DREAM! JUST A DREAM! NOTHING MORE THAN A DREAM! I WILL FORCE MYSELF TO BELIEVE IT IS NOTHING MORE!
251 DAYS LEFT UNTIL HE FALLS IN LOVE.
NO.5 END

MARUKAWA PUBLISHING TERMINOLOGY & JARGON (PART 9)

***NOTE:** ALL OF THE TERMINOLOGY LISTED HEREIN IS SPECIFIC TO MARUKAWA PUBLISHING AND MAY NOT BE APPLICABLE TO THE GENERAL PUBLISHING INDUSTRY.

[MULTIPLE PRINTINGS]

SECOND PRINTINGS OR MULTIPLE PRINTINGS INVOLVE USING THE ORIGINAL PRINTER PLATES TO PRINT ANOTHER SET OF A BOOK OR DOCUMENT. IT CAN ALSO BE CALLED A "REPRINT" OR A "REISSUE."

[MARUKAWA PUBLISHING SALES DEPARTMENT]

THE MARUKAWA PUBLISHING SALES DEPARTMENT IS RESPONSIBLE FOR SUPERVISING THE DISTRIBUTION AND SALE OF ALL MARUKAWA BOOKS AND MANGA. THE DEPARTMENT HOLDS SO MUCH CLOUT IN MARUKAWA RUMOR HAS IT THAT WHOEVER GOES AGAINST THEIR WISHES WILL SUDDENLY FIND THEIR BOOKS NOT SELLING. TAKAFUMI YOKOZAWA, FRIEND OF *EMERALD MONTHLY*'S EDITOR IN CHIEF, SUPERVISES SALES FOR ALL MANGA VOLUMES.

[AN EDITOR'S DUTIES]

ACCORDING TO *EMERALD MONTHLY* EDITOR IN CHIEF, MASAMUNE TAKANO, NINETY-FOUR PERCENT OF AN EDITOR'S DUTIES CONSIST OF "CONNING CREATORS INTO DROPPING THEIR GUARD JUST LONG ENOUGH TO PRY THE CHAPTER OUT OF THEIR CLENCHED FISTS WHILE BROWBEATING THE PRINTER INTO WAITING UNTIL THE LAST POSSIBLE SECOND BEFORE SHOVING THE COMPLETED COPY DOWN THEIR THROATS." THE OTHER SIX PERCENT REMAINS A MYSTERY.

The World's Greatest First Love
The Case of Ritsu Onodera

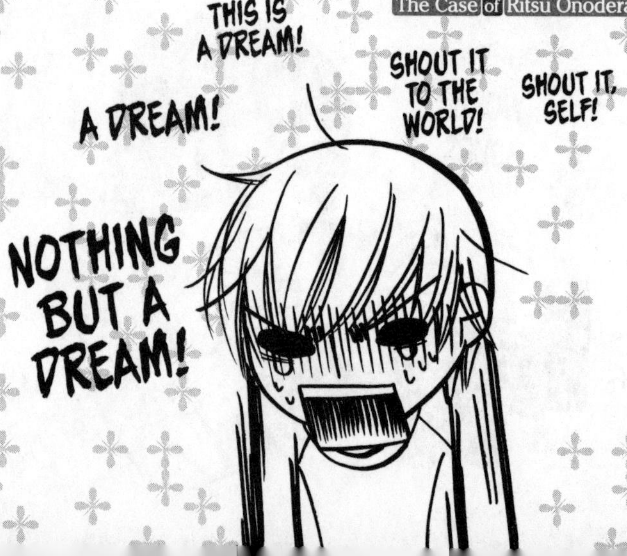
SHOUT IT, SELF!
SHOUT IT TO THE WORLD!
THIS IS A DREAM!
A DREAM!
NOTHING BUT A DREAM!

MARUKAWA PUBLISHING TERMINOLOGY & JARGON (PART 10)

***NOTE:** ALL OF THE TERMINOLOGY LISTED HEREIN IS SPECIFIC TO MARUKAWA PUBLISHING AND MAY NOT BE APPLICABLE TO THE GENERAL PUBLISHING INDUSTRY.

[TINKLE]

TINKLE IS THE NAME OF THE MASCOT CHARACTER FOR MARUKAWA PUBLISHING'S SHOJO MANGA ANTHOLOGY, *MONTHLY EMERALD.* A BUNNY WITH WINGS, TINKLE SOMETIMES CARRIES A FAIRY WAND WITH A STAR ON THE END. IT IS ALSO OCCASIONALLY CONSIDERED THE GUARDIAN DEITY OF THE *EMERALD* EDITORIAL DEPARTMENT.

[COLOR PROOF]

A COLOR PROOF IS PRINTED DURING AN ADDITIONAL EDITING STAGE AND ADDED TO THE PROCESS IF THE DOCUMENT INCLUDES COLOR IMAGES OR TABLES. ONCE THE FINAL PRINTING PLATES HAVE BEEN SET, COLOR PROOFS ARE PRINTED USING THE SAME INKS THAT WILL BE USED ON THE OFFICIAL PRINTING. EDITORS CHECK THEM MAINLY TO SEE THAT THE COLORS ACCURATELY MATCH THE ORIGINAL ILLUSTRATION AND THAT THE PLATES WERE SET CORRECTLY.

[BOOK DESIGN]

BOOK DESIGN REFERS TO THE OVERALL STYLE AND LAYOUT OF A BOOK. IT OBVIOUSLY INCLUDES THE COVER ART, BUT THINGS SUCH AS THE DUST COVER, TEXT LAYOUT, TYPEFACE, PAPER TYPE, AND EVEN FONT SIZE ALSO COME INTO CONSIDERATION.

The World's Greatest First Love
The Case of Ritsu Onodera

DURING WORK HOURS
MONTHLY PANDA

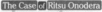

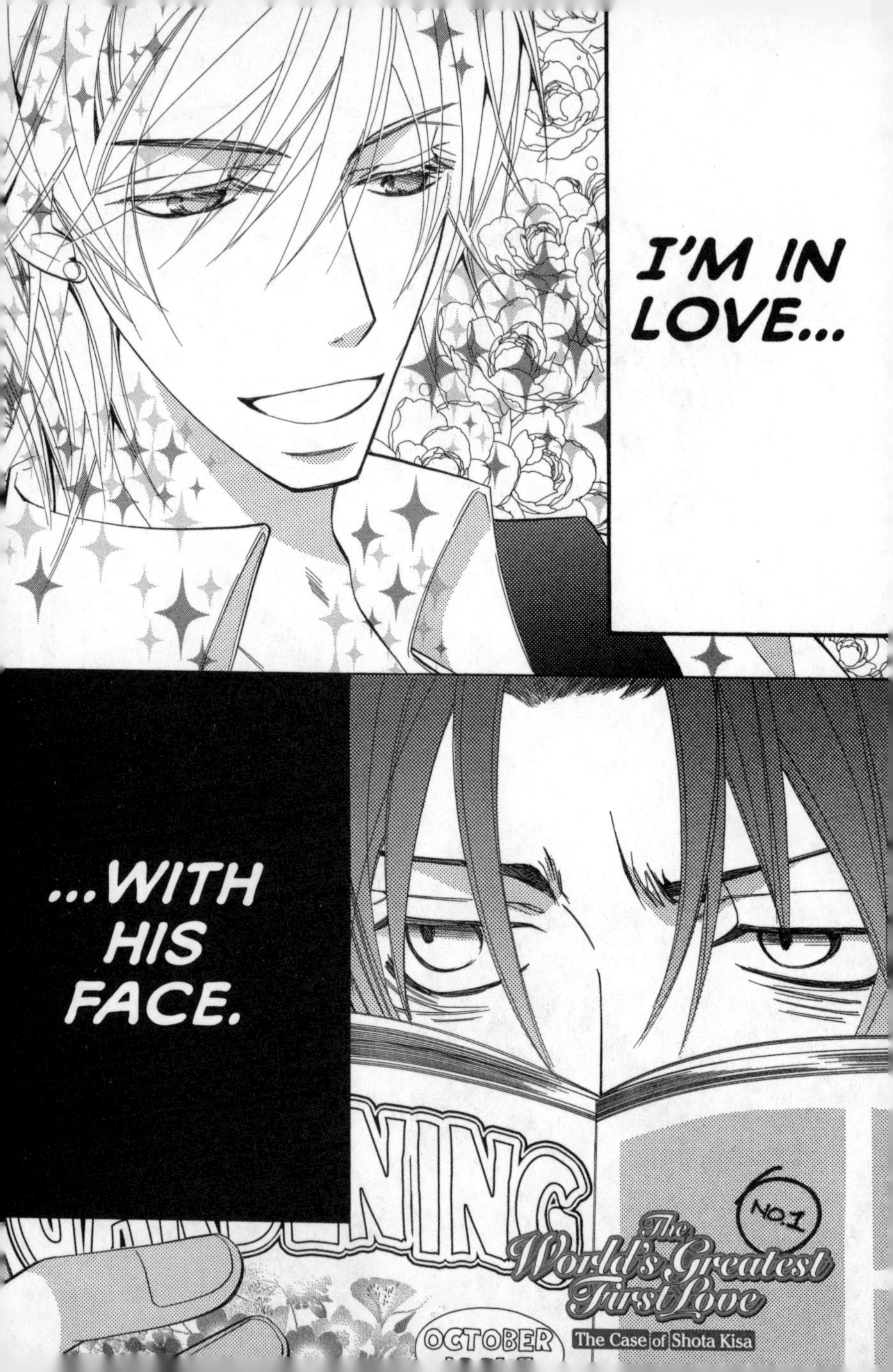
I'M IN LOVE...
...WITH HIS FACE.
NO.1
OCTOBER
The World's Greatest First Love
The Case of Shota Kisa

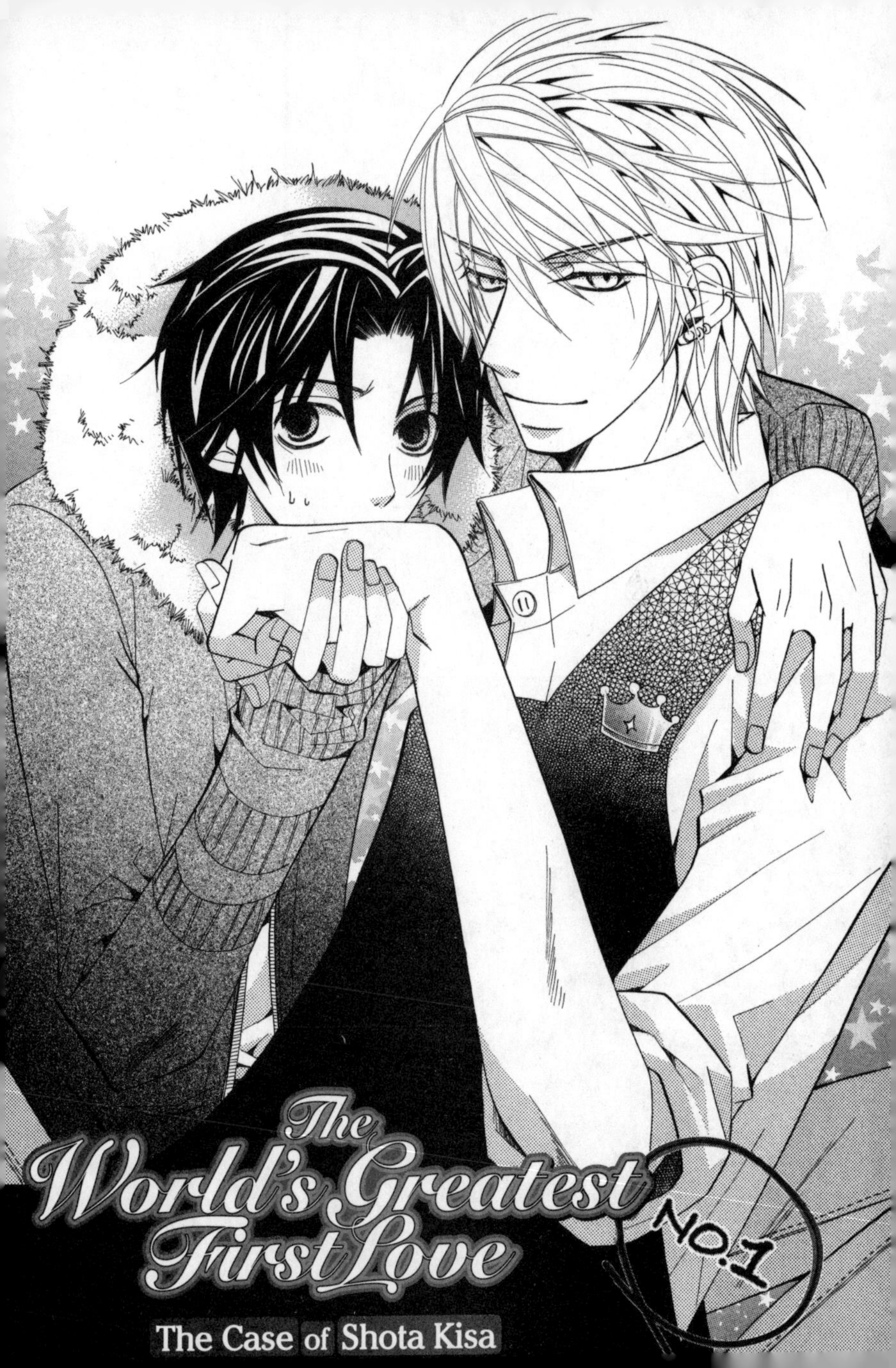
The World's Greatest First Love
NO.1
The Case of Shota Kisa

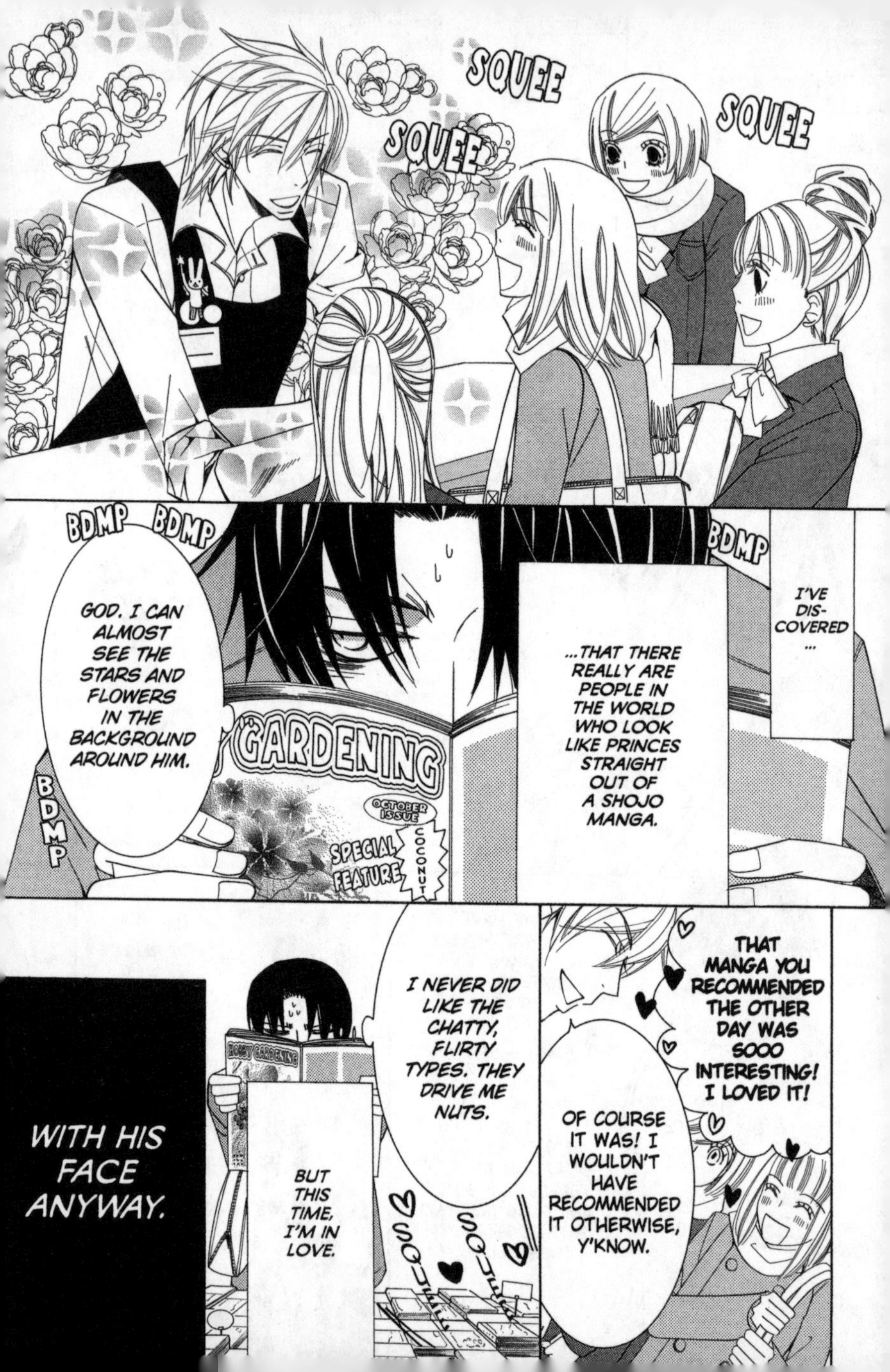

SQUEE
SQUEE
SQUEE
BDMP
I'VE DISCOVERED...
...THAT THERE REALLY ARE PEOPLE IN THE WORLD WHO LOOK LIKE PRINCES STRAIGHT OUT OF A SHOJO MANGA.
BDMP BDMP
GOD. I CAN ALMOST SEE THE STARS AND FLOWERS IN THE BACKGROUND AROUND HIM.
BDMP
GARDENING
OCTOBER ISSUE
SPECIAL FEATURE
COCONUT
THAT MANGA YOU RECOMMENDED THE OTHER DAY WAS SOOO INTERESTING! I LOVED IT!
OF COURSE IT WAS! I WOULDN'T HAVE RECOMMENDED IT OTHERWISE, Y'KNOW.
I NEVER DID LIKE THE CHATTY, FLIRTY TYPES. THEY DRIVE ME NUTS.
BUT THIS TIME, I'M IN LOVE.
HOBBY GARDENING
WITH HIS FACE ANYWAY.

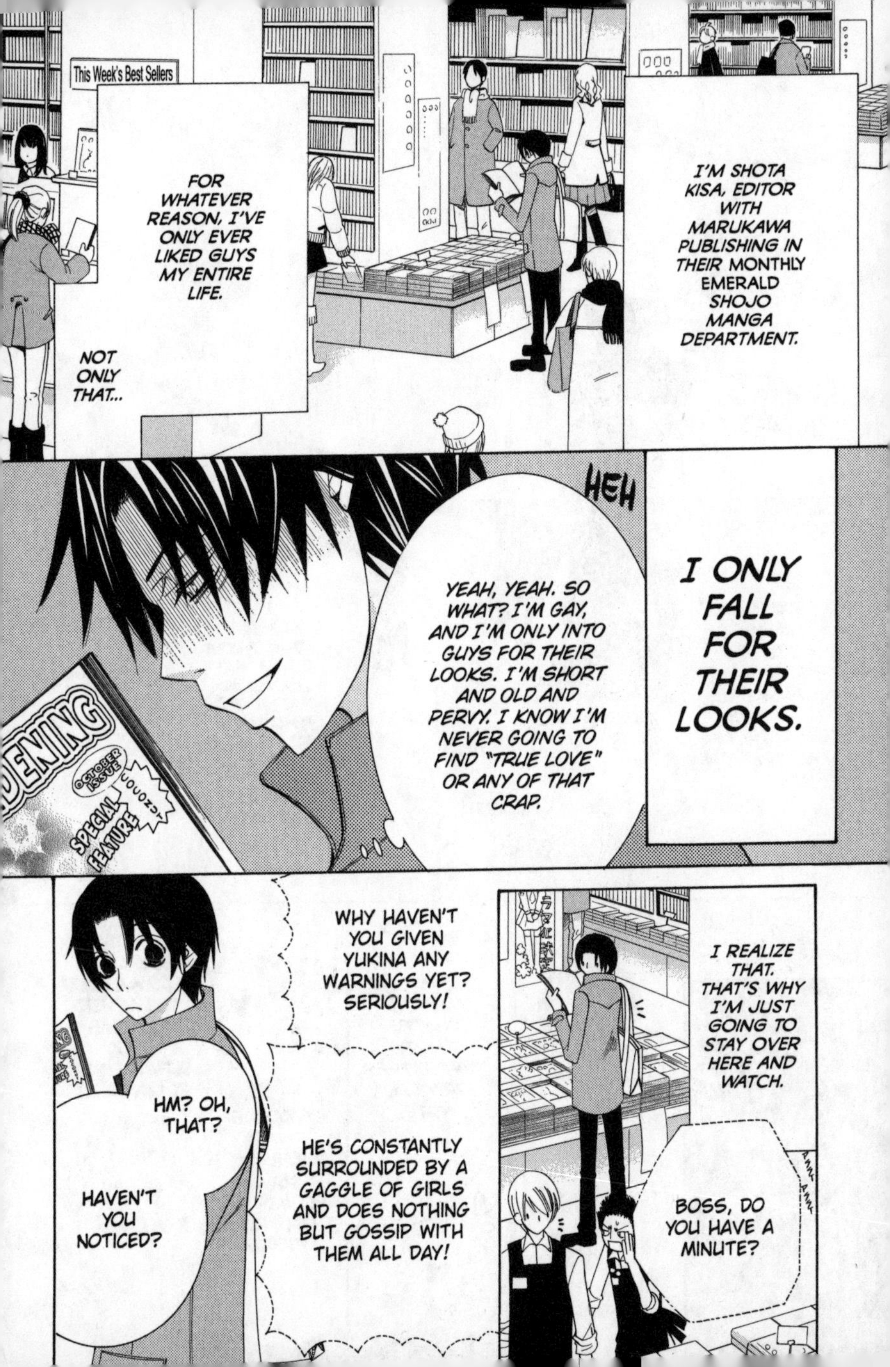

This Week's Best Sellers
I'M SHOTA KISA, EDITOR WITH MARUKAWA PUBLISHING IN THEIR MONTHLY EMERALD SHOJO MANGA DEPARTMENT.
FOR WHATEVER REASON, I'VE ONLY EVER LIKED GUYS MY ENTIRE LIFE.
NOT ONLY THAT...
I ONLY FALL FOR THEIR LOOKS.
HEH
YEAH, YEAH. SO WHAT? I'M GAY, AND I'M ONLY INTO GUYS FOR THEIR LOOKS. I'M SHORT AND OLD AND PERVY. I KNOW I'M NEVER GOING TO FIND "TRUE LOVE" OR ANY OF THAT CRAP.
DENING
OCTOBER ISSUE
SPECIAL FEATURE
I REALIZE THAT. THAT'S WHY I'M JUST GOING TO STAY OVER HERE AND WATCH.
BOSS, DO YOU HAVE A MINUTE?
WHY HAVEN'T YOU GIVEN YUKINA ANY WARNINGS YET? SERIOUSLY!
HM? OH, THAT?
HE'S CONSTANTLY SURROUNDED BY A GAGGLE OF GIRLS AND DOES NOTHING BUT GOSSIP WITH THEM ALL DAY!
HAVEN'T YOU NOTICED?

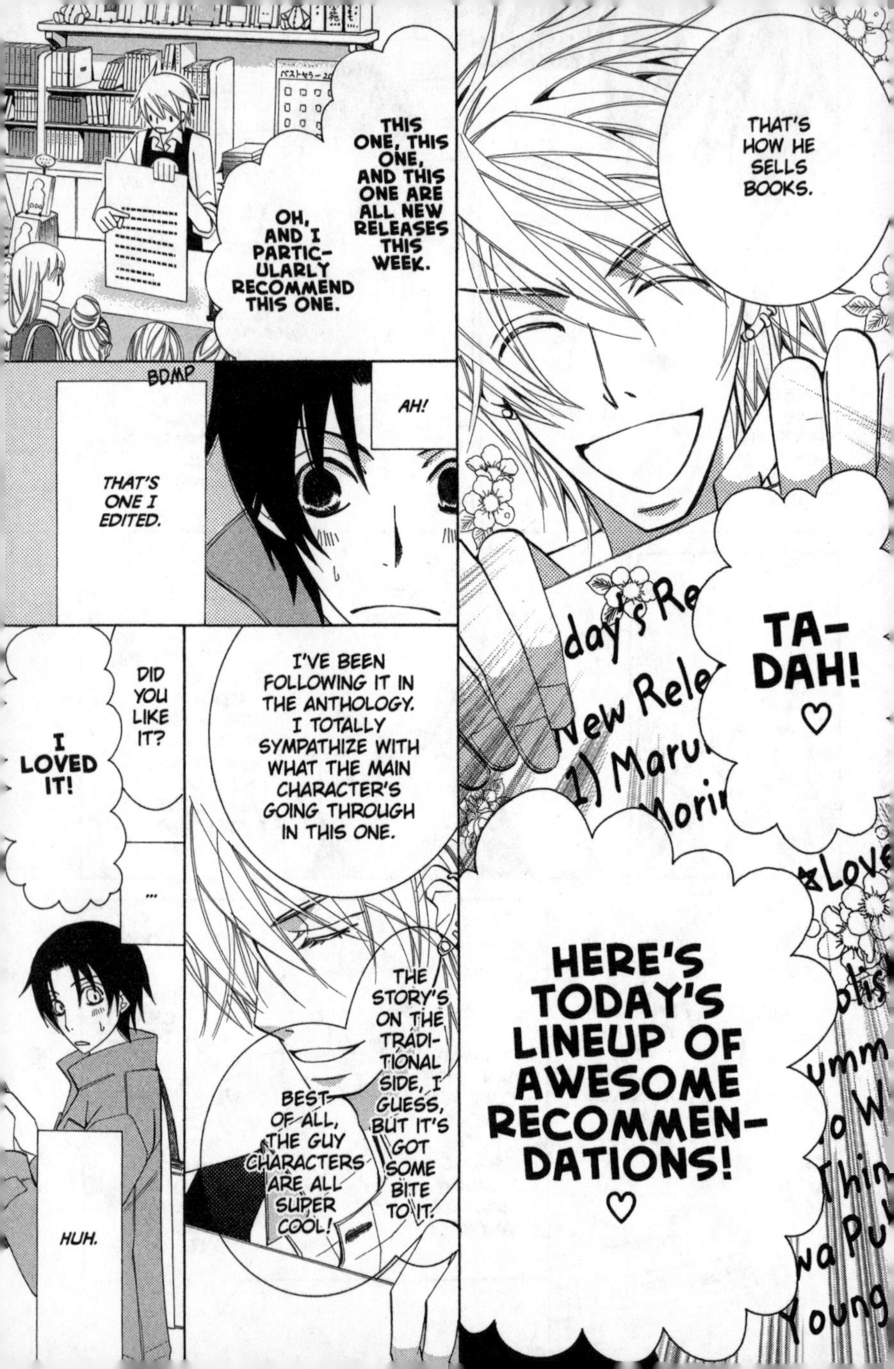
THAT'S HOW HE SELLS BOOKS.
TA-DAH! ♡
HERE'S TODAY'S LINEUP OF AWESOME RECOMMENDATIONS! ♡
THIS ONE, THIS ONE, AND THIS ONE ARE ALL NEW RELEASES THIS WEEK.
OH, AND I PARTICULARLY RECOMMEND THIS ONE.
BDMP
AH!
THAT'S ONE I EDITED.
I'VE BEEN FOLLOWING IT IN THE ANTHOLOGY. I TOTALLY SYMPATHIZE WITH WHAT THE MAIN CHARACTER'S GOING THROUGH IN THIS ONE.
THE STORY'S ON THE TRADITIONAL SIDE, I GUESS, BUT IT'S GOT SOME BITE TO IT.
BEST OF ALL, THE GUY CHARACTERS ARE ALL SUPER COOL!
DID YOU LIKE IT?
I LOVED IT!
...
HUH.

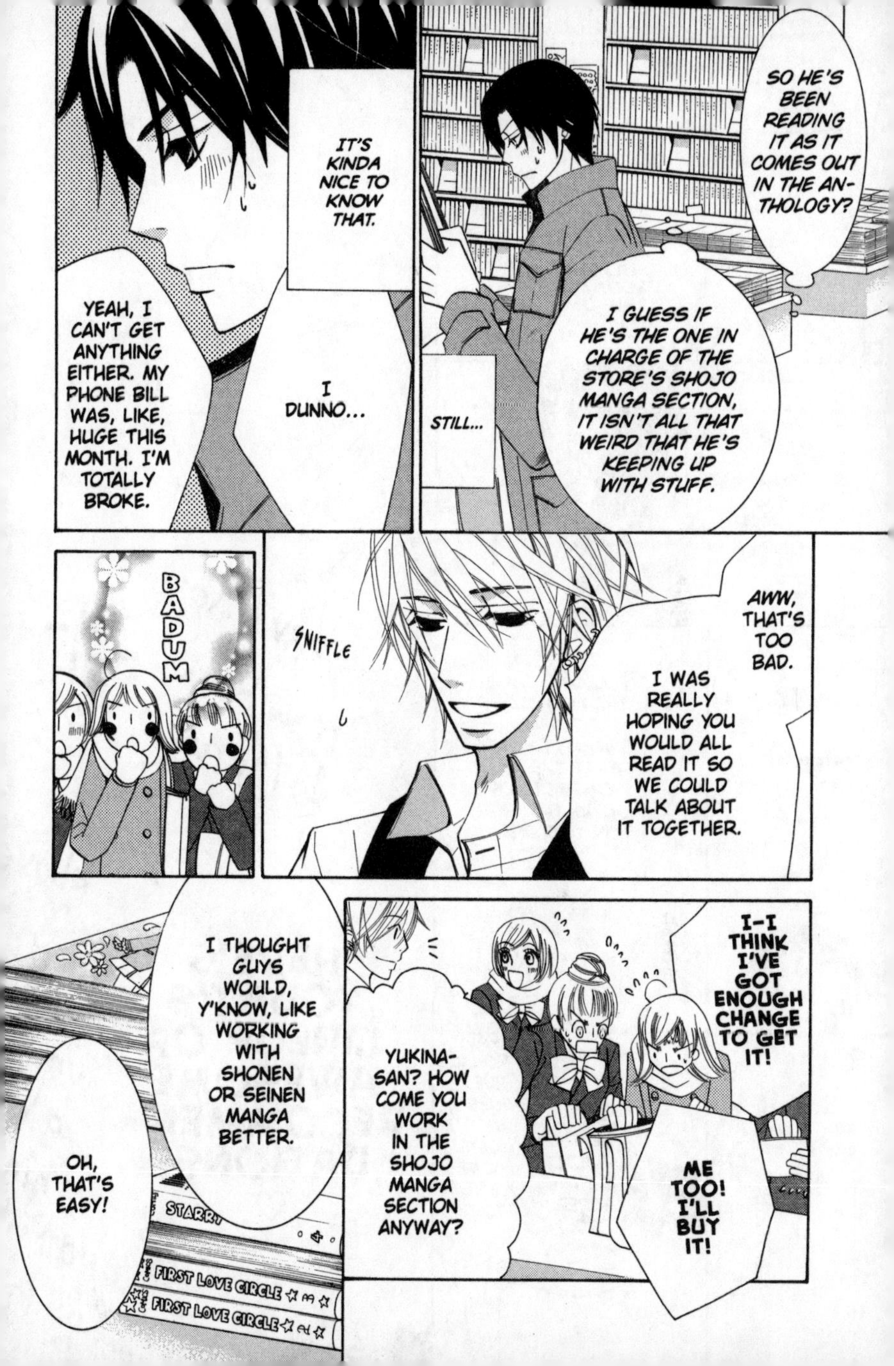
SO HE'S BEEN READING IT AS IT COMES OUT IN THE ANTHOLOGY?
I GUESS IF HE'S THE ONE IN CHARGE OF THE STORE'S SHOJO MANGA SECTION, IT ISN'T ALL THAT WEIRD THAT HE'S KEEPING UP WITH STUFF.
STILL...
IT'S KINDA NICE TO KNOW THAT.
I DUNNO...
YEAH, I CAN'T GET ANYTHING EITHER. MY PHONE BILL WAS, LIKE, HUGE THIS MONTH. I'M TOTALLY BROKE.
AWW, THAT'S TOO BAD.
I WAS REALLY HOPING YOU WOULD ALL READ IT SO WE COULD TALK ABOUT IT TOGETHER.
SNIFFLE
BADUM
I-I THINK I'VE GOT ENOUGH CHANGE TO GET IT!
ME TOO! I'LL BUY IT!
YUKINA-SAN? HOW COME YOU WORK IN THE SHOJO MANGA SECTION ANYWAY?
I THOUGHT GUYS WOULD, Y'KNOW, LIKE WORKING WITH SHONEN OR SEINEN MANGA BETTER.
OH, THAT'S EASY!
STARRY
FIRST LOVE CIRCLE
FIRST LOVE CIRCLE

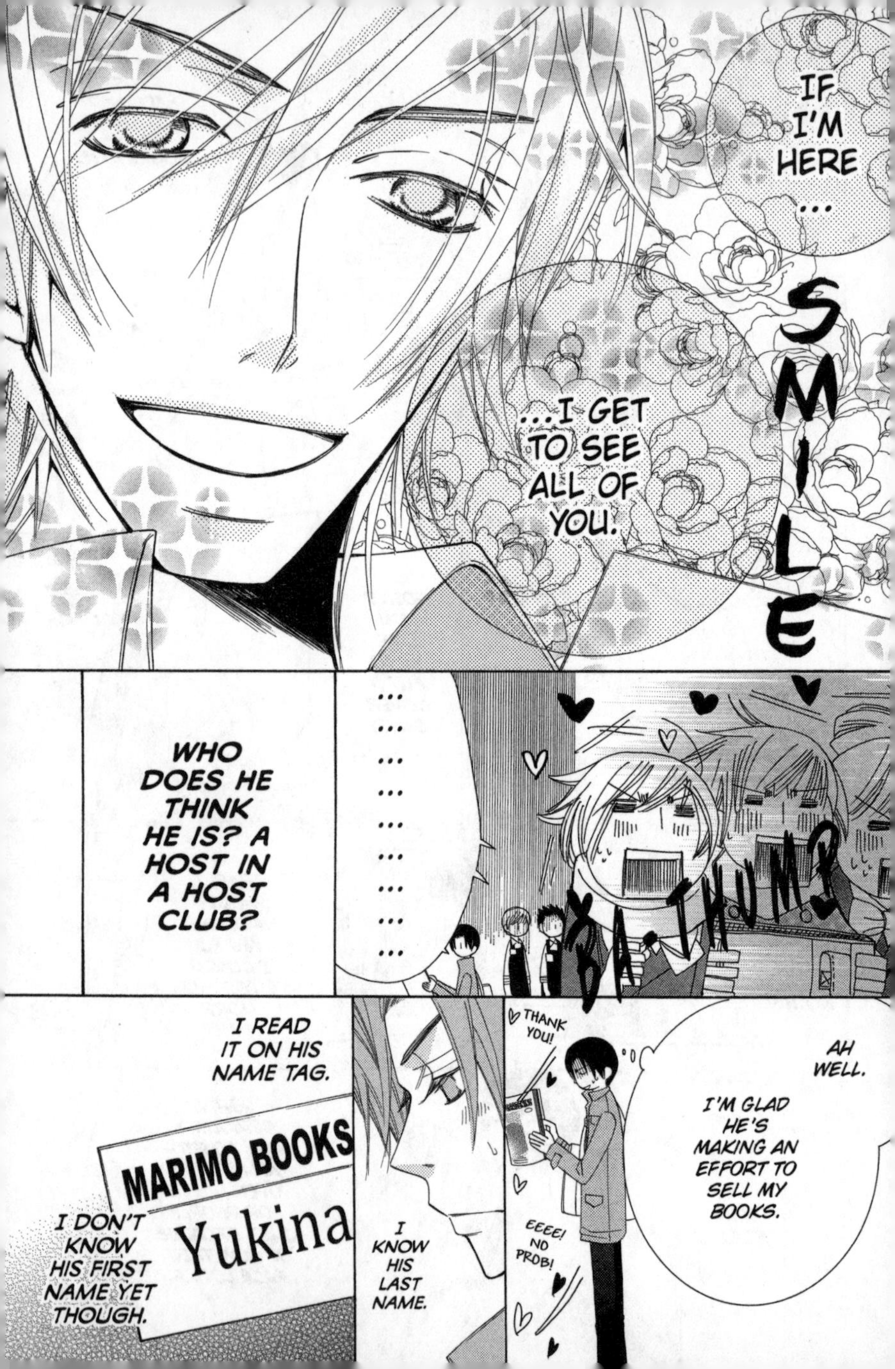
IF I'M HERE ...
...I GET TO SEE ALL OF YOU.
SMILE
BA-THUMP
... ...
WHO DOES HE THINK HE IS? A HOST IN A HOST CLUB?
AH WELL.
I'M GLAD HE'S MAKING AN EFFORT TO SELL MY BOOKS.
THANK YOU!
EEEE! NO PROB!
I KNOW HIS LAST NAME.
I READ IT ON HIS NAME TAG.
MARIMO BOOKS
Yukina
I DON'T KNOW HIS FIRST NAME YET THOUGH.

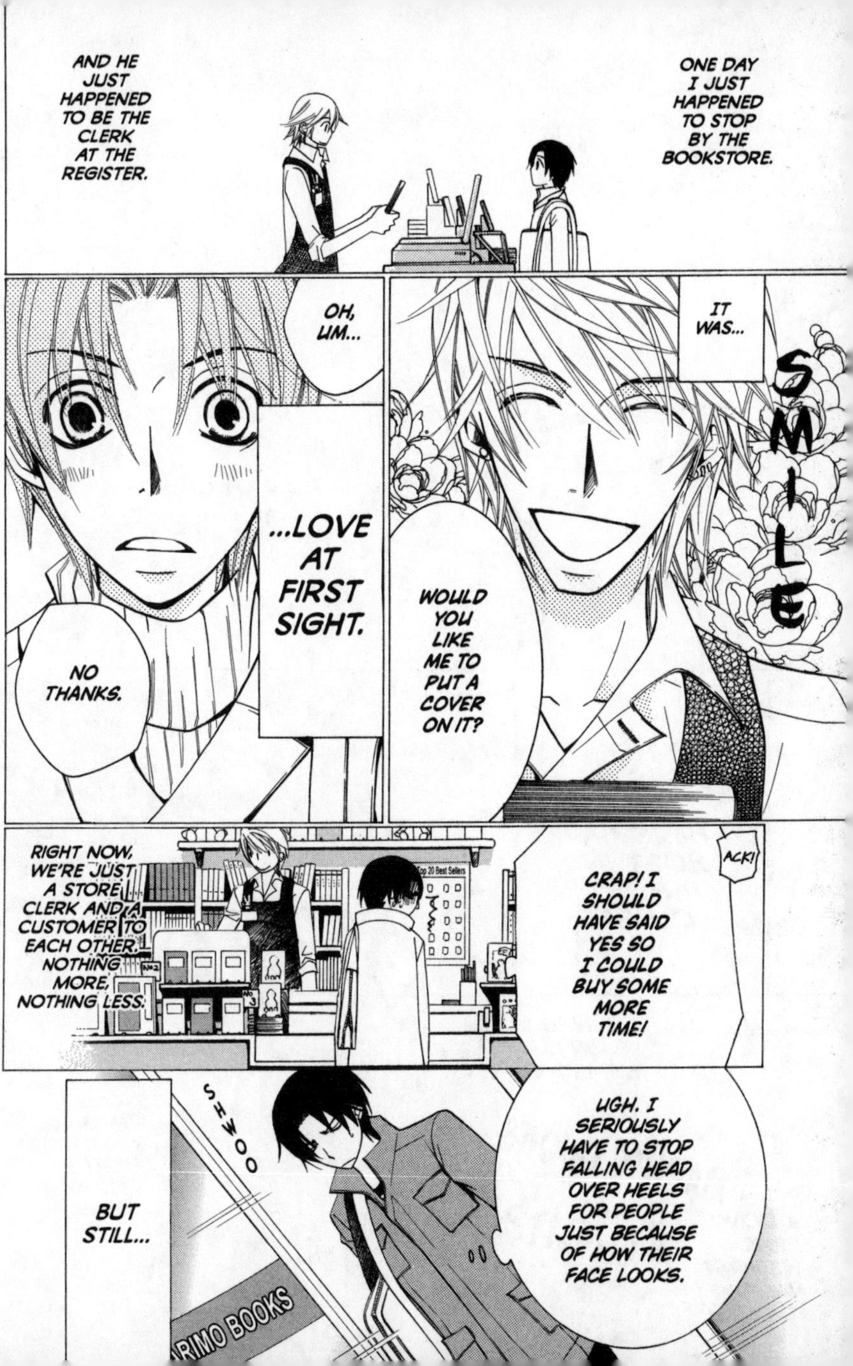
ONE DAY I JUST HAPPENED TO STOP BY THE BOOKSTORE.
AND HE JUST HAPPENED TO BE THE CLERK AT THE REGISTER.
IT WAS...
SMILE
WOULD YOU LIKE ME TO PUT A COVER ON IT?
OH, UM...
...LOVE AT FIRST SIGHT.
NO THANKS.
ACK!
CRAP! I SHOULD HAVE SAID YES SO I COULD BUY SOME MORE TIME!
Top 20 Best Sellers
RIGHT NOW, WE'RE JUST A STORE CLERK AND A CUSTOMER TO EACH OTHER. NOTHING MORE, NOTHING LESS.
UGH. I SERIOUSLY HAVE TO STOP FALLING HEAD OVER HEELS FOR PEOPLE JUST BECAUSE OF HOW THEIR FACE LOOKS.
SHWOO
RIMO BOOKS
BUT STILL...

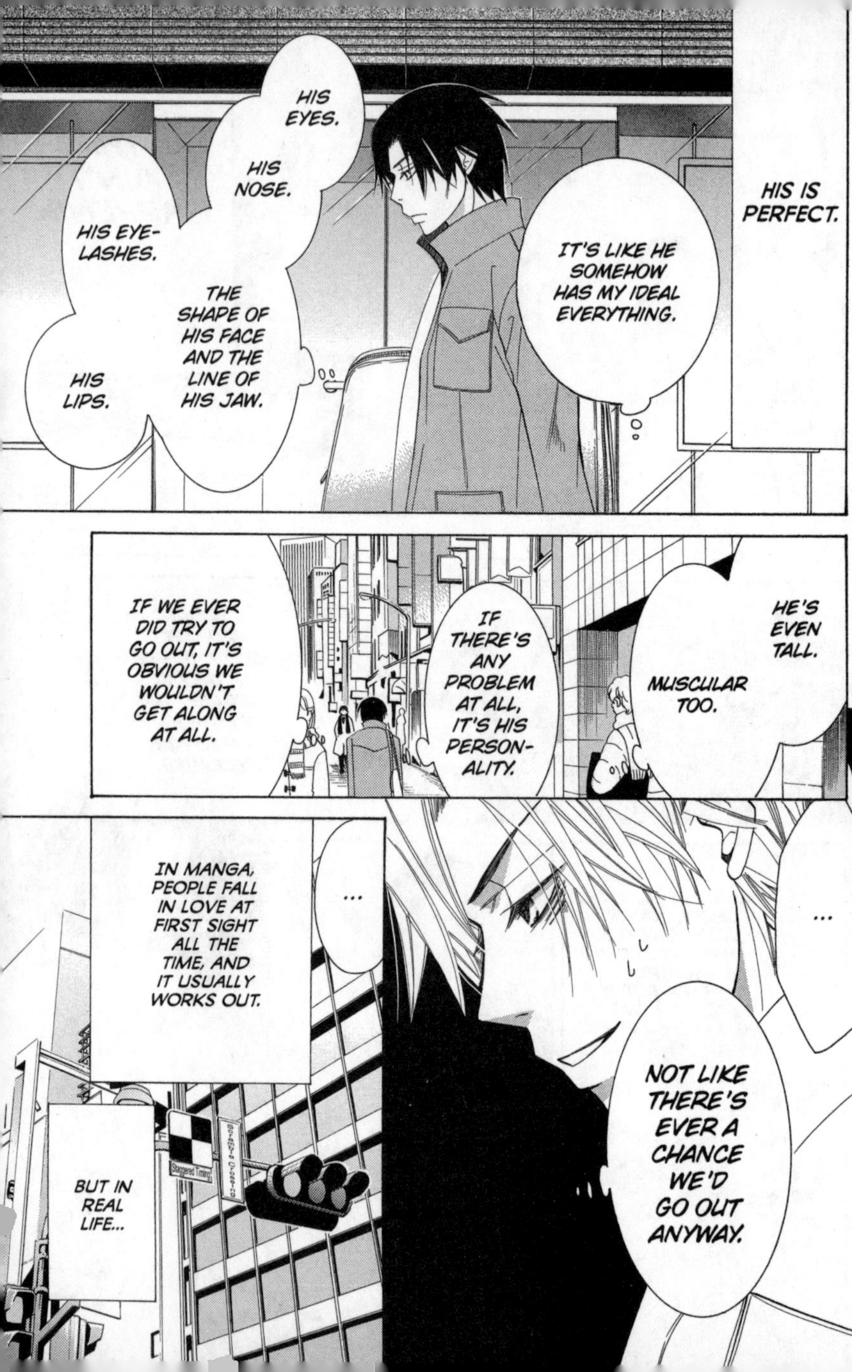
HIS IS PERFECT.
IT'S LIKE HE SOMEHOW HAS MY IDEAL EVERYTHING.
HIS EYES.
HIS NOSE.
HIS EYE-LASHES.
THE SHAPE OF HIS FACE AND THE LINE OF HIS JAW.
HIS LIPS.
HE'S EVEN TALL.
MUSCULAR TOO.
IF THERE'S ANY PROBLEM AT ALL, IT'S HIS PERSON-ALITY.
IF WE EVER DID TRY TO GO OUT, IT'S OBVIOUS WE WOULDN'T GET ALONG AT ALL.
...
NOT LIKE THERE'S EVER A CHANCE WE'D GO OUT ANYWAY.
...
IN MANGA, PEOPLE FALL IN LOVE AT FIRST SIGHT ALL THE TIME, AND IT USUALLY WORKS OUT.
Scramble Crossing
Staggered Timing
BUT IN REAL LIFE...

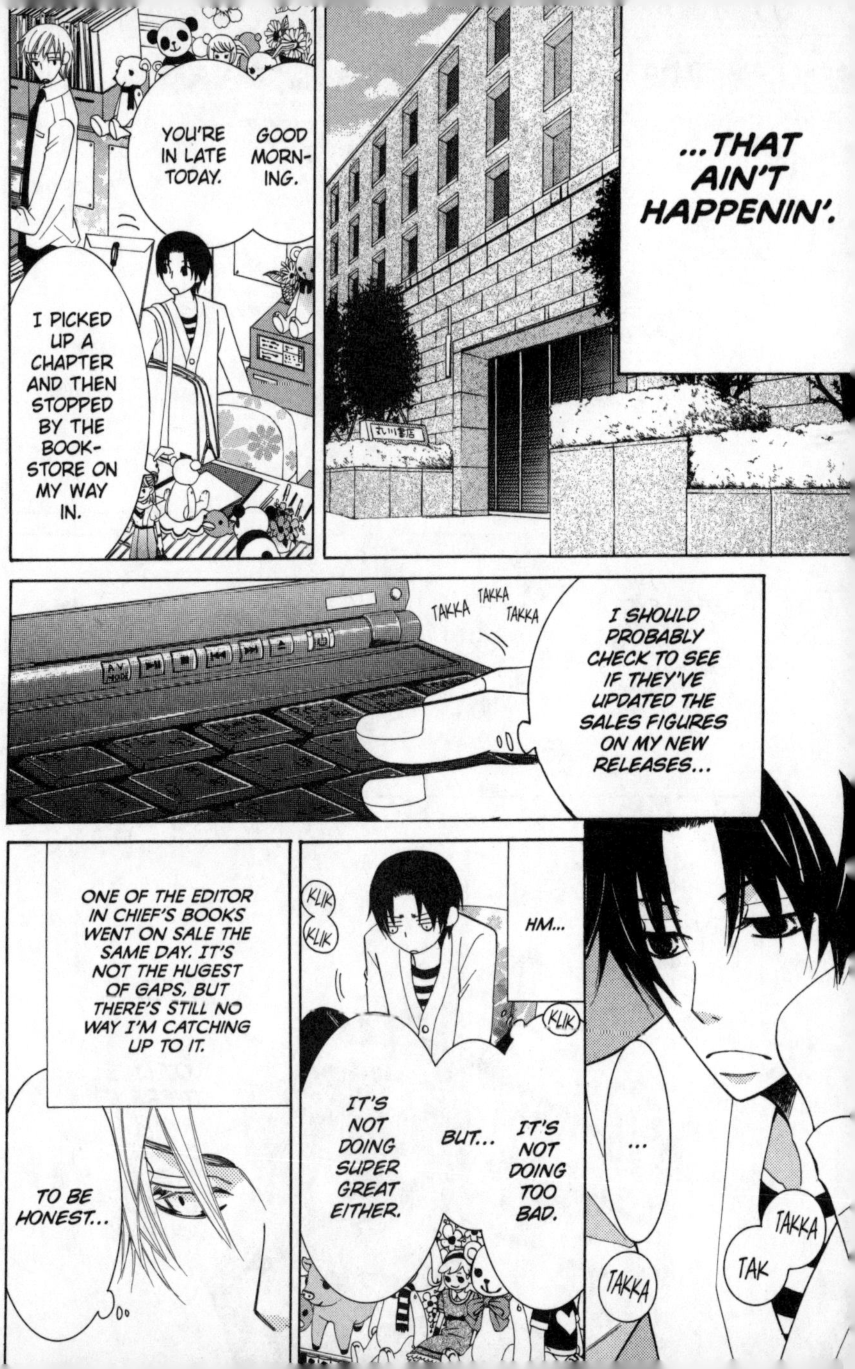
...THAT AIN'T HAPPENIN'.
GOOD MORNING.
YOU'RE IN LATE TODAY.
I PICKED UP A CHAPTER AND THEN STOPPED BY THE BOOKSTORE ON MY WAY IN.
TAKKA TAKKA TAKKA
I SHOULD PROBABLY CHECK TO SEE IF THEY'VE UPDATED THE SALES FIGURES ON MY NEW RELEASES...
...
TAKKA
TAK
TAKKA
HM...
KLIK
KLIK
KLIK
IT'S NOT DOING TOO BAD.
BUT...
IT'S NOT DOING SUPER GREAT EITHER.
ONE OF THE EDITOR IN CHIEF'S BOOKS WENT ON SALE THE SAME DAY. IT'S NOT THE HUGEST OF GAPS, BUT THERE'S STILL NO WAY I'M CATCHING UP TO IT.
TO BE HONEST...

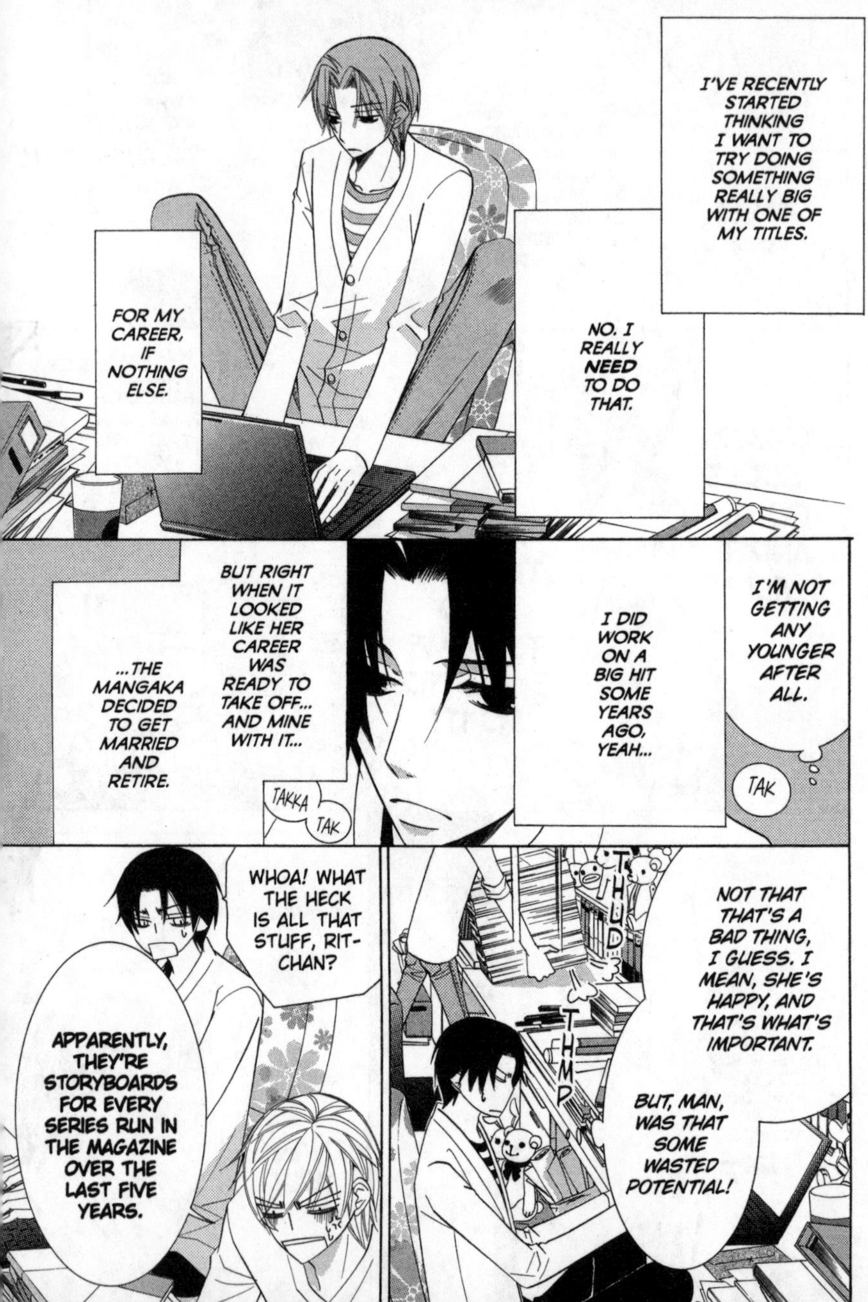
I'VE RECENTLY STARTED THINKING I WANT TO TRY DOING SOMETHING REALLY BIG WITH ONE OF MY TITLES.
NO. I REALLY **NEED** TO DO THAT.
FOR MY CAREER, IF NOTHING ELSE.
I'M NOT GETTING ANY YOUNGER AFTER ALL.
TAK
I DID WORK ON A BIG HIT SOME YEARS AGO, YEAH...
BUT RIGHT WHEN IT LOOKED LIKE HER CAREER WAS READY TO TAKE OFF... AND MINE WITH IT...
...THE MANGAKA DECIDED TO GET MARRIED AND RETIRE.
TAKKA TAK
THUD
THMP
NOT THAT THAT'S A BAD THING, I GUESS. I MEAN, SHE'S HAPPY, AND THAT'S WHAT'S IMPORTANT.
BUT, MAN, WAS THAT SOME WASTED POTENTIAL!
WHOA! WHAT THE HECK IS ALL THAT STUFF, RIT-CHAN?
APPARENTLY, THEY'RE STORYBOARDS FOR EVERY SERIES RUN IN THE MAGAZINE OVER THE LAST FIVE YEARS.

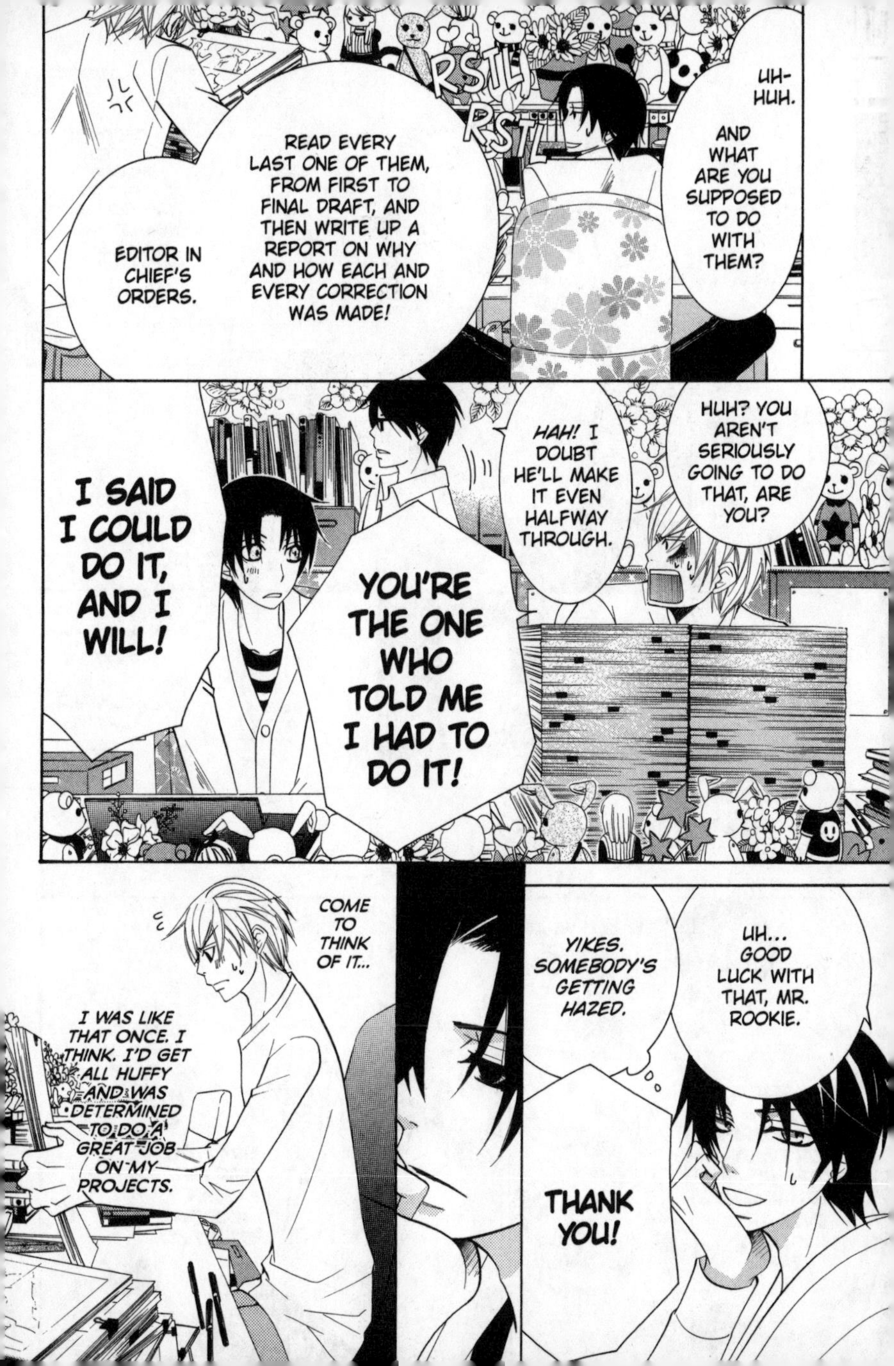
UH-HUH.
AND WHAT ARE YOU SUPPOSED TO DO WITH THEM?
RSTL
RSTL
READ EVERY LAST ONE OF THEM, FROM FIRST TO FINAL DRAFT, AND THEN WRITE UP A REPORT ON WHY AND HOW EACH AND EVERY CORRECTION WAS MADE!
EDITOR IN CHIEF'S ORDERS.
HUH? YOU AREN'T SERIOUSLY GOING TO DO THAT, ARE YOU?
HAH! I DOUBT HE'LL MAKE IT EVEN HALFWAY THROUGH.
YOU'RE THE ONE WHO TOLD ME I HAD TO DO IT!
I SAID I COULD DO IT, AND I WILL!
UH... GOOD LUCK WITH THAT, MR. ROOKIE.
YIKES. SOMEBODY'S GETTING HAZED.
THANK YOU!
COME TO THINK OF IT...
I WAS LIKE THAT ONCE. I THINK. I'D GET ALL HUFFY AND WAS DETERMINED TO DO A GREAT JOB ON MY PROJECTS.

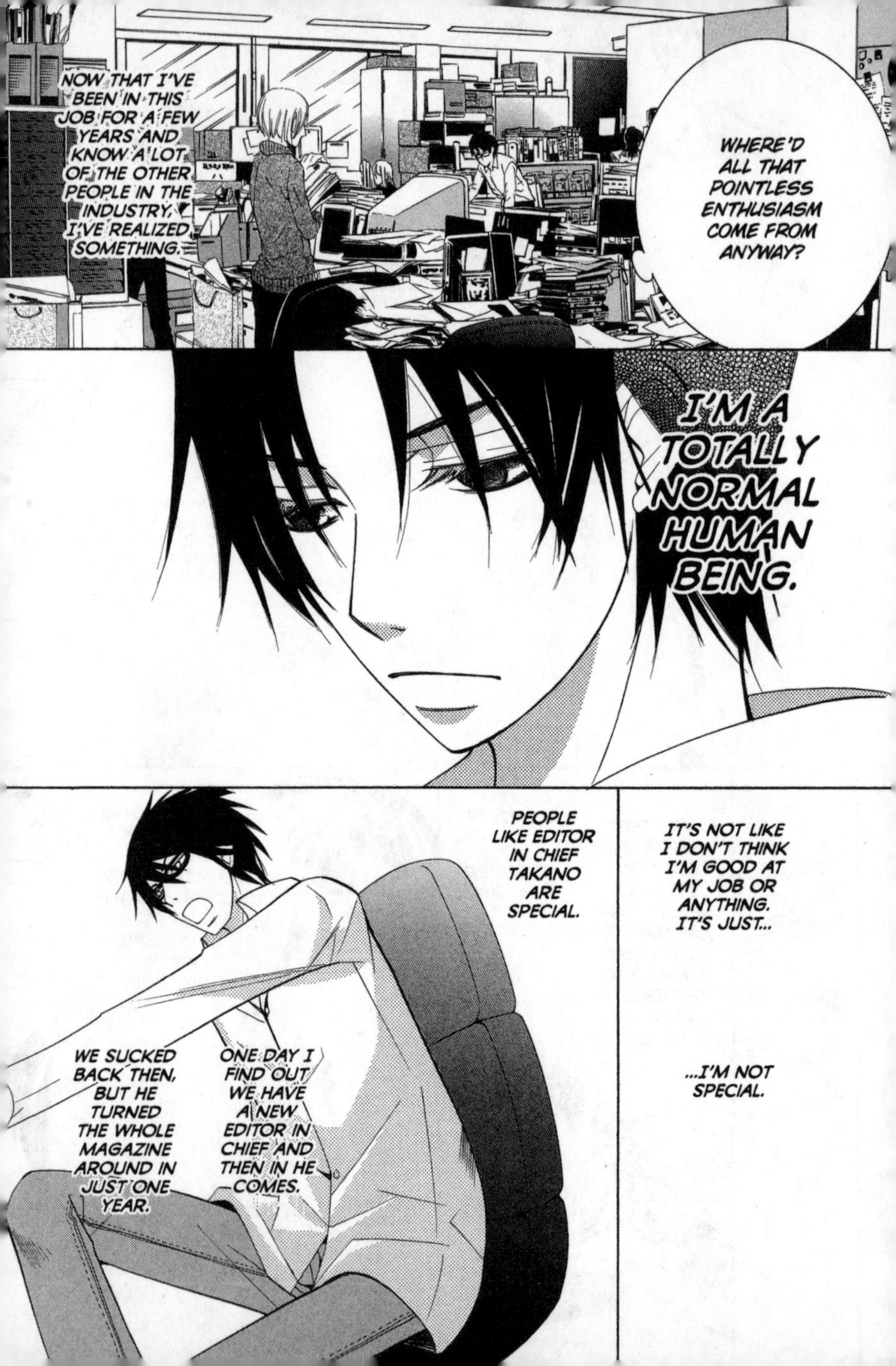
WHERE'D ALL THAT POINTLESS ENTHUSIASM COME FROM ANYWAY?
NOW THAT I'VE BEEN IN THIS JOB FOR A FEW YEARS AND KNOW A LOT OF THE OTHER PEOPLE IN THE INDUSTRY, I'VE REALIZED SOMETHING.
I'M A TOTALLY NORMAL HUMAN BEING.
IT'S NOT LIKE I DON'T THINK I'M GOOD AT MY JOB OR ANYTHING. IT'S JUST...
...I'M NOT SPECIAL.
PEOPLE LIKE EDITOR IN CHIEF TAKANO ARE SPECIAL.
ONE DAY I FIND OUT WE HAVE A NEW EDITOR IN CHIEF AND THEN IN HE COMES.
WE SUCKED BACK THEN, BUT HE TURNED THE WHOLE MAGAZINE AROUND IN JUST ONE YEAR.

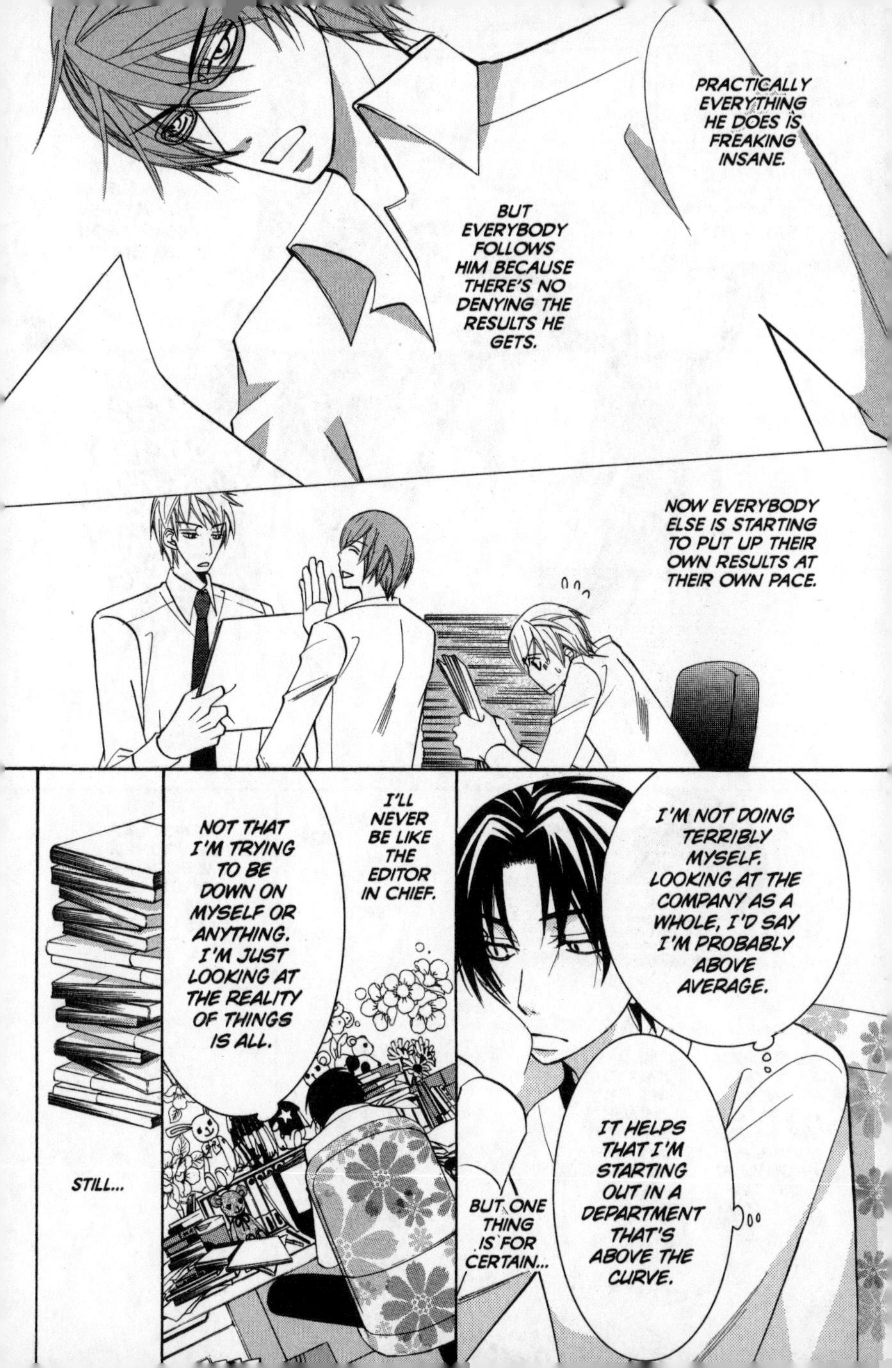
PRACTICALLY EVERYTHING HE DOES IS FREAKING INSANE.
BUT EVERYBODY FOLLOWS HIM BECAUSE THERE'S NO DENYING THE RESULTS HE GETS.
NOW EVERYBODY ELSE IS STARTING TO PUT UP THEIR OWN RESULTS AT THEIR OWN PACE.
I'M NOT DOING TERRIBLY MYSELF. LOOKING AT THE COMPANY AS A WHOLE, I'D SAY I'M PROBABLY ABOVE AVERAGE.
IT HELPS THAT I'M STARTING OUT IN A DEPARTMENT THAT'S ABOVE THE CURVE.
BUT ONE THING IS FOR CERTAIN...
I'LL NEVER BE LIKE THE EDITOR IN CHIEF.
NOT THAT I'M TRYING TO BE DOWN ON MYSELF OR ANYTHING. I'M JUST LOOKING AT THE REALITY OF THINGS IS ALL.
STILL...

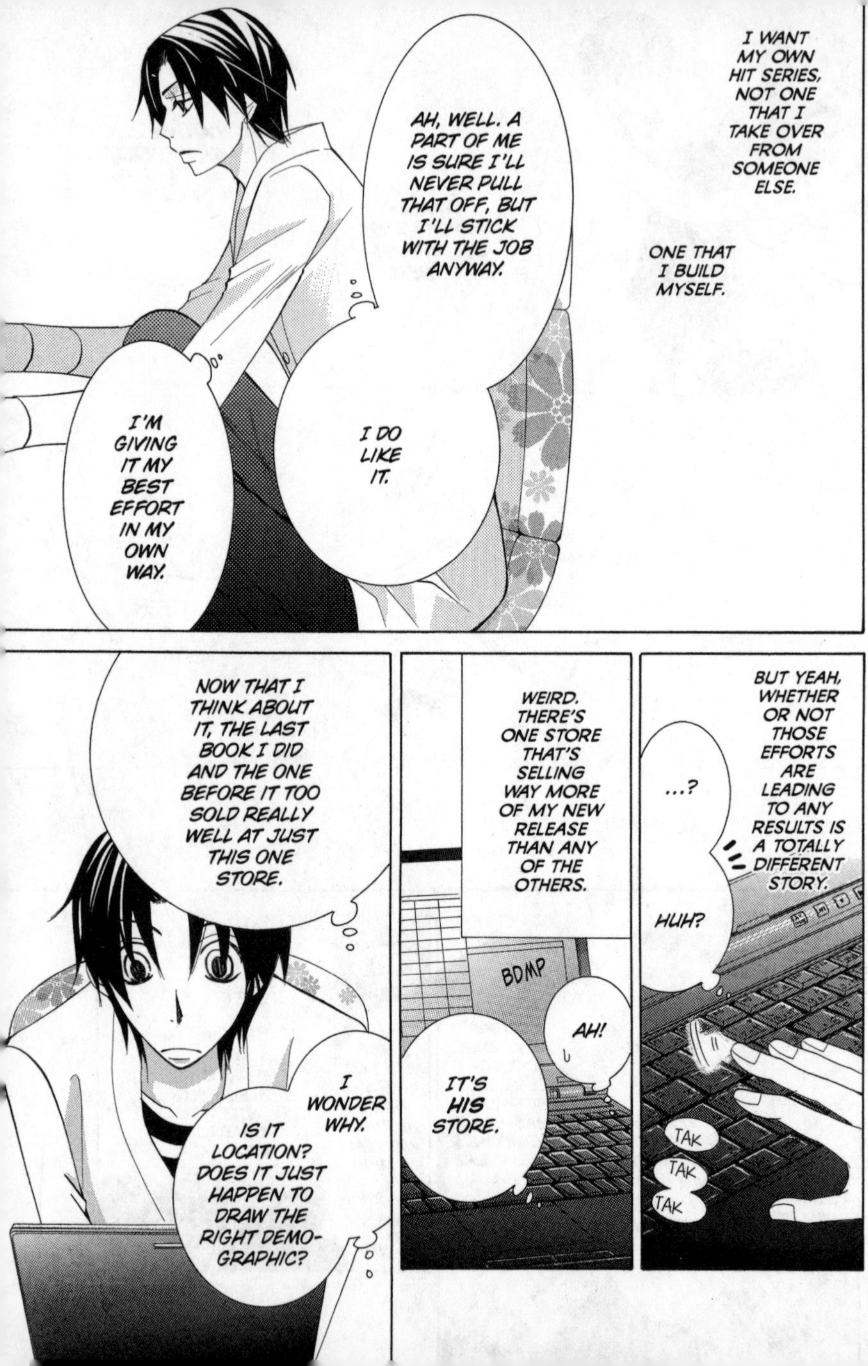
I WANT MY OWN HIT SERIES, NOT ONE THAT I TAKE OVER FROM SOMEONE ELSE.
ONE THAT I BUILD MYSELF.
AH, WELL. A PART OF ME IS SURE I'LL NEVER PULL THAT OFF, BUT I'LL STICK WITH THE JOB ANYWAY.
I DO LIKE IT.
I'M GIVING IT MY BEST EFFORT IN MY OWN WAY.
BUT YEAH, WHETHER OR NOT THOSE EFFORTS ARE LEADING TO ANY RESULTS IS A TOTALLY DIFFERENT STORY.
...?
HUH?
TAK
TAK
TAK
WEIRD. THERE'S ONE STORE THAT'S SELLING WAY MORE OF MY NEW RELEASE THAN ANY OF THE OTHERS.
BDMP
AH!
IT'S HIS STORE.
NOW THAT I THINK ABOUT IT, THE LAST BOOK I DID AND THE ONE BEFORE IT TOO SOLD REALLY WELL AT JUST THIS ONE STORE.
I WONDER WHY.
IS IT LOCATION? DOES IT JUST HAPPEN TO DRAW THE RIGHT DEMO-GRAPHIC?

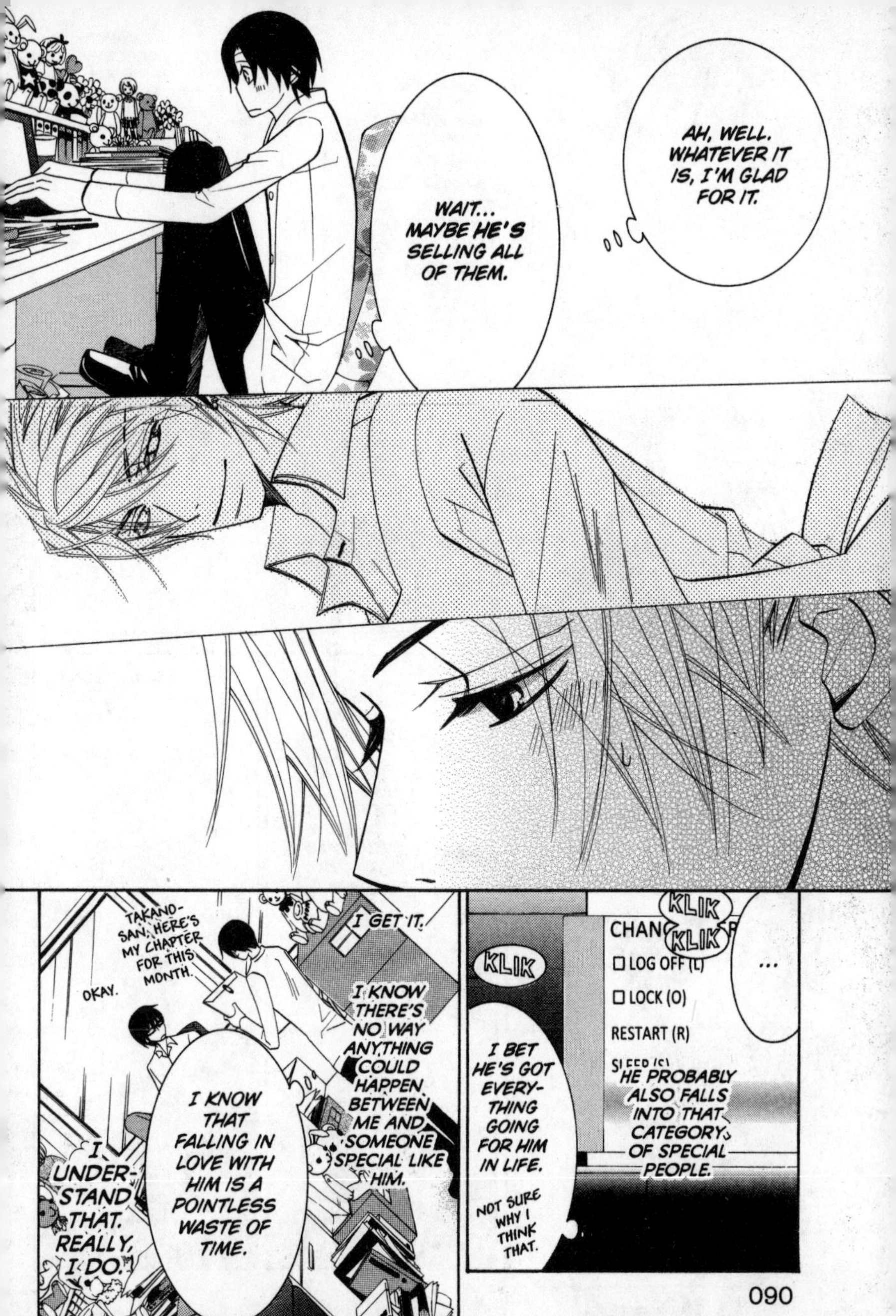
AH, WELL. WHATEVER IT IS, I'M GLAD FOR IT.
WAIT... MAYBE HE'S SELLING ALL OF THEM.
KLIK
KLIK
LOG OFF (L)
LOCK (O)
RESTART (R)
...
HE PROBABLY ALSO FALLS INTO THAT CATEGORY OF SPECIAL PEOPLE.
KLIK
I BET HE'S GOT EVERY-THING GOING FOR HIM IN LIFE.
NOT SURE WHY I THINK THAT.
I GET IT.
TAKANO-SAN, HERE'S MY CHAPTER FOR THIS MONTH.
OKAY.
I KNOW THERE'S NO WAY ANYTHING COULD HAPPEN BETWEEN ME AND SOMEONE SPECIAL LIKE HIM.
I KNOW THAT FALLING IN LOVE WITH HIM IS A POINTLESS WASTE OF TIME.
I UNDER-STAND THAT. REALLY, I DO.

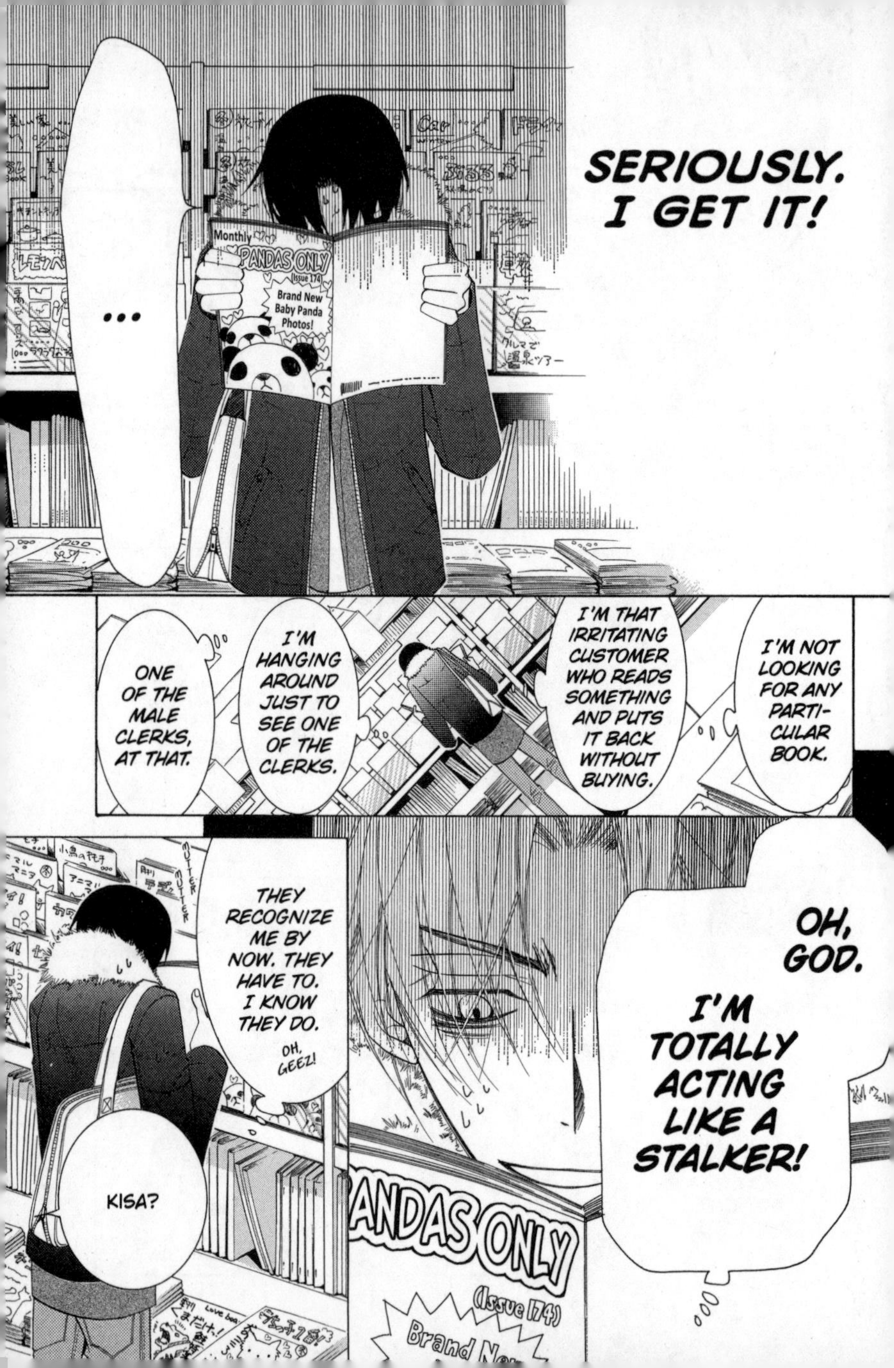
SERIOUSLY. I GET IT!
Monthly
PANDAS ONLY
(Issue 174)
Brand New Baby Panda Photos!
...
I'M NOT LOOKING FOR ANY PARTICULAR BOOK.
I'M THAT IRRITATING CUSTOMER WHO READS SOMETHING AND PUTS IT BACK WITHOUT BUYING.
I'M HANGING AROUND JUST TO SEE ONE OF THE CLERKS.
ONE OF THE MALE CLERKS, AT THAT.
OH, GOD.
I'M TOTALLY ACTING LIKE A STALKER!
MUTTER MUTTER
THEY RECOGNIZE ME BY NOW. THEY HAVE TO. I KNOW THEY DO.
OH, GEEZ!
KISA?

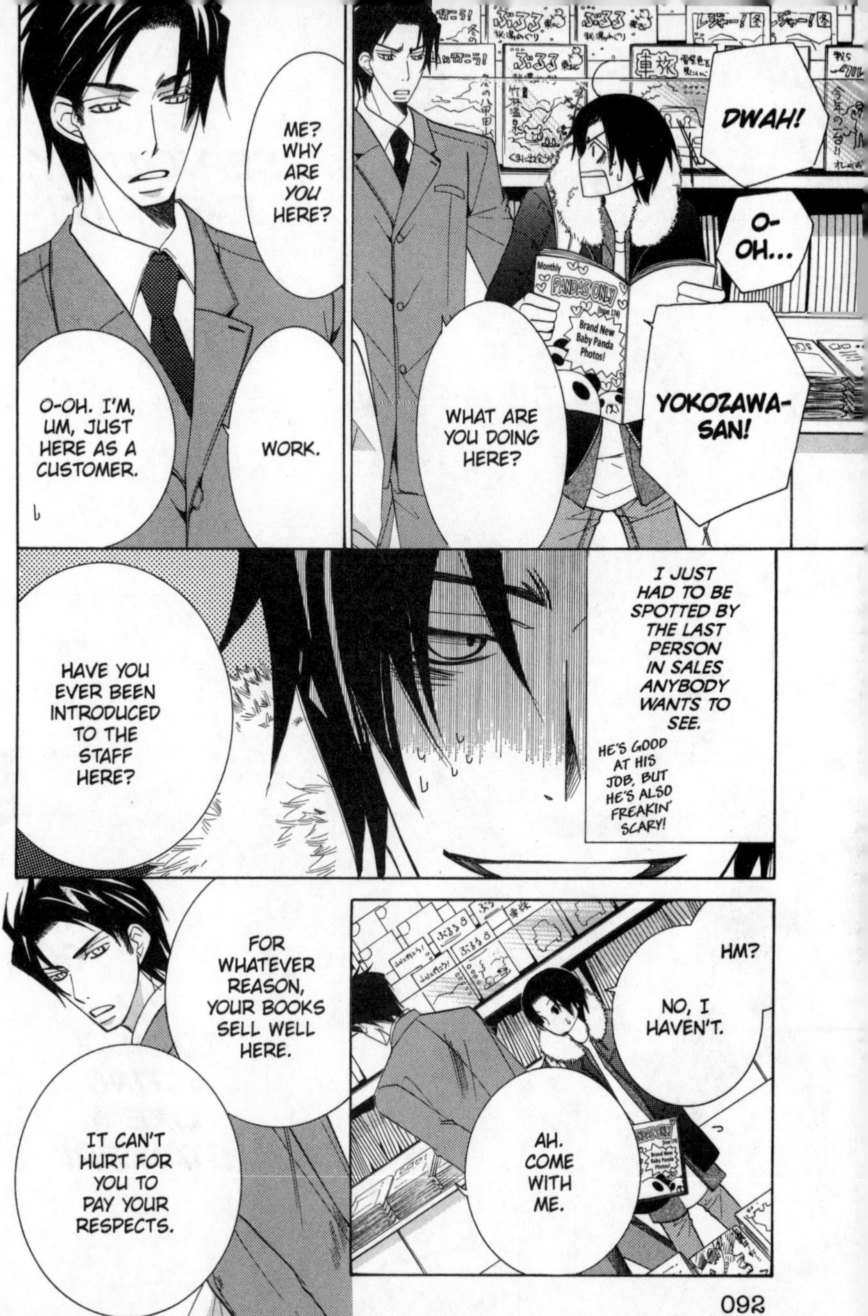
DWAH!
O-OH...
YOKOZAWA-SAN!
Monthly PANDAS ONLY Issue 174 Brand New Baby Panda Photos!
WHAT ARE YOU DOING HERE?
ME? WHY ARE YOU HERE?
WORK.
O-OH. I'M, UM, JUST HERE AS A CUSTOMER.
I JUST HAD TO BE SPOTTED BY THE LAST PERSON IN SALES ANYBODY WANTS TO SEE.
HE'S GOOD AT HIS JOB, BUT HE'S ALSO FREAKIN' SCARY!
HAVE YOU EVER BEEN INTRODUCED TO THE STAFF HERE?
HM?
NO, I HAVEN'T.
AH. COME WITH ME.
FOR WHATEVER REASON, YOUR BOOKS SELL WELL HERE.
IT CAN'T HURT FOR YOU TO PAY YOUR RESPECTS.

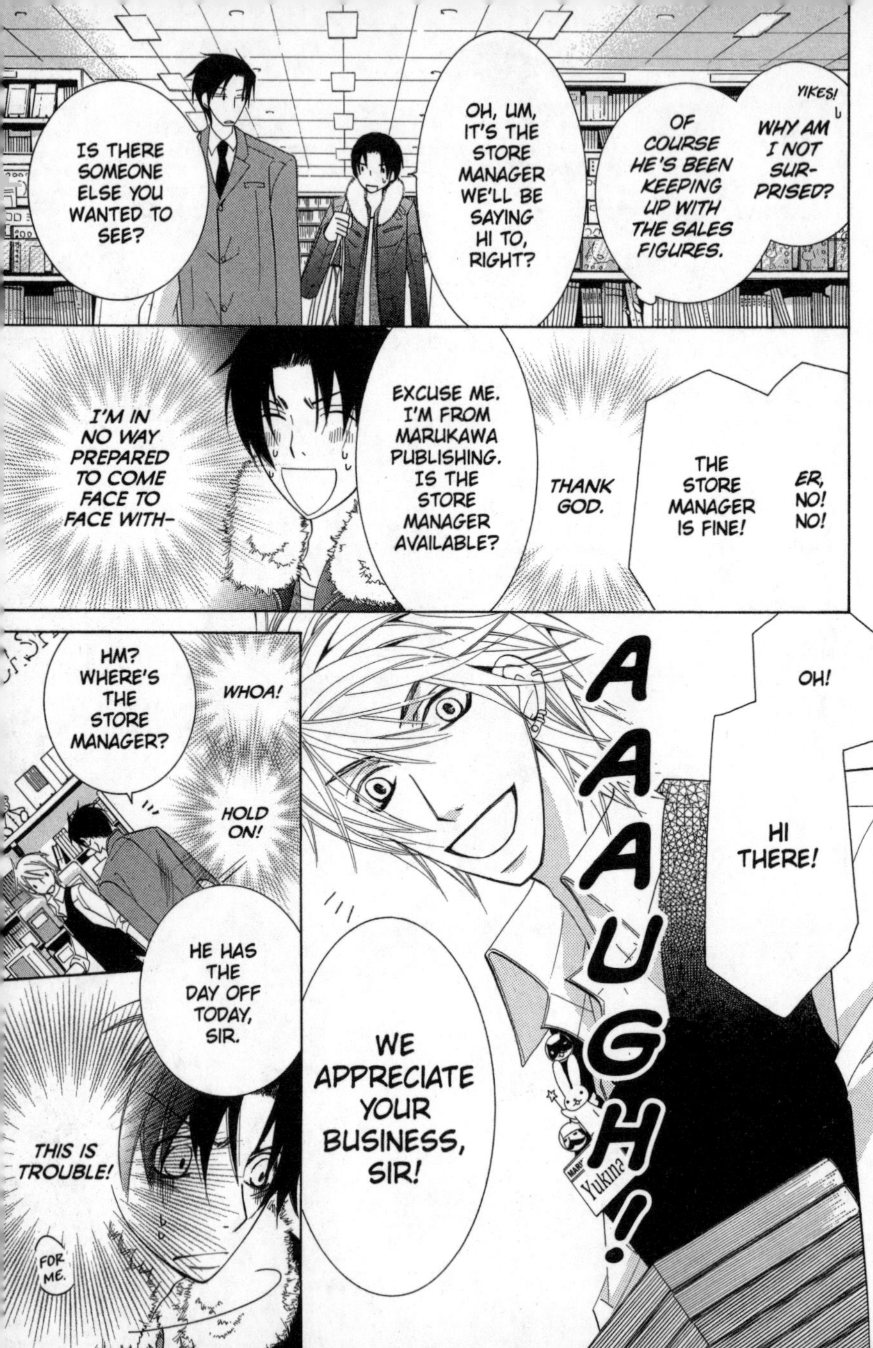
YIKES!
WHY AM I NOT SURPRISED?
OF COURSE HE'S BEEN KEEPING UP WITH THE SALES FIGURES.
OH, UM, IT'S THE STORE MANAGER WE'LL BE SAYING HI TO, RIGHT?
IS THERE SOMEONE ELSE YOU WANTED TO SEE?
ER, NO! NO!
THE STORE MANAGER IS FINE!
THANK GOD.
EXCUSE ME. I'M FROM MARUKAWA PUBLISHING. IS THE STORE MANAGER AVAILABLE?
I'M IN NO WAY PREPARED TO COME FACE TO FACE WITH-
OH!
HI THERE!
AAAAUGH!!
WE APPRECIATE YOUR BUSINESS, SIR!
Yukina
HM? WHERE'S THE STORE MANAGER?
WHOA!
HOLD ON!
HE HAS THE DAY OFF TODAY, SIR.
THIS IS TROUBLE!
FOR ME.

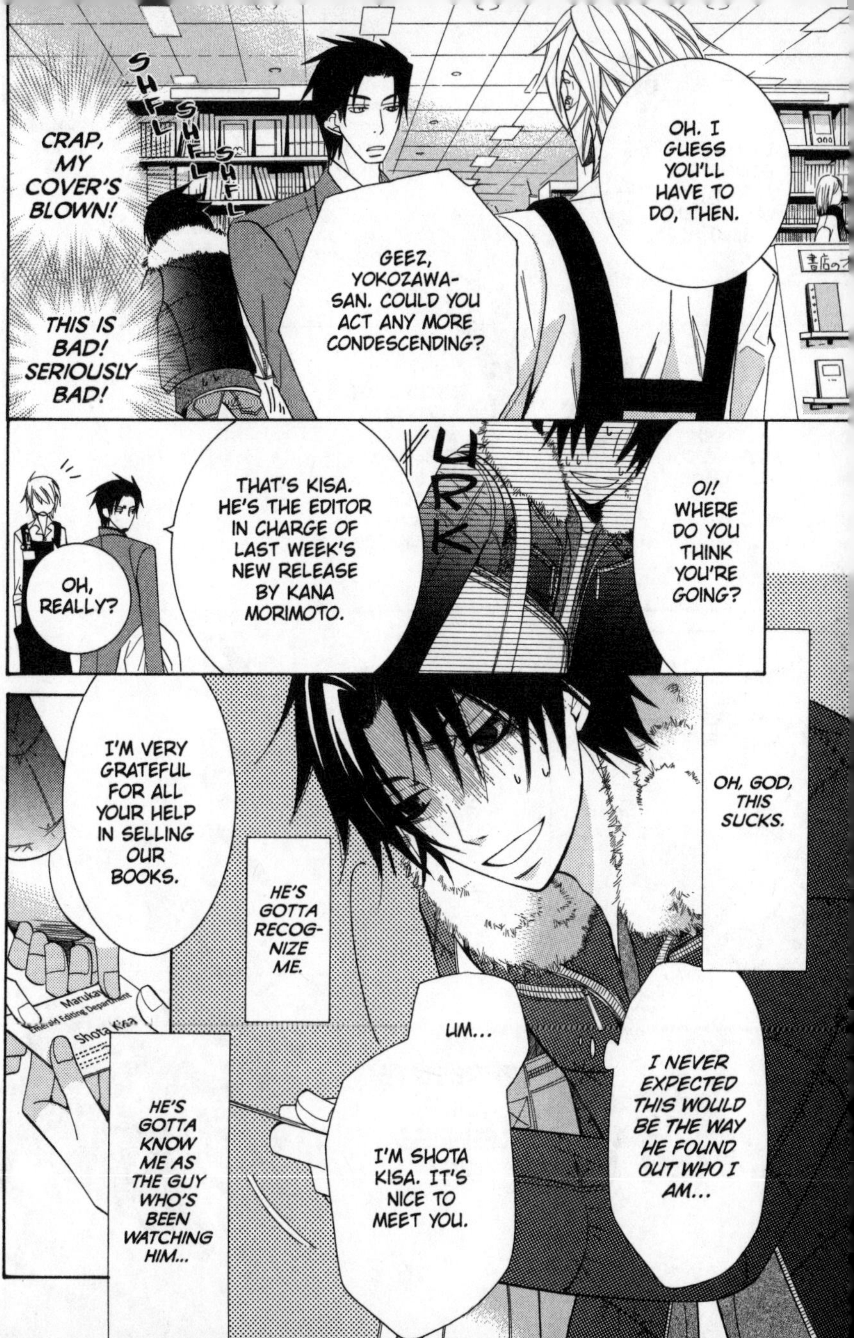
OH. I GUESS YOU'LL HAVE TO DO, THEN.
GEEZ, YOKOZAWA-SAN. COULD YOU ACT ANY MORE CONDESCENDING?
SHFL SHFL SHFL
CRAP, MY COVER'S BLOWN!
THIS IS BAD! SERIOUSLY BAD!
OI! WHERE DO YOU THINK YOU'RE GOING?
URK
THAT'S KISA. HE'S THE EDITOR IN CHARGE OF LAST WEEK'S NEW RELEASE BY KANA MORIMOTO.
OH, REALLY?
OH, GOD, THIS SUCKS.
I'M VERY GRATEFUL FOR ALL YOUR HELP IN SELLING OUR BOOKS.
HE'S GOTTA RECOGNIZE ME.
Emerald Editing Department
Shota Kisa
UM...
I NEVER EXPECTED THIS WOULD BE THE WAY HE FOUND OUT WHO I AM...
I'M SHOTA KISA. IT'S NICE TO MEET YOU.
HE'S GOTTA KNOW ME AS THE GUY WHO'S BEEN WATCHING HIM...

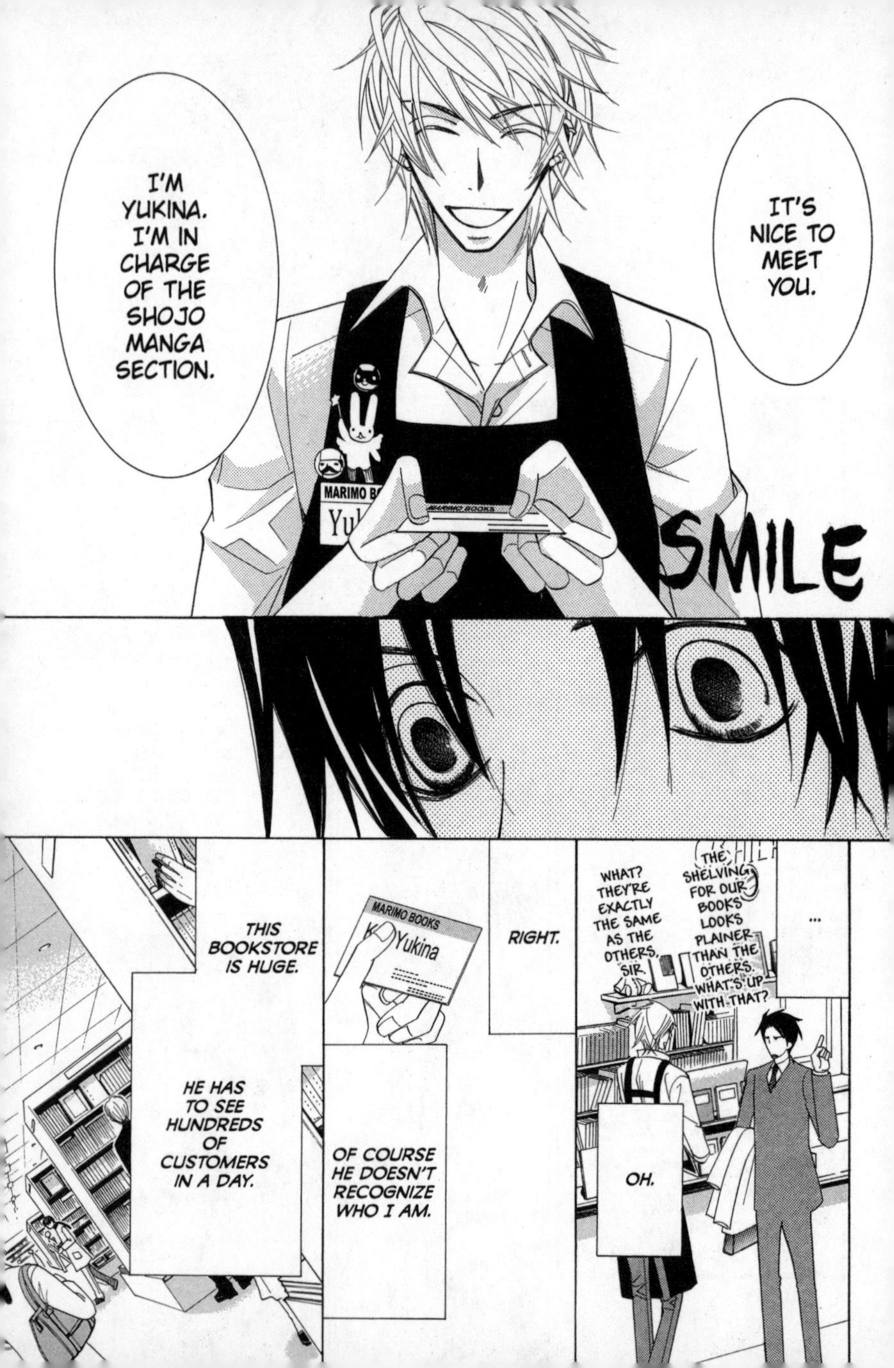
IT'S NICE TO MEET YOU.
I'M YUKINA. I'M IN CHARGE OF THE SHOJO MANGA SECTION.
SMILE
...
THE SHELVING FOR OUR BOOKS LOOKS PLAINER THAN THE OTHERS. WHAT'S UP WITH THAT?
WHAT? THEY'RE EXACTLY THE SAME AS THE OTHERS, SIR.
OH.
RIGHT.
MARIMO BOOKS
Yukina
OF COURSE HE DOESN'T RECOGNIZE WHO I AM.
THIS BOOKSTORE IS HUGE.
HE HAS TO SEE HUNDREDS OF CUSTOMERS IN A DAY.

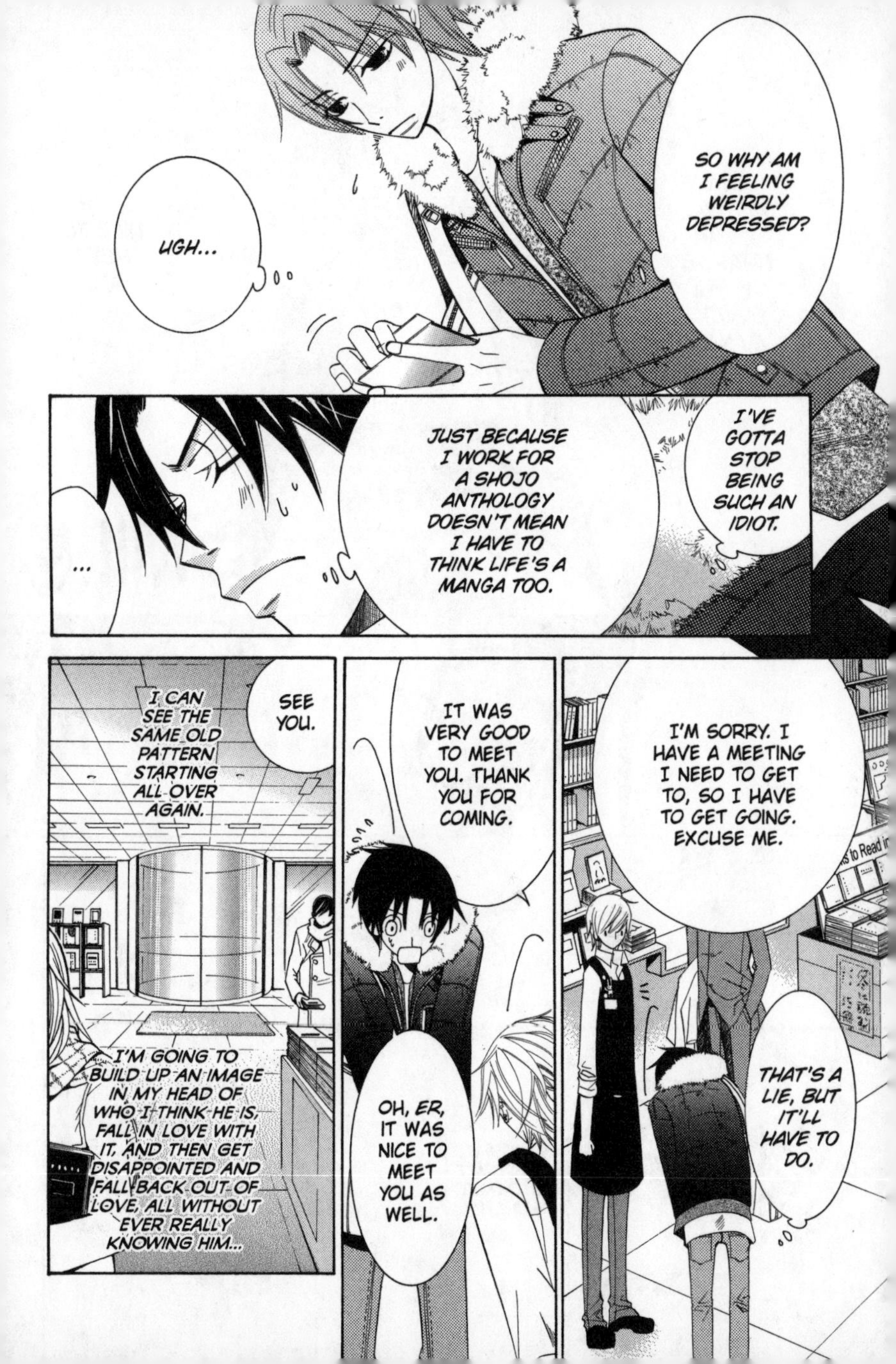
SO WHY AM I FEELING WEIRDLY DEPRESSED?
UGH...
I'VE GOTTA STOP BEING SUCH AN IDIOT.
JUST BECAUSE I WORK FOR A SHOJO ANTHOLOGY DOESN'T MEAN I HAVE TO THINK LIFE'S A MANGA TOO.
...
I'M SORRY. I HAVE A MEETING I NEED TO GET TO, SO I HAVE TO GET GOING. EXCUSE ME.
THAT'S A LIE, BUT IT'LL HAVE TO DO.
IT WAS VERY GOOD TO MEET YOU. THANK YOU FOR COMING.
OH, ER, IT WAS NICE TO MEET YOU AS WELL.
SEE YOU.
I CAN SEE THE SAME OLD PATTERN STARTING ALL OVER AGAIN.
I'M GOING TO BUILD UP AN IMAGE IN MY HEAD OF WHO I THINK HE IS, FALL IN LOVE WITH IT, AND THEN GET DISAPPOINTED AND FALL BACK OUT OF LOVE, ALL WITHOUT EVER REALLY KNOWING HIM...

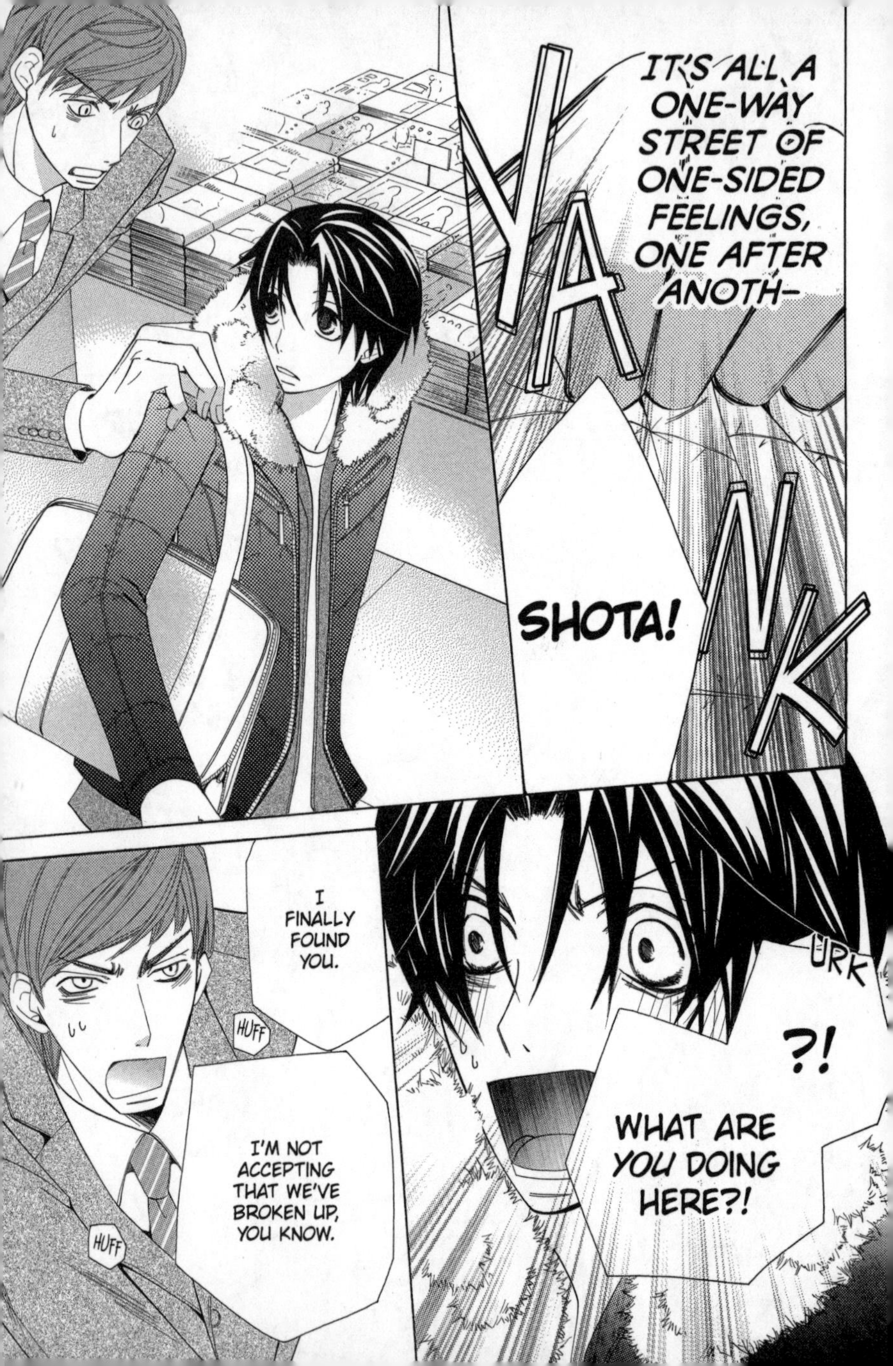
IT'S ALL A ONE-WAY STREET OF ONE-SIDED FEELINGS, ONE AFTER ANOTH-
YANK
SHOTA!
URK
?!
WHAT ARE YOU DOING HERE?!
I FINALLY FOUND YOU.
HUFF
HUFF
I'M NOT ACCEPTING THAT WE'VE BROKEN UP, YOU KNOW.

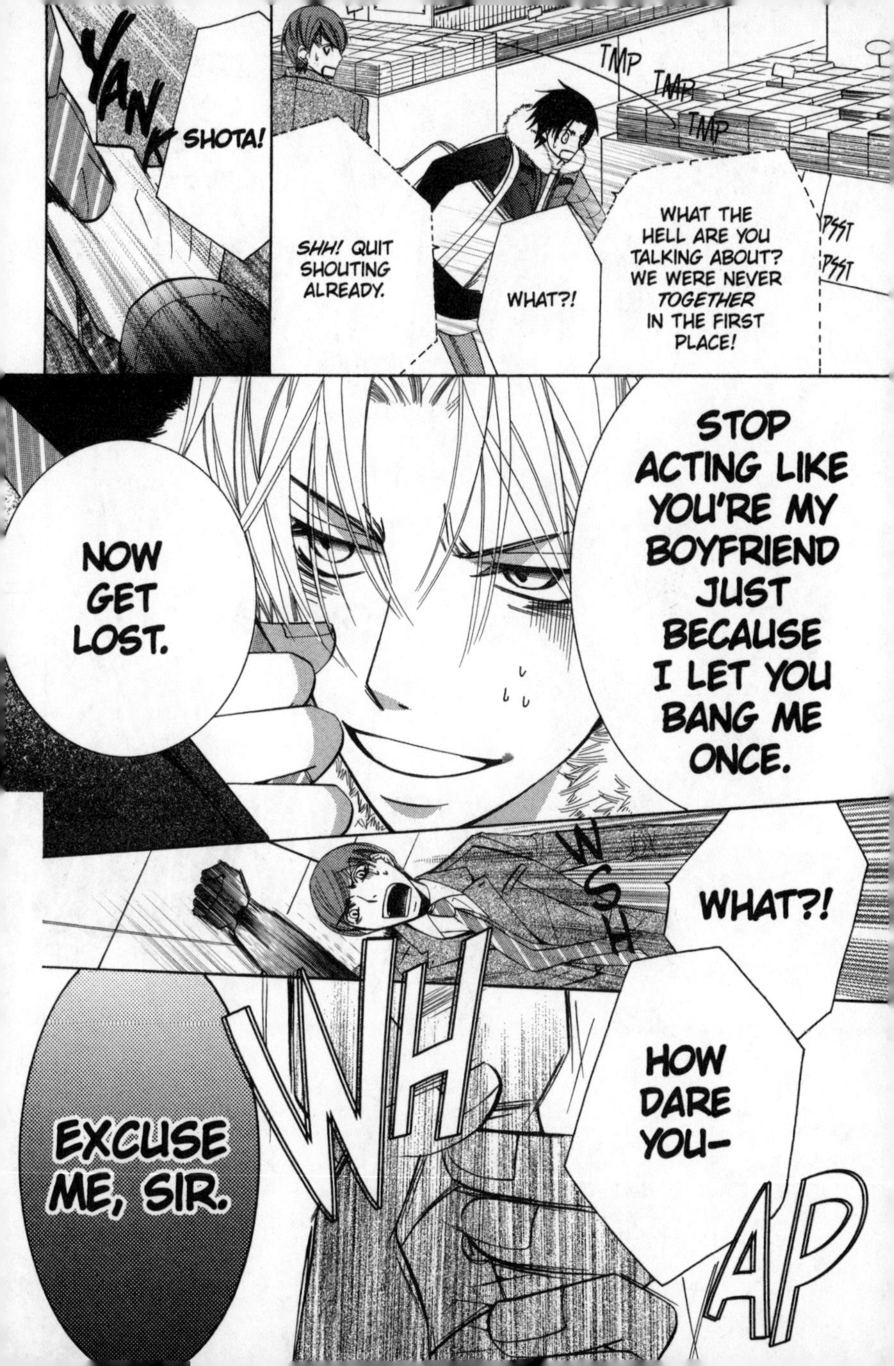
TMP
TMP
TMP
PSST
PSST
WHAT THE HELL ARE YOU TALKING ABOUT? WE WERE NEVER *TOGETHER* IN THE FIRST PLACE!
WHAT?!
SHH! QUIT SHOUTING ALREADY.
YANK
SHOTA!
STOP ACTING LIKE YOU'RE MY BOYFRIEND JUST BECAUSE I LET YOU BANG ME ONCE.
NOW GET LOST.
WSH
WHAT?!
HOW DARE YOU-
WHAP
EXCUSE ME, SIR.

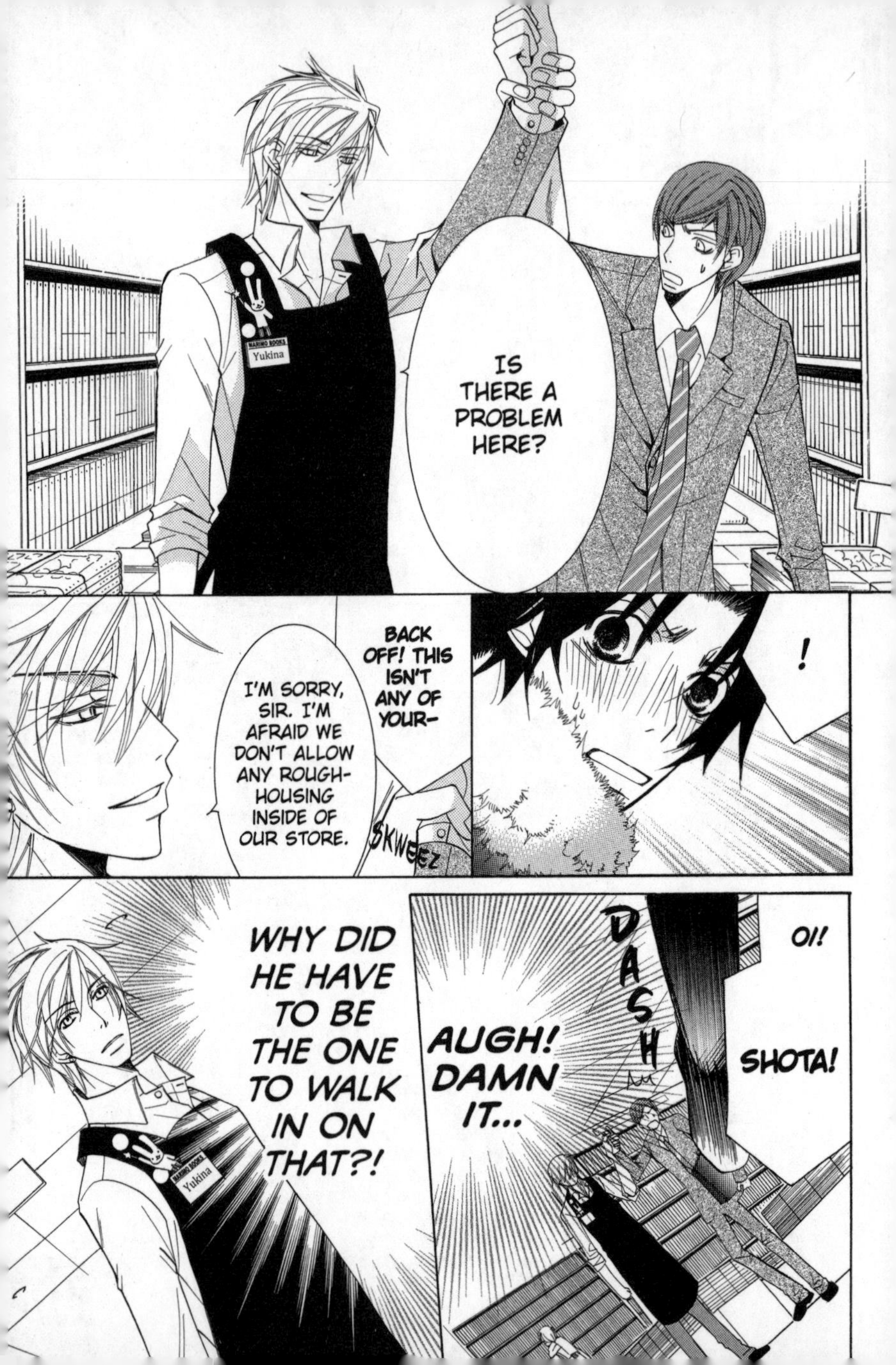
IS THERE A PROBLEM HERE?
MARIMO BOOKS
Yukina
!
BACK OFF! THIS ISN'T ANY OF YOUR-
I'M SORRY, SIR. I'M AFRAID WE DON'T ALLOW ANY ROUGH-HOUSING INSIDE OF OUR STORE.
SKWEEZ
OI!
SHOTA!
DASH
AUGH! DAMN IT...
WHY DID HE HAVE TO BE THE ONE TO WALK IN ON THAT?!
MARIMO BOOKS
Yukina

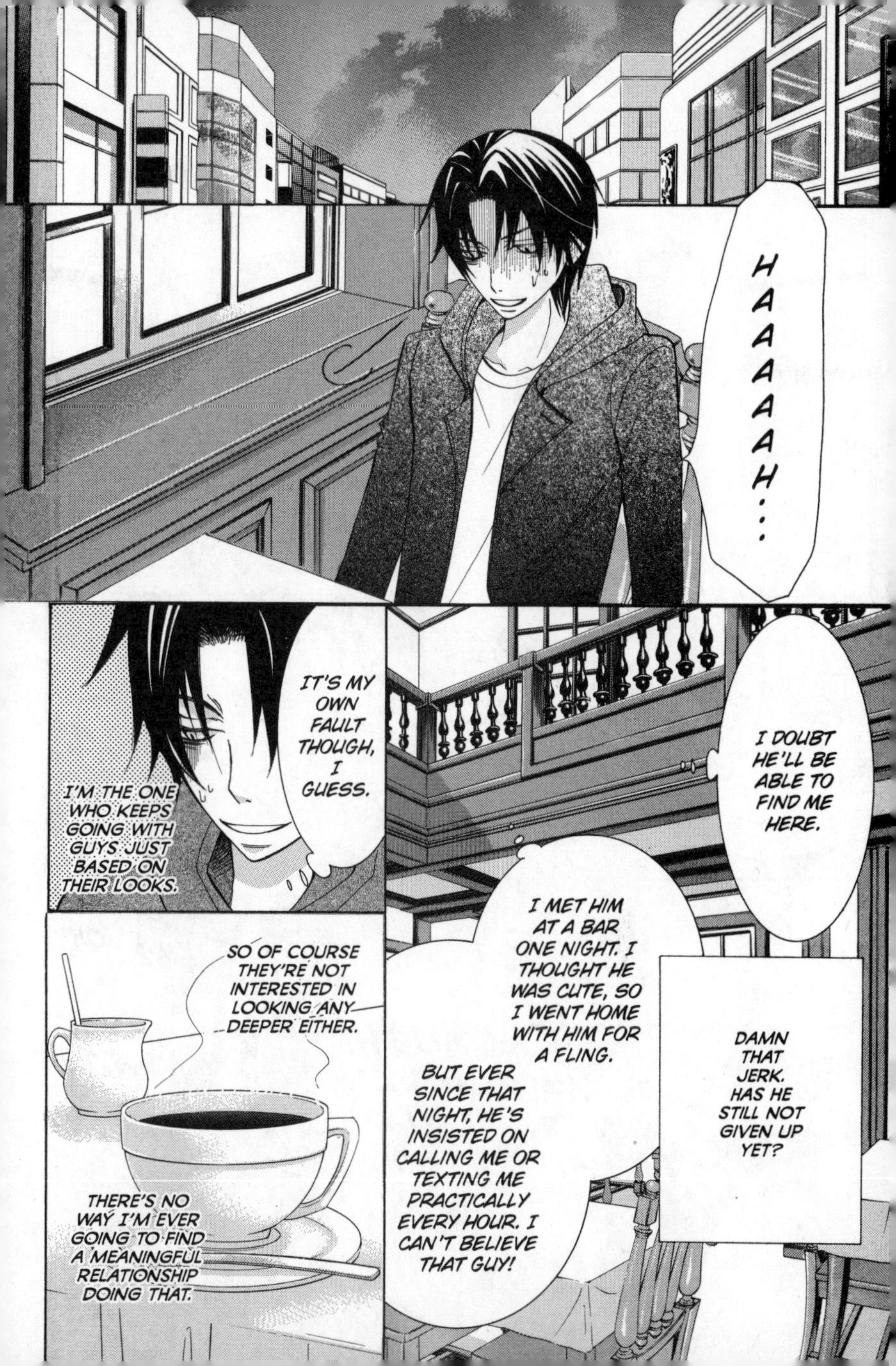
HAAAAAAH...
I DOUBT HE'LL BE ABLE TO FIND ME HERE.
DAMN THAT JERK. HAS HE STILL NOT GIVEN UP YET?
I MET HIM AT A BAR ONE NIGHT. I THOUGHT HE WAS CUTE, SO I WENT HOME WITH HIM FOR A FLING.
BUT EVER SINCE THAT NIGHT, HE'S INSISTED ON CALLING ME OR TEXTING ME PRACTICALLY EVERY HOUR. I CAN'T BELIEVE THAT GUY!
IT'S MY OWN FAULT THOUGH, I GUESS.
I'M THE ONE WHO KEEPS GOING WITH GUYS JUST BASED ON THEIR LOOKS.
SO OF COURSE THEY'RE NOT INTERESTED IN LOOKING ANY DEEPER EITHER.
THERE'S NO WAY I'M EVER GOING TO FIND A MEANINGFUL RELATIONSHIP DOING THAT.

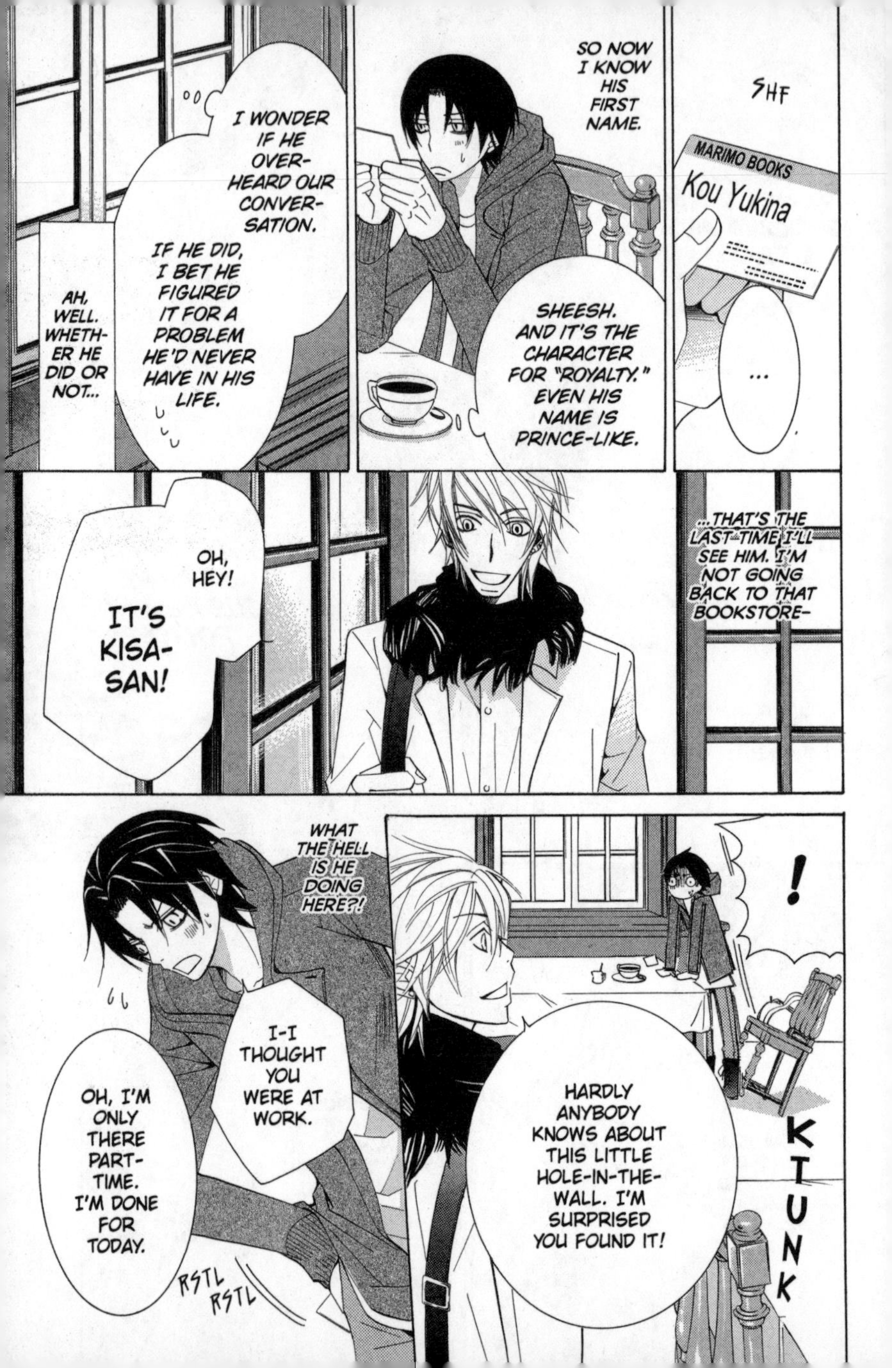
SHF
MARIMO BOOKS
Kou Yukina
...
SO NOW I KNOW HIS FIRST NAME.
SHEESH. AND IT'S THE CHARACTER FOR "ROYALTY." EVEN HIS NAME IS PRINCE-LIKE.
I WONDER IF HE OVER-HEARD OUR CONVER-SATION.
IF HE DID, I BET HE FIGURED IT FOR A PROBLEM HE'D NEVER HAVE IN HIS LIFE.
AH, WELL. WHETH-ER HE DID OR NOT...
...THAT'S THE LAST TIME I'LL SEE HIM. I'M NOT GOING BACK TO THAT BOOKSTORE–
OH, HEY!
IT'S KISA-SAN!
!
KTUNK
WHAT THE HELL IS HE DOING HERE?!
HARDLY ANYBODY KNOWS ABOUT THIS LITTLE HOLE-IN-THE-WALL. I'M SURPRISED YOU FOUND IT!
I-I THOUGHT YOU WERE AT WORK.
OH, I'M ONLY THERE PART-TIME. I'M DONE FOR TODAY.
RSTL RSTL

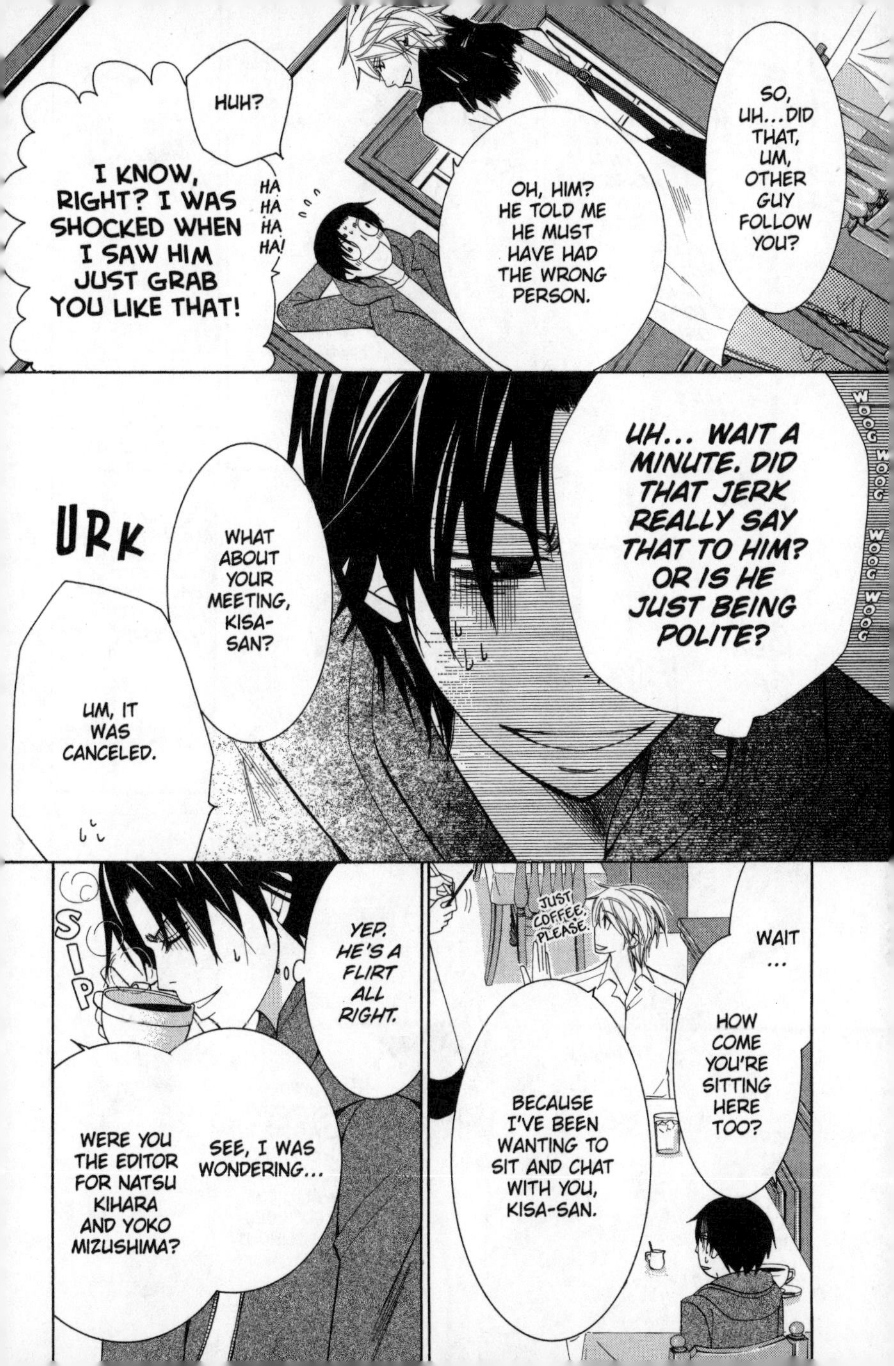

SO, UH...DID THAT, UM, OTHER GUY FOLLOW YOU?
OH, HIM? HE TOLD ME HE MUST HAVE HAD THE WRONG PERSON.
HUH?
HA HA HA HA!
I KNOW, RIGHT? I WAS SHOCKED WHEN I SAW HIM JUST GRAB YOU LIKE THAT!
WOOG WOOG WOOG WOOG
UH... WAIT A MINUTE. DID THAT JERK REALLY SAY THAT TO HIM? OR IS HE JUST BEING POLITE?
WHAT ABOUT YOUR MEETING, KISA-SAN?
URK
UM, IT WAS CANCELED.
WAIT ...
HOW COME YOU'RE SITTING HERE TOO?
JUST COFFEE, PLEASE.
BECAUSE I'VE BEEN WANTING TO SIT AND CHAT WITH YOU, KISA-SAN.
YEP. HE'S A FLIRT ALL RIGHT.
SIP
SEE, I WAS WONDERING...
WERE YOU THE EDITOR FOR NATSU KIHARA AND YOKO MIZUSHIMA?

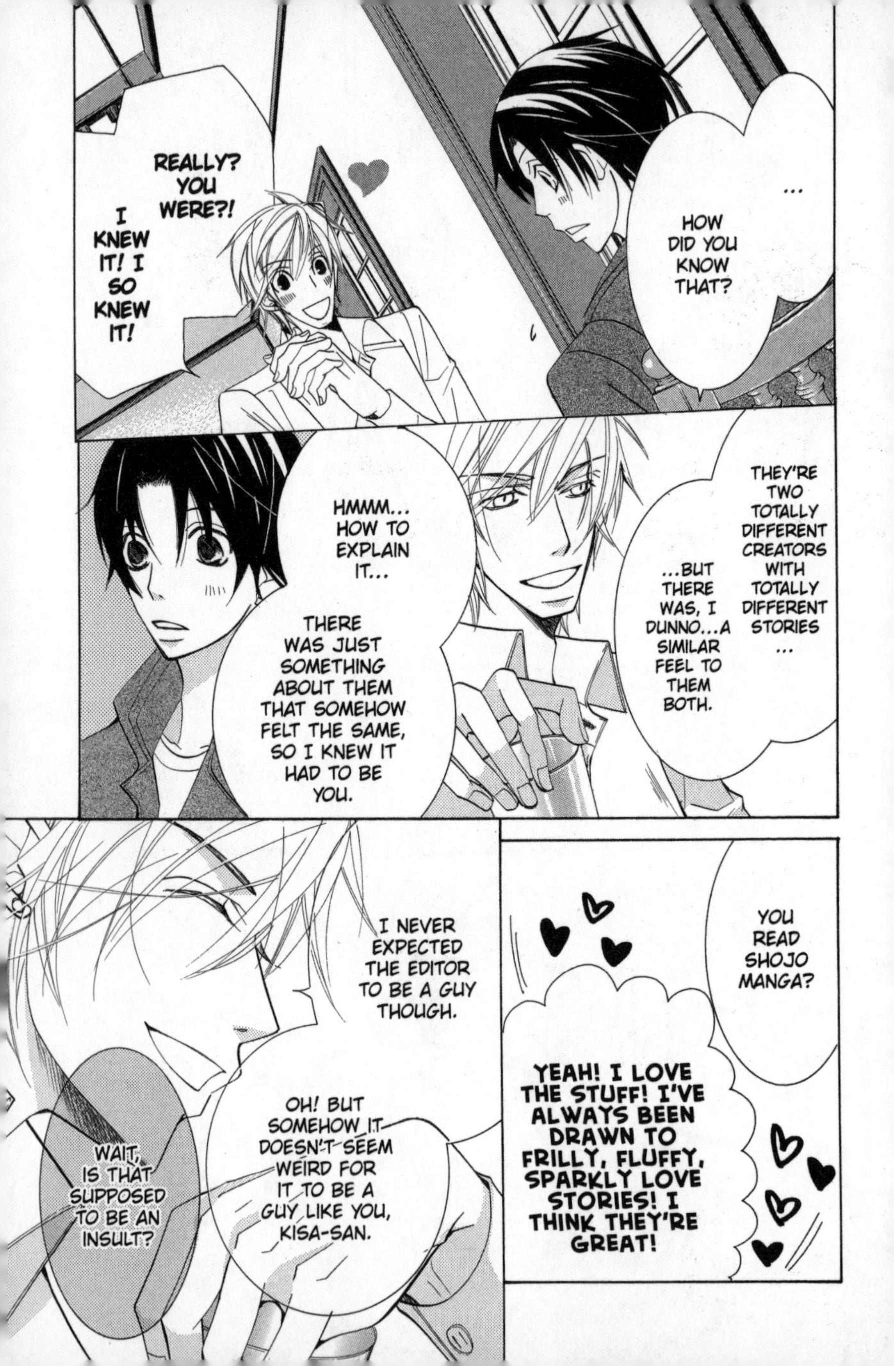
...
HOW DID YOU KNOW THAT?
REALLY? YOU WERE?!
I KNEW IT! I SO KNEW IT!
THEY'RE TWO TOTALLY DIFFERENT CREATORS WITH TOTALLY DIFFERENT STORIES...
...BUT THERE WAS, I DUNNO...A SIMILAR FEEL TO THEM BOTH.
HMMM... HOW TO EXPLAIN IT...
THERE WAS JUST SOMETHING ABOUT THEM THAT SOMEHOW FELT THE SAME, SO I KNEW IT HAD TO BE YOU.
YOU READ SHOJO MANGA?
YEAH! I LOVE THE STUFF! I'VE ALWAYS BEEN DRAWN TO FRILLY, FLUFFY, SPARKLY LOVE STORIES! I THINK THEY'RE GREAT!
I NEVER EXPECTED THE EDITOR TO BE A GUY THOUGH.
OH! BUT SOMEHOW IT DOESN'T SEEM WEIRD FOR IT TO BE A GUY LIKE YOU, KISA-SAN.
WAIT, IS THAT SUPPOSED TO BE AN INSULT?

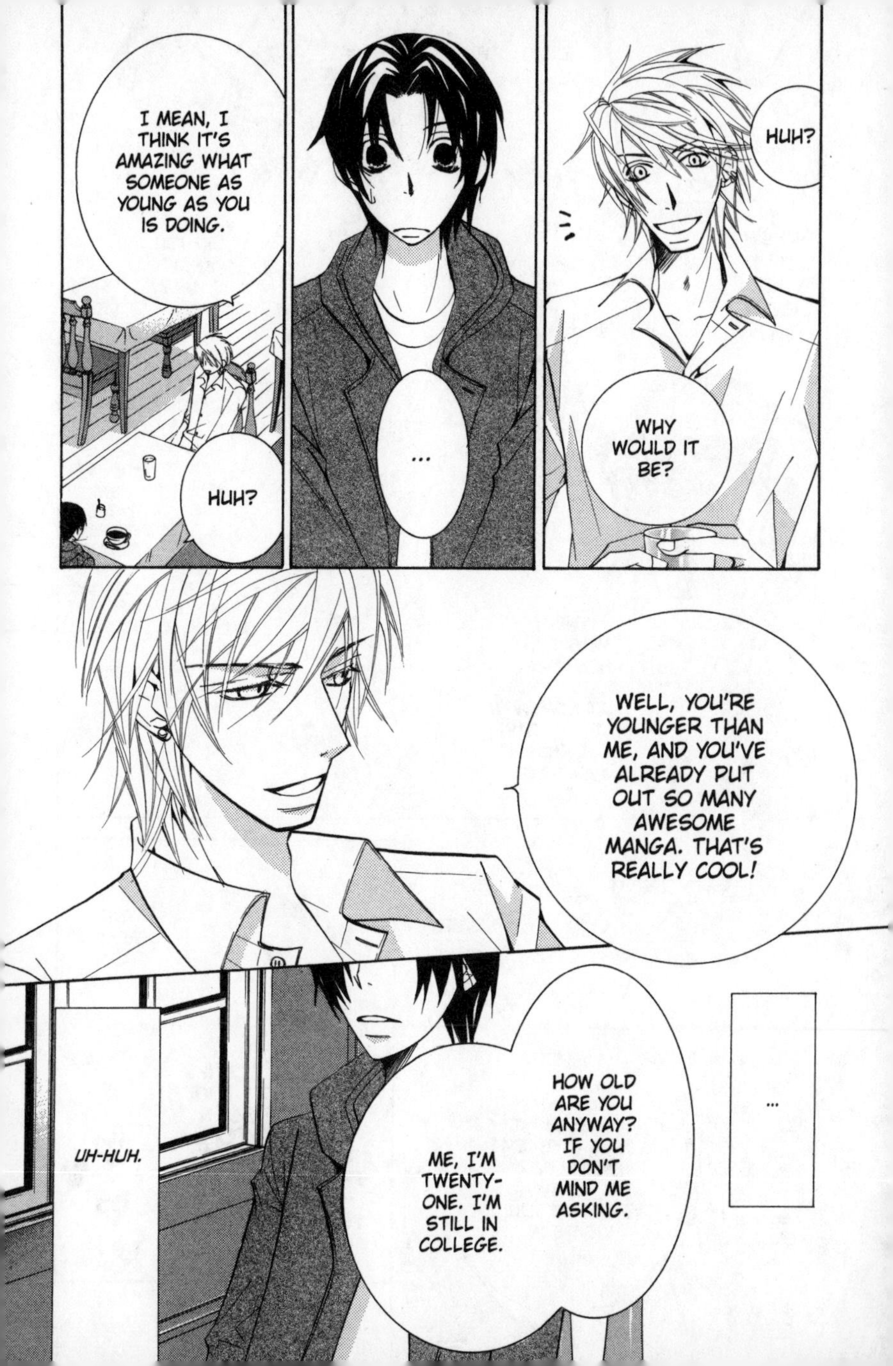
HUH?
WHY WOULD IT BE?
...
I MEAN, I THINK IT'S AMAZING WHAT SOMEONE AS YOUNG AS YOU IS DOING.
HUH?
WELL, YOU'RE YOUNGER THAN ME, AND YOU'VE ALREADY PUT OUT SO MANY AWESOME MANGA. THAT'S REALLY COOL!
...
HOW OLD ARE YOU ANYWAY? IF YOU DON'T MIND ME ASKING.
ME, I'M TWENTY-ONE. I'M STILL IN COLLEGE.
UH-HUH.

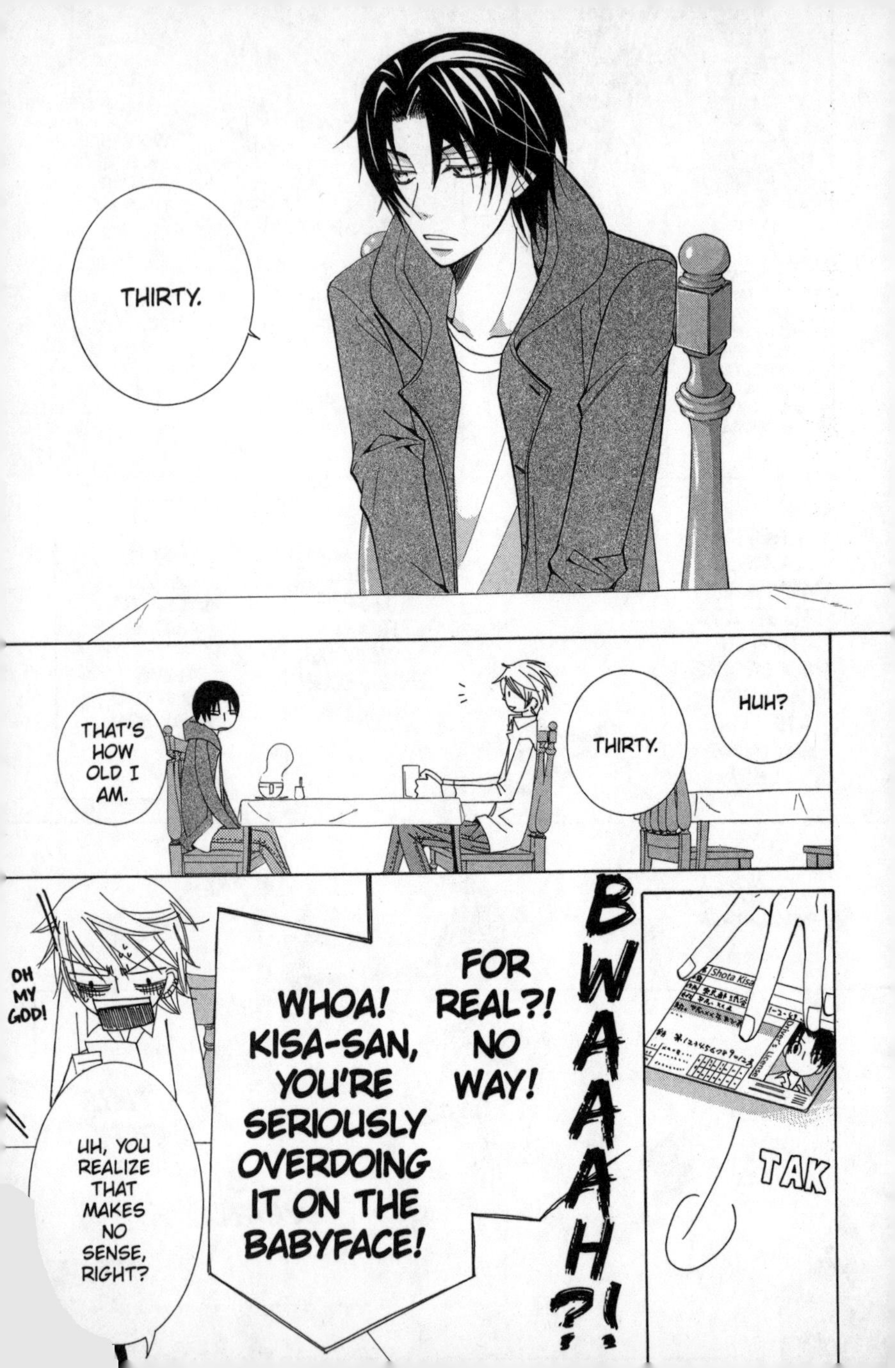
THIRTY.
HUH?
THIRTY.
THAT'S HOW OLD I AM.
Shota Kisa
Driver's License
TAK
BWAAAAAH?!
FOR REAL?! NO WAY!
WHOA! KISA-SAN, YOU'RE SERIOUSLY OVERDOING IT ON THE BABYFACE!
OH MY GOD!
UH, YOU REALIZE THAT MAKES NO SENSE, RIGHT?

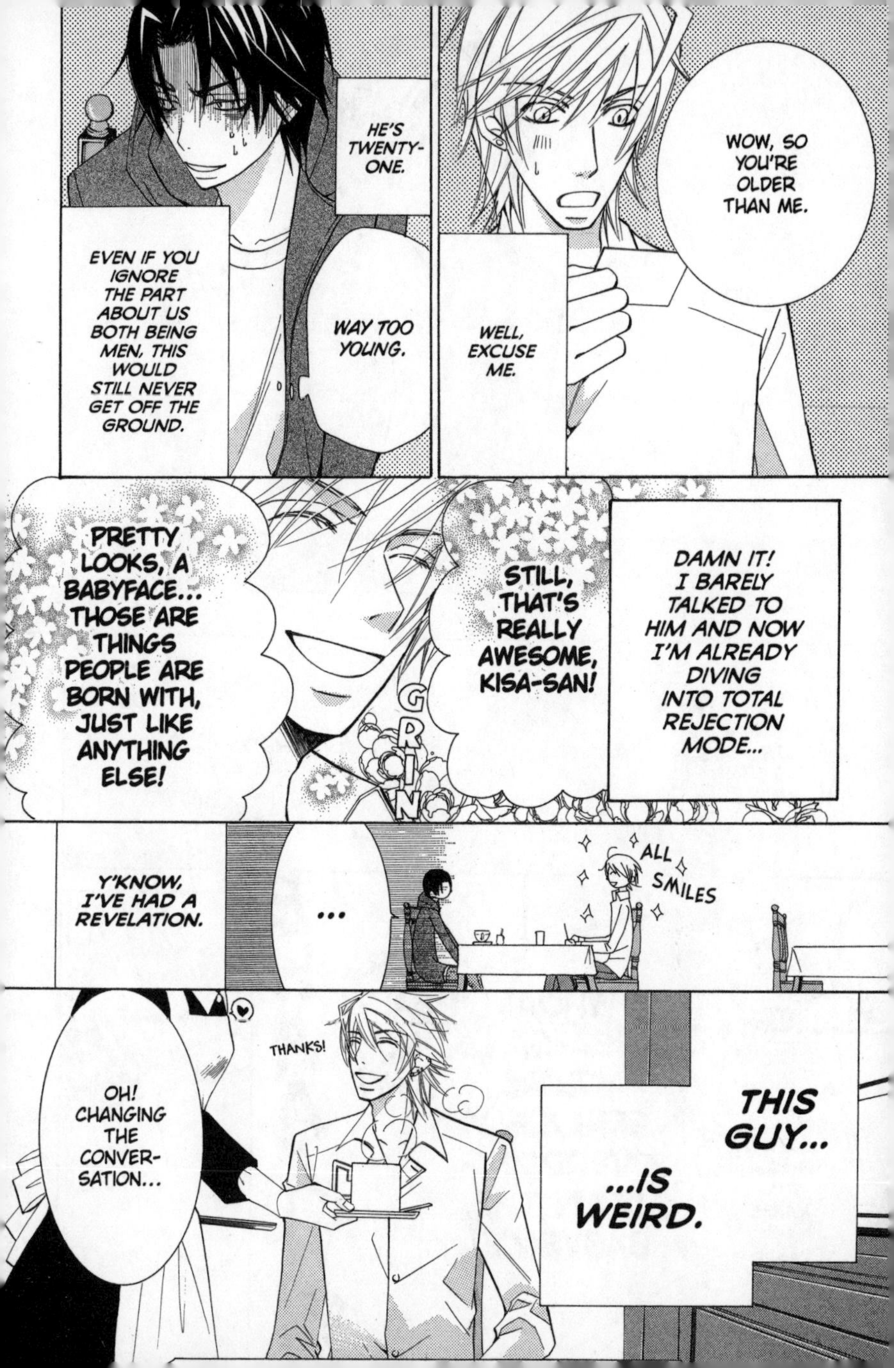
WOW, SO YOU'RE OLDER THAN ME.
WELL, EXCUSE ME.
HE'S TWENTY-ONE.
WAY TOO YOUNG.
EVEN IF YOU IGNORE THE PART ABOUT US BOTH BEING MEN, THIS WOULD STILL NEVER GET OFF THE GROUND.
DAMN IT! I BARELY TALKED TO HIM AND NOW I'M ALREADY DIVING INTO TOTAL REJECTION MODE...
STILL, THAT'S REALLY AWESOME, KISA-SAN!
GRIN
PRETTY LOOKS, A BABYFACE... THOSE ARE THINGS PEOPLE ARE BORN WITH, JUST LIKE ANYTHING ELSE!
ALL SMILES
...
Y'KNOW, I'VE HAD A REVELATION.
THIS GUY...
...IS WEIRD.
THANKS!
OH! CHANGING THE CONVER-SATION...

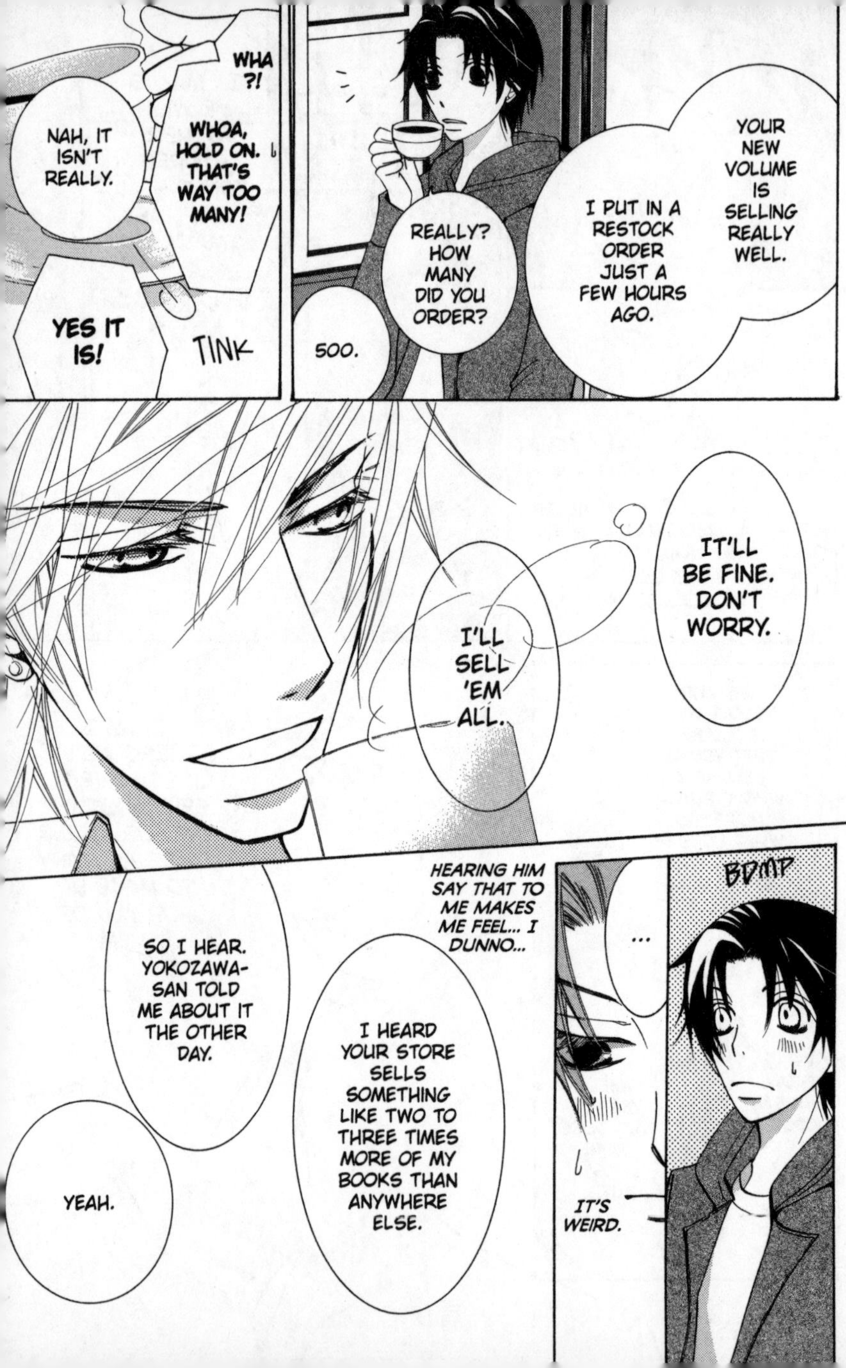

YOUR NEW VOLUME IS SELLING REALLY WELL.
I PUT IN A RESTOCK ORDER JUST A FEW HOURS AGO.
REALLY? HOW MANY DID YOU ORDER?
500.
WHA ?!
WHOA, HOLD ON. THAT'S WAY TOO MANY!
NAH, IT ISN'T REALLY.
TINK
YES IT IS!
IT'LL BE FINE. DON'T WORRY.
I'LL SELL 'EM ALL.
BDMP
HEARING HIM SAY THAT TO ME MAKES ME FEEL... I DUNNO...
...
IT'S WEIRD.
I HEARD YOUR STORE SELLS SOMETHING LIKE TWO TO THREE TIMES MORE OF MY BOOKS THAN ANYWHERE ELSE.
SO I HEAR. YOKOZAWA-SAN TOLD ME ABOUT IT THE OTHER DAY.
YEAH.

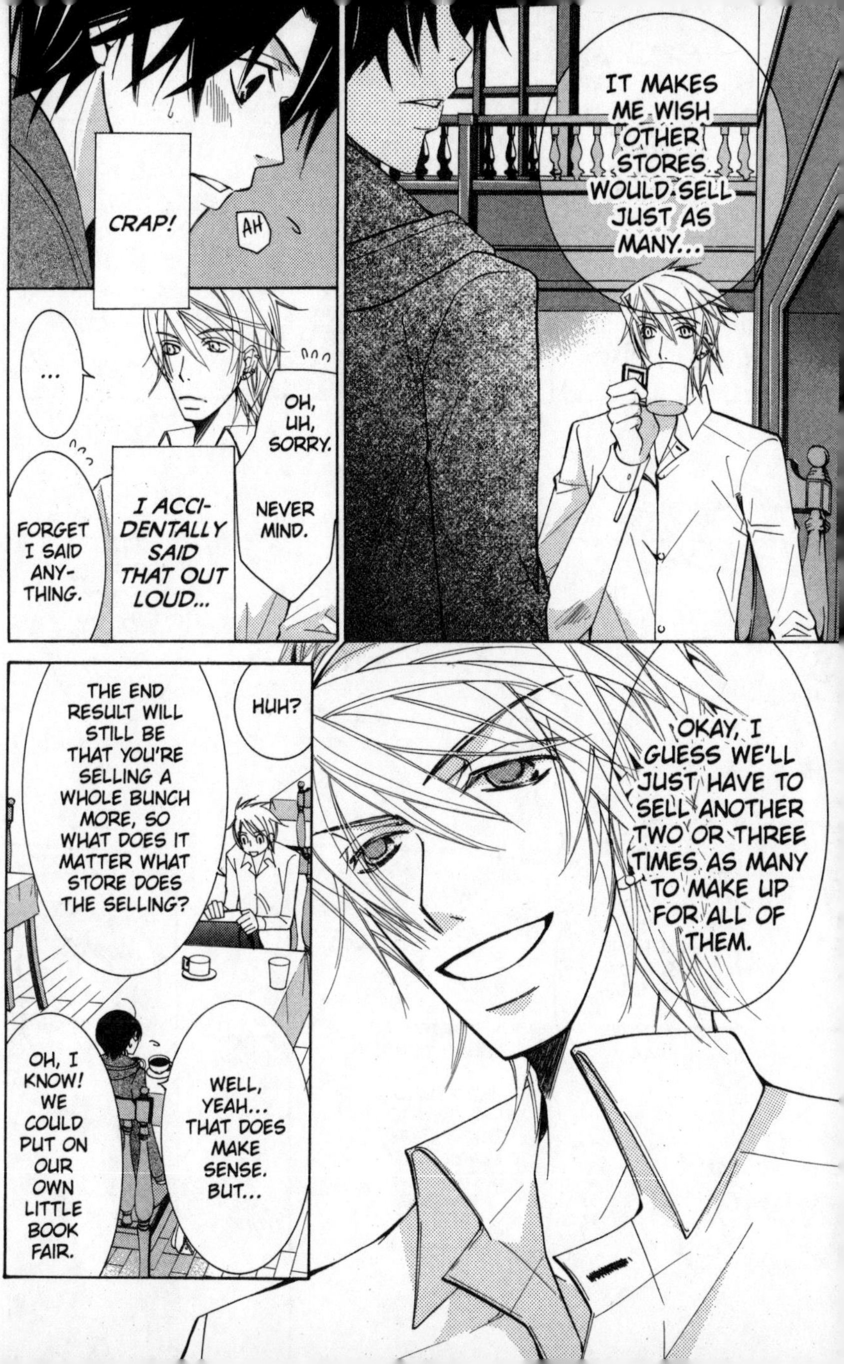
IT MAKES ME WISH OTHER STORES WOULD SELL JUST AS MANY...
AH
CRAP!
...
OH, UH, SORRY.
NEVER MIND.
I ACCIDENTALLY SAID THAT OUT LOUD...
FORGET I SAID ANYTHING.
OKAY, I GUESS WE'LL JUST HAVE TO SELL ANOTHER TWO OR THREE TIMES AS MANY TO MAKE UP FOR ALL OF THEM.
HUH?
THE END RESULT WILL STILL BE THAT YOU'RE SELLING A WHOLE BUNCH MORE, SO WHAT DOES IT MATTER WHAT STORE DOES THE SELLING?
WELL, YEAH... THAT DOES MAKE SENSE. BUT...
OH, I KNOW! WE COULD PUT ON OUR OWN LITTLE BOOK FAIR.

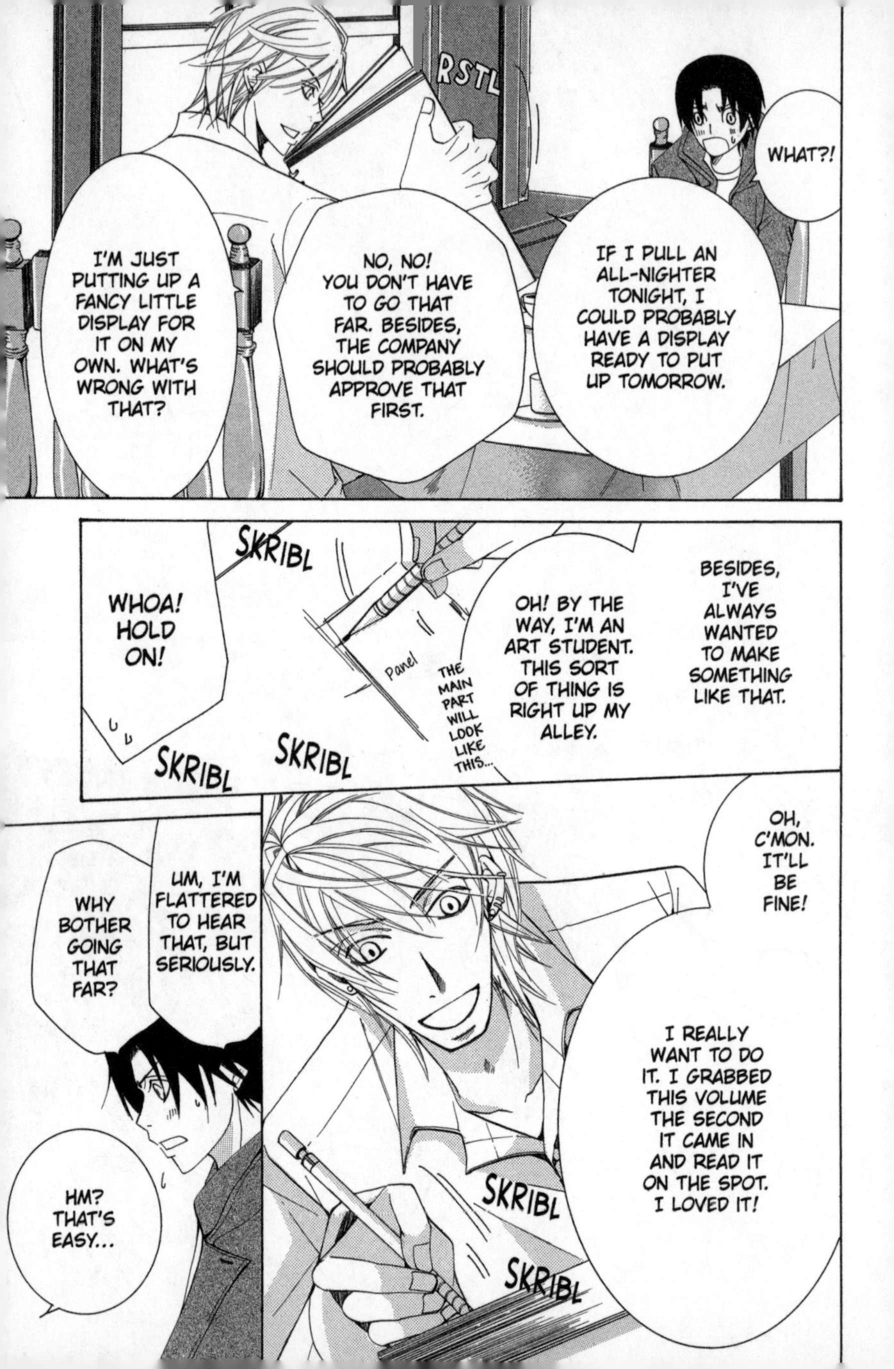

WHAT?!
RSTL
IF I PULL AN ALL-NIGHTER TONIGHT, I COULD PROBABLY HAVE A DISPLAY READY TO PUT UP TOMORROW.
NO, NO! YOU DON'T HAVE TO GO THAT FAR. BESIDES, THE COMPANY SHOULD PROBABLY APPROVE THAT FIRST.
I'M JUST PUTTING UP A FANCY LITTLE DISPLAY FOR IT ON MY OWN. WHAT'S WRONG WITH THAT?
BESIDES, I'VE ALWAYS WANTED TO MAKE SOMETHING LIKE THAT.
OH! BY THE WAY, I'M AN ART STUDENT. THIS SORT OF THING IS RIGHT UP MY ALLEY.
THE MAIN PART WILL LOOK LIKE THIS...
Panel
SKRIBL
WHOA! HOLD ON!
SKRIBL
SKRIBL
OH, C'MON. IT'LL BE FINE!
I REALLY WANT TO DO IT. I GRABBED THIS VOLUME THE SECOND IT CAME IN AND READ IT ON THE SPOT. I LOVED IT!
SKRIBL
SKRIBL
UM, I'M FLATTERED TO HEAR THAT, BUT SERIOUSLY.
WHY BOTHER GOING THAT FAR?
HM? THAT'S EASY...

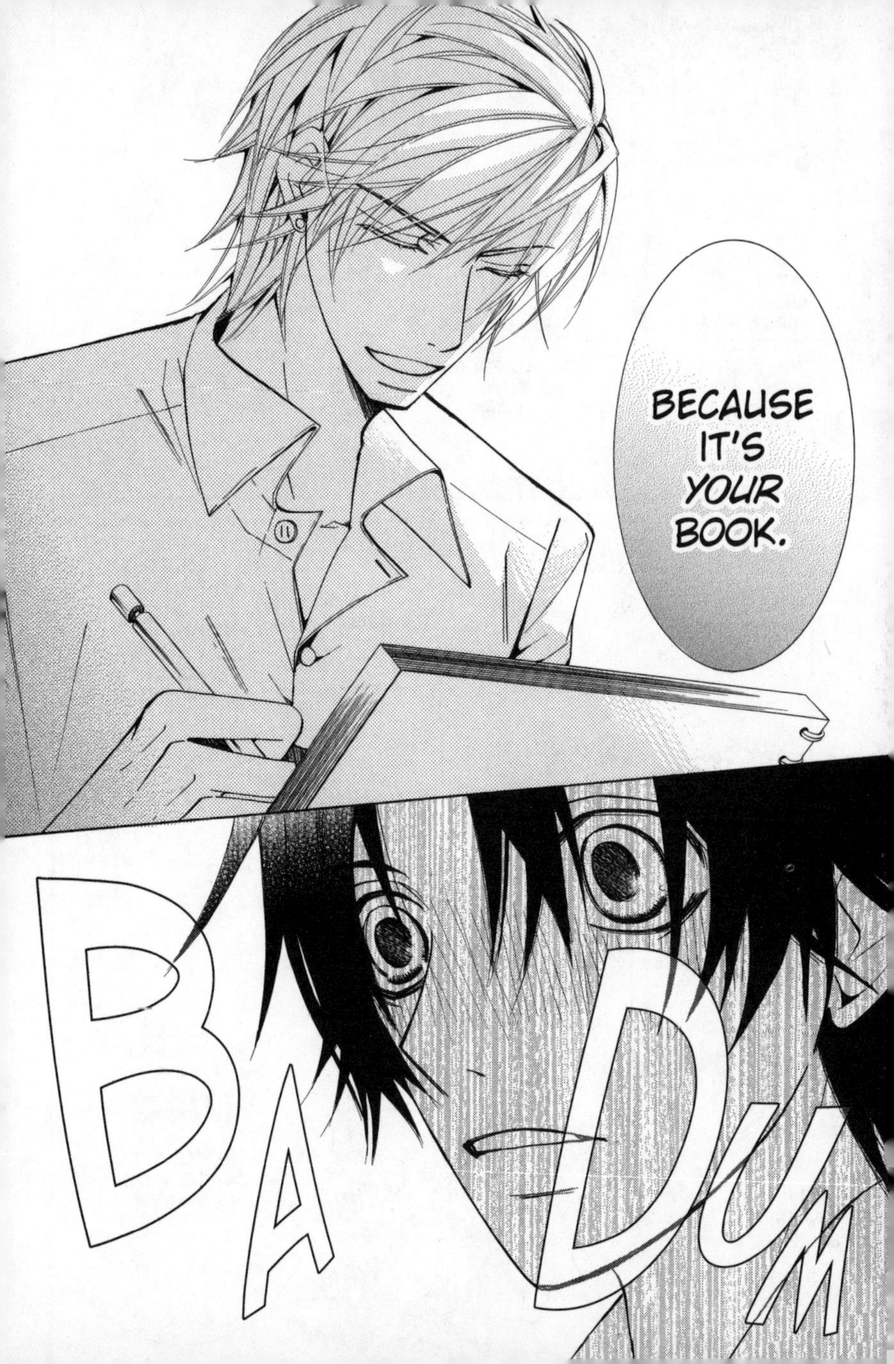
BECAUSE IT'S *YOUR* BOOK.
BA-DUM

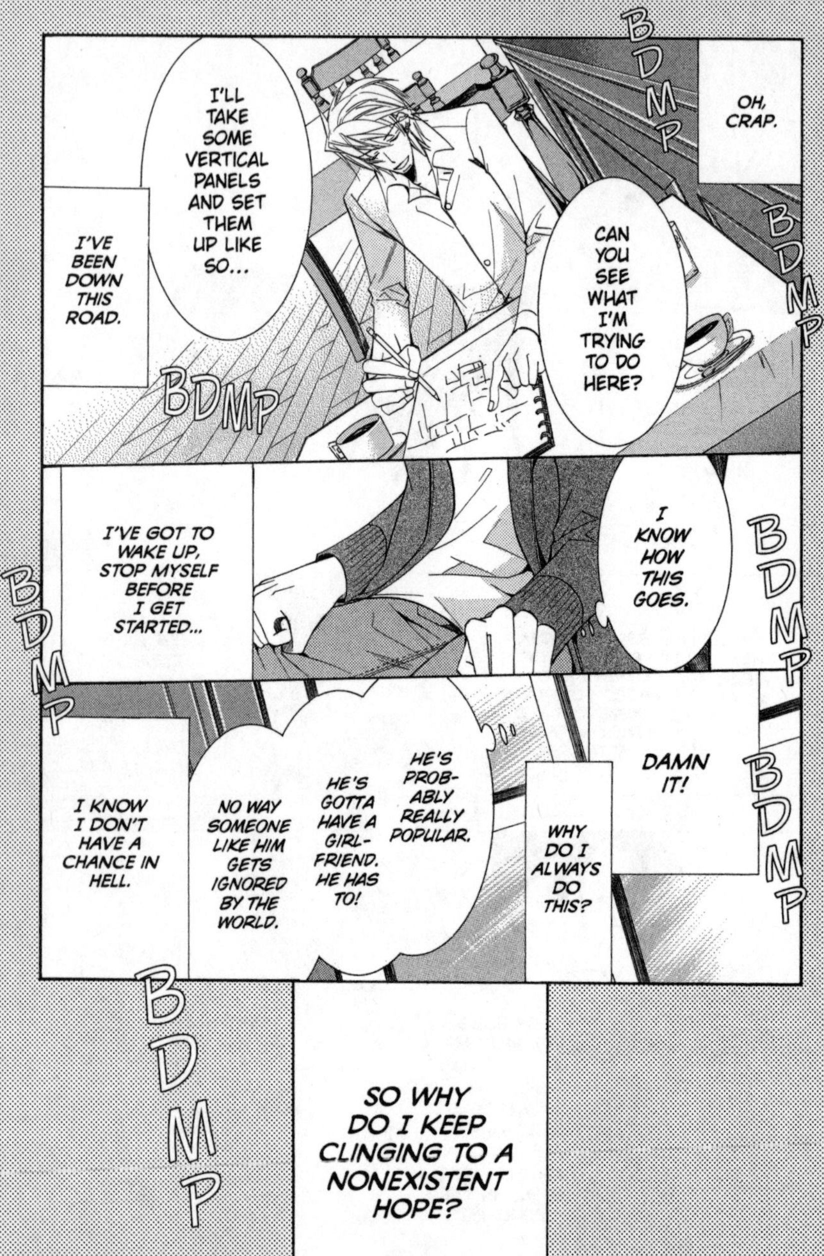
BDMP
OH, CRAP.
CAN YOU SEE WHAT I'M TRYING TO DO HERE?
I'LL TAKE SOME VERTICAL PANELS AND SET THEM UP LIKE SO...
BDMP
I'VE BEEN DOWN THIS ROAD.
BDMP
BDMP
I KNOW HOW THIS GOES.
I'VE GOT TO WAKE UP, STOP MYSELF BEFORE I GET STARTED...
BDMP
BDMP
DAMN IT!
WHY DO I ALWAYS DO THIS?
HE'S PROB-ABLY REALLY POPULAR.
HE'S GOTTA HAVE A GIRL-FRIEND. HE HAS TO!
NO WAY SOMEONE LIKE HIM GETS IGNORED BY THE WORLD.
I KNOW I DON'T HAVE A CHANCE IN HELL.
SO WHY DO I KEEP CLINGING TO A NONEXISTENT HOPE?
BDMP

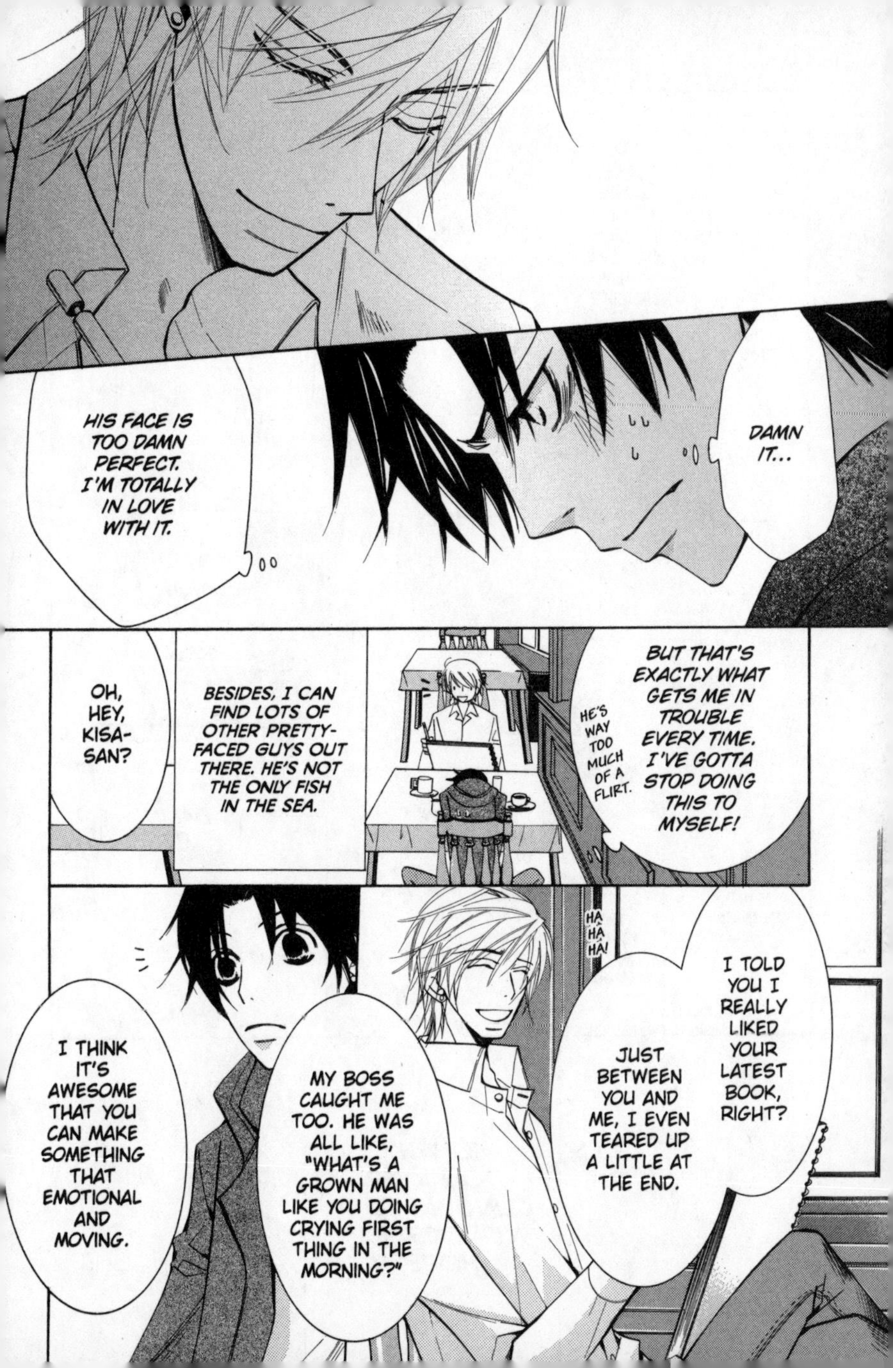
DAMN IT...
HIS FACE IS TOO DAMN PERFECT. I'M TOTALLY IN LOVE WITH IT.
BUT THAT'S EXACTLY WHAT GETS ME IN TROUBLE EVERY TIME. I'VE GOTTA STOP DOING THIS TO MYSELF!
HE'S WAY TOO MUCH OF A FLIRT.
BESIDES, I CAN FIND LOTS OF OTHER PRETTY-FACED GUYS OUT THERE. HE'S NOT THE ONLY FISH IN THE SEA.
OH, HEY, KISA-SAN?
HA HA HA!
I TOLD YOU I REALLY LIKED YOUR LATEST BOOK, RIGHT?
JUST BETWEEN YOU AND ME, I EVEN TEARED UP A LITTLE AT THE END.
MY BOSS CAUGHT ME TOO. HE WAS ALL LIKE, "WHAT'S A GROWN MAN LIKE YOU DOING CRYING FIRST THING IN THE MORNING?"
I THINK IT'S AWESOME THAT YOU CAN MAKE SOMETHING THAT EMOTIONAL AND MOVING.

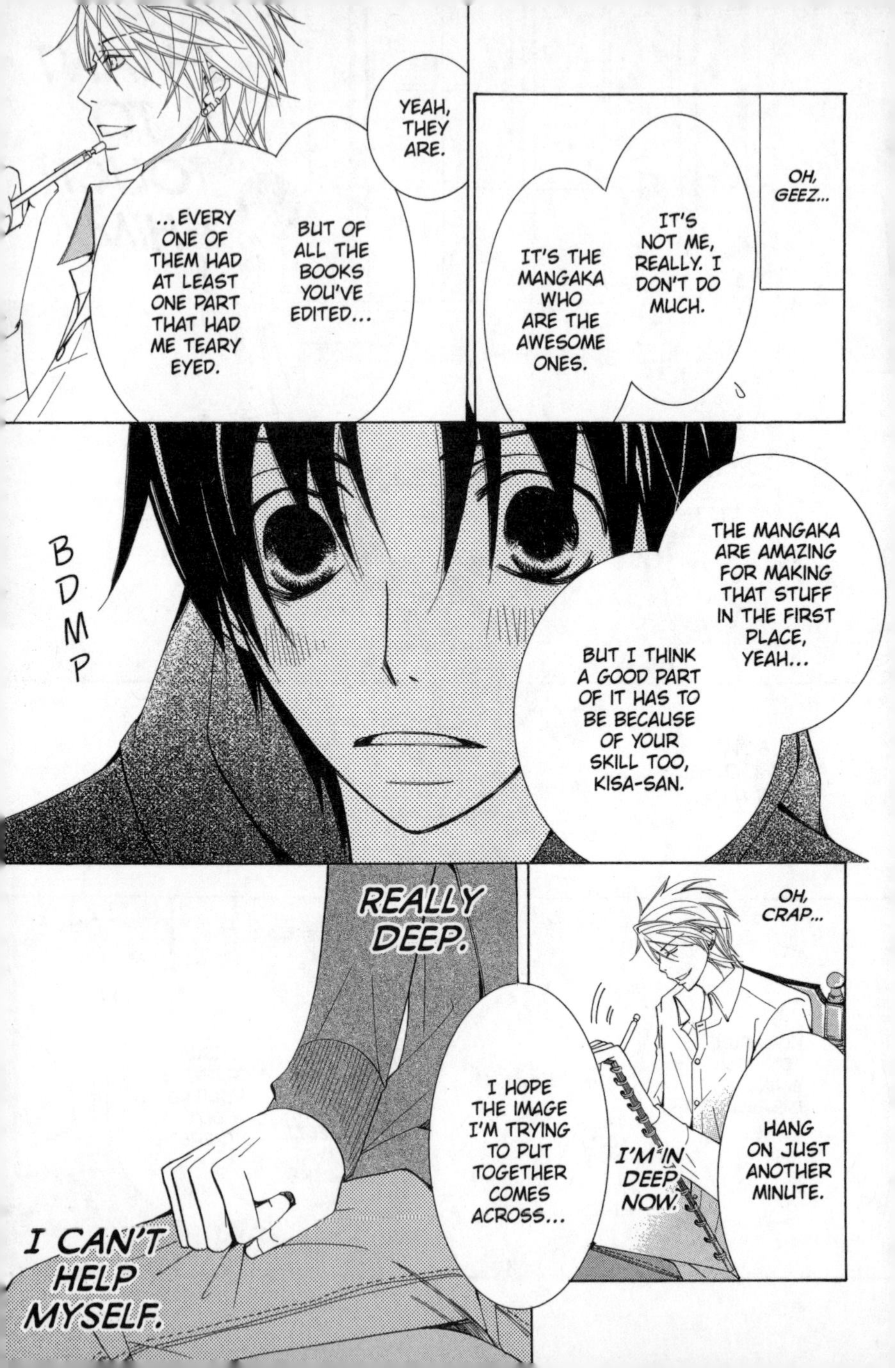
OH, GEEZ...
IT'S NOT ME, REALLY. I DON'T DO MUCH.
IT'S THE MANGAKA WHO ARE THE AWESOME ONES.
YEAH, THEY ARE.
BUT OF ALL THE BOOKS YOU'VE EDITED...
...EVERY ONE OF THEM HAD AT LEAST ONE PART THAT HAD ME TEARY EYED.
THE MANGAKA ARE AMAZING FOR MAKING THAT STUFF IN THE FIRST PLACE, YEAH...
BUT I THINK A GOOD PART OF IT HAS TO BE BECAUSE OF YOUR SKILL TOO, KISA-SAN.
BDMP
OH, CRAP...
HANG ON JUST ANOTHER MINUTE.
I'M IN DEEP NOW.
I HOPE THE IMAGE I'M TRYING TO PUT TOGETHER COMES ACROSS...
REALLY DEEP.
I CAN'T HELP MYSELF.

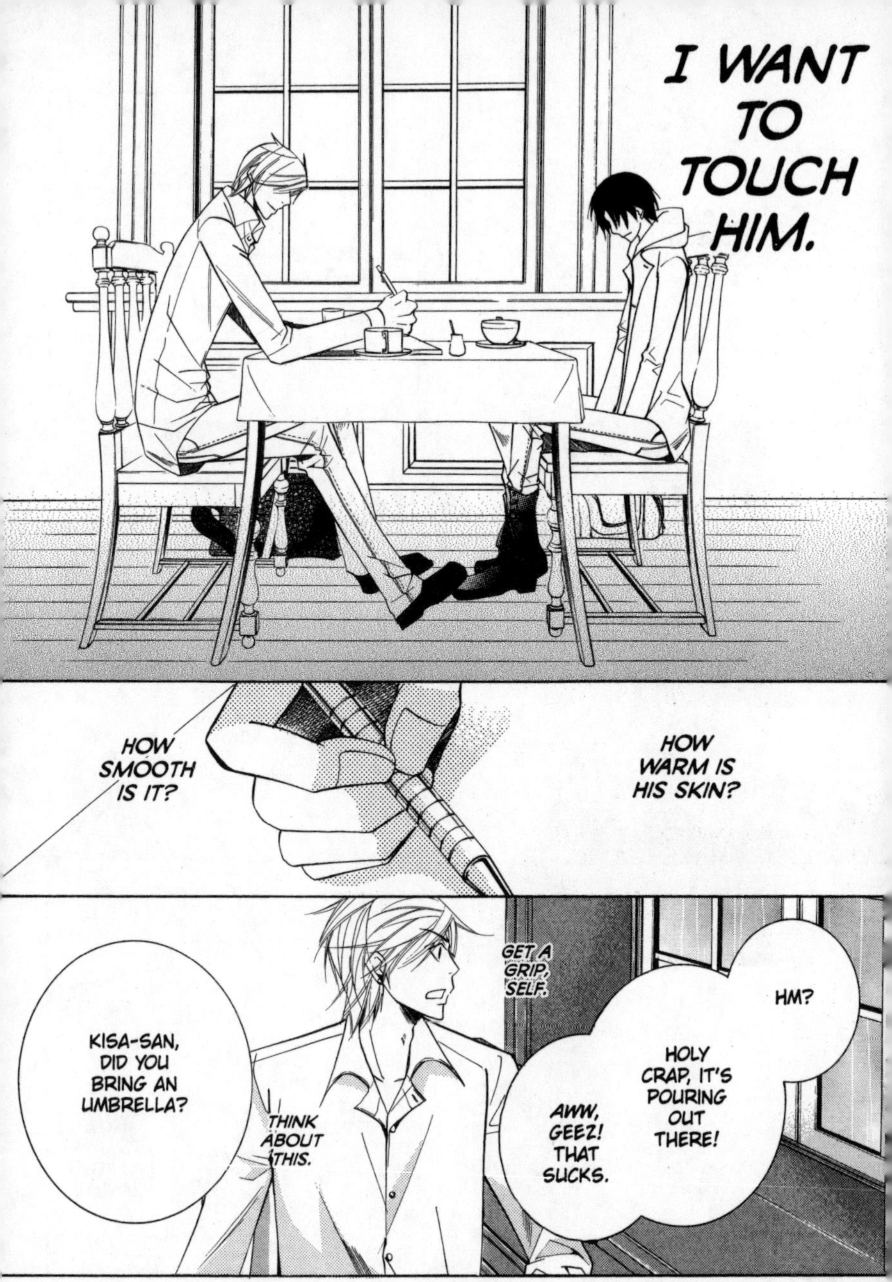
I WANT TO TOUCH HIM.
HOW WARM IS HIS SKIN?
HOW SMOOTH IS IT?
HM?
HOLY CRAP, IT'S POURING OUT THERE!
AWW, GEEZ! THAT SUCKS.
GET A GRIP, SELF.
THINK ABOUT THIS.
KISA-SAN, DID YOU BRING AN UMBRELLA?

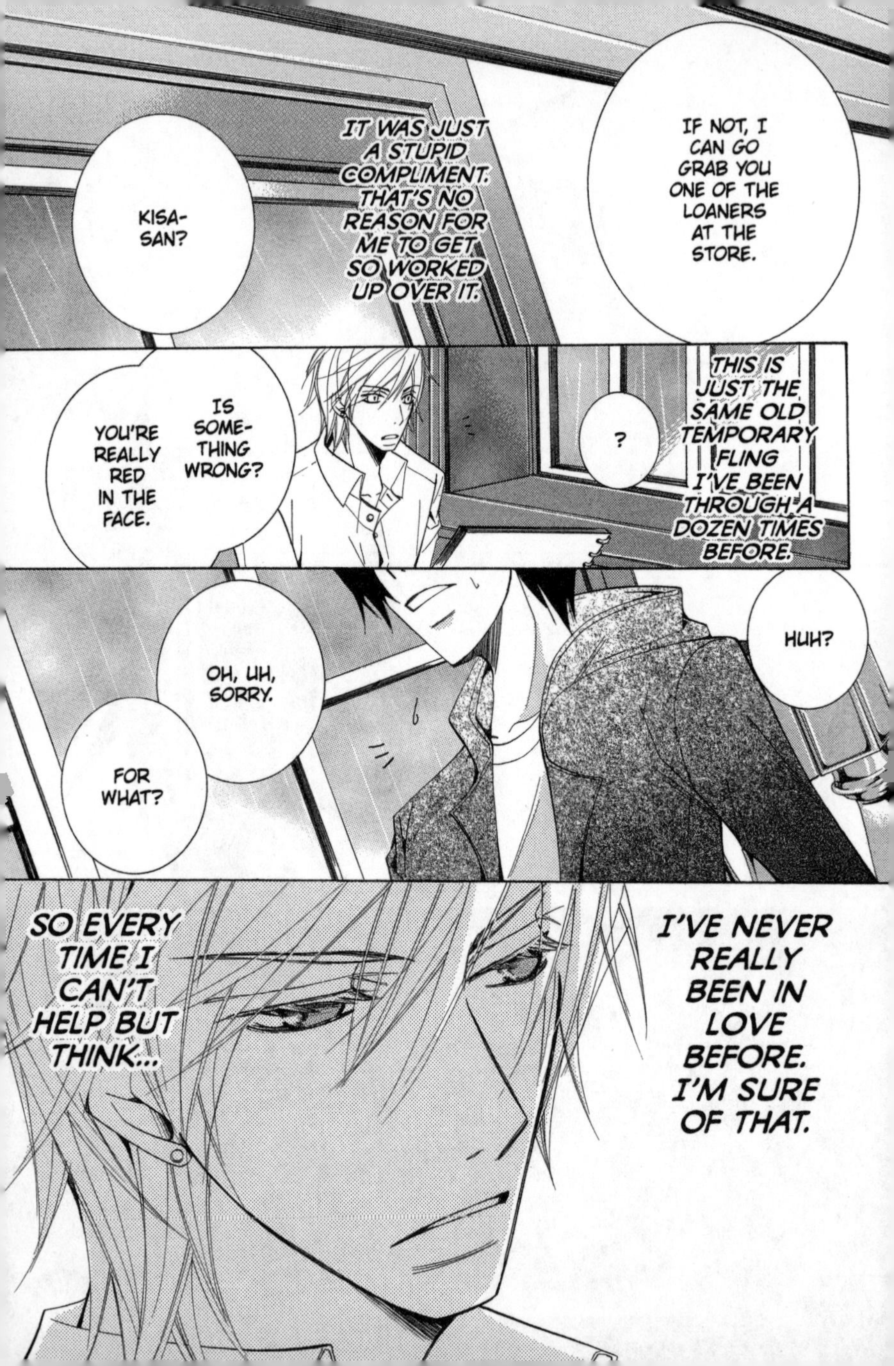
IF NOT, I CAN GO GRAB YOU ONE OF THE LOANERS AT THE STORE.
IT WAS JUST A STUPID COMPLIMENT. THAT'S NO REASON FOR ME TO GET SO WORKED UP OVER IT.
KISA-SAN?
THIS IS JUST THE SAME OLD TEMPORARY FLING I'VE BEEN THROUGH A DOZEN TIMES BEFORE.
?
IS SOMETHING WRONG?
YOU'RE REALLY RED IN THE FACE.
HUH?
OH, UH, SORRY.
FOR WHAT?
I'VE NEVER REALLY BEEN IN LOVE BEFORE. I'M SURE OF THAT.
SO EVERY TIME I CAN'T HELP BUT THINK...

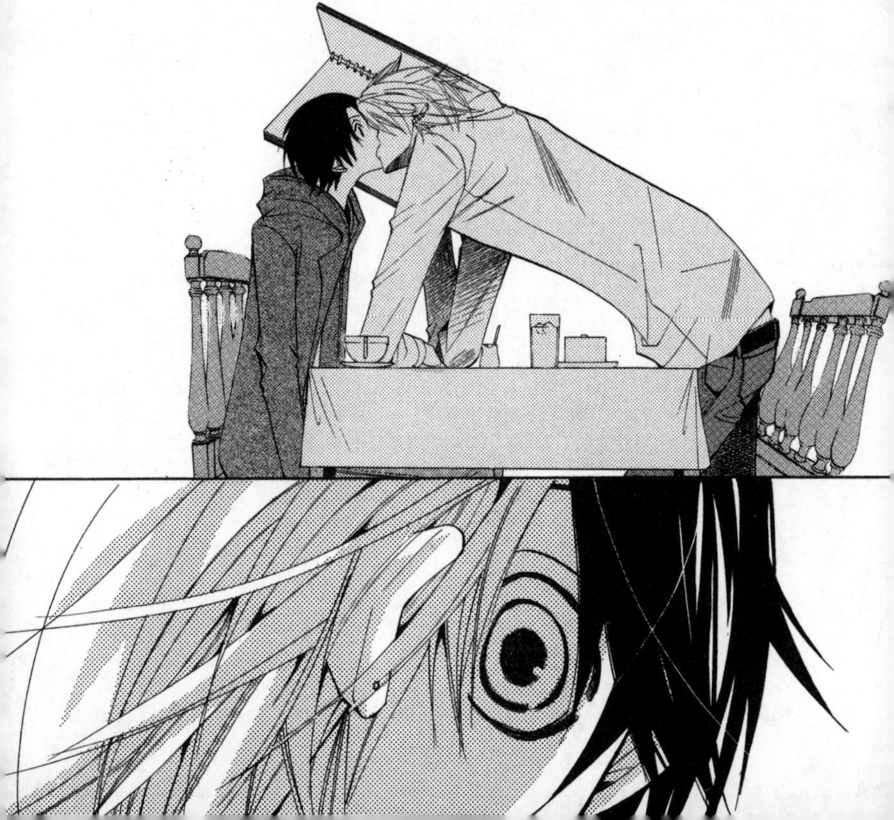

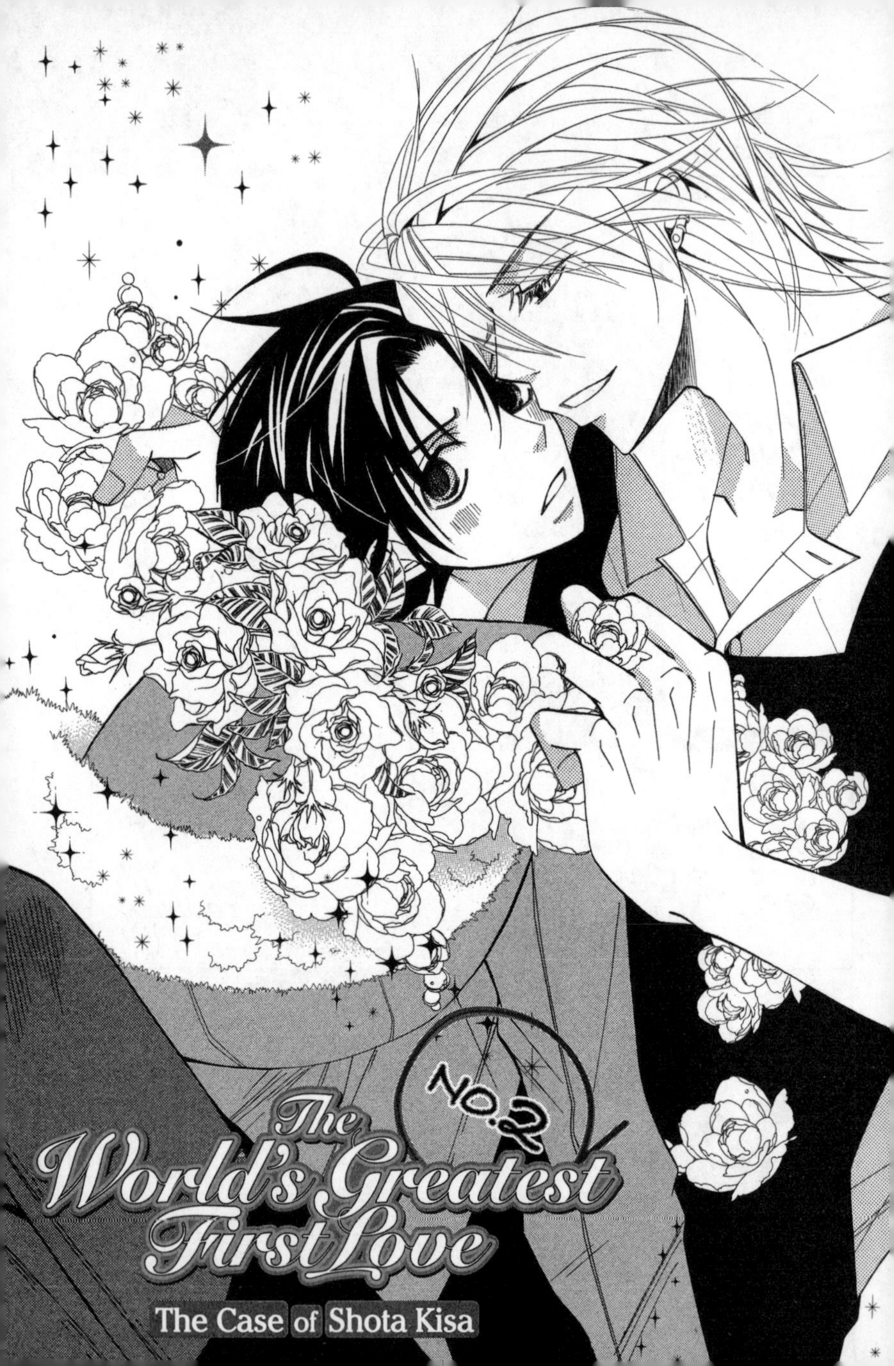

No.2
The World's Greatest First Love
The Case of Shota Kisa

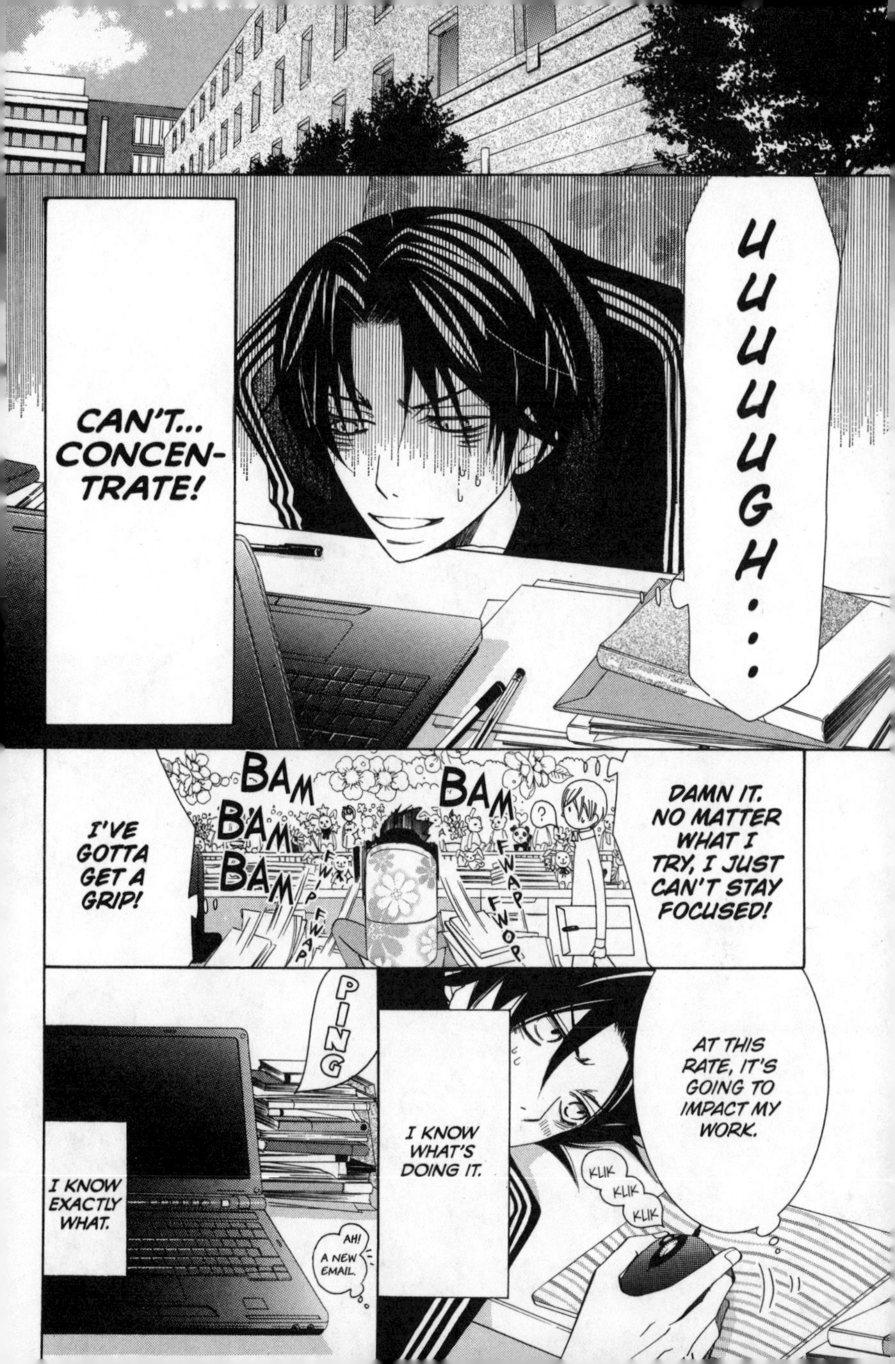
UUUUUGH...
CAN'T... CONCEN-TRATE!
DAMN IT. NO MATTER WHAT I TRY, I JUST CAN'T STAY FOCUSED!
BAM
BAM
BAM
BAM
FWAP
FWOP
FWIP
FWAP
I'VE GOTTA GET A GRIP!
AT THIS RATE, IT'S GOING TO IMPACT MY WORK.
I KNOW WHAT'S DOING IT.
KLIK
KLIK
KLIK
PING
AH! A NEW EMAIL.
I KNOW EXACTLY WHAT.

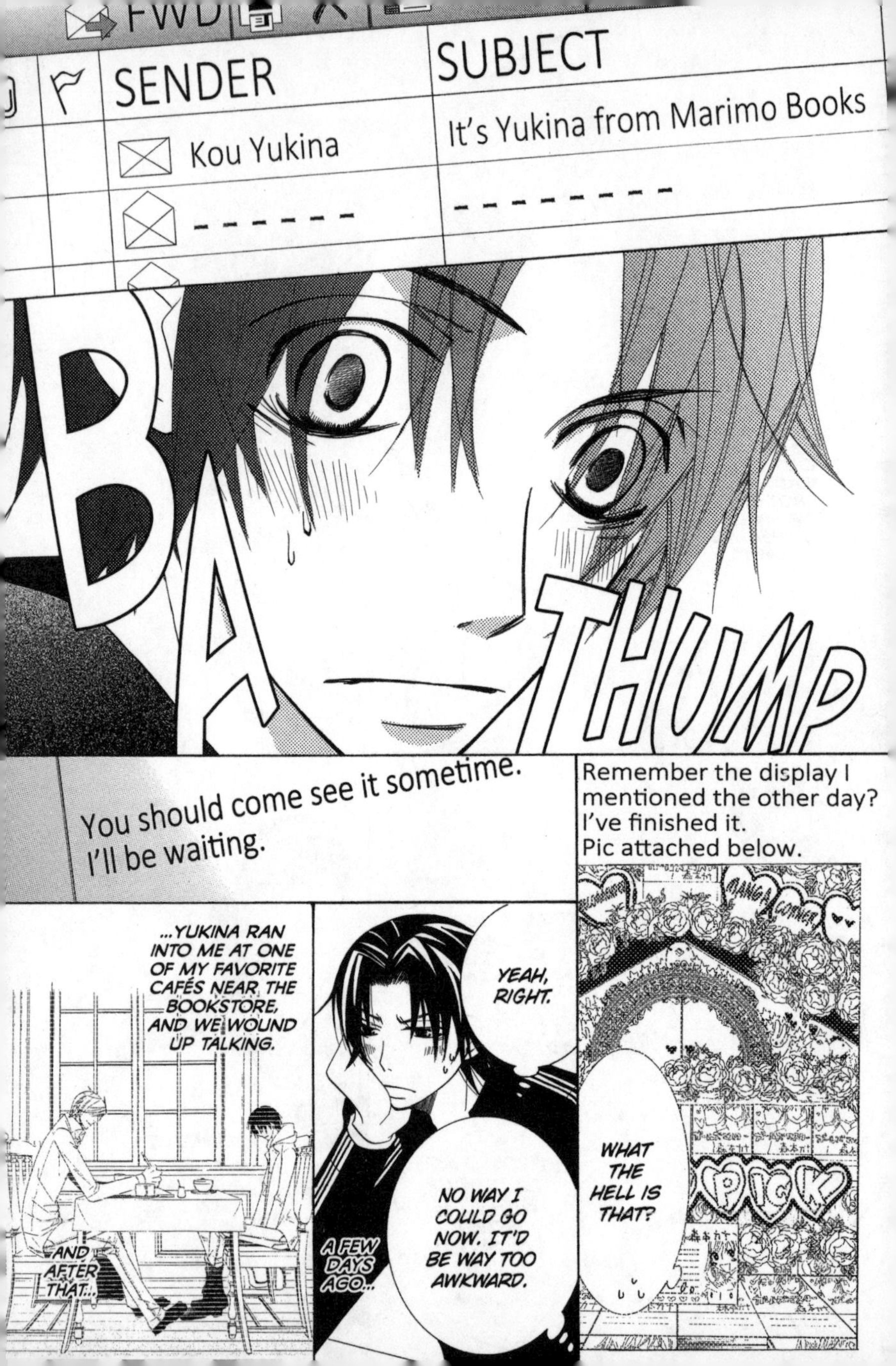
FWD
SENDER
SUBJECT
Kou Yukina
It's Yukina from Marimo Books
BA
THUMP
Remember the display I mentioned the other day? I've finished it. Pic attached below.
MANGA CORNER
PICK
WHAT THE HELL IS THAT?
You should come see it sometime. I'll be waiting.
YEAH, RIGHT.
NO WAY I COULD GO NOW. IT'D BE WAY TOO AWKWARD.
A FEW DAYS AGO...
...YUKINA RAN INTO ME AT ONE OF MY FAVORITE CAFÉS NEAR THE BOOKSTORE, AND WE WOUND UP TALKING.
AND AFTER THAT...

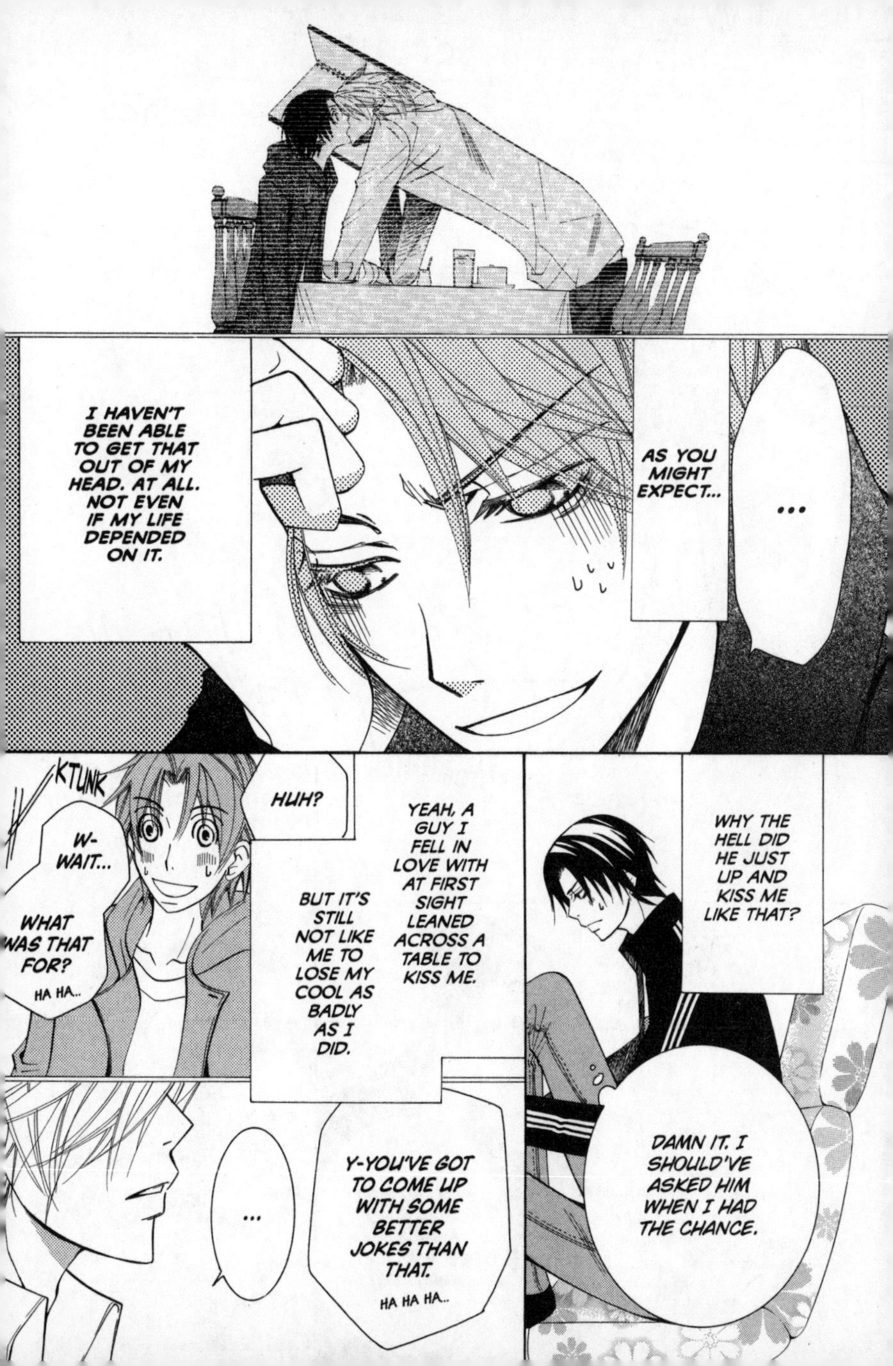
...
AS YOU MIGHT EXPECT...
I HAVEN'T BEEN ABLE TO GET THAT OUT OF MY HEAD. AT ALL. NOT EVEN IF MY LIFE DEPENDED ON IT.
WHY THE HELL DID HE JUST UP AND KISS ME LIKE THAT?
DAMN IT. I SHOULD'VE ASKED HIM WHEN I HAD THE CHANCE.
HUH?
YEAH, A GUY I FELL IN LOVE WITH AT FIRST SIGHT LEANED ACROSS A TABLE TO KISS ME.
BUT IT'S STILL NOT LIKE ME TO LOSE MY COOL AS BADLY AS I DID.
KTUNK
W-WAIT...
WHAT WAS THAT FOR?
HA HA...
Y-YOU'VE GOT TO COME UP WITH SOME BETTER JOKES THAN THAT.
HA HA HA...
...

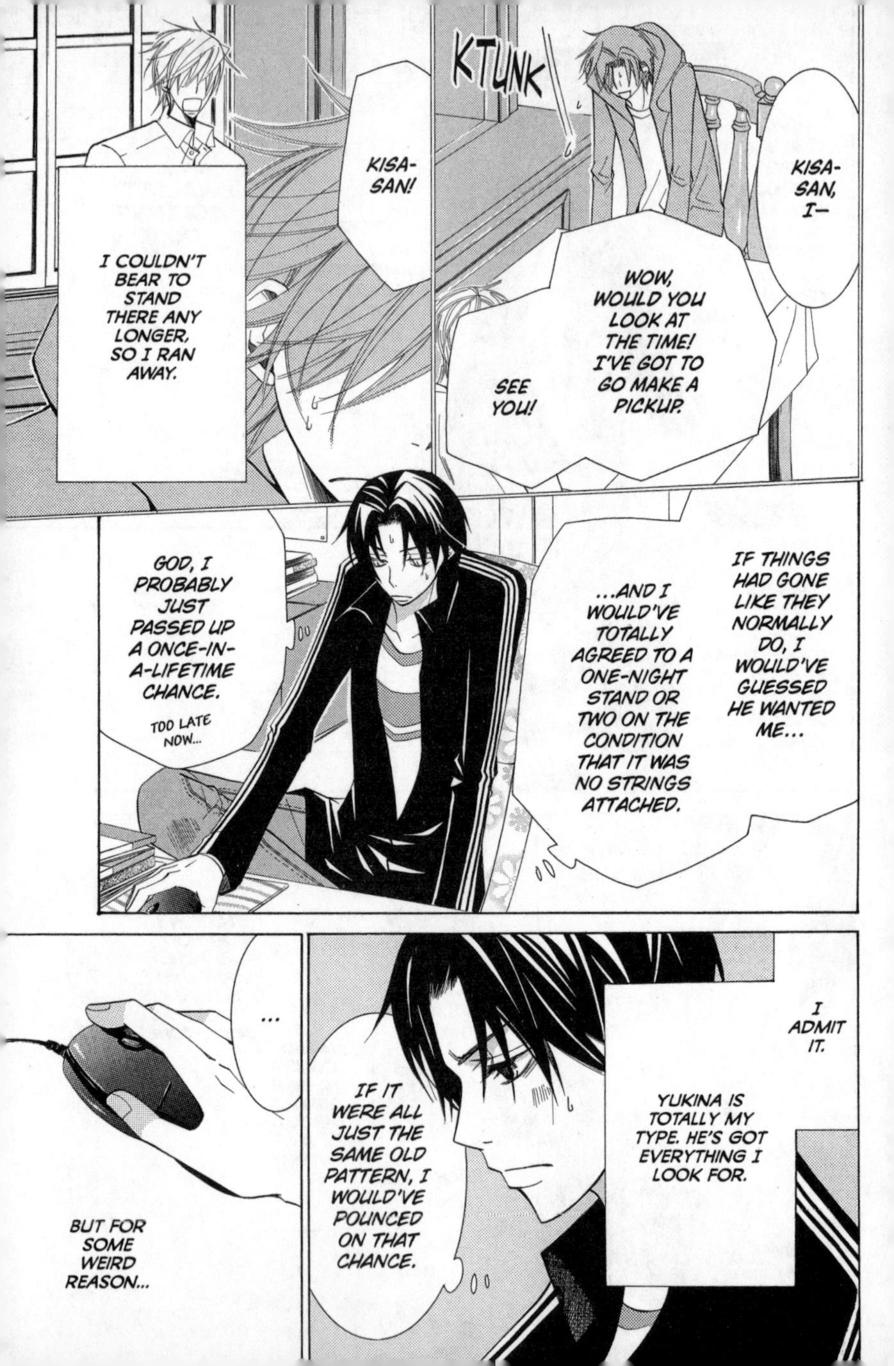
KTUNK
KISA-SAN, I—
WOW, WOULD YOU LOOK AT THE TIME! I'VE GOT TO GO MAKE A PICKUP.
SEE YOU!
KISA-SAN!
I COULDN'T BEAR TO STAND THERE ANY LONGER, SO I RAN AWAY.
IF THINGS HAD GONE LIKE THEY NORMALLY DO, I WOULD'VE GUESSED HE WANTED ME...
...AND I WOULD'VE TOTALLY AGREED TO A ONE-NIGHT STAND OR TWO ON THE CONDITION THAT IT WAS NO STRINGS ATTACHED.
GOD, I PROBABLY JUST PASSED UP A ONCE-IN-A-LIFETIME CHANCE.
TOO LATE NOW...
I ADMIT IT.
YUKINA IS TOTALLY MY TYPE. HE'S GOT EVERYTHING I LOOK FOR.
IF IT WERE ALL JUST THE SAME OLD PATTERN, I WOULD'VE POUNCED ON THAT CHANCE.
...
BUT FOR SOME WEIRD REASON...

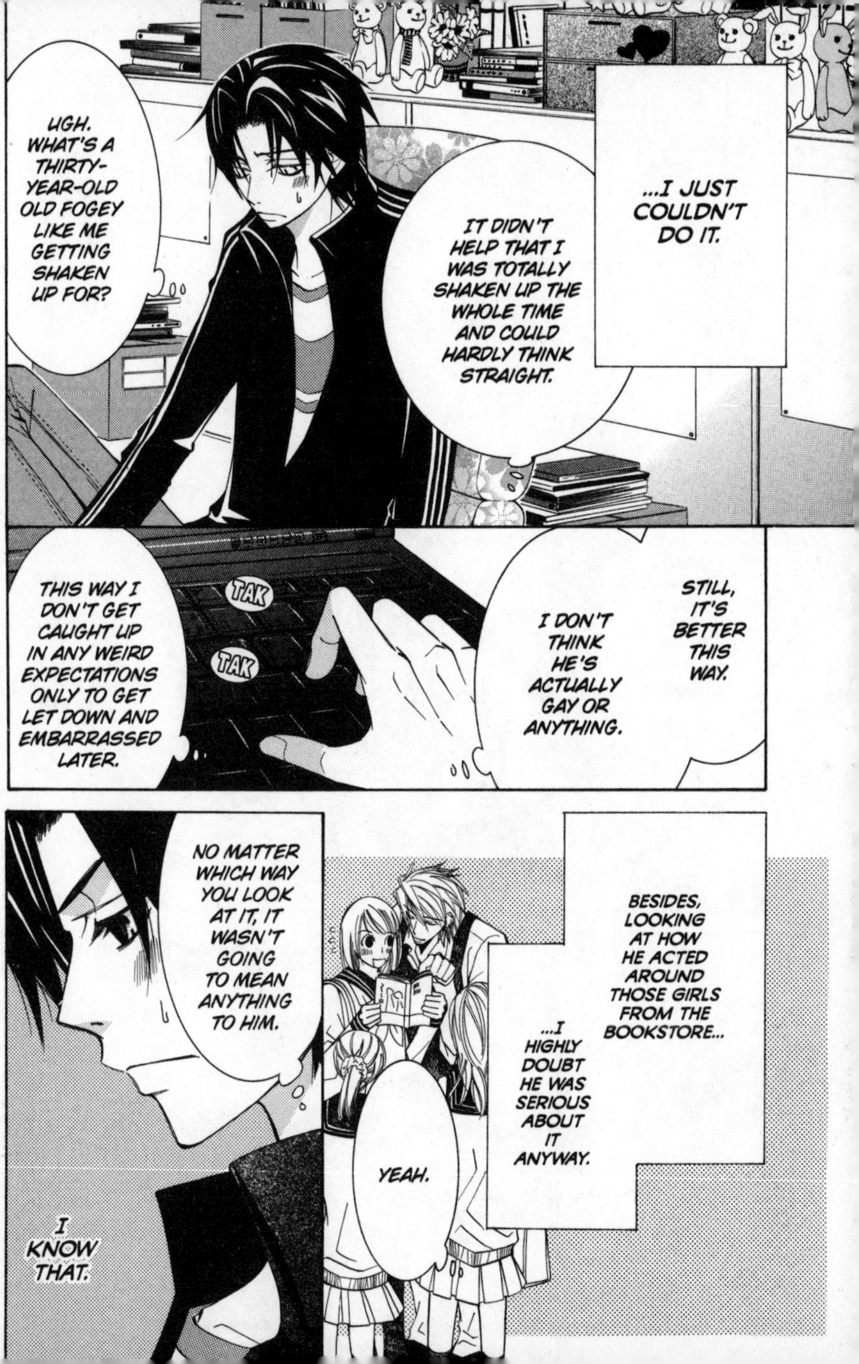
...I JUST COULDN'T DO IT.
IT DIDN'T HELP THAT I WAS TOTALLY SHAKEN UP THE WHOLE TIME AND COULD HARDLY THINK STRAIGHT.
UGH. WHAT'S A THIRTY-YEAR-OLD OLD FOGEY LIKE ME GETTING SHAKEN UP FOR?
STILL, IT'S BETTER THIS WAY.
I DON'T THINK HE'S ACTUALLY GAY OR ANYTHING.
TAK
TAK
THIS WAY I DON'T GET CAUGHT UP IN ANY WEIRD EXPECTATIONS ONLY TO GET LET DOWN AND EMBARRASSED LATER.
BESIDES, LOOKING AT HOW HE ACTED AROUND THOSE GIRLS FROM THE BOOKSTORE...
...I HIGHLY DOUBT HE WAS SERIOUS ABOUT IT ANYWAY.
YEAH.
NO MATTER WHICH WAY YOU LOOK AT IT, IT WASN'T GOING TO MEAN ANYTHING TO HIM.
I KNOW THAT.

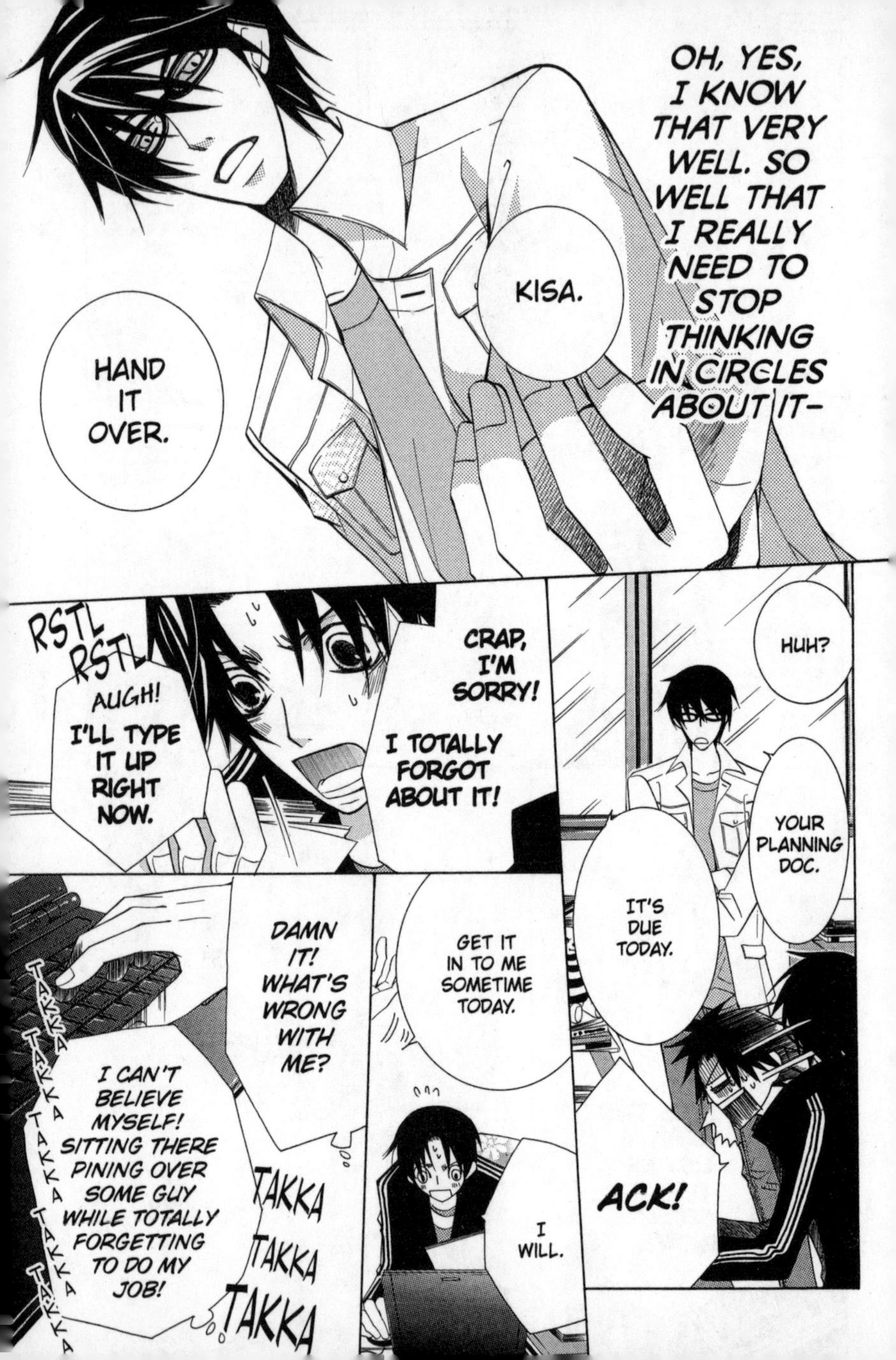
OH, YES, I KNOW THAT VERY WELL. SO WELL THAT I REALLY NEED TO STOP THINKING IN CIRCLES ABOUT IT–
KISA.
HAND IT OVER.
HUH?
YOUR PLANNING DOC.
IT'S DUE TODAY.
ACK!
CRAP, I'M SORRY!
I TOTALLY FORGOT ABOUT IT!
RSTL RSTL
AUGH! I'LL TYPE IT UP RIGHT NOW.
GET IT IN TO ME SOMETIME TODAY.
I WILL.
DAMN IT! WHAT'S WRONG WITH ME?
TAKKA TAKKA TAKKA
I CAN'T BELIEVE MYSELF! SITTING THERE PINING OVER SOME GUY WHILE TOTALLY FORGETTING TO DO MY JOB!
TAKKA TAKKA TAKKA TAKKA TAKKA TAKKA TAKKA

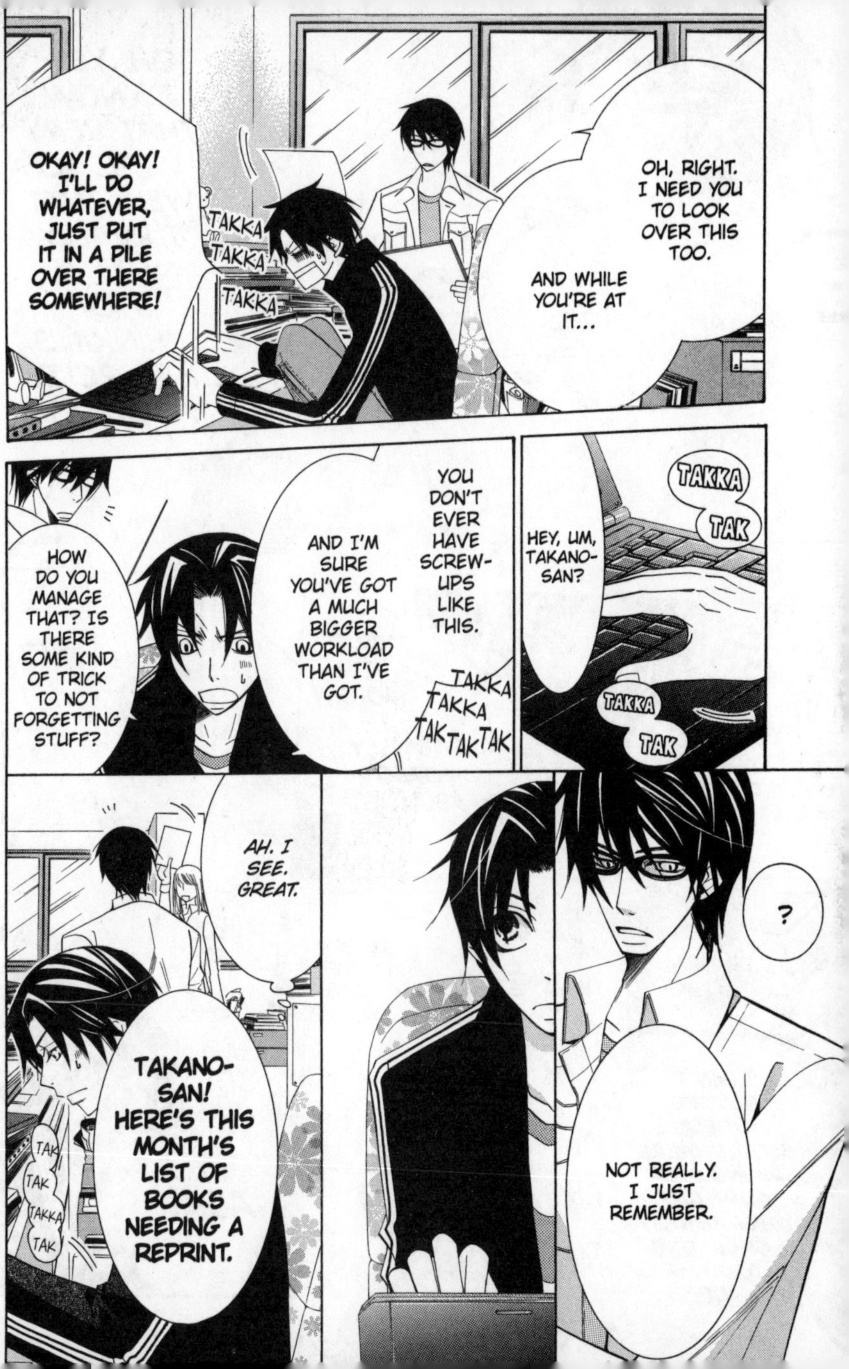

OH, RIGHT. I NEED YOU TO LOOK OVER THIS TOO.
AND WHILE YOU'RE AT IT...
OKAY! OKAY! I'LL DO WHATEVER, JUST PUT IT IN A PILE OVER THERE SOMEWHERE!
TAKKA TAKKA TAKKA
TAKKA TAK
HEY, UM, TAKANO-SAN?
TAKKA TAK
YOU DON'T EVER HAVE SCREW-UPS LIKE THIS.
AND I'M SURE YOU'VE GOT A MUCH BIGGER WORKLOAD THAN I'VE GOT.
TAKKA TAKKA TAKTAKTAK
HOW DO YOU MANAGE THAT? IS THERE SOME KIND OF TRICK TO NOT FORGETTING STUFF?
?
NOT REALLY. I JUST REMEMBER.
AH. I SEE. GREAT.
TAKANO-SAN! HERE'S THIS MONTH'S LIST OF BOOKS NEEDING A REPRINT.
TAK TAK TAKKA TAK

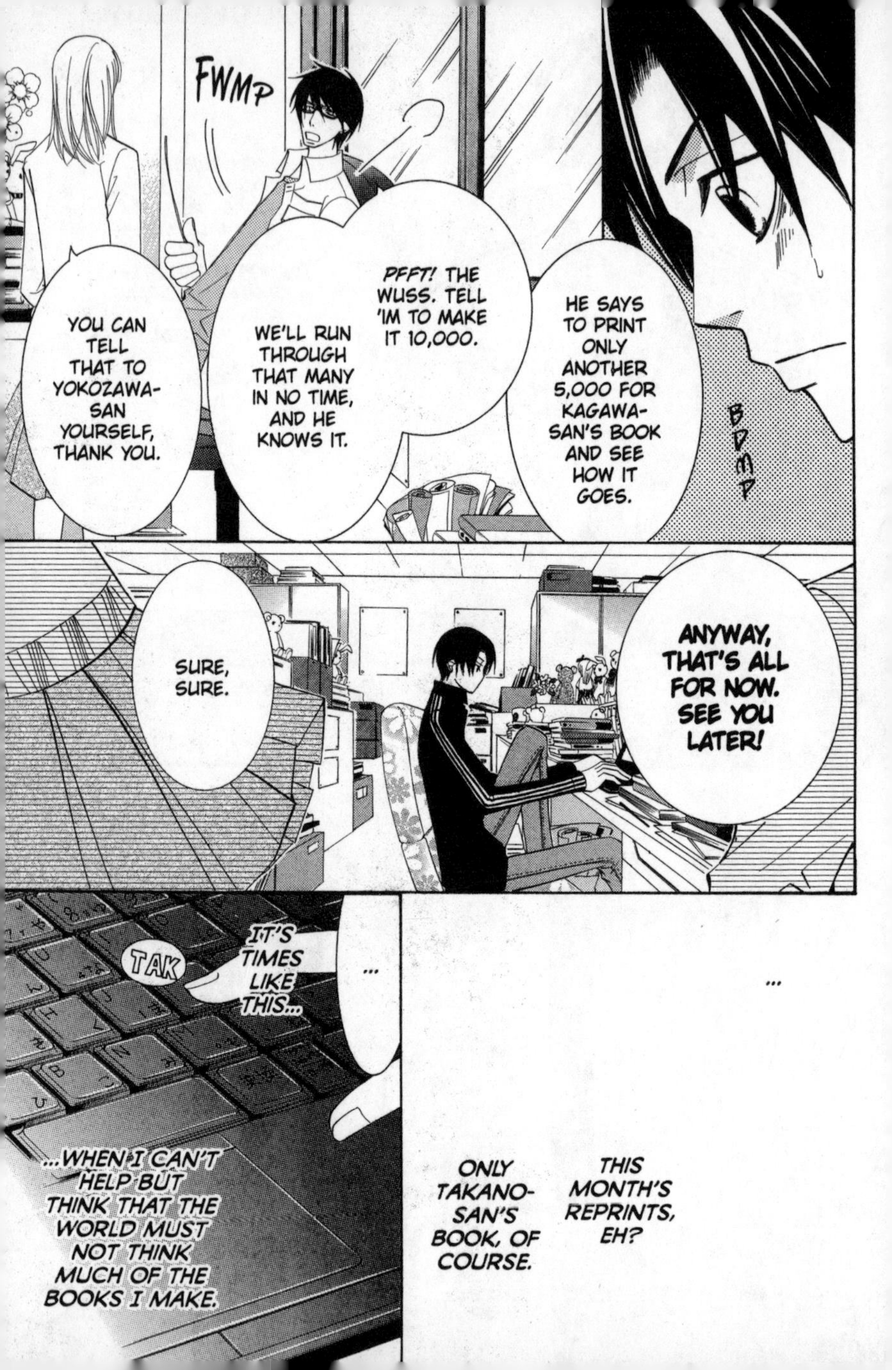
HE SAYS TO PRINT ONLY ANOTHER 5,000 FOR KAGAWA-SAN'S BOOK AND SEE HOW IT GOES.
BDMP
FWMP
PFFT! THE WUSS. TELL 'IM TO MAKE IT 10,000.
WE'LL RUN THROUGH THAT MANY IN NO TIME, AND HE KNOWS IT.
YOU CAN TELL THAT TO YOKOZAWA-SAN YOURSELF, THANK YOU.
ANYWAY, THAT'S ALL FOR NOW. SEE YOU LATER!
SURE, SURE.
...
THIS MONTH'S REPRINTS, EH?
ONLY TAKANO-SAN'S BOOK, OF COURSE.
...
IT'S TIMES LIKE THIS...
TAK
...WHEN I CAN'T HELP BUT THINK THAT THE WORLD MUST NOT THINK MUCH OF THE BOOKS I MAKE.

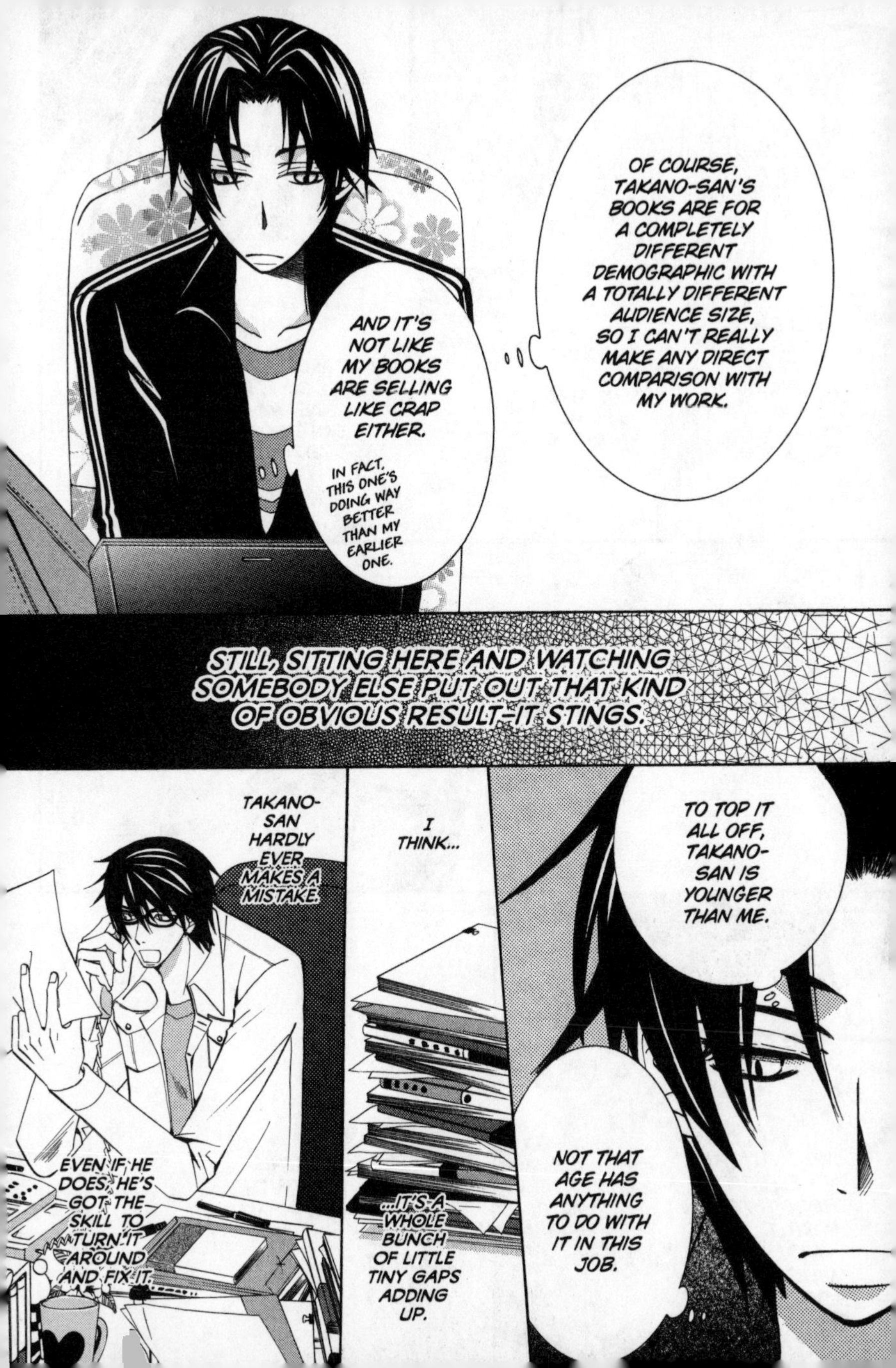
OF COURSE, TAKANO-SAN'S BOOKS ARE FOR A COMPLETELY DIFFERENT DEMOGRAPHIC WITH A TOTALLY DIFFERENT AUDIENCE SIZE, SO I CAN'T REALLY MAKE ANY DIRECT COMPARISON WITH MY WORK.
AND IT'S NOT LIKE MY BOOKS ARE SELLING LIKE CRAP EITHER.
IN FACT, THIS ONE'S DOING WAY BETTER THAN MY EARLIER ONE.
STILL, SITTING HERE AND WATCHING SOMEBODY ELSE PUT OUT THAT KIND OF OBVIOUS RESULT—IT STINGS.
TO TOP IT ALL OFF, TAKANO-SAN IS YOUNGER THAN ME.
NOT THAT AGE HAS ANYTHING TO DO WITH IT IN THIS JOB.
I THINK...
...IT'S A WHOLE BUNCH OF LITTLE TINY GAPS ADDING UP.
TAKANO-SAN HARDLY EVER MAKES A MISTAKE.
EVEN IF HE DOES, HE'S GOT THE SKILL TO TURN IT AROUND AND FIX IT.

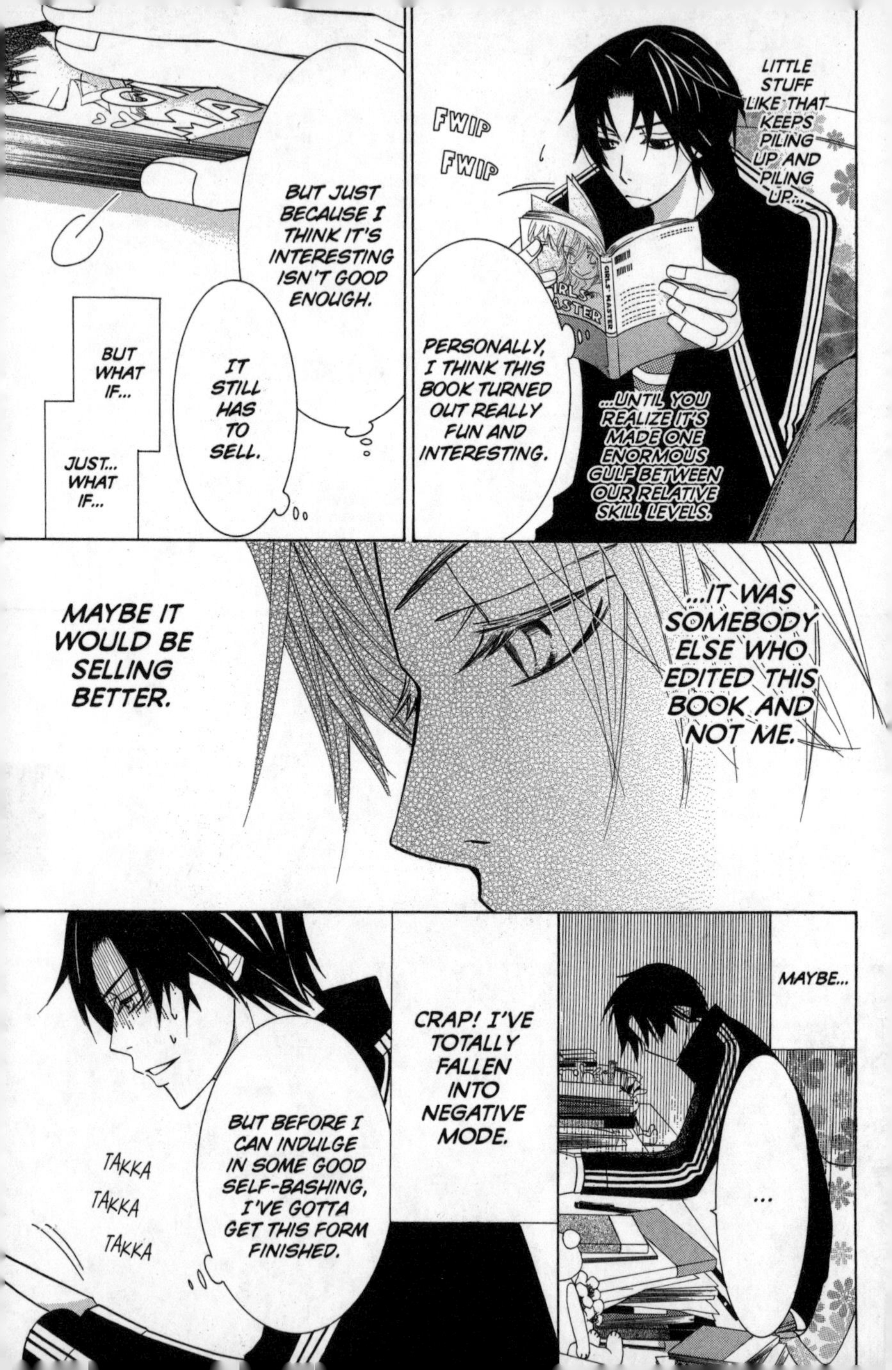

LITTLE STUFF LIKE THAT KEEPS PILING UP AND PILING UP...
FWIP
FWIP
GIRLS' MASTER
...UNTIL YOU REALIZE IT'S MADE ONE ENORMOUS GULF BETWEEN OUR RELATIVE SKILL LEVELS.
PERSONALLY, I THINK THIS BOOK TURNED OUT REALLY FUN AND INTERESTING.
BUT JUST BECAUSE I THINK IT'S INTERESTING ISN'T GOOD ENOUGH.
IT STILL HAS TO SELL.
BUT WHAT IF...
JUST... WHAT IF...
...IT WAS SOMEBODY ELSE WHO EDITED THIS BOOK AND NOT ME.
MAYBE IT WOULD BE SELLING BETTER.
MAYBE...
...
CRAP! I'VE TOTALLY FALLEN INTO NEGATIVE MODE.
BUT BEFORE I CAN INDULGE IN SOME GOOD SELF-BASHING, I'VE GOTTA GET THIS FORM FINISHED.
TAKKA
TAKKA
TAKKA

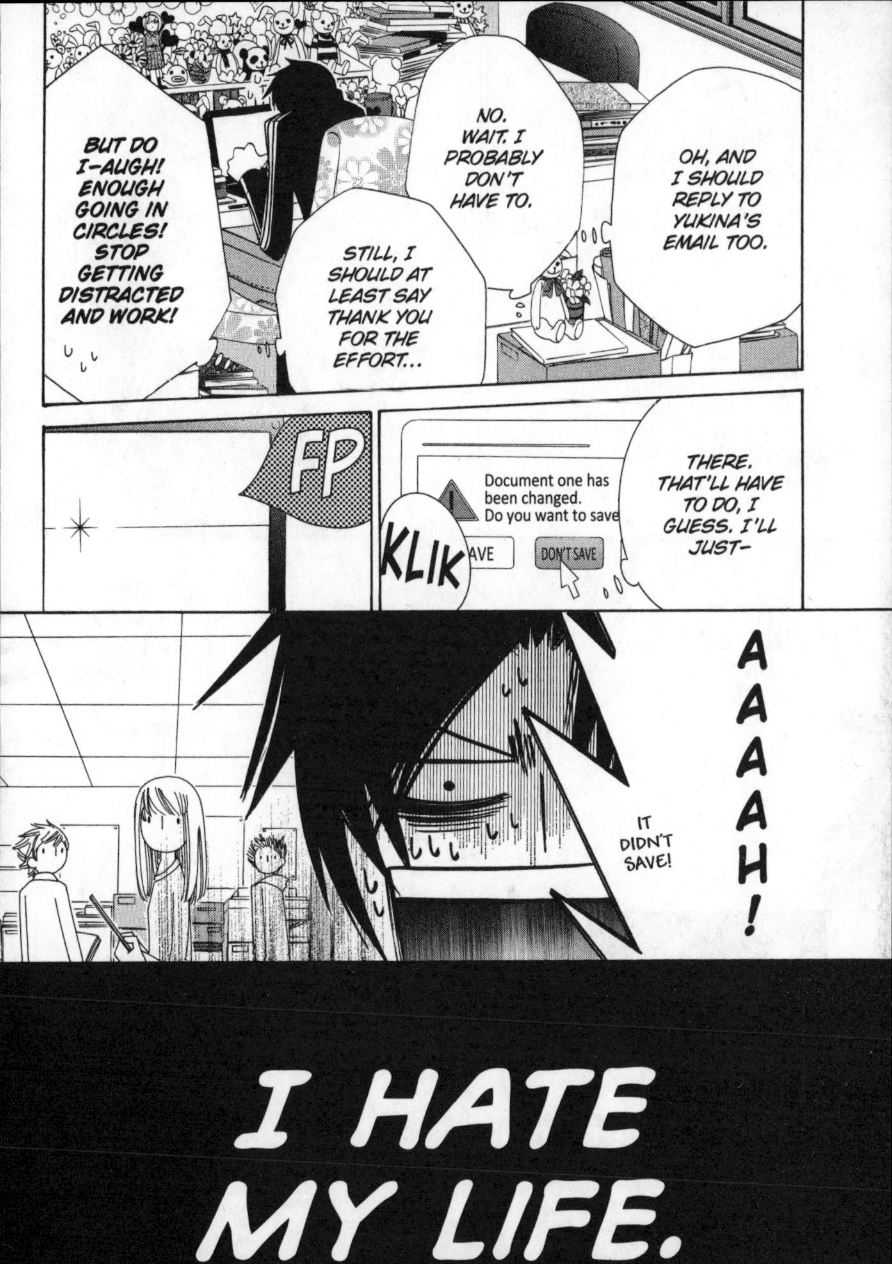
OH, AND I SHOULD REPLY TO YUKINA'S EMAIL TOO.
NO. WAIT. I PROBABLY DON'T HAVE TO.
STILL, I SHOULD AT LEAST SAY THANK YOU FOR THE EFFORT...
BUT DO I-AUGH! ENOUGH GOING IN CIRCLES! STOP GETTING DISTRACTED AND WORK!
THERE. THAT'LL HAVE TO DO, I GUESS. I'LL JUST-
Document one has been changed. Do you want to save
DON'T SAVE
KLIK
FP
AAAAAH!
IT DIDN'T SAVE!
I HATE MY LIFE.

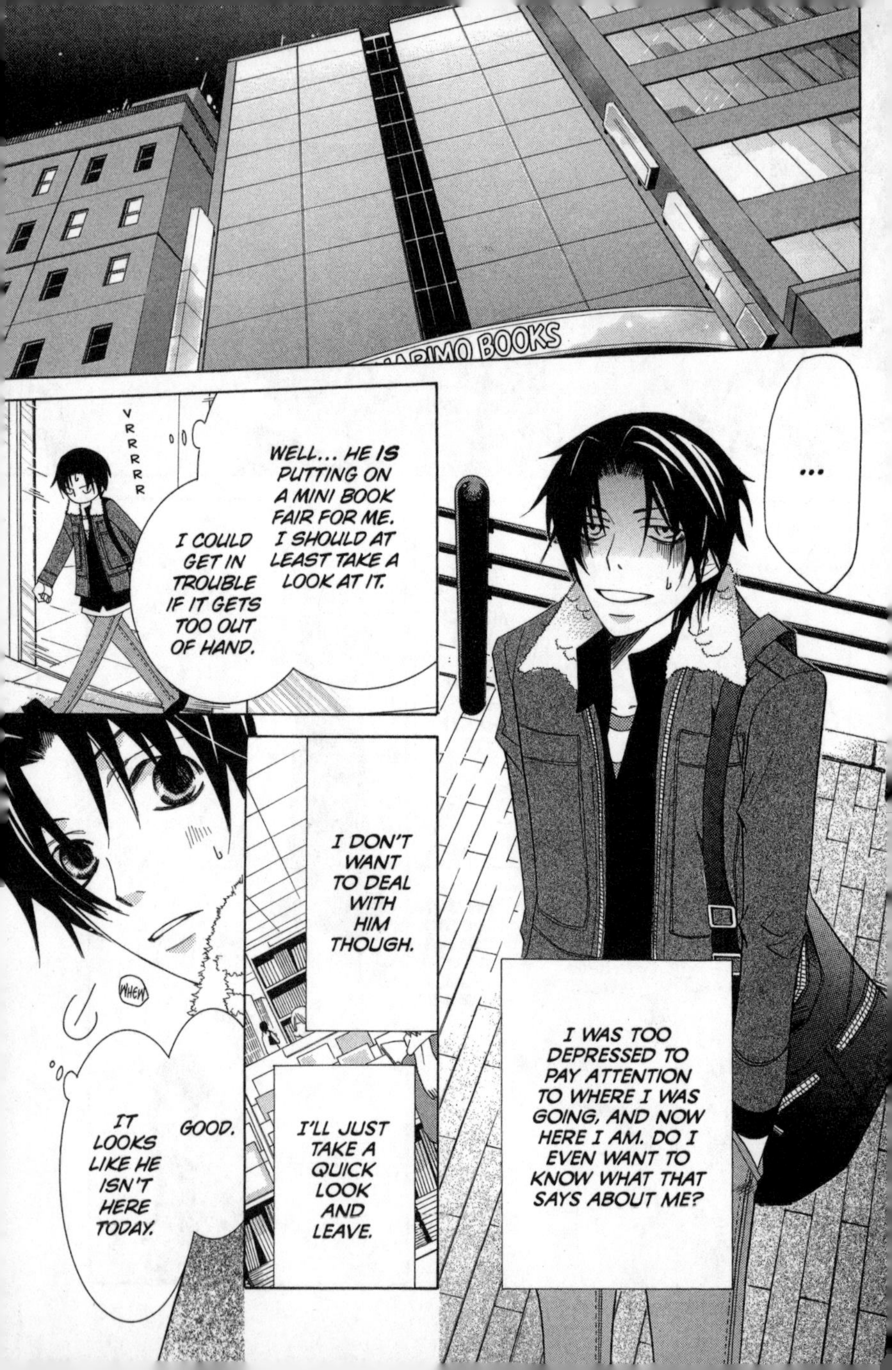
ARIMO BOOKS
...
I WAS TOO DEPRESSED TO PAY ATTENTION TO WHERE I WAS GOING, AND NOW HERE I AM. DO I EVEN WANT TO KNOW WHAT THAT SAYS ABOUT ME?
VRRRRR
WELL... HE IS PUTTING ON A MINI BOOK FAIR FOR ME. I SHOULD AT LEAST TAKE A LOOK AT IT.
I COULD GET IN TROUBLE IF IT GETS TOO OUT OF HAND.
I DON'T WANT TO DEAL WITH HIM THOUGH.
I'LL JUST TAKE A QUICK LOOK AND LEAVE.
GOOD.
IT LOOKS LIKE HE ISN'T HERE TODAY.
WHEW

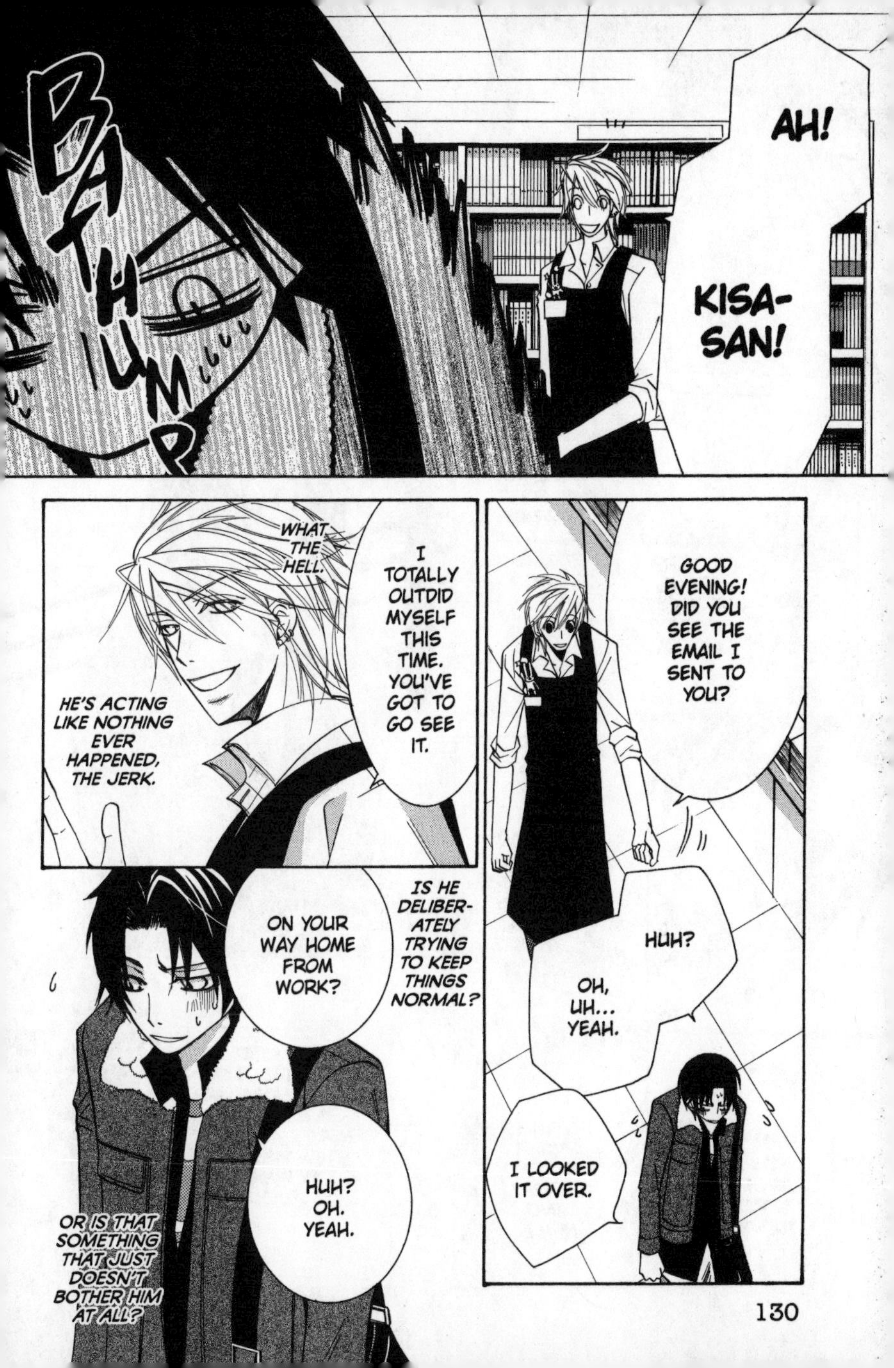
AH!
KISA-SAN!
BA-THUMP
GOOD EVENING! DID YOU SEE THE EMAIL I SENT TO YOU?
HUH?
OH, UH... YEAH.
I LOOKED IT OVER.
I TOTALLY OUTDID MYSELF THIS TIME. YOU'VE GOT TO GO SEE IT.
WHAT THE HELL.
HE'S ACTING LIKE NOTHING EVER HAPPENED, THE JERK.
IS HE DELIBERATELY TRYING TO KEEP THINGS NORMAL?
ON YOUR WAY HOME FROM WORK?
HUH? OH. YEAH.
OR IS THAT SOMETHING THAT JUST DOESN'T BOTHER HIM AT ALL?

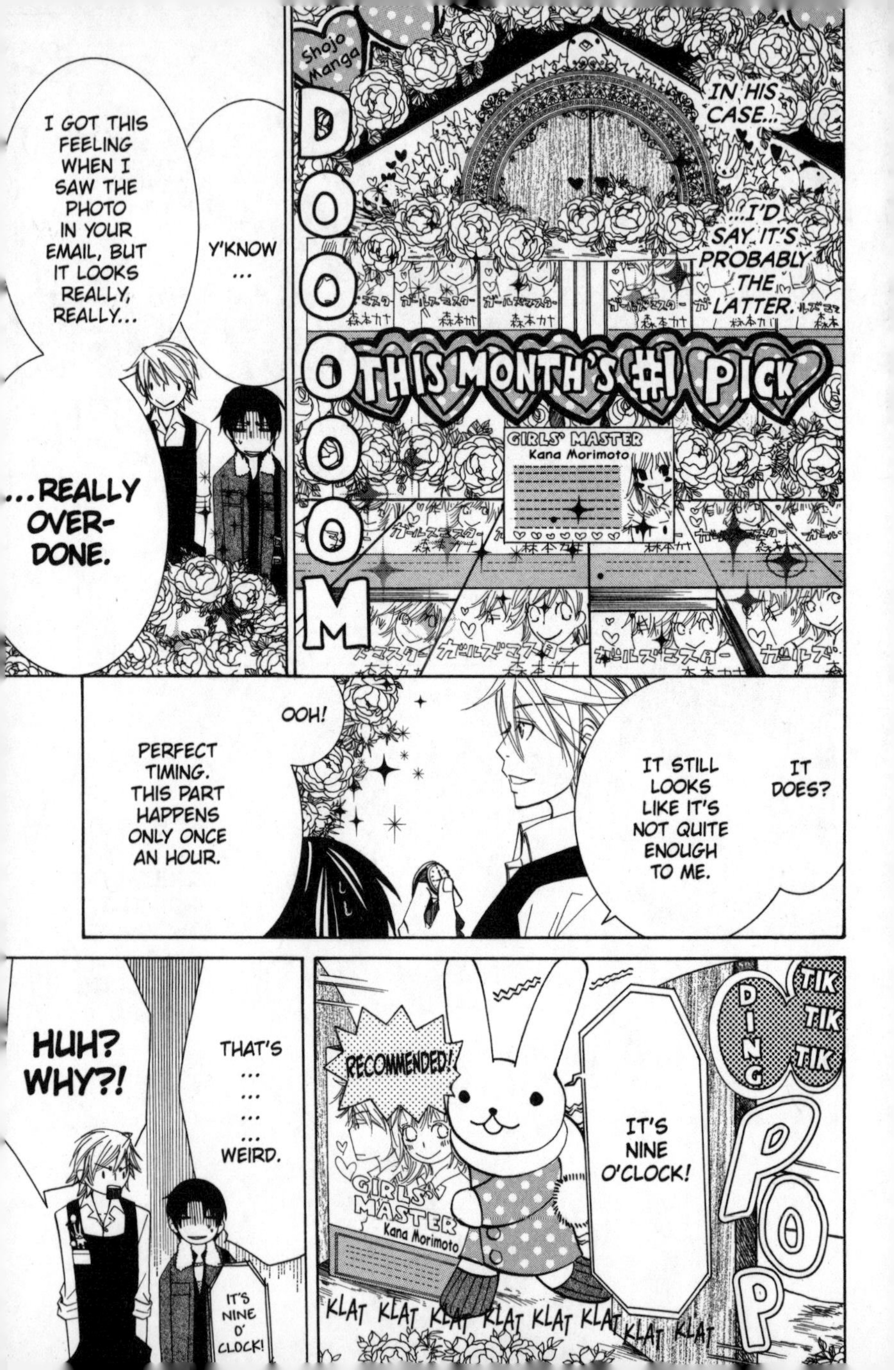
Shojo Manga
IN HIS CASE...
...I'D SAY IT'S PROBABLY THE LATTER.
DOOOOOOOM
THIS MONTH'S #1 PICK
GIRLS' MASTER
Kana Morimoto
Y'KNOW ...
I GOT THIS FEELING WHEN I SAW THE PHOTO IN YOUR EMAIL, BUT IT LOOKS REALLY, REALLY...
...REALLY OVER-DONE.
IT DOES?
IT STILL LOOKS LIKE IT'S NOT QUITE ENOUGH TO ME.
OOH!
PERFECT TIMING. THIS PART HAPPENS ONLY ONCE AN HOUR.
TIK TIK TIK
DING
POP POP
IT'S NINE O'CLOCK!
RECOMMENDED!
GIRLS' MASTER
Kana Morimoto
KLAT KLAT KLAT KLAT KLAT KLAT KLAT KLAT
THAT'S ... ... WEIRD.
HUH? WHY?!
IT'S NINE O' CLOCK!

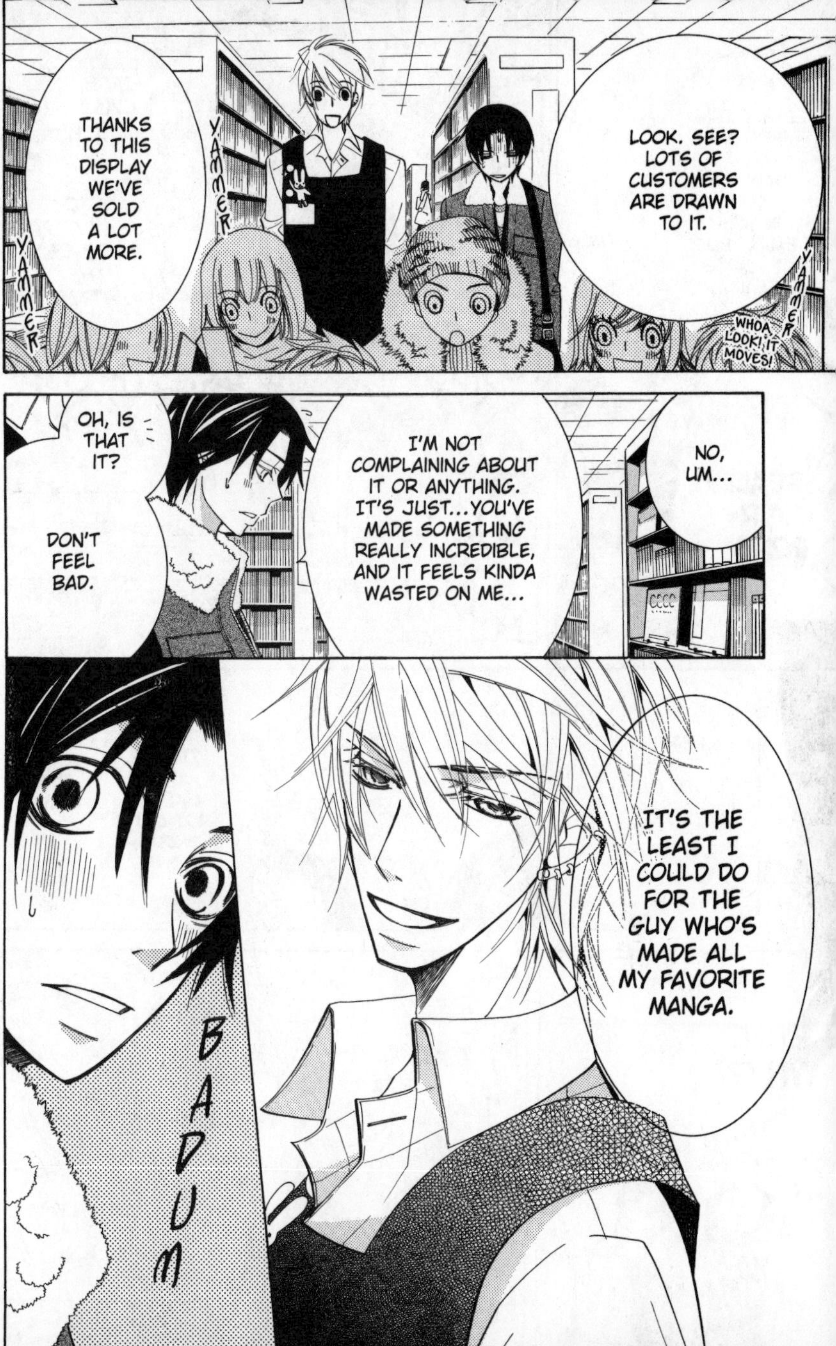
LOOK. SEE? LOTS OF CUSTOMERS ARE DRAWN TO IT.
YAMMER
WHOA, LOOK! IT MOVES!
YAMMER
THANKS TO THIS DISPLAY WE'VE SOLD A LOT MORE.
YAMMER
NO, UM...
I'M NOT COMPLAINING ABOUT IT OR ANYTHING. IT'S JUST...YOU'VE MADE SOMETHING REALLY INCREDIBLE, AND IT FEELS KINDA WASTED ON ME...
OH, IS THAT IT?
DON'T FEEL BAD.
IT'S THE LEAST I COULD DO FOR THE GUY WHO'S MADE ALL MY FAVORITE MANGA.
BADUM

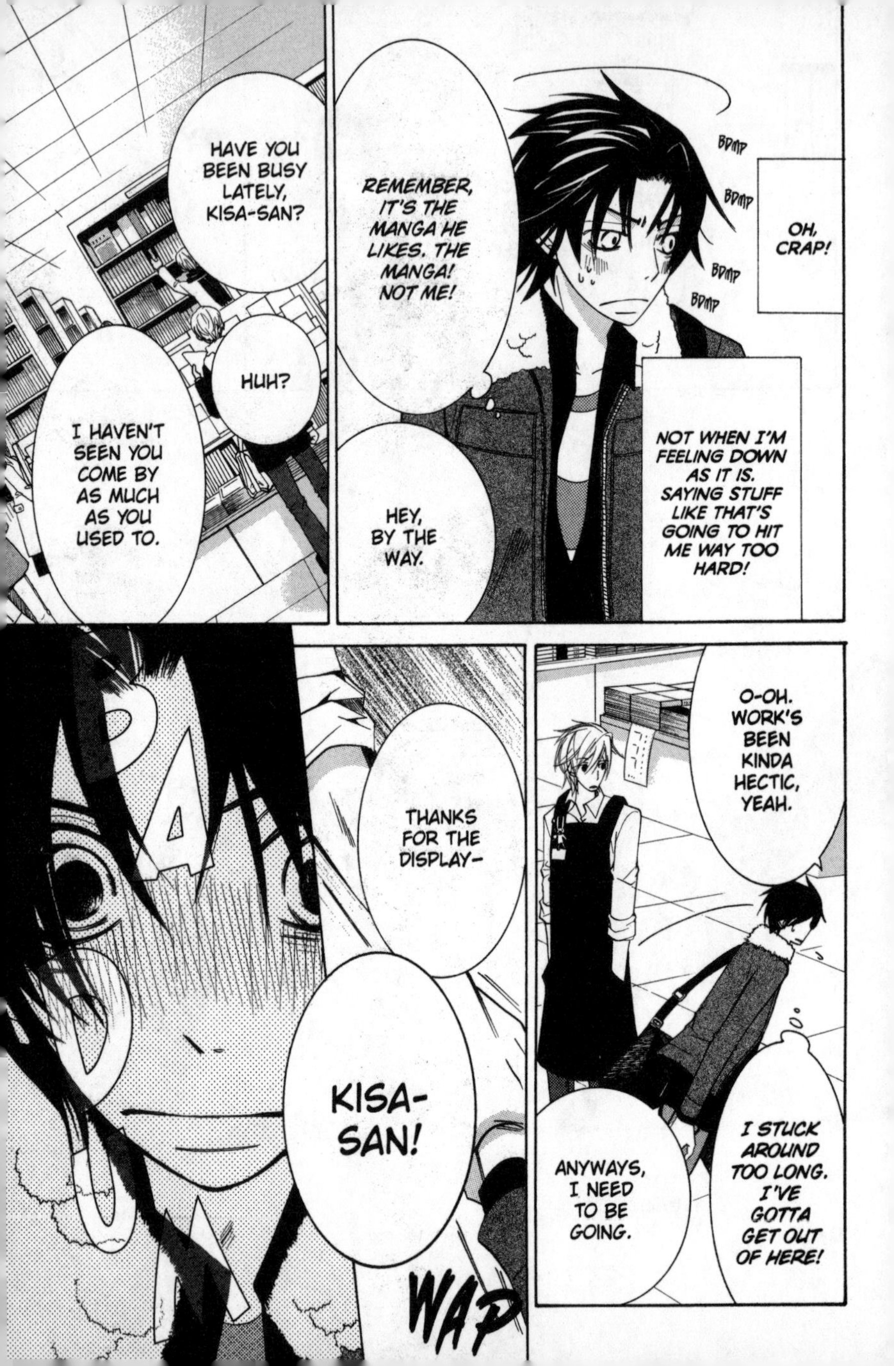
BDMP BDMP BDMP BDMP
OH, CRAP!
REMEMBER, IT'S THE MANGA HE LIKES. THE MANGA! NOT ME!
NOT WHEN I'M FEELING DOWN AS IT IS. SAYING STUFF LIKE THAT'S GOING TO HIT ME WAY TOO HARD!
HEY, BY THE WAY.
HAVE YOU BEEN BUSY LATELY, KISA-SAN?
HUH?
I HAVEN'T SEEN YOU COME BY AS MUCH AS YOU USED TO.
O-OH. WORK'S BEEN KINDA HECTIC, YEAH.
I STUCK AROUND TOO LONG. I'VE GOTTA GET OUT OF HERE!
ANYWAYS, I NEED TO BE GOING.
THANKS FOR THE DISPLAY-
KISA-SAN!
WAP

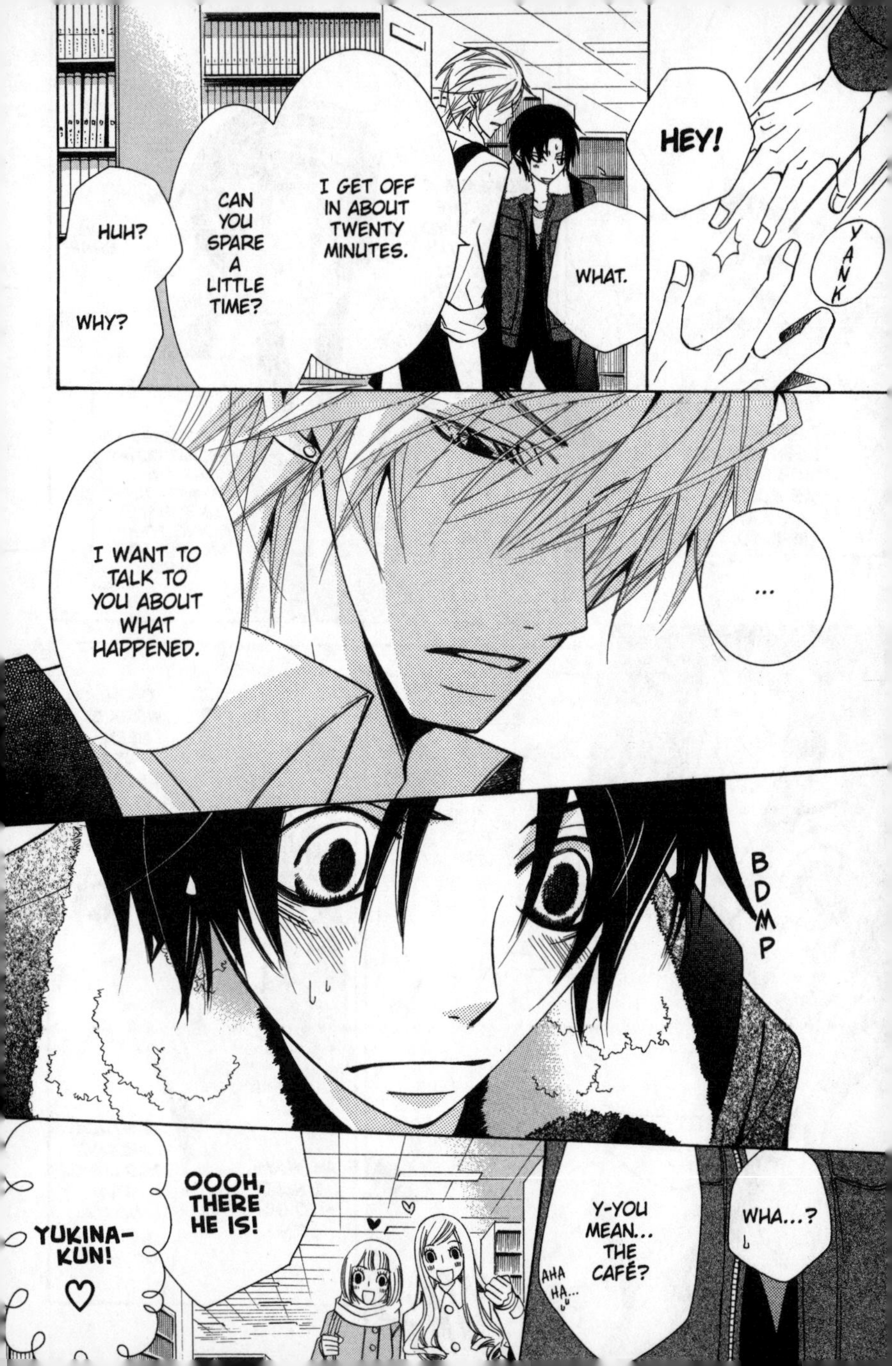
HEY!
YANK
WHAT.
I GET OFF IN ABOUT TWENTY MINUTES.
CAN YOU SPARE A LITTLE TIME?
HUH?
WHY?
...
I WANT TO TALK TO YOU ABOUT WHAT HAPPENED.
BDMP
WHA...?
Y-YOU MEAN... THE CAFÉ?
AHA HA...
OOOH, THERE HE IS!
YUKINA-KUN! ♡

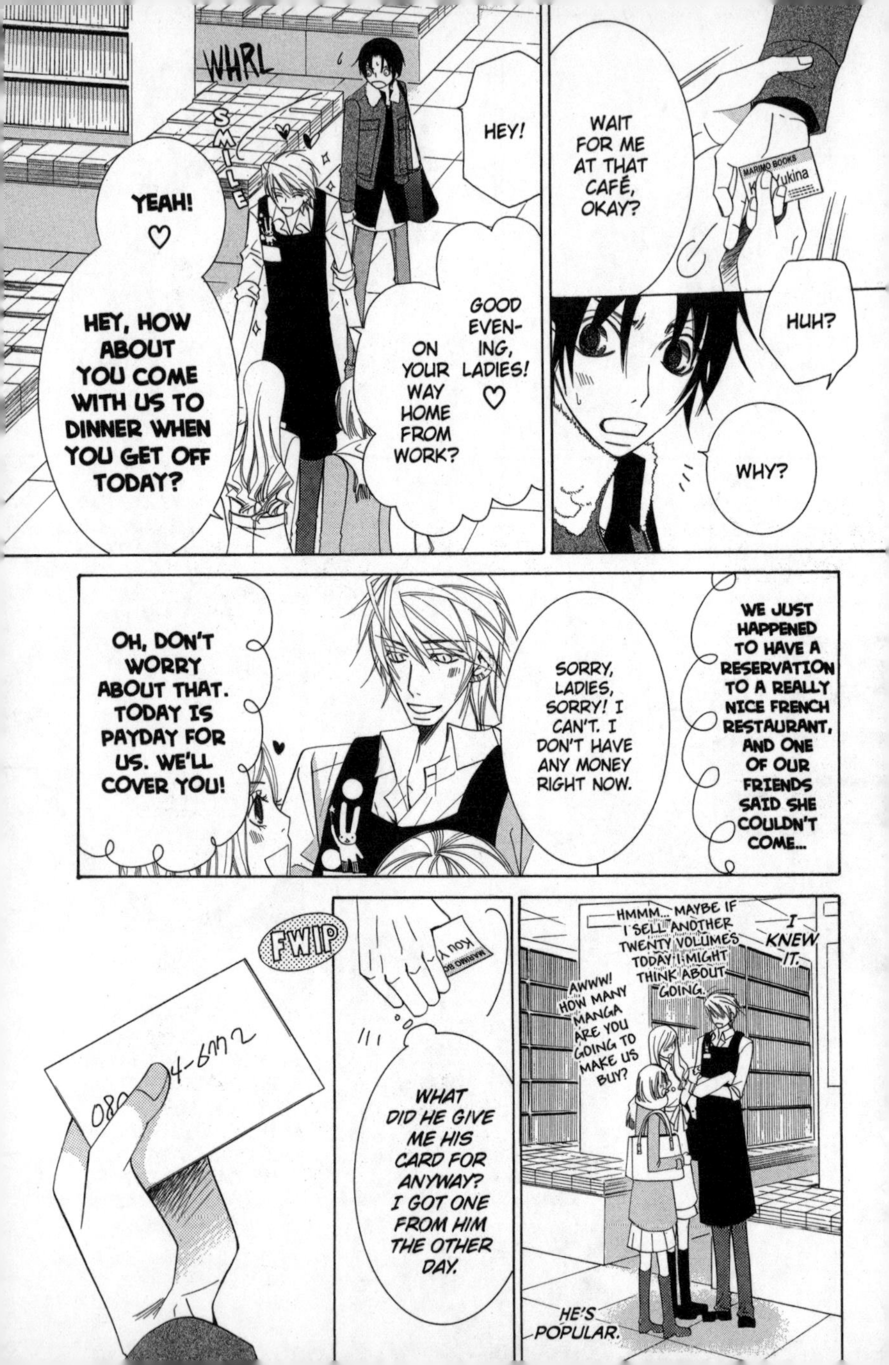
WAIT FOR ME AT THAT CAFÉ, OKAY?
MARIMO BOOKS
Yukina
HUH?
WHY?
HEY!
WHRL
SMILE
GOOD EVENING, LADIES! ♡
ON YOUR WAY HOME FROM WORK?
YEAH! ♡
HEY, HOW ABOUT YOU COME WITH US TO DINNER WHEN YOU GET OFF TODAY?
WE JUST HAPPENED TO HAVE A RESERVATION TO A REALLY NICE FRENCH RESTAURANT, AND ONE OF OUR FRIENDS SAID SHE COULDN'T COME...
SORRY, LADIES, SORRY! I CAN'T. I DON'T HAVE ANY MONEY RIGHT NOW.
OH, DON'T WORRY ABOUT THAT. TODAY IS PAYDAY FOR US. WE'LL COVER YOU!
I KNEW IT.
HMMM... MAYBE IF I SELL ANOTHER TWENTY VOLUMES TODAY I MIGHT THINK ABOUT GOING.
AWWW! HOW MANY MANGA ARE YOU GOING TO MAKE US BUY?
HE'S POPULAR.
WHAT DID HE GIVE ME HIS CARD FOR ANYWAY? I GOT ONE FROM HIM THE OTHER DAY.
FWIP

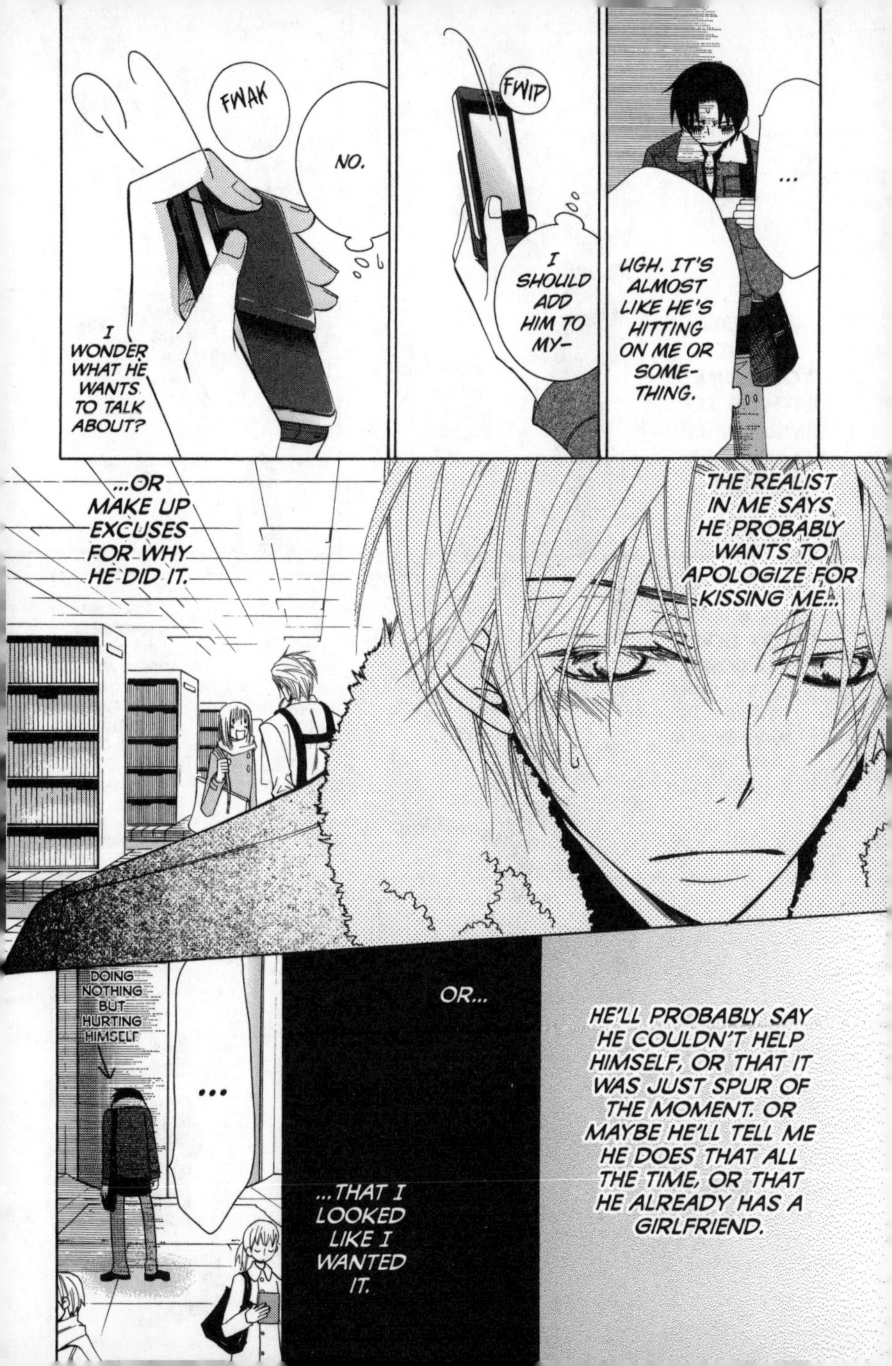
...
UGH. IT'S ALMOST LIKE HE'S HITTING ON ME OR SOMETHING.
FWIP
I SHOULD ADD HIM TO MY-
FWAK
NO.
I WONDER WHAT HE WANTS TO TALK ABOUT?
THE REALIST IN ME SAYS HE PROBABLY WANTS TO APOLOGIZE FOR KISSING ME...
...OR MAKE UP EXCUSES FOR WHY HE DID IT.
HE'LL PROBABLY SAY HE COULDN'T HELP HIMSELF, OR THAT IT WAS JUST SPUR OF THE MOMENT. OR MAYBE HE'LL TELL ME HE DOES THAT ALL THE TIME, OR THAT HE ALREADY HAS A GIRLFRIEND.
OR...
...THAT I LOOKED LIKE I WANTED IT.
...
DOING NOTHING BUT HURTING HIMSELF

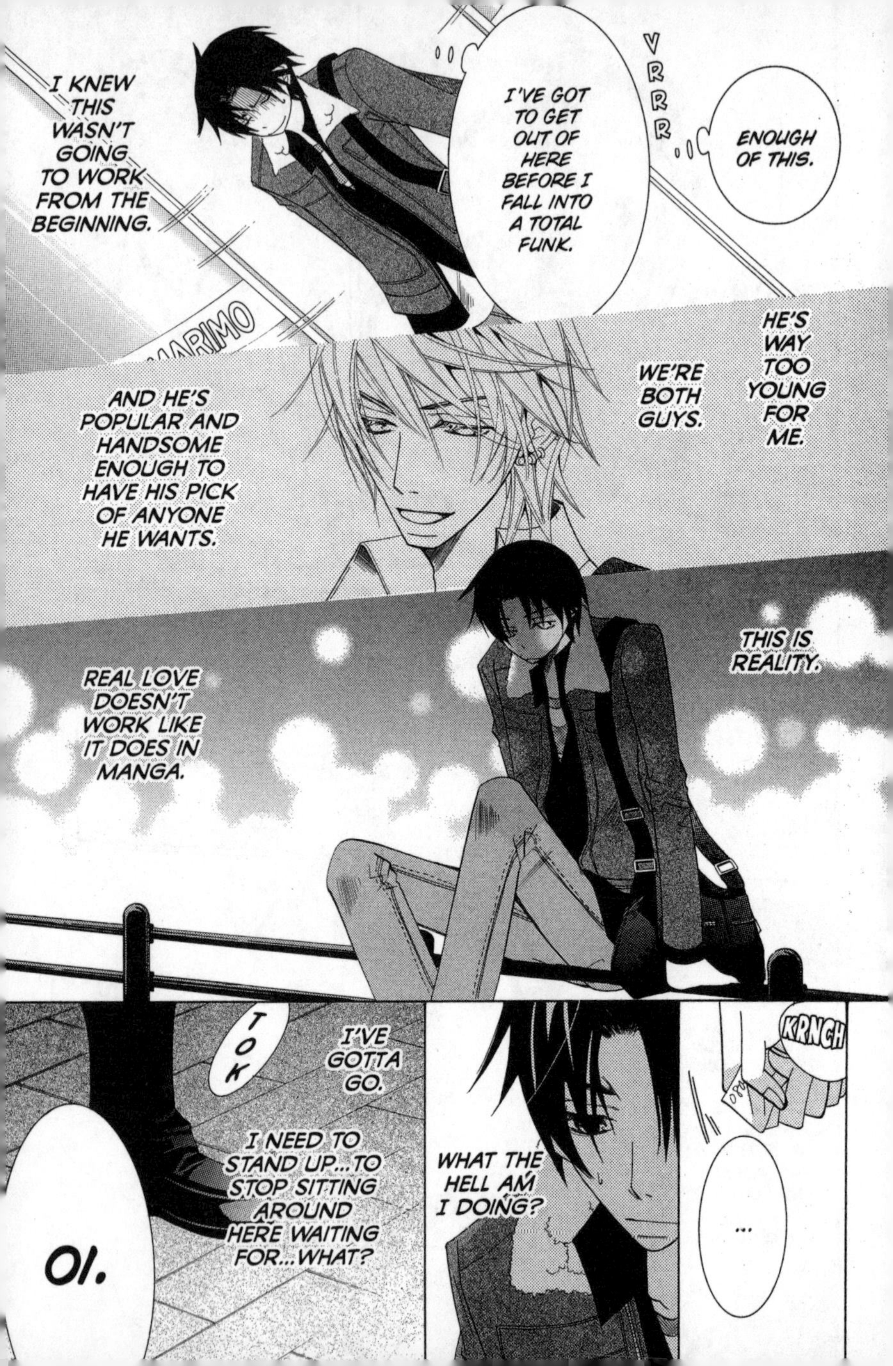

ENOUGH OF THIS.
VRRR
I'VE GOT TO GET OUT OF HERE BEFORE I FALL INTO A TOTAL FUNK.
I KNEW THIS WASN'T GOING TO WORK FROM THE BEGINNING.
HE'S WAY TOO YOUNG FOR ME.
WE'RE BOTH GUYS.
AND HE'S POPULAR AND HANDSOME ENOUGH TO HAVE HIS PICK OF ANYONE HE WANTS.
THIS IS REALITY.
REAL LOVE DOESN'T WORK LIKE IT DOES IN MANGA.
KRNCH
...
WHAT THE HELL AM I DOING?
I'VE GOTTA GO.
TOK
I NEED TO STAND UP...TO STOP SITTING AROUND HERE WAITING FOR...WHAT?
OI.

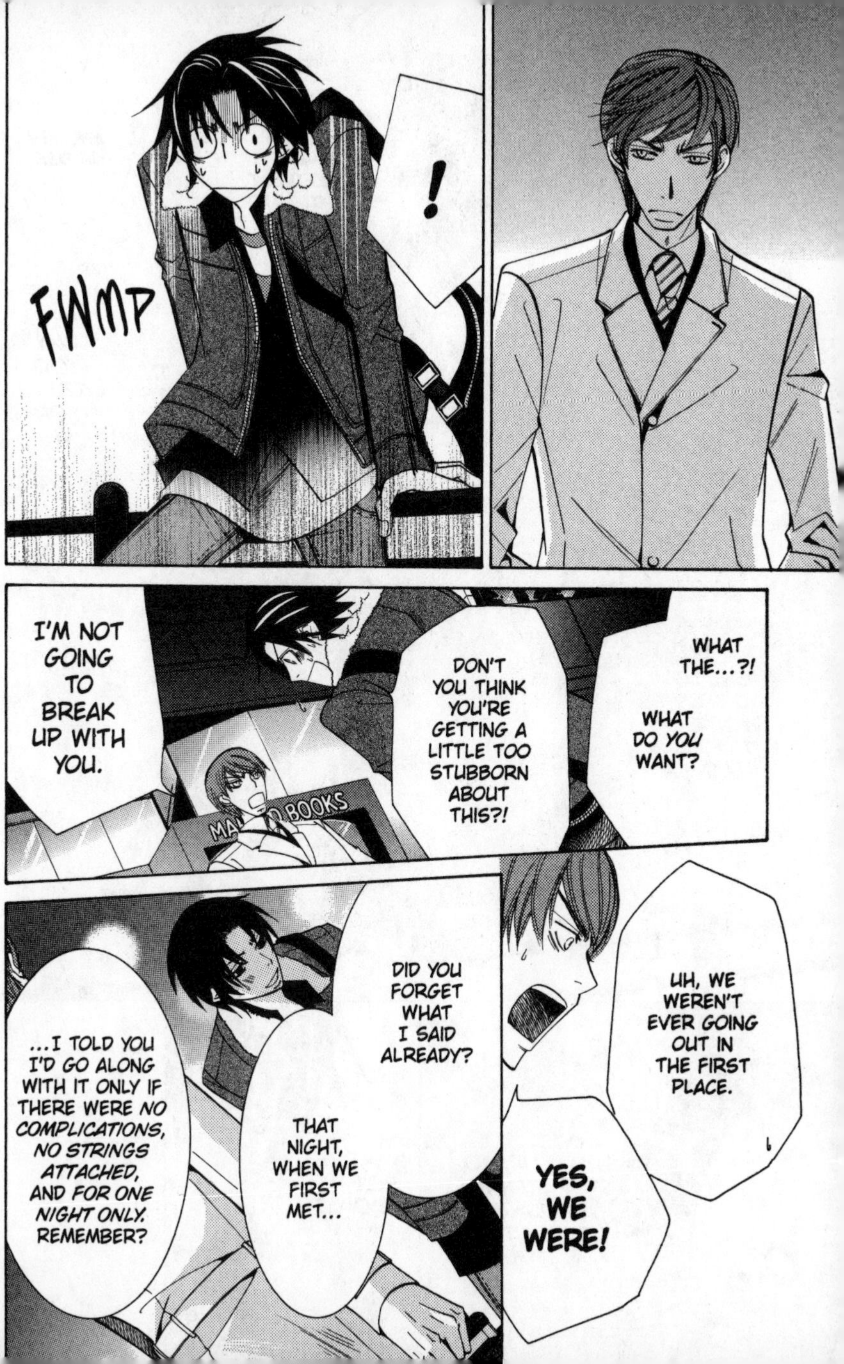
!
FWMP
WHAT THE...?!
WHAT DO *YOU* WANT?
DON'T YOU THINK *YOU'RE* GETTING A LITTLE TOO STUBBORN ABOUT THIS?!
I'M NOT GOING TO BREAK UP WITH YOU.
UH, WE WEREN'T EVER GOING OUT IN THE FIRST PLACE.
YES, WE WERE!
DID YOU FORGET WHAT I SAID ALREADY?
THAT NIGHT, WHEN WE FIRST MET...
...I TOLD YOU I'D GO ALONG WITH IT ONLY IF THERE WERE *NO COMPLICATIONS, NO STRINGS ATTACHED,* AND *FOR ONE NIGHT ONLY.* REMEMBER?

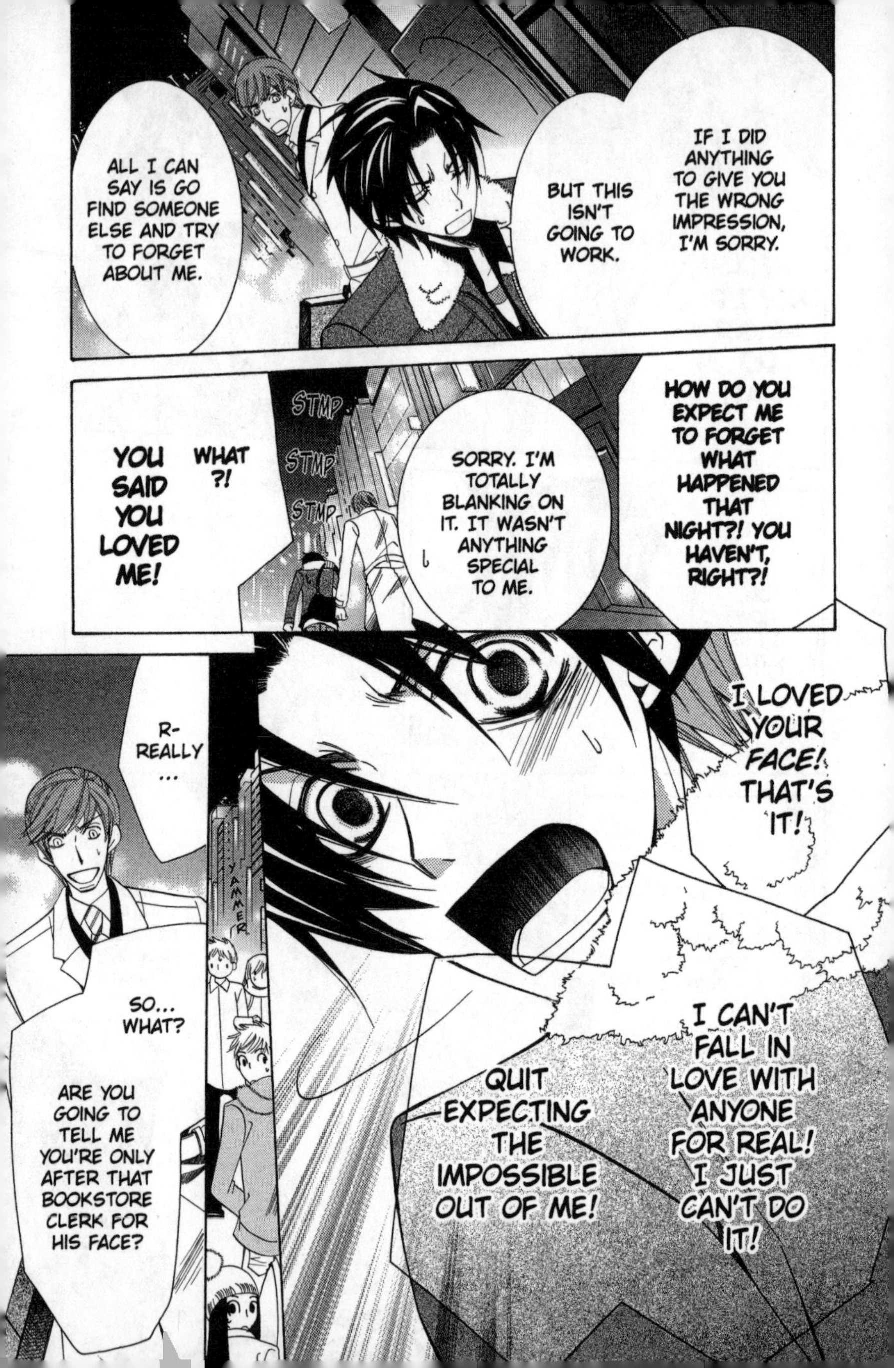
IF I DID ANYTHING TO GIVE YOU THE WRONG IMPRESSION, I'M SORRY.
BUT THIS ISN'T GOING TO WORK.
ALL I CAN SAY IS GO FIND SOMEONE ELSE AND TRY TO FORGET ABOUT ME.
HOW DO YOU EXPECT ME TO FORGET WHAT HAPPENED THAT NIGHT?! YOU HAVEN'T, RIGHT?!
STMP
STMP
STMP
SORRY. I'M TOTALLY BLANKING ON IT. IT WASN'T ANYTHING SPECIAL TO ME.
WHAT?!
YOU SAID YOU LOVED ME!
I LOVED YOUR FACE! THAT'S IT!
I CAN'T FALL IN LOVE WITH ANYONE FOR REAL! I JUST CAN'T DO IT!
QUIT EXPECTING THE IMPOSSIBLE OUT OF ME!
YAMMER
R-REALLY...
SO... WHAT?
ARE YOU GOING TO TELL ME YOU'RE ONLY AFTER THAT BOOKSTORE CLERK FOR HIS FACE?

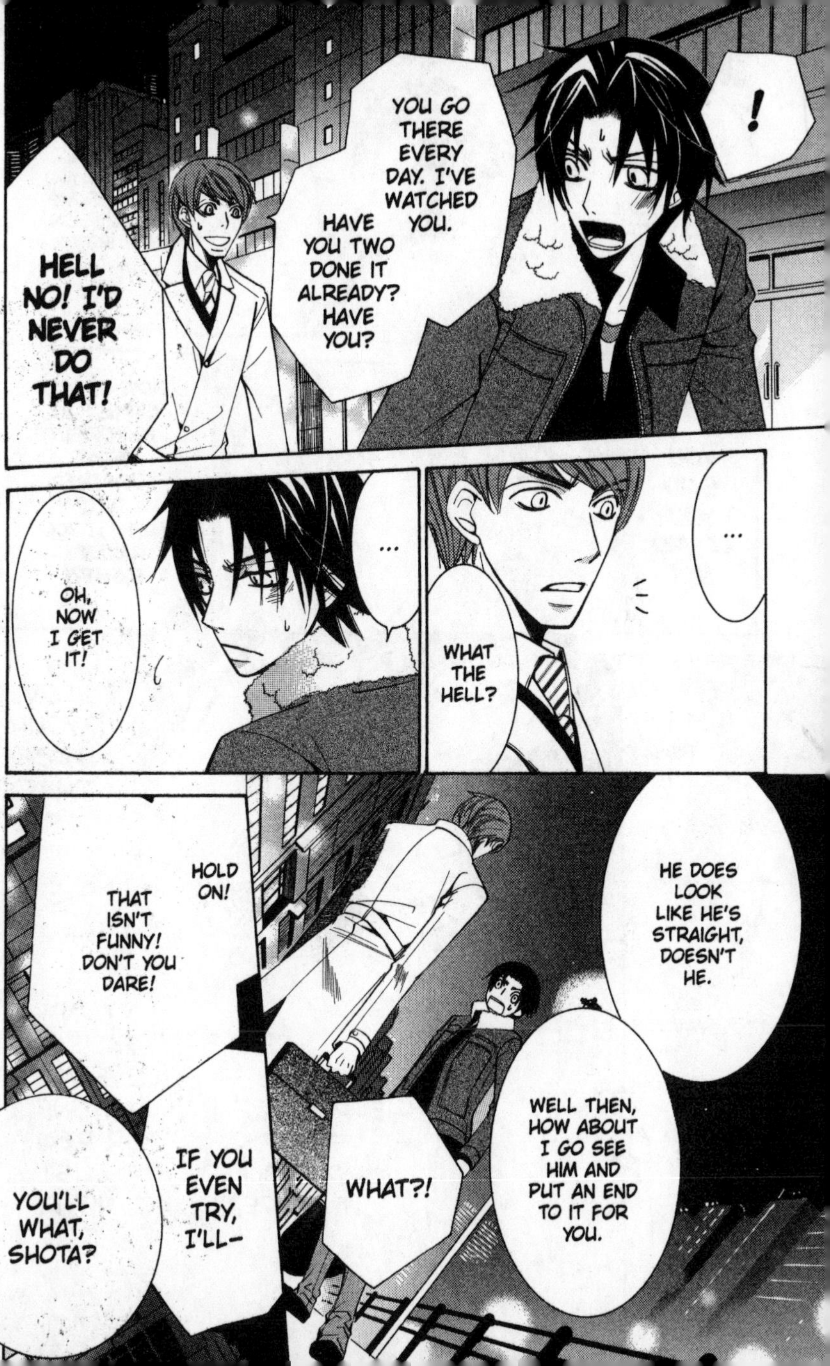
!
YOU GO THERE EVERY DAY. I'VE WATCHED YOU.
HAVE YOU TWO DONE IT ALREADY? HAVE YOU?
HELL NO! I'D NEVER DO THAT!
...
WHAT THE HELL?
...
OH, NOW I GET IT!
HE DOES LOOK LIKE HE'S STRAIGHT, DOESN'T HE.
HOLD ON!
THAT ISN'T FUNNY! DON'T YOU DARE!
WELL THEN, HOW ABOUT I GO SEE HIM AND PUT AN END TO IT FOR YOU.
WHAT?!
IF YOU EVEN TRY, I'LL-
YOU'LL WHAT, SHOTA?

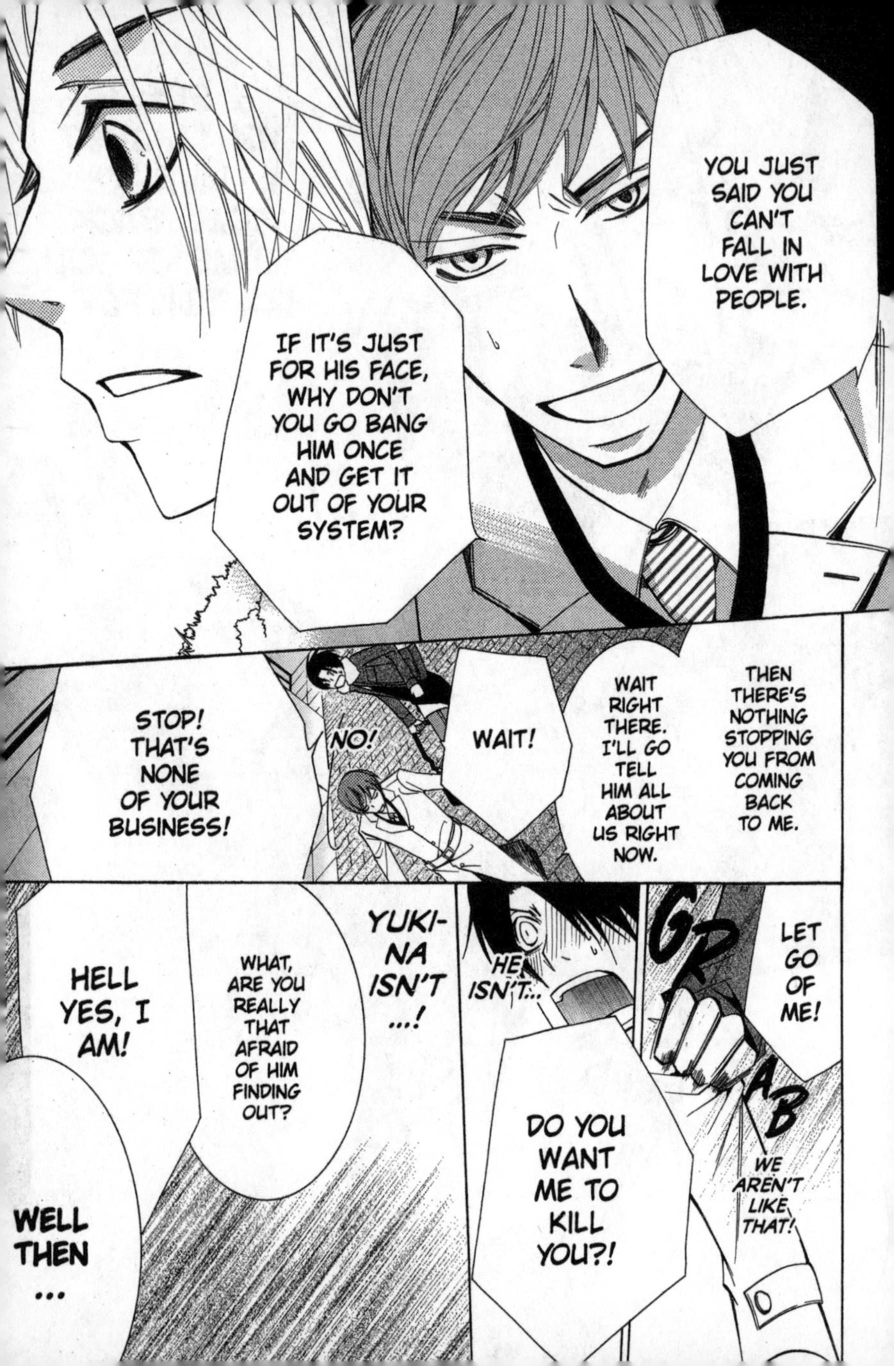
YOU JUST SAID YOU CAN'T FALL IN LOVE WITH PEOPLE.
IF IT'S JUST FOR HIS FACE, WHY DON'T YOU GO BANG HIM ONCE AND GET IT OUT OF YOUR SYSTEM?
THEN THERE'S NOTHING STOPPING YOU FROM COMING BACK TO ME.
WAIT RIGHT THERE. I'LL GO TELL HIM ALL ABOUT US RIGHT NOW.
WAIT!
NO!
STOP! THAT'S NONE OF YOUR BUSINESS!
LET GO OF ME!
GRAB
WE AREN'T LIKE THAT!
HE ISN'T...
DO YOU WANT ME TO KILL YOU?!
YUKI-NA ISN'T ...!
WHAT, ARE YOU REALLY THAT AFRAID OF HIM FINDING OUT?
HELL YES, I AM!
WELL THEN ...

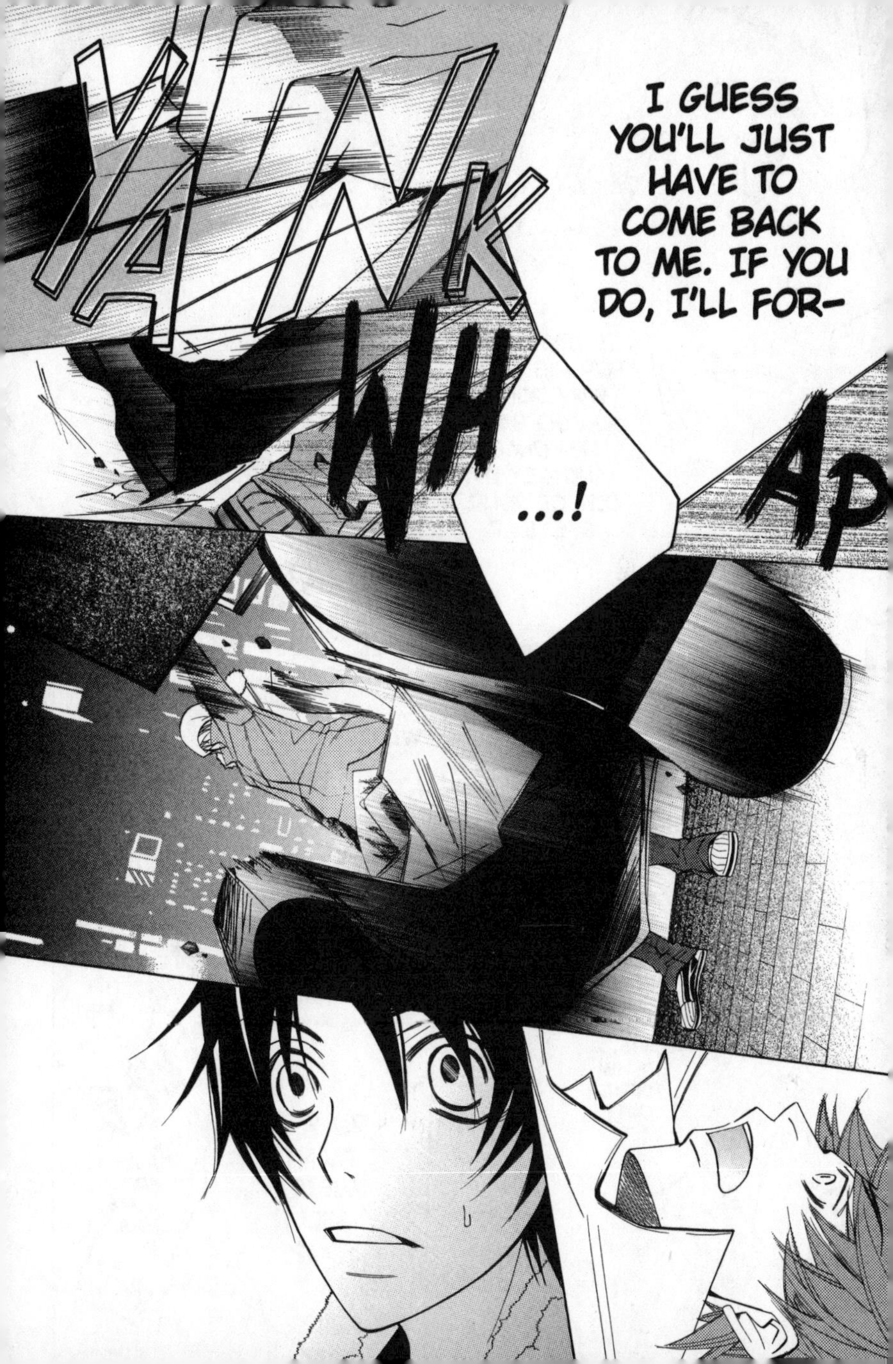
I GUESS YOU'LL JUST HAVE TO COME BACK TO ME. IF YOU DO, I'LL FOR-
YANK
WHAP
...!

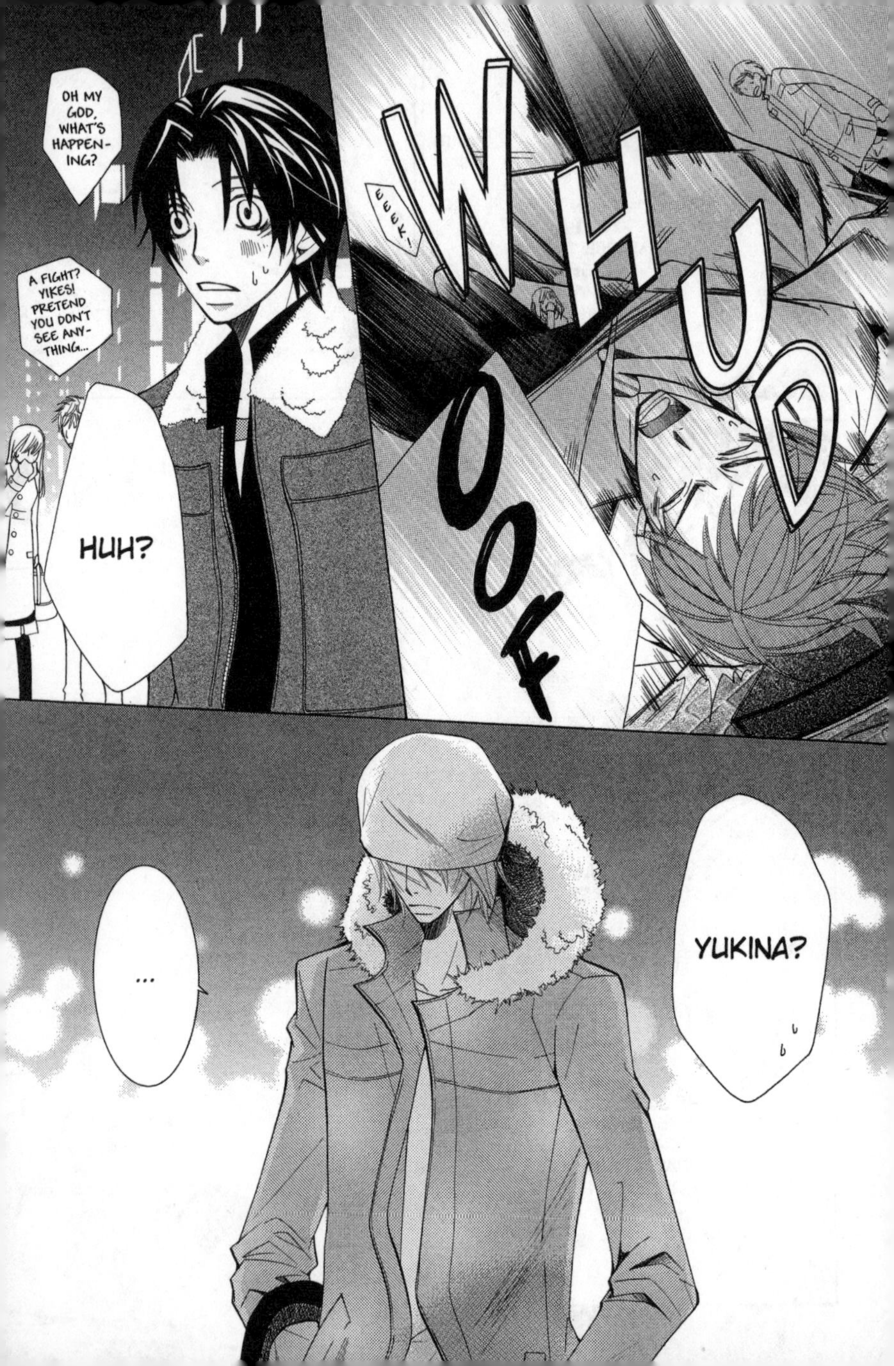
EEEK!
WHUD
OOF
OH MY GOD, WHAT'S HAPPEN-ING?
A FIGHT? YIKES! PRETEND YOU DON'T SEE ANY-THING...
HUH?
YUKINA?
...

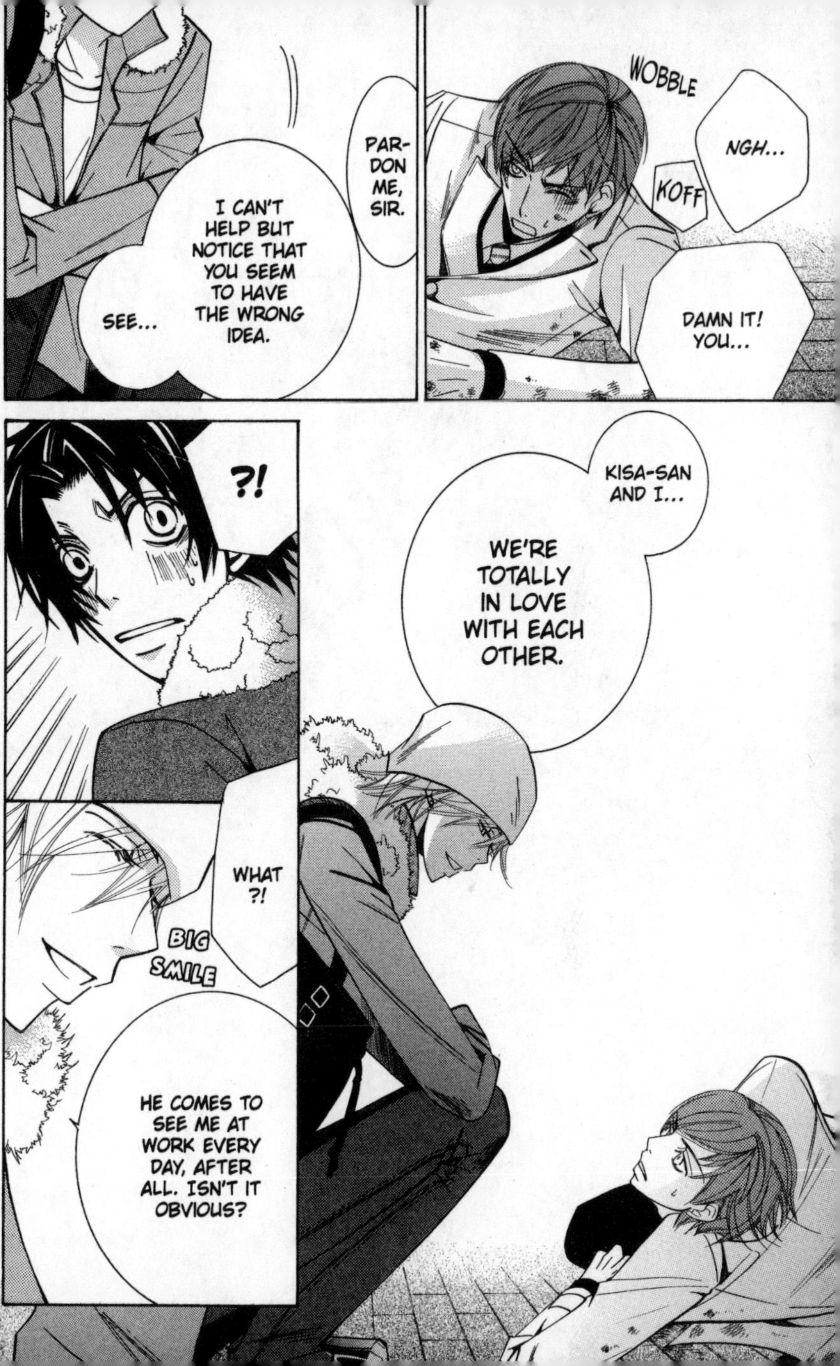
WOBBLE
NGH...
KOFF
DAMN IT! YOU...
PAR-DON ME, SIR.
I CAN'T HELP BUT NOTICE THAT YOU SEEM TO HAVE THE WRONG IDEA.
SEE...
KISA-SAN AND I...
WE'RE TOTALLY IN LOVE WITH EACH OTHER.
?!
WHAT ?!
BIG SMILE
HE COMES TO SEE ME AT WORK EVERY DAY, AFTER ALL. ISN'T IT OBVIOUS?

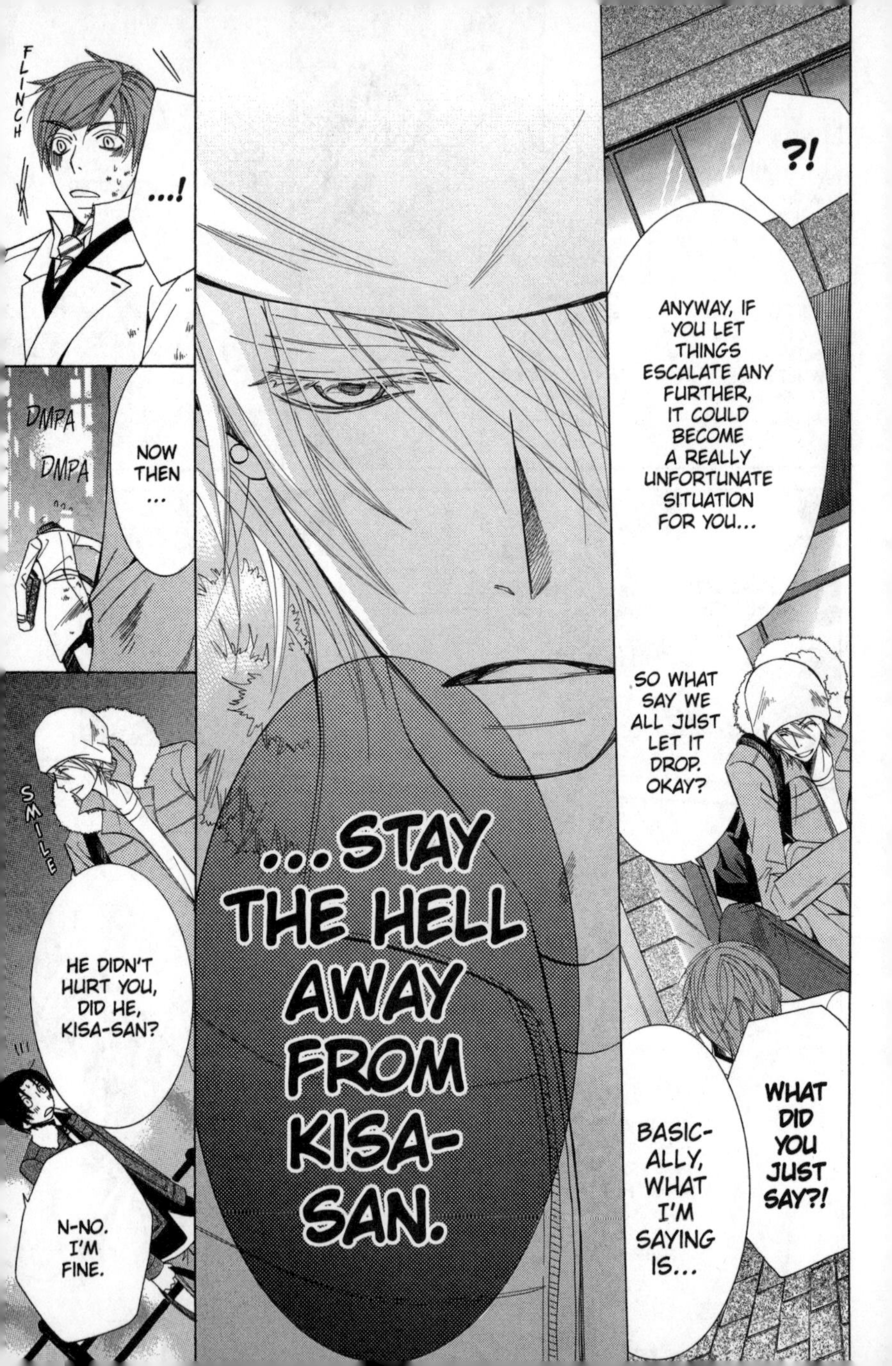
?!
ANYWAY, IF YOU LET THINGS ESCALATE ANY FURTHER, IT COULD BECOME A REALLY UNFORTUNATE SITUATION FOR YOU...
SO WHAT SAY WE ALL JUST LET IT DROP. OKAY?
WHAT DID YOU JUST SAY?!
BASIC-ALLY, WHAT I'M SAYING IS...
...STAY THE HELL AWAY FROM KISA-SAN.
FLINCH
...!
NOW THEN...
DMPA
DMPA
SMILE
HE DIDN'T HURT YOU, DID HE, KISA-SAN?
N-NO. I'M FINE.

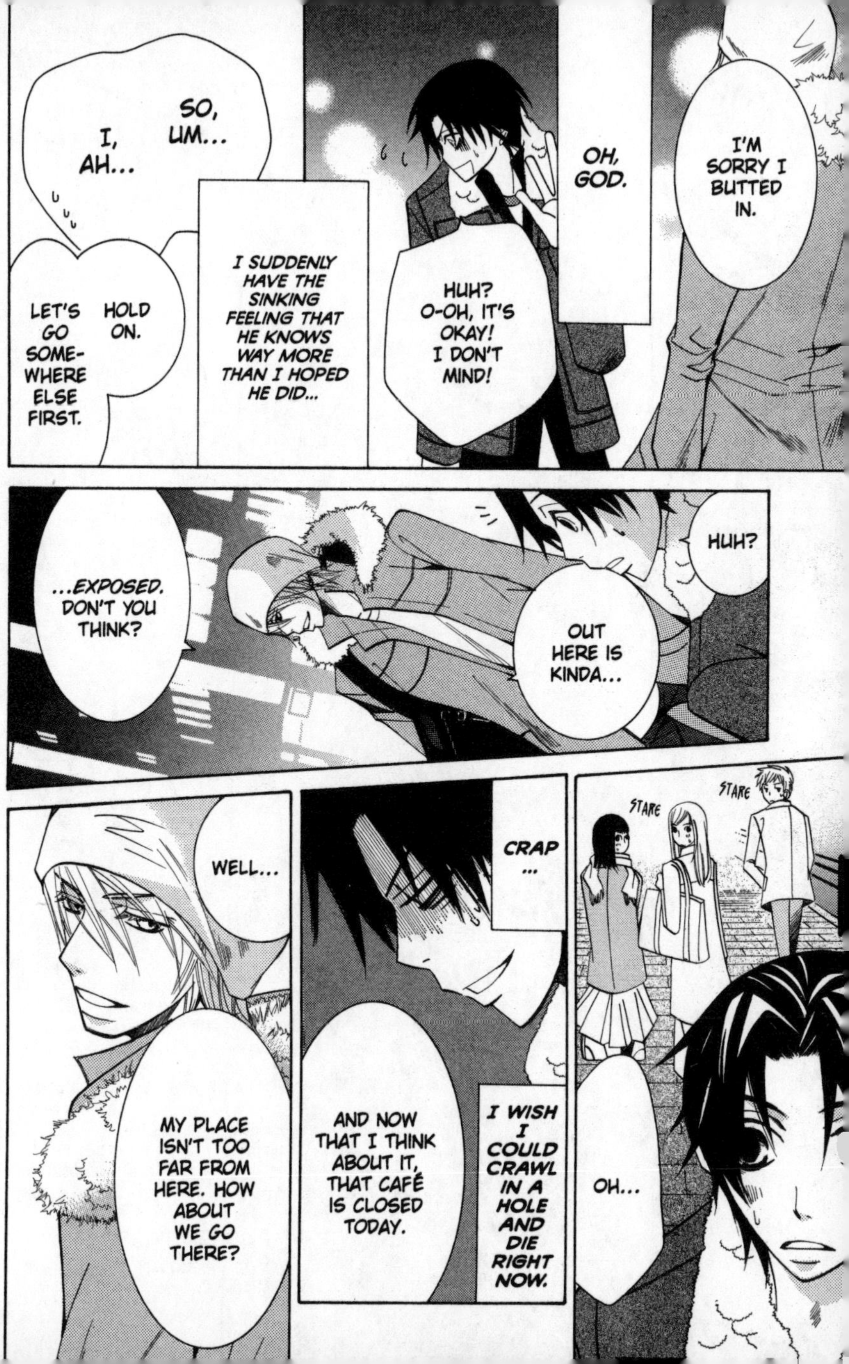
I'M SORRY I BUTTED IN.
OH, GOD.
HUH? O-OH, IT'S OKAY! I DON'T MIND!
I SUDDENLY HAVE THE SINKING FEELING THAT HE KNOWS WAY MORE THAN I HOPED HE DID...
SO, UM...
I, AH...
HOLD ON.
LET'S GO SOMEWHERE ELSE FIRST.
HUH?
OUT HERE IS KINDA...
...EXPOSED. DON'T YOU THINK?
STARE
STARE
OH...
CRAP...
I WISH I COULD CRAWL IN A HOLE AND DIE RIGHT NOW.
AND NOW THAT I THINK ABOUT IT, THAT CAFÉ IS CLOSED TODAY.
WELL...
MY PLACE ISN'T TOO FAR FROM HERE. HOW ABOUT WE GO THERE?

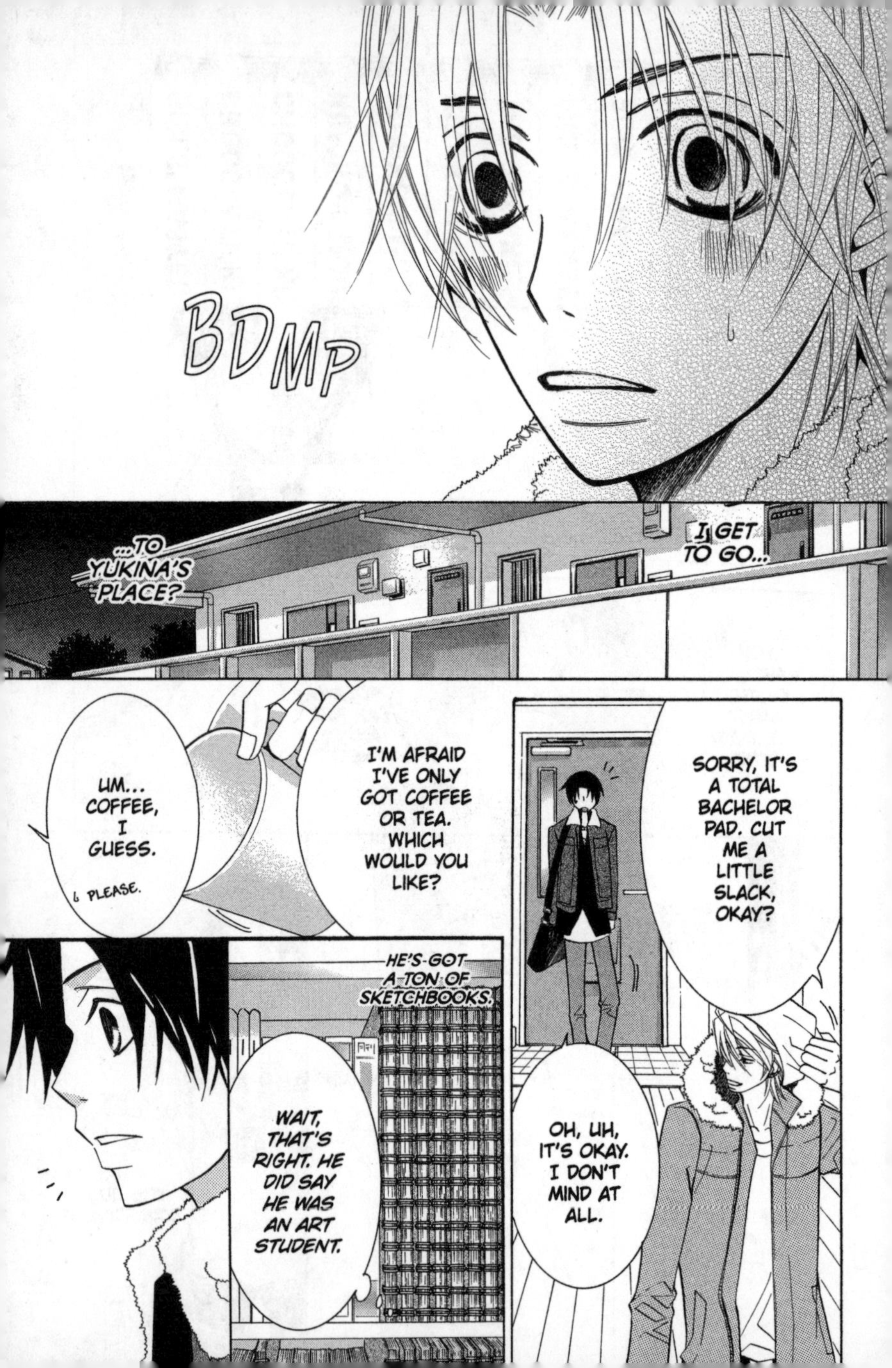
BDMP
I GET TO GO...
...TO YUKINA'S PLACE?
SORRY, IT'S A TOTAL BACHELOR PAD. CUT ME A LITTLE SLACK, OKAY?
OH, UH, IT'S OKAY. I DON'T MIND AT ALL.
I'M AFRAID I'VE ONLY GOT COFFEE OR TEA. WHICH WOULD YOU LIKE?
UM... COFFEE, I GUESS.
PLEASE.
HE'S GOT A TON OF SKETCHBOOKS.
WAIT, THAT'S RIGHT. HE DID SAY HE WAS AN ART STUDENT.

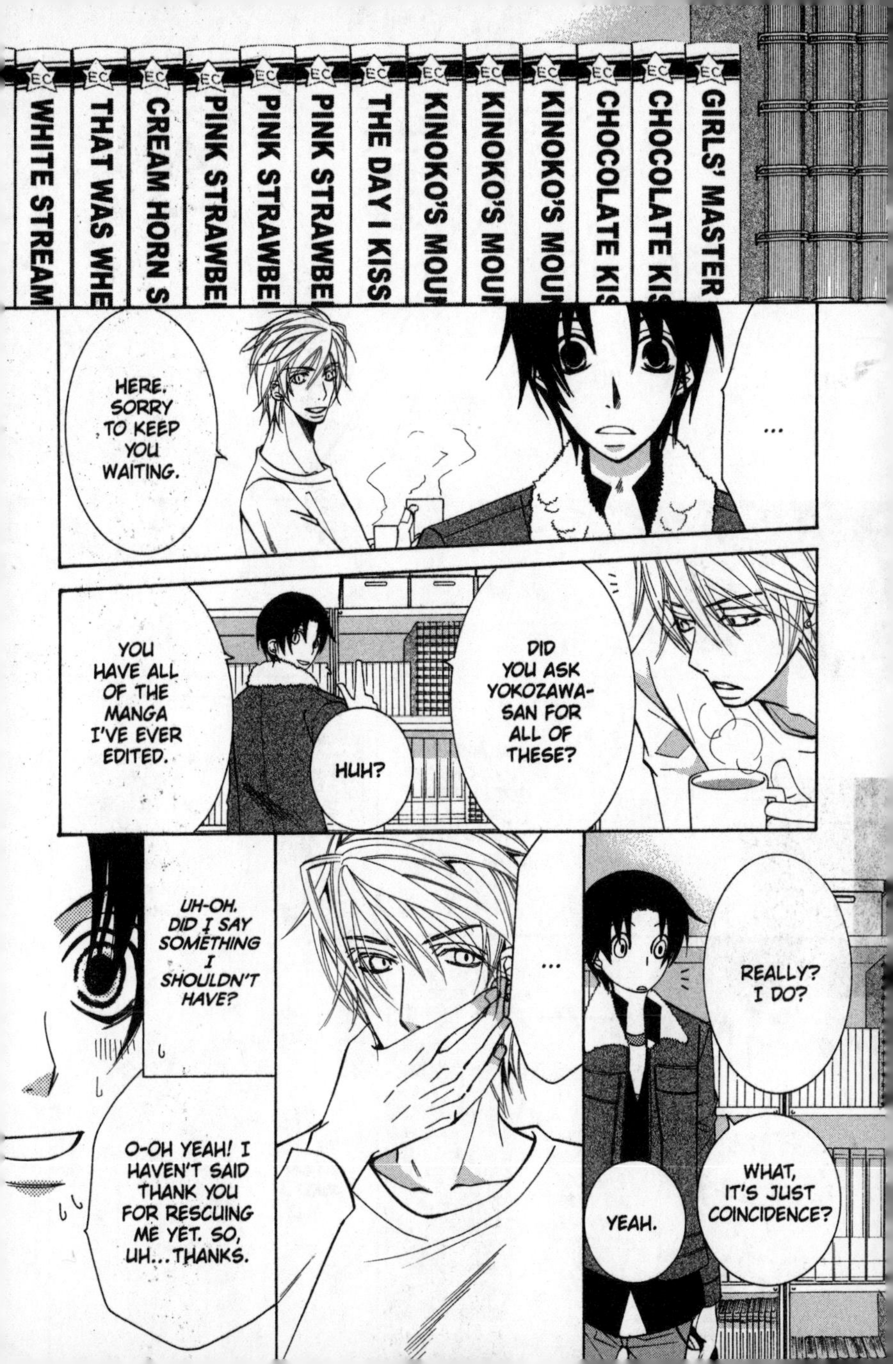
GIRLS' MASTER
CHOCOLATE KIS
CHOCOLATE KIS
KINOKO'S MOUN
KINOKO'S MOUN
KINOKO'S MOUN
THE DAY I KISS
PINK STRAWBE
PINK STRAWBE
PINK STRAWBE
CREAM HORN S
THAT WAS WHE
WHITE STREAM
...
HERE. SORRY TO KEEP YOU WAITING.
DID YOU ASK YOKOZAWA-SAN FOR ALL OF THESE?
HUH?
YOU HAVE ALL OF THE MANGA I'VE EVER EDITED.
REALLY? I DO?
WHAT, IT'S JUST COINCIDENCE?
YEAH.
...
UH-OH. DID I SAY SOMETHING I SHOULDN'T HAVE?
O-OH YEAH! I HAVEN'T SAID THANK YOU FOR RESCUING ME YET. SO, UH...THANKS.

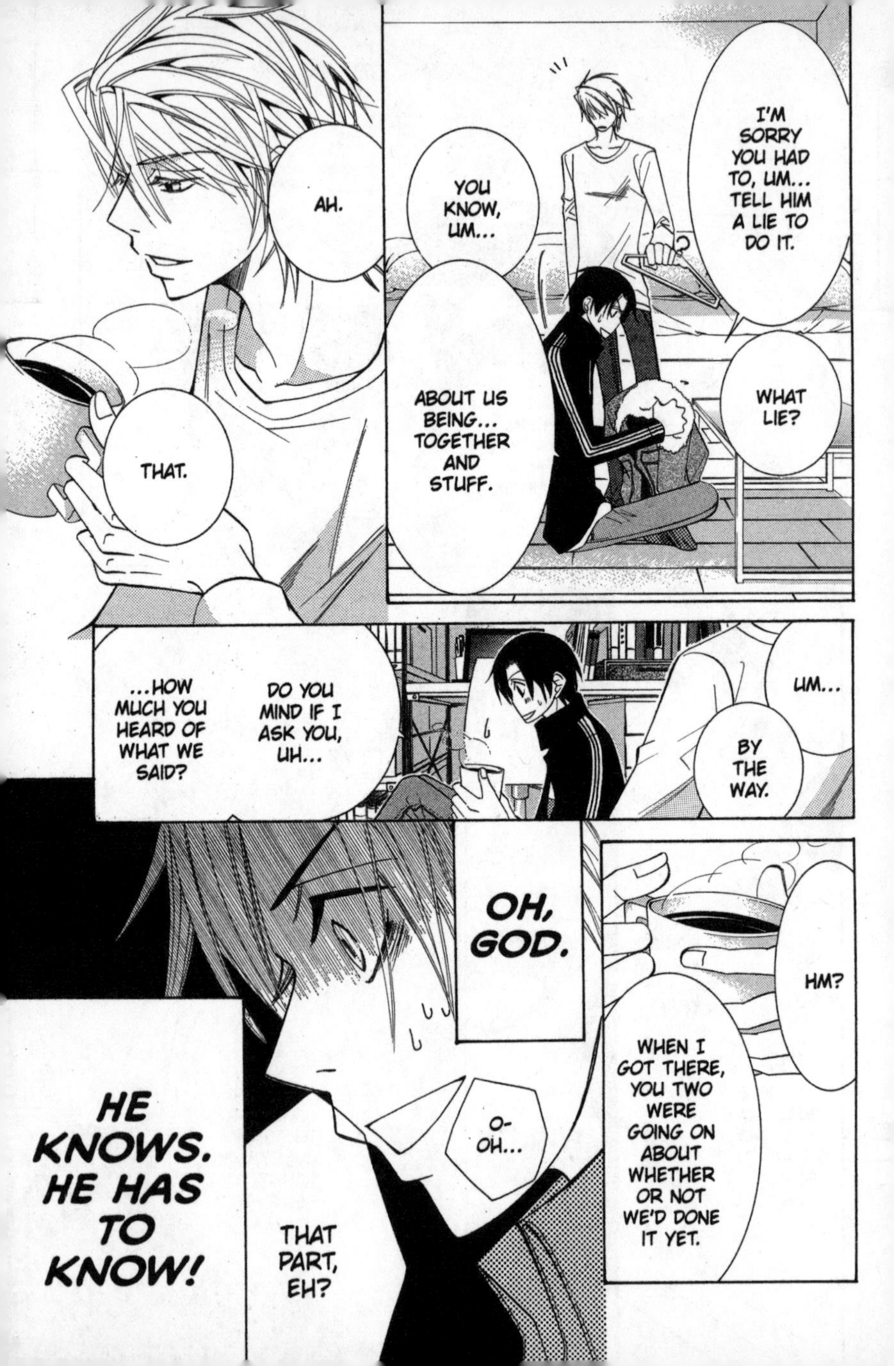
I'M SORRY YOU HAD TO, UM... TELL HIM A LIE TO DO IT.
WHAT LIE?
YOU KNOW, UM...
ABOUT US BEING... TOGETHER AND STUFF.
AH.
THAT.
UM...
BY THE WAY.
DO YOU MIND IF I ASK YOU, UH...
...HOW MUCH YOU HEARD OF WHAT WE SAID?
HM?
WHEN I GOT THERE, YOU TWO WERE GOING ON ABOUT WHETHER OR NOT WE'D DONE IT YET.
OH, GOD.
O-OH...
THAT PART, EH?
HE KNOWS. HE HAS TO KNOW!

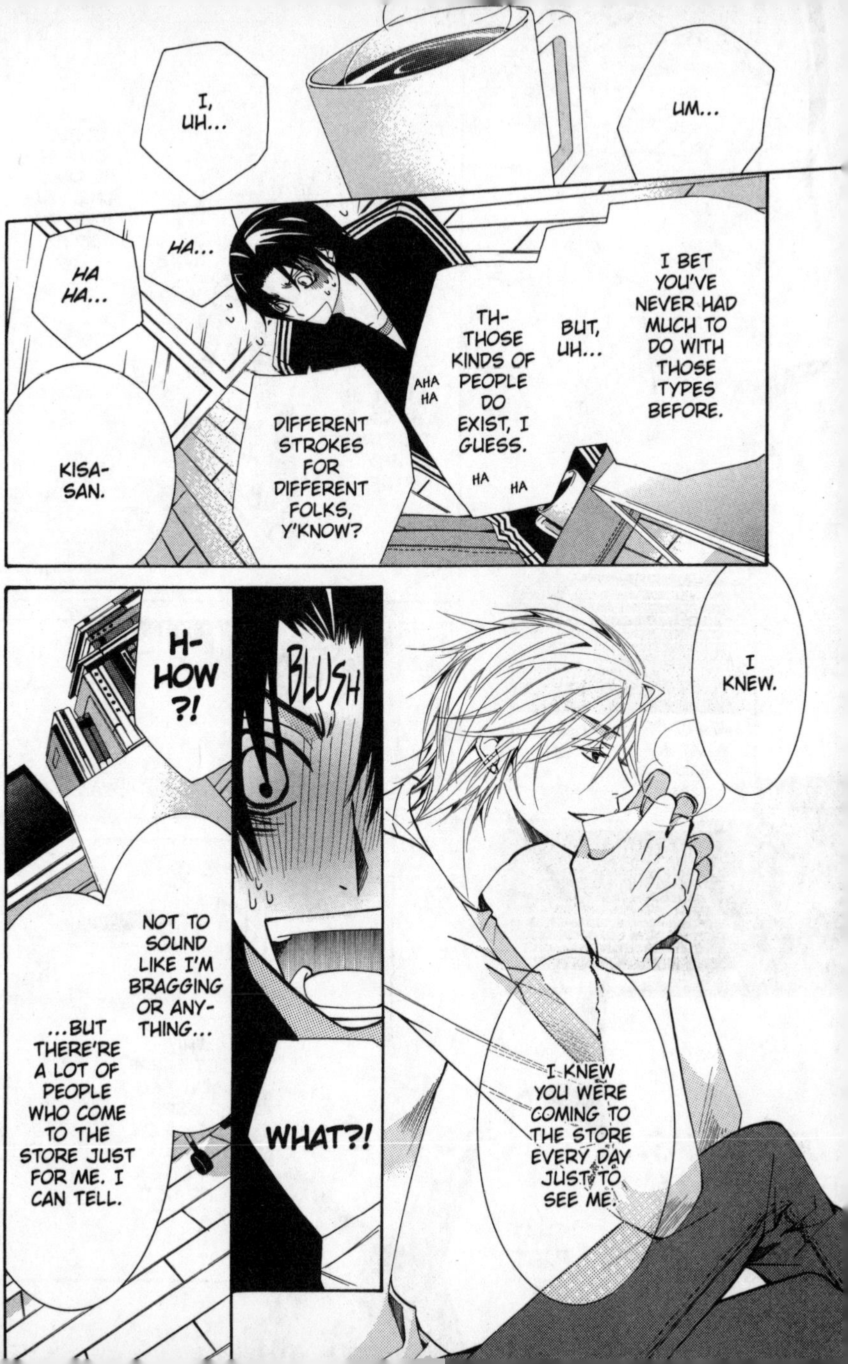
UM...
I, UH...
I BET YOU'VE NEVER HAD MUCH TO DO WITH THOSE TYPES BEFORE.
BUT, UH...
TH-THOSE KINDS OF PEOPLE DO EXIST, I GUESS.
AHA HA
HA
HA
DIFFERENT STROKES FOR DIFFERENT FOLKS, Y'KNOW?
HA...
HA HA...
KISA-SAN.
I KNEW.
I KNEW YOU WERE COMING TO THE STORE EVERY DAY JUST TO SEE ME.
BLUSH
H-HOW?!
WHAT?!
NOT TO SOUND LIKE I'M BRAGGING OR ANYTHING...
...BUT THERE'RE A LOT OF PEOPLE WHO COME TO THE STORE JUST FOR ME. I CAN TELL.

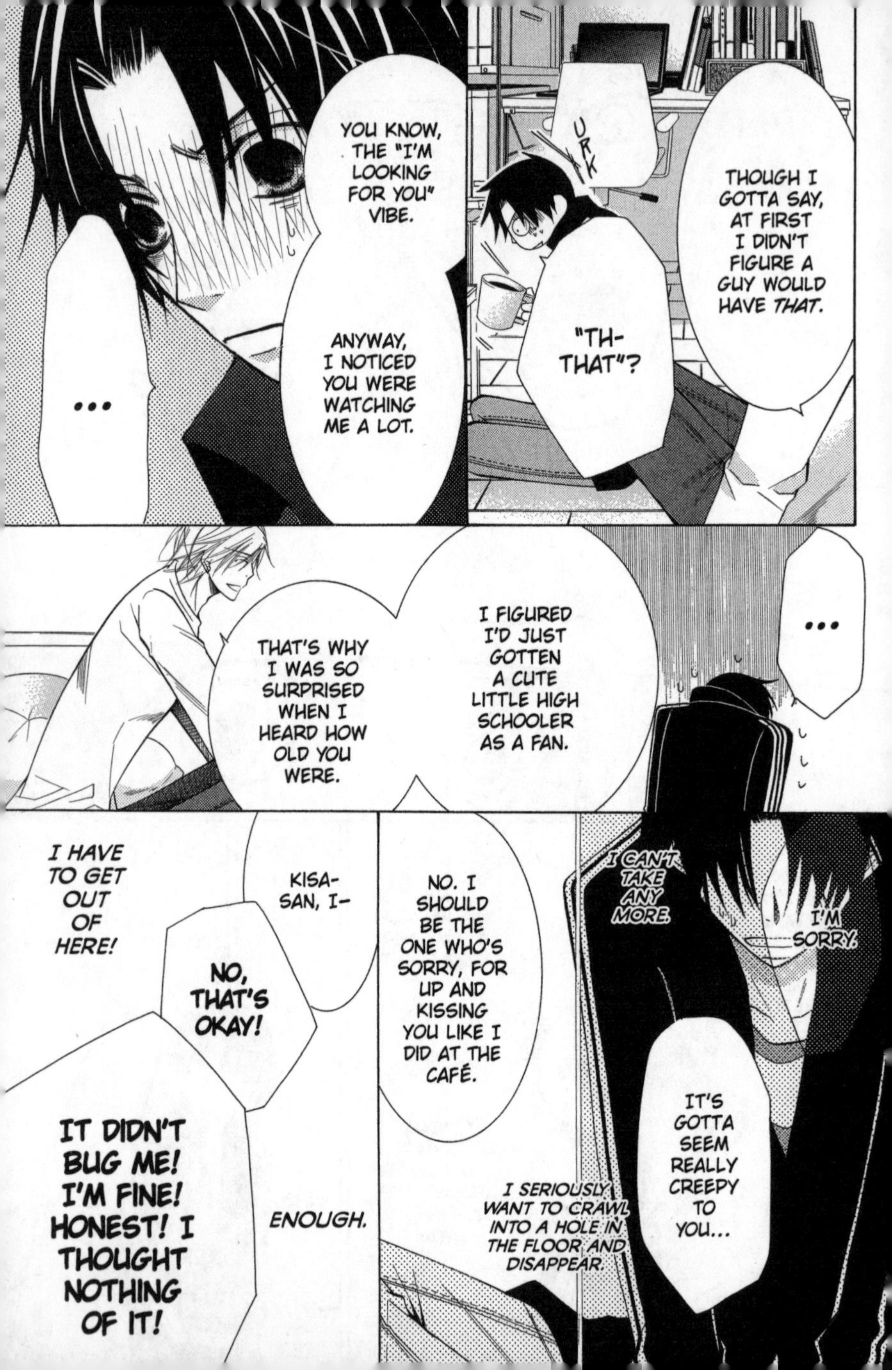
THOUGH I GOTTA SAY, AT FIRST I DIDN'T FIGURE A GUY WOULD HAVE *THAT*.
URK
"TH- THAT"?
YOU KNOW, THE "I'M LOOKING FOR YOU" VIBE.
ANYWAY, I NOTICED YOU WERE WATCHING ME A LOT.
...
...
I FIGURED I'D JUST GOTTEN A CUTE LITTLE HIGH SCHOOLER AS A FAN.
THAT'S WHY I WAS SO SURPRISED WHEN I HEARD HOW OLD YOU WERE.
I'M SORRY.
I CAN'T TAKE ANY MORE.
IT'S GOTTA SEEM REALLY CREEPY TO YOU...
I SERIOUSLY WANT TO CRAWL INTO A HOLE IN THE FLOOR AND DISAPPEAR.
NO. I SHOULD BE THE ONE WHO'S SORRY, FOR UP AND KISSING YOU LIKE I DID AT THE CAFÉ.
KISA-SAN, I-
ENOUGH.
I HAVE TO GET OUT OF HERE!
NO, THAT'S OKAY!
IT DIDN'T BUG ME! I'M FINE! HONEST! I THOUGHT NOTHING OF IT!

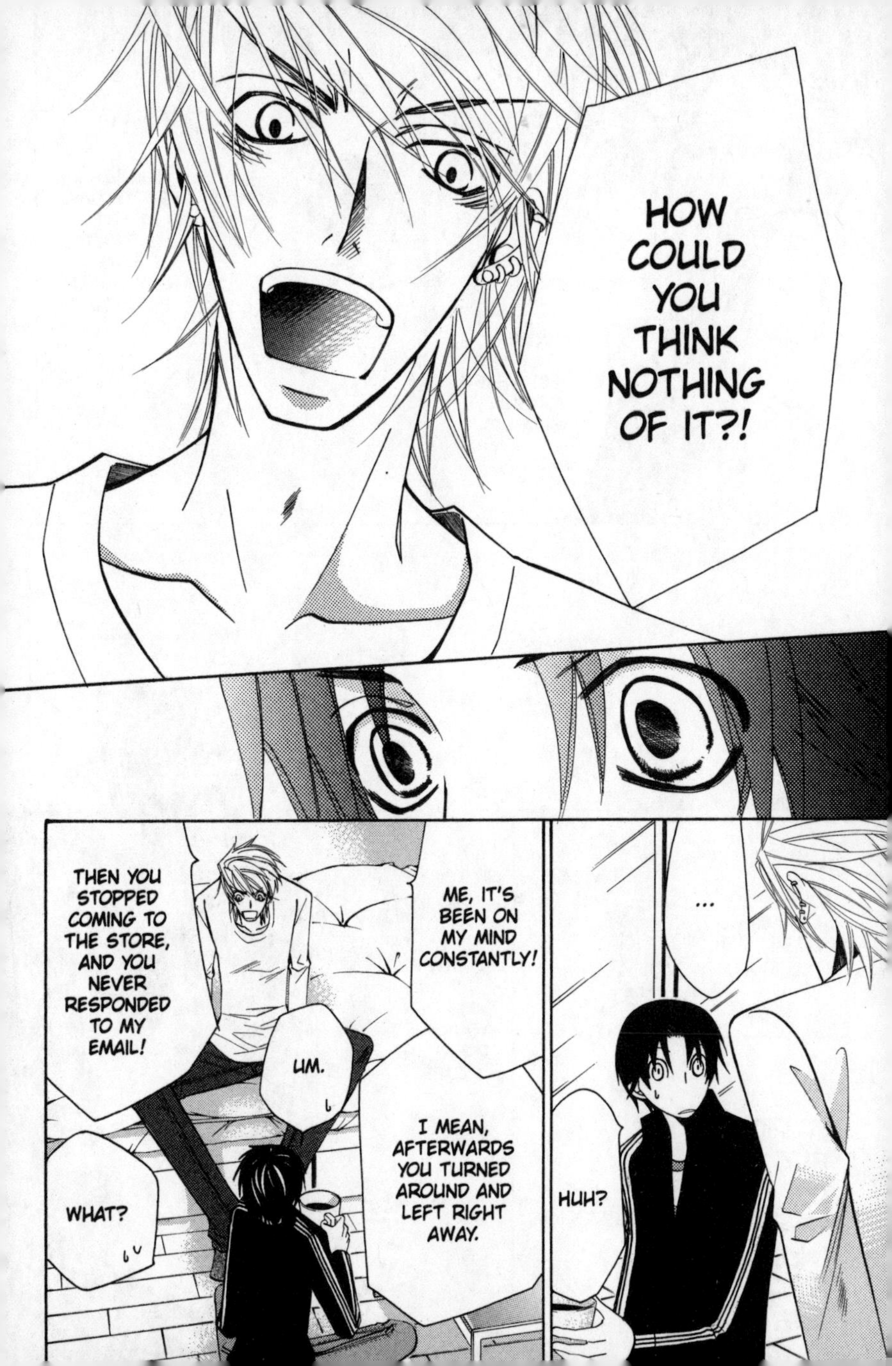
HOW COULD YOU THINK NOTHING OF IT?!
...
HUH?
ME, IT'S BEEN ON MY MIND CONSTANTLY!
THEN YOU STOPPED COMING TO THE STORE, AND YOU NEVER RESPONDED TO MY EMAIL!
UM.
I MEAN, AFTERWARDS YOU TURNED AROUND AND LEFT RIGHT AWAY.
WHAT?

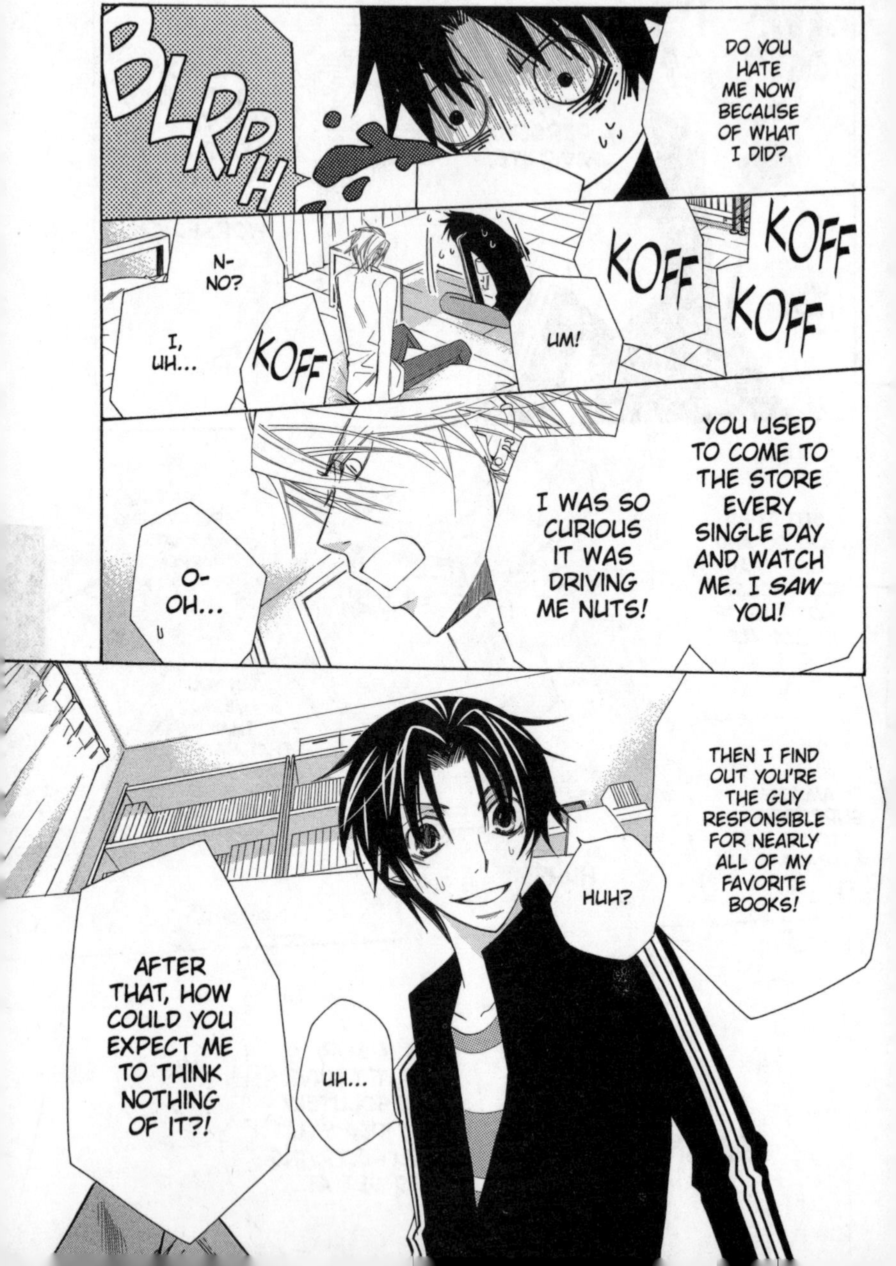
DO YOU HATE ME NOW BECAUSE OF WHAT I DID?
BLRPH
KOFF
KOFF
KOFF
UM!
KOFF
N-NO?
I, UH...
YOU USED TO COME TO THE STORE EVERY SINGLE DAY AND WATCH ME. I *SAW* YOU!
I WAS SO CURIOUS IT WAS DRIVING ME NUTS!
O-OH...
THEN I FIND OUT YOU'RE THE GUY RESPONSIBLE FOR NEARLY ALL OF MY FAVORITE BOOKS!
HUH?
AFTER THAT, HOW COULD YOU EXPECT ME TO THINK NOTHING OF IT?!
UH...

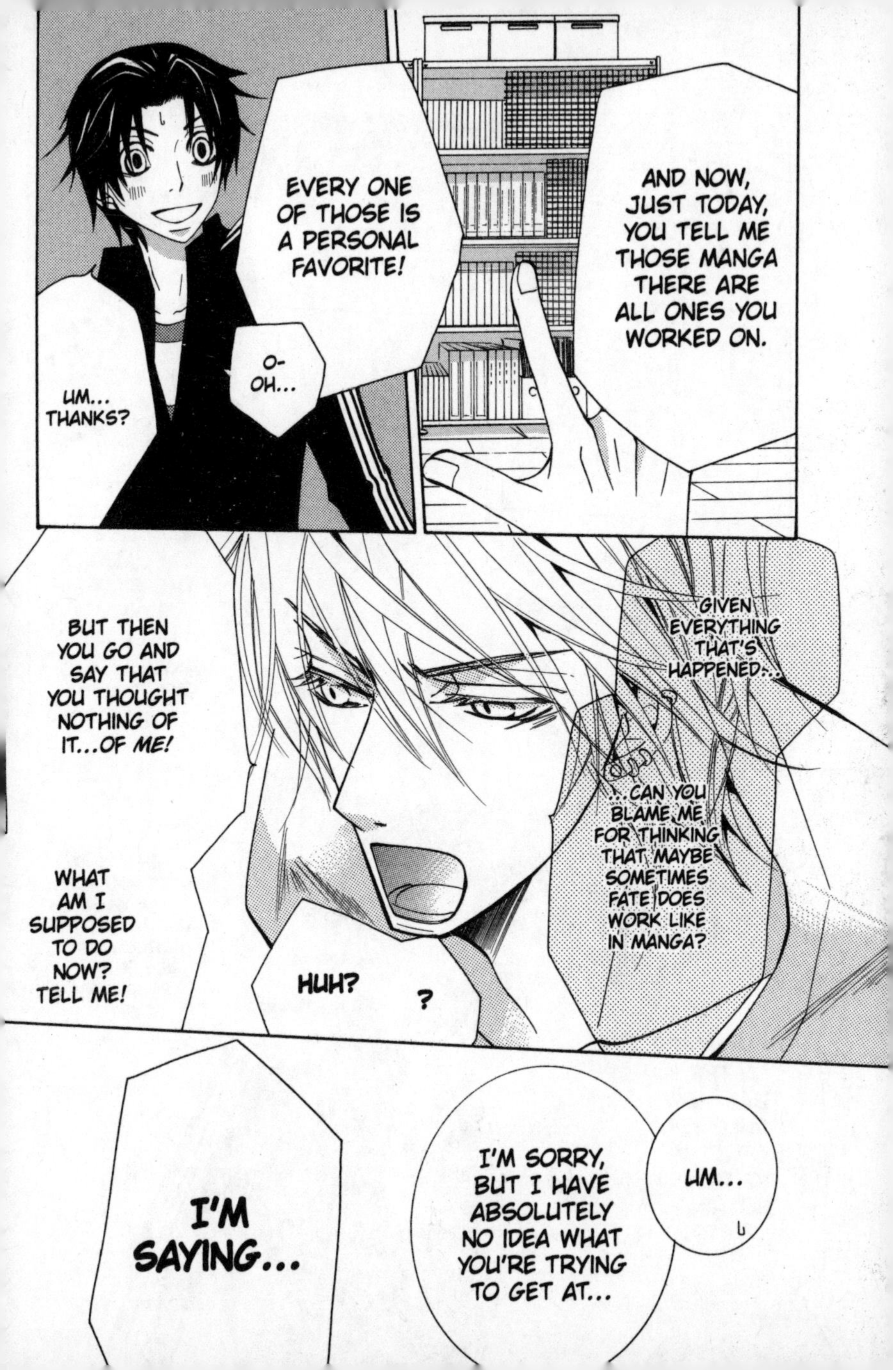
AND NOW, JUST TODAY, YOU TELL ME THOSE MANGA THERE ARE ALL ONES YOU WORKED ON.
EVERY ONE OF THOSE IS A PERSONAL FAVORITE!
O-OH...
UM... THANKS?
GIVEN EVERYTHING THAT'S HAPPENED...
...CAN YOU BLAME ME FOR THINKING THAT MAYBE SOMETIMES FATE DOES WORK LIKE IN MANGA?
BUT THEN YOU GO AND SAY THAT YOU THOUGHT NOTHING OF IT...OF ME!
WHAT AM I SUPPOSED TO DO NOW? TELL ME!
HUH?
?
UM...
I'M SORRY, BUT I HAVE ABSOLUTELY NO IDEA WHAT YOU'RE TRYING TO GET AT...
I'M SAYING...

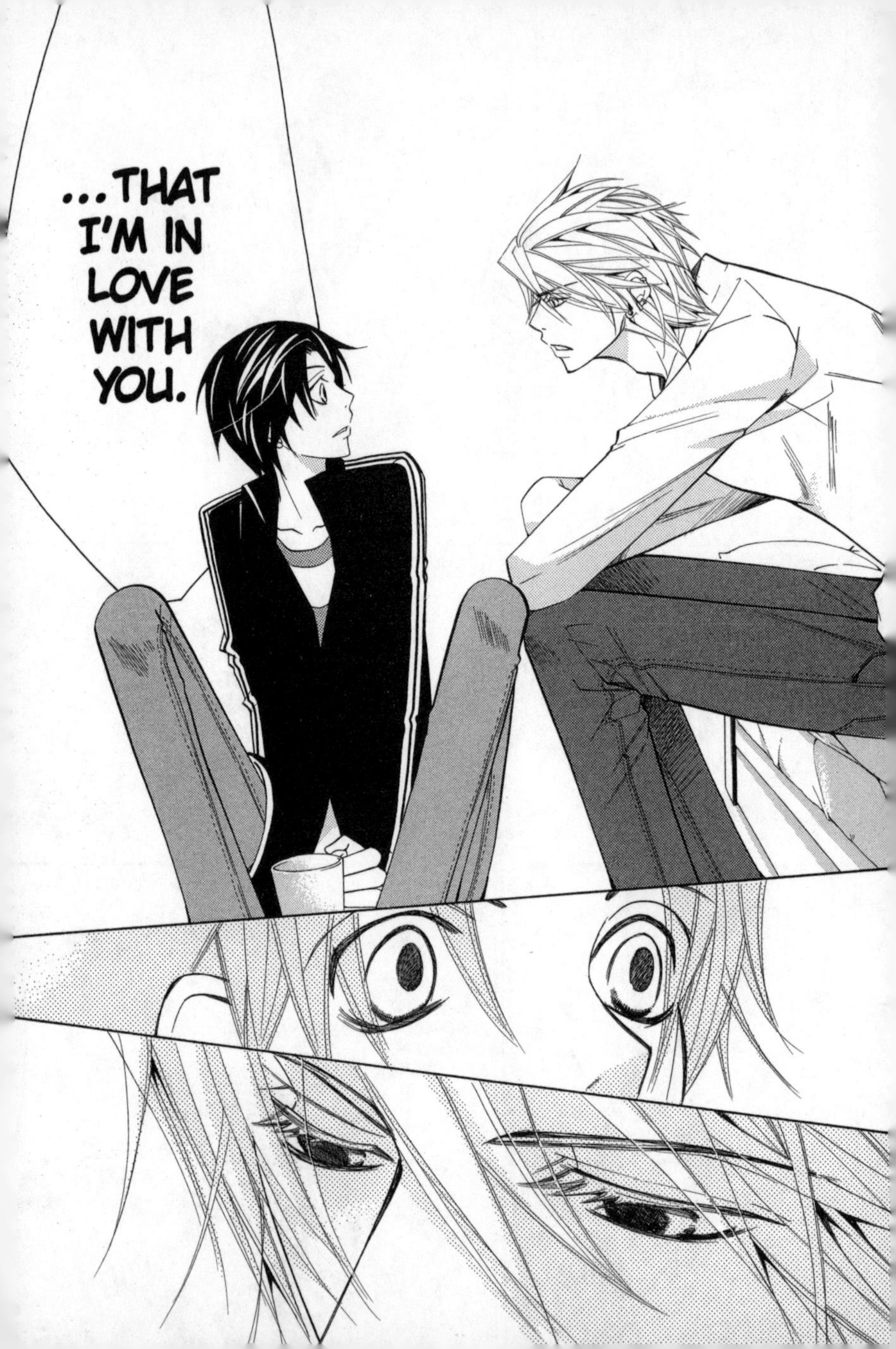
...THAT I'M IN LOVE WITH YOU.

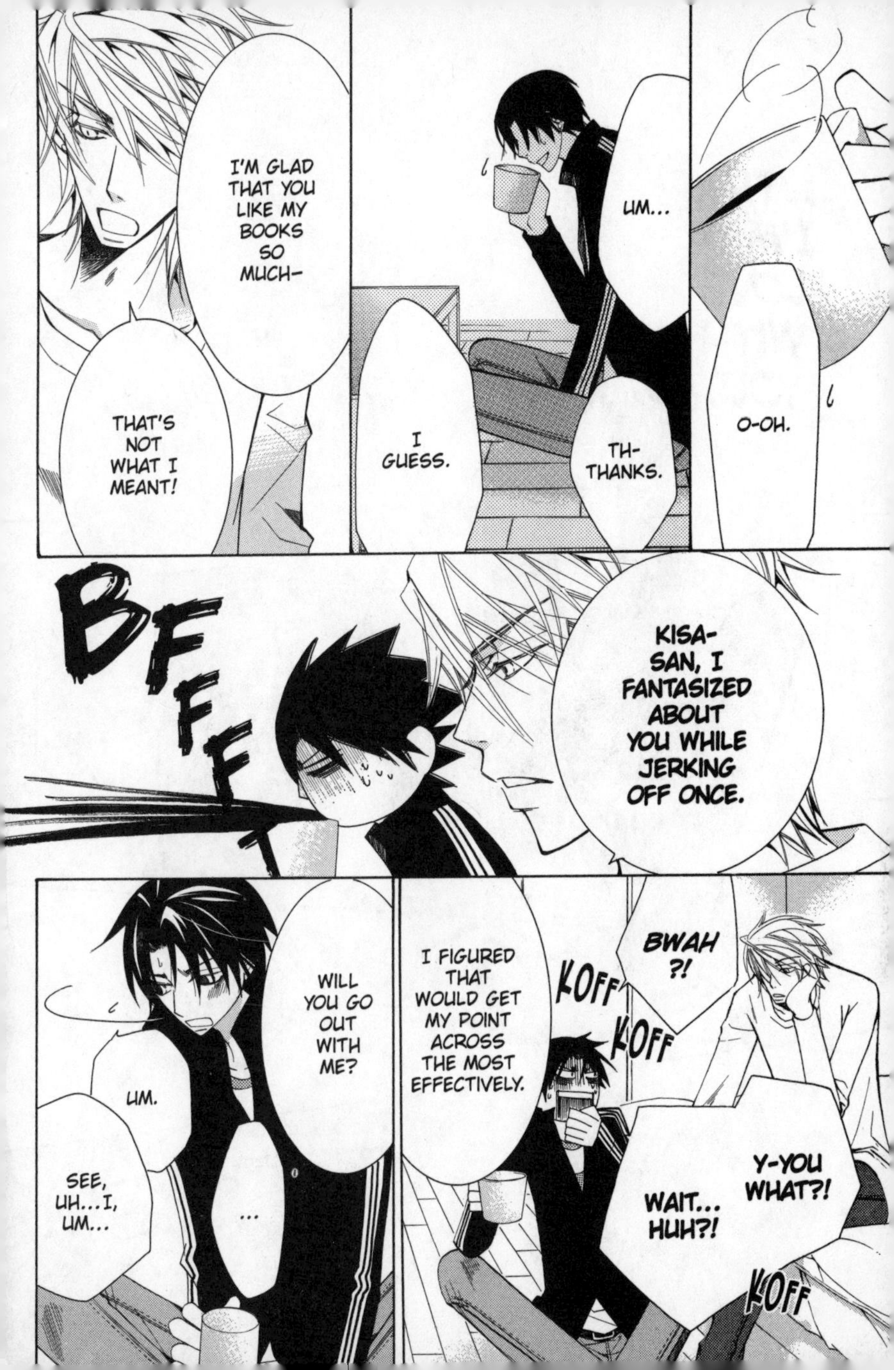
O-OH.
UM...
TH- THANKS.
I GUESS.
I'M GLAD THAT YOU LIKE MY BOOKS SO MUCH-
THAT'S NOT WHAT I MEANT!
KISA-SAN, I FANTASIZED ABOUT YOU WHILE JERKING OFF ONCE.
BFFF
BWAH ?!
KOFF
KOFF
I FIGURED THAT WOULD GET MY POINT ACROSS THE MOST EFFECTIVELY.
Y-YOU WHAT?!
WAIT... HUH?!
KOFF
WILL YOU GO OUT WITH ME?
UM.
...
SEE, UH...I, UM...

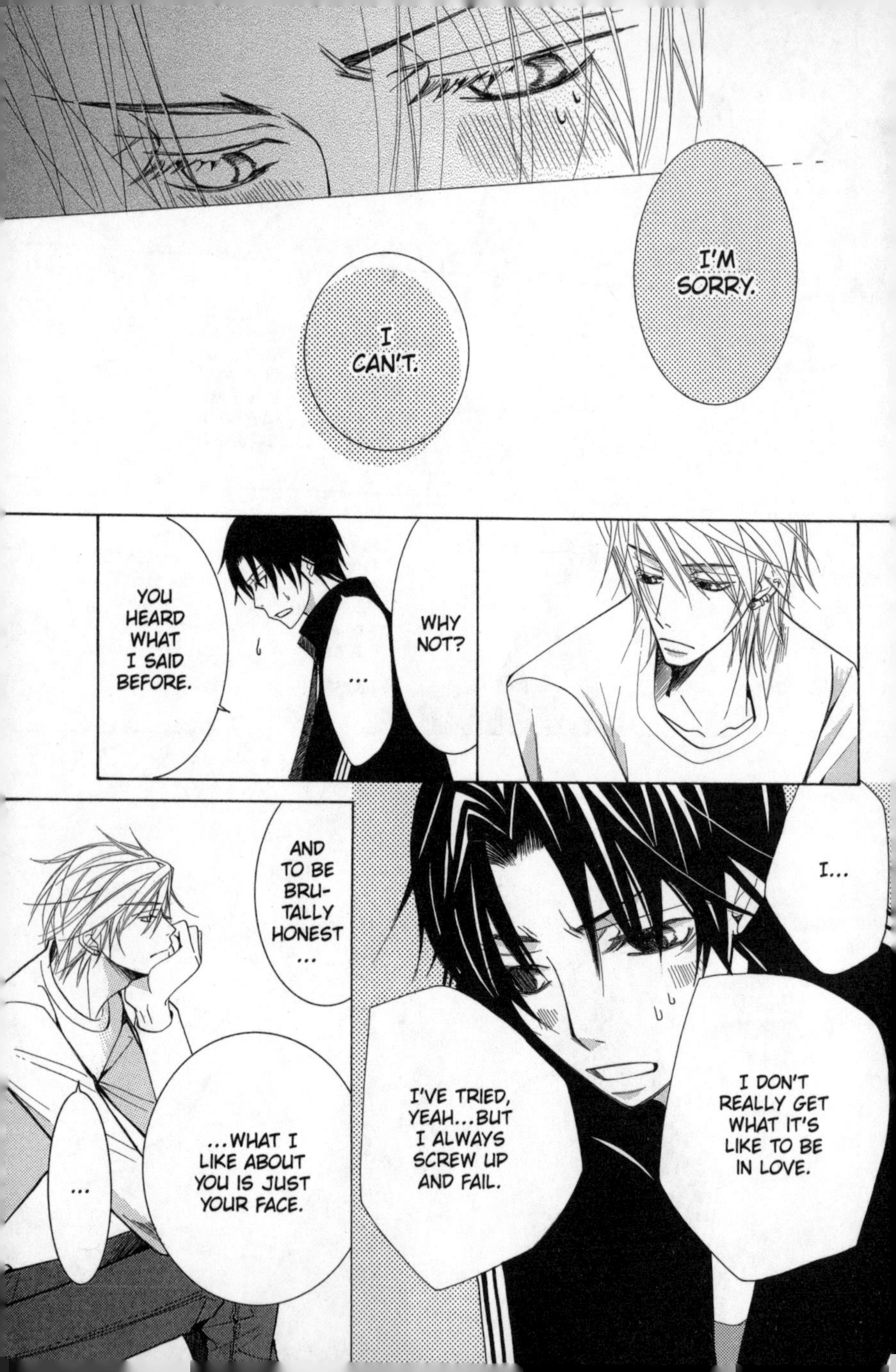
I'M SORRY.
I CAN'T.
WHY NOT?
...
YOU HEARD WHAT I SAID BEFORE.
I...
I DON'T REALLY GET WHAT IT'S LIKE TO BE IN LOVE.
I'VE TRIED, YEAH...BUT I ALWAYS SCREW UP AND FAIL.
AND TO BE BRU-TALLY HONEST...
...WHAT I LIKE ABOUT YOU IS JUST YOUR FACE.
...

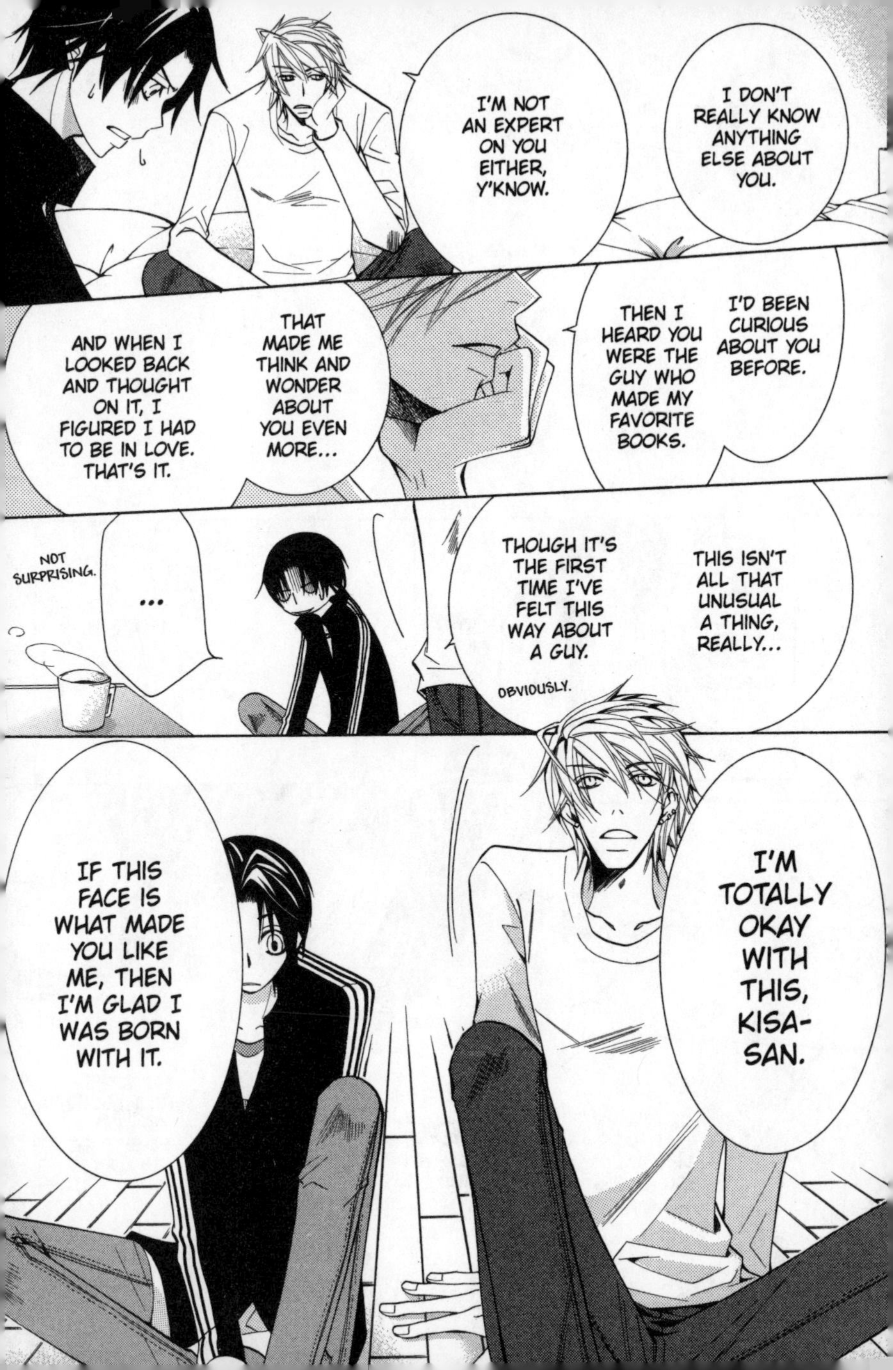
I DON'T REALLY KNOW ANYTHING ELSE ABOUT YOU.
I'M NOT AN EXPERT ON YOU EITHER, Y'KNOW.
I'D BEEN CURIOUS ABOUT YOU BEFORE.
THEN I HEARD YOU WERE THE GUY WHO MADE MY FAVORITE BOOKS.
THAT MADE ME THINK AND WONDER ABOUT YOU EVEN MORE...
AND WHEN I LOOKED BACK AND THOUGHT ON IT, I FIGURED I HAD TO BE IN LOVE. THAT'S IT.
THIS ISN'T ALL THAT UNUSUAL A THING, REALLY...
THOUGH IT'S THE FIRST TIME I'VE FELT THIS WAY ABOUT A GUY.
OBVIOUSLY.
...
NOT SURPRISING.
I'M TOTALLY OKAY WITH THIS, KISA-SAN.
IF THIS FACE IS WHAT MADE YOU LIKE ME, THEN I'M GLAD I WAS BORN WITH IT.

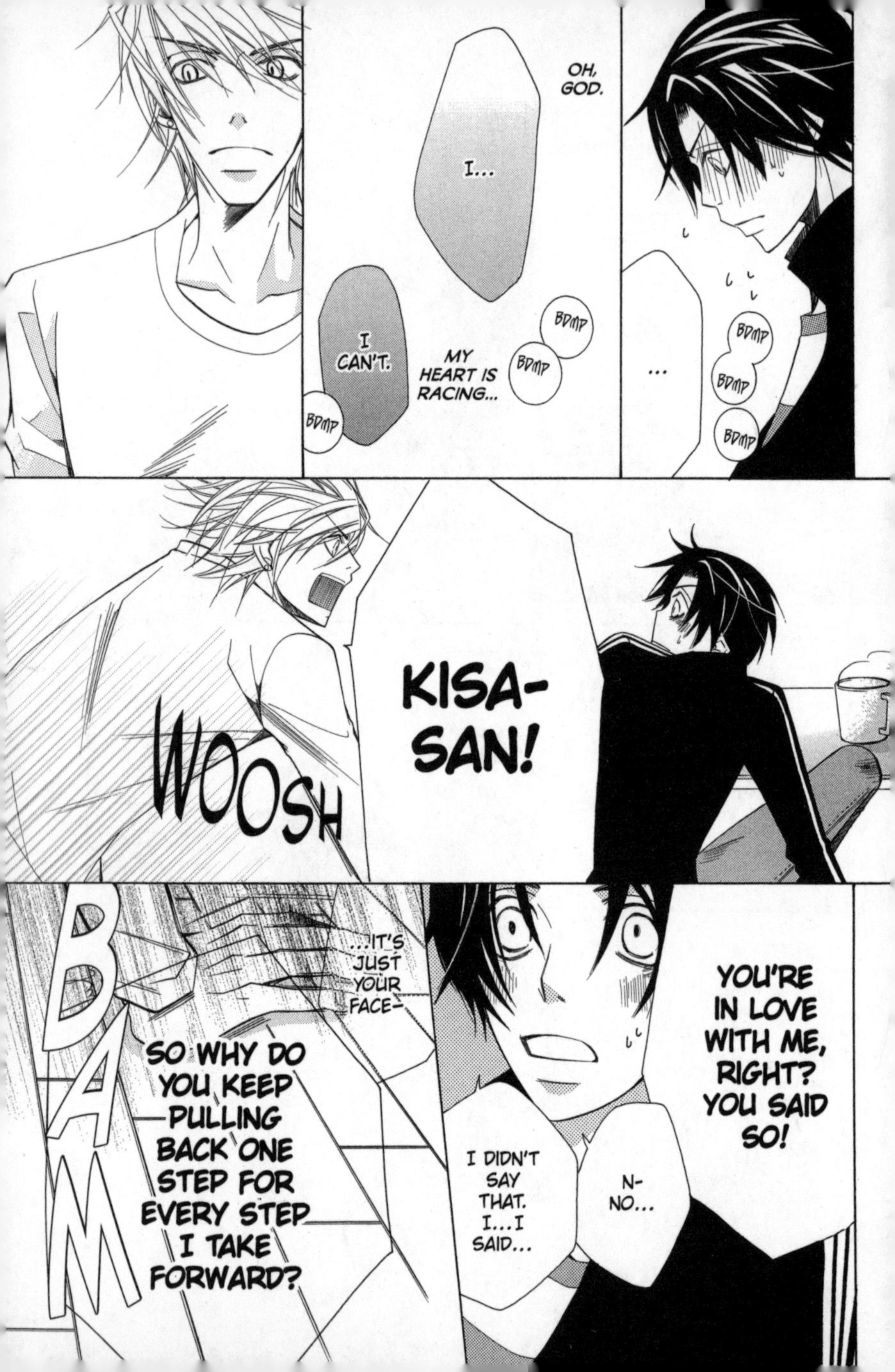
...
BDMP
BDMP
BDMP
OH, GOD.
BDMP
BDMP
I...
MY HEART IS RACING...
I CAN'T.
BDMP
KISA-SAN!
WOOSH
YOU'RE IN LOVE WITH ME, RIGHT? YOU SAID SO!
N-NO...
I DIDN'T SAY THAT. I...I SAID...
...IT'S JUST YOUR FACE-
SO WHY DO YOU KEEP PULLING BACK ONE STEP FOR EVERY STEP I TAKE FORWARD?
BAM

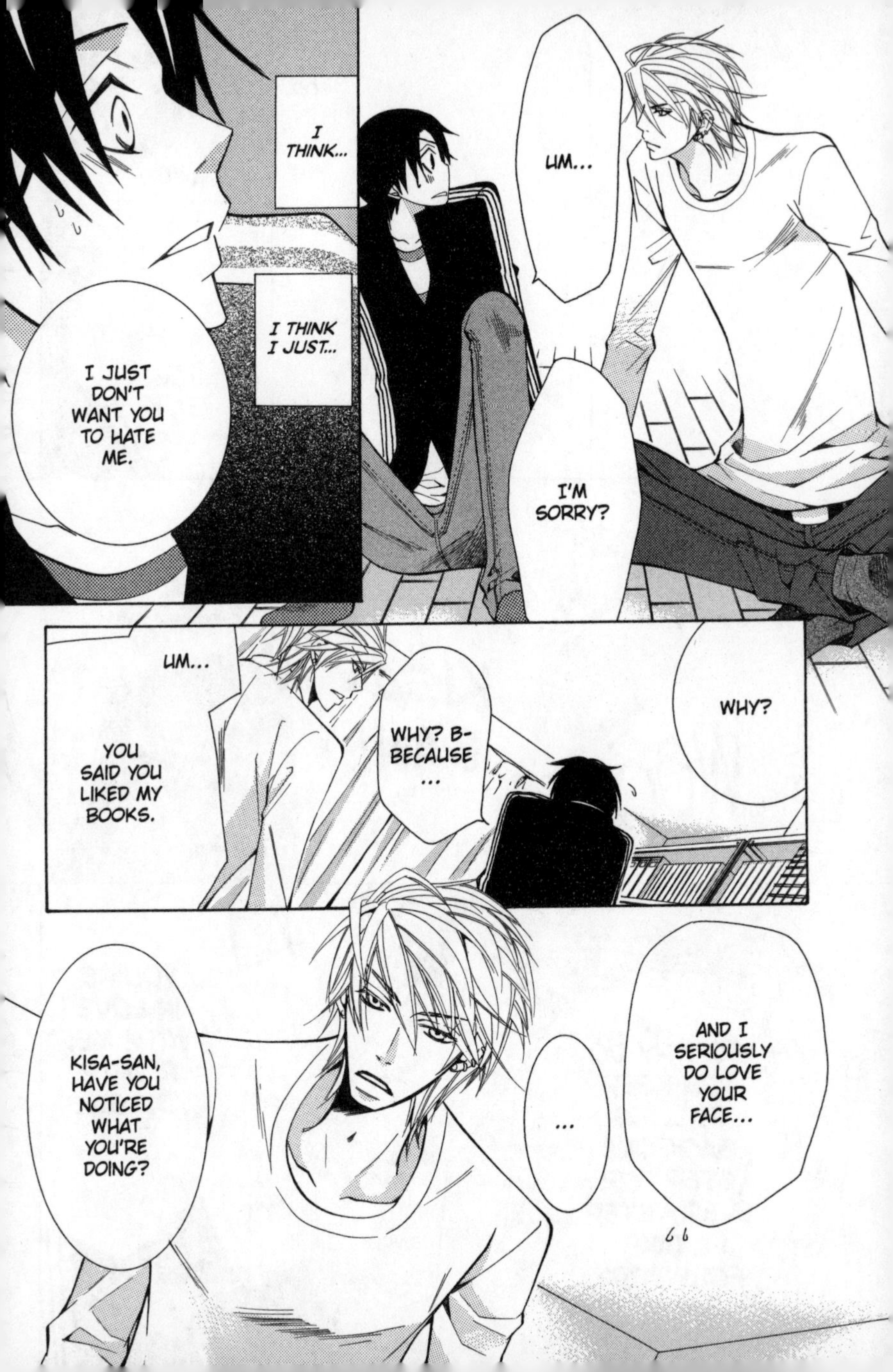
UM...
I'M SORRY?
I THINK...
I THINK I JUST...
I JUST DON'T WANT YOU TO HATE ME.
WHY?
WHY? B-BECAUSE ...
UM...
YOU SAID YOU LIKED MY BOOKS.
AND I SERIOUSLY DO LOVE YOUR FACE...
...
KISA-SAN, HAVE YOU NOTICED WHAT YOU'RE DOING?

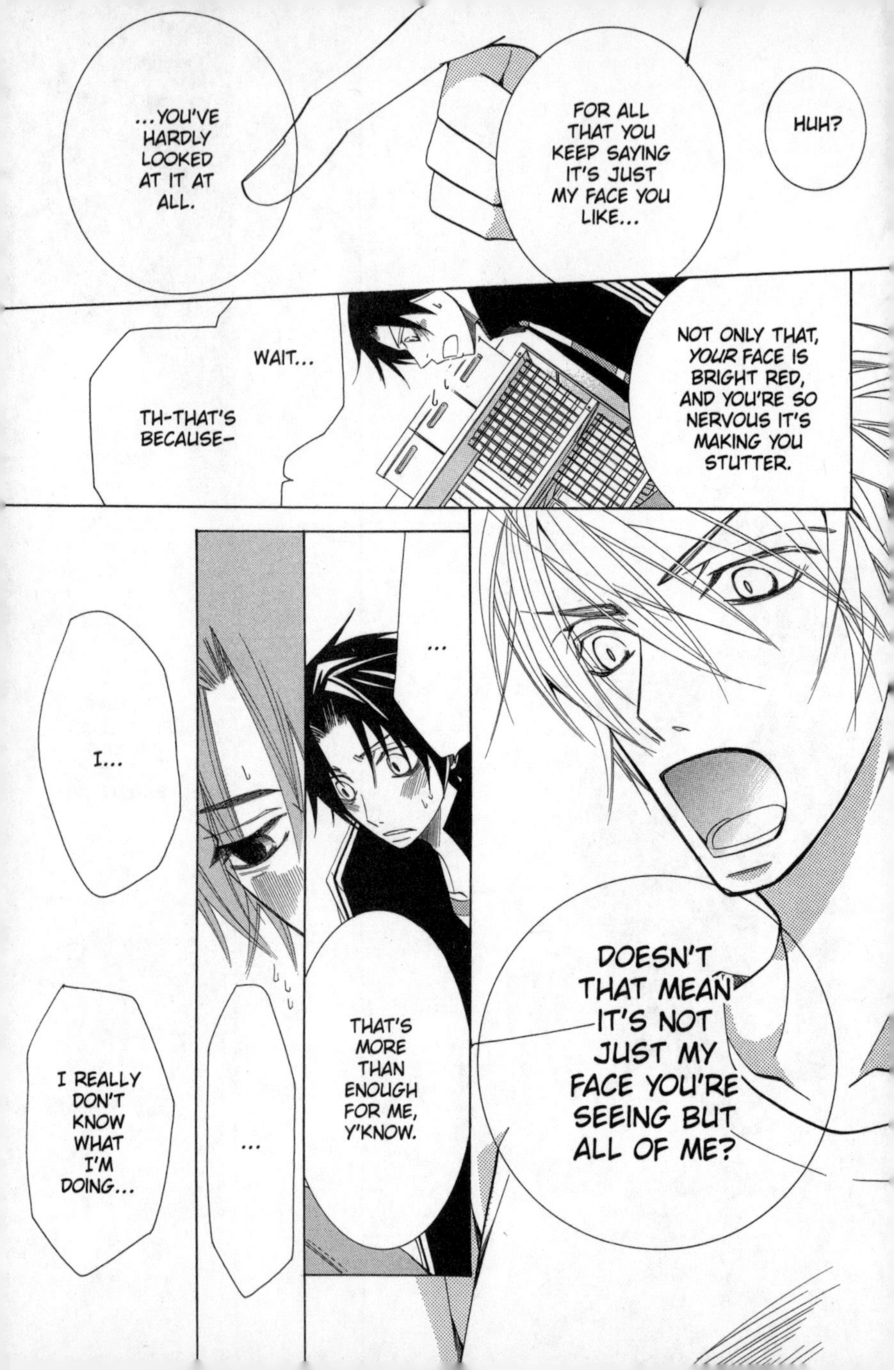
HUH?
FOR ALL THAT YOU KEEP SAYING IT'S JUST MY FACE YOU LIKE...
...YOU'VE HARDLY LOOKED AT IT AT ALL.
NOT ONLY THAT, *YOUR* FACE IS BRIGHT RED, AND YOU'RE SO NERVOUS IT'S MAKING YOU STUTTER.
WAIT...
TH-THAT'S BECAUSE-
DOESN'T THAT MEAN IT'S NOT JUST MY FACE YOU'RE SEEING BUT ALL OF ME?
...
THAT'S MORE THAN ENOUGH FOR ME, Y'KNOW.
I...
...
I REALLY DON'T KNOW WHAT I'M DOING...

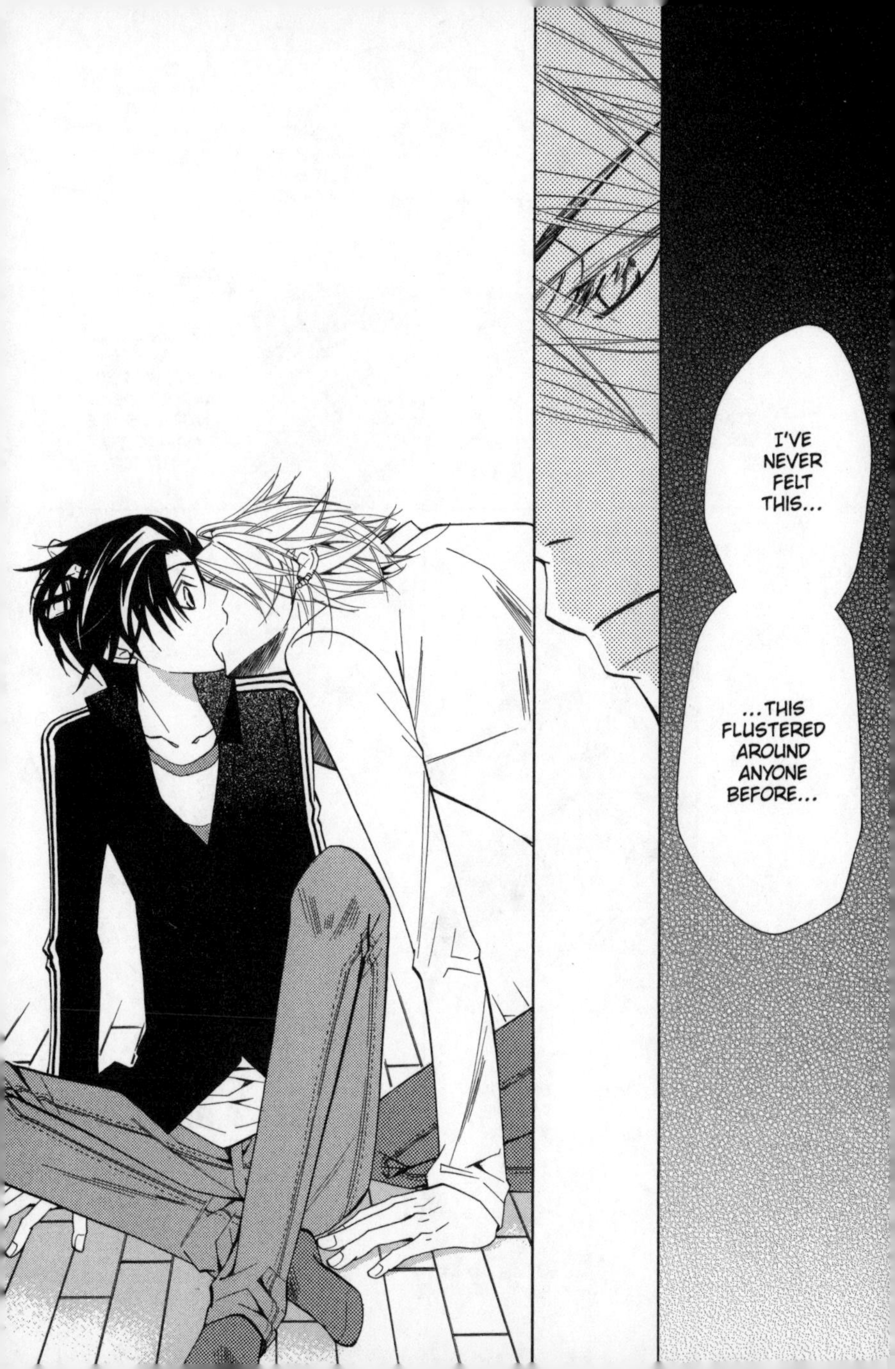
I'VE NEVER FELT THIS...
...THIS FLUSTERED AROUND ANYONE BEFORE...

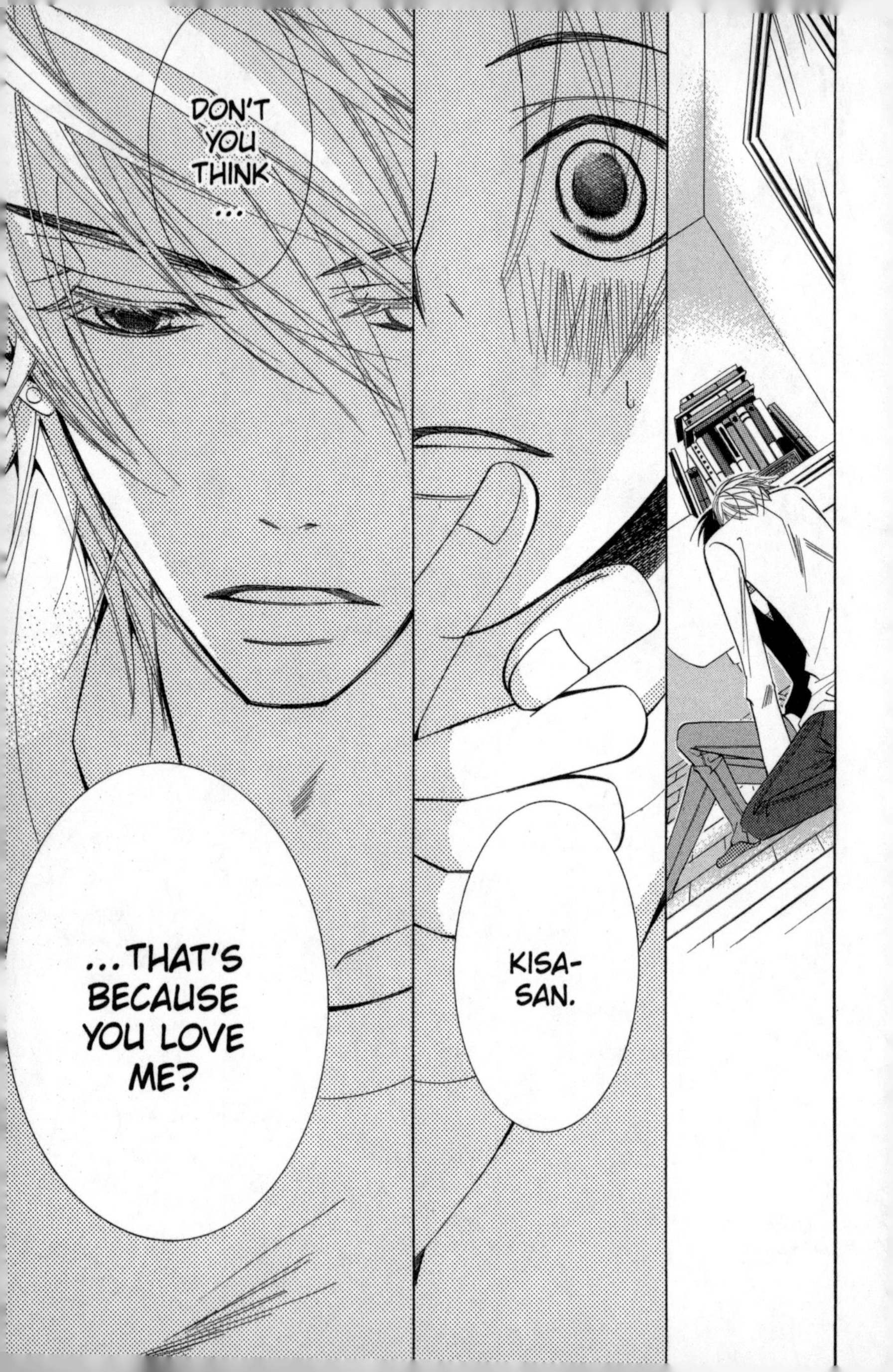
KISA-SAN.
DON'T YOU THINK ...
...THAT'S BECAUSE YOU LOVE ME?

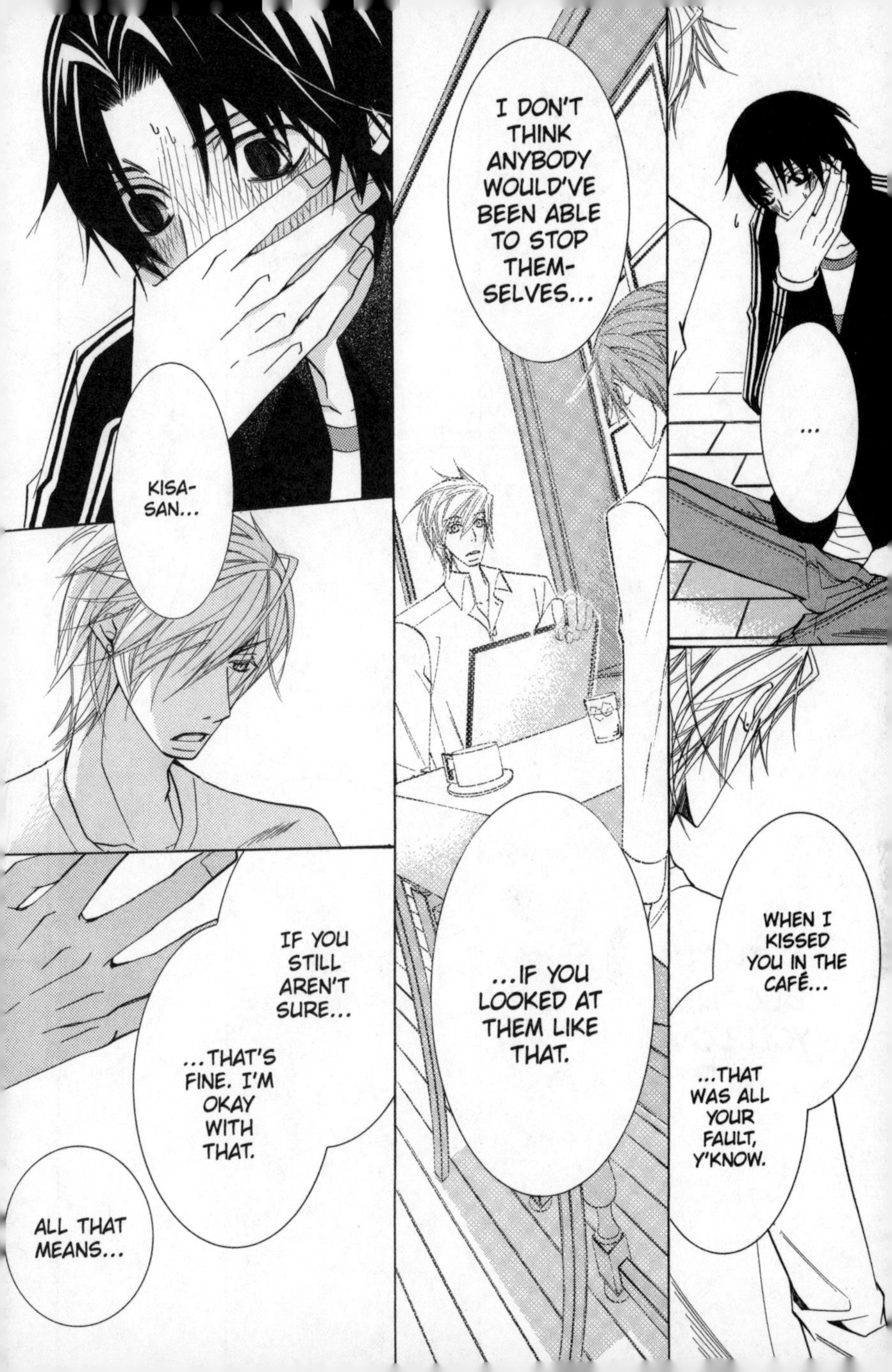
...
WHEN I KISSED YOU IN THE CAFÉ...
...THAT WAS ALL YOUR FAULT, Y'KNOW.
I DON'T THINK ANYBODY WOULD'VE BEEN ABLE TO STOP THEMSELVES...
...IF YOU LOOKED AT THEM LIKE THAT.
KISA-SAN...
IF YOU STILL AREN'T SURE...
...THAT'S FINE. I'M OKAY WITH THAT.
ALL THAT MEANS...

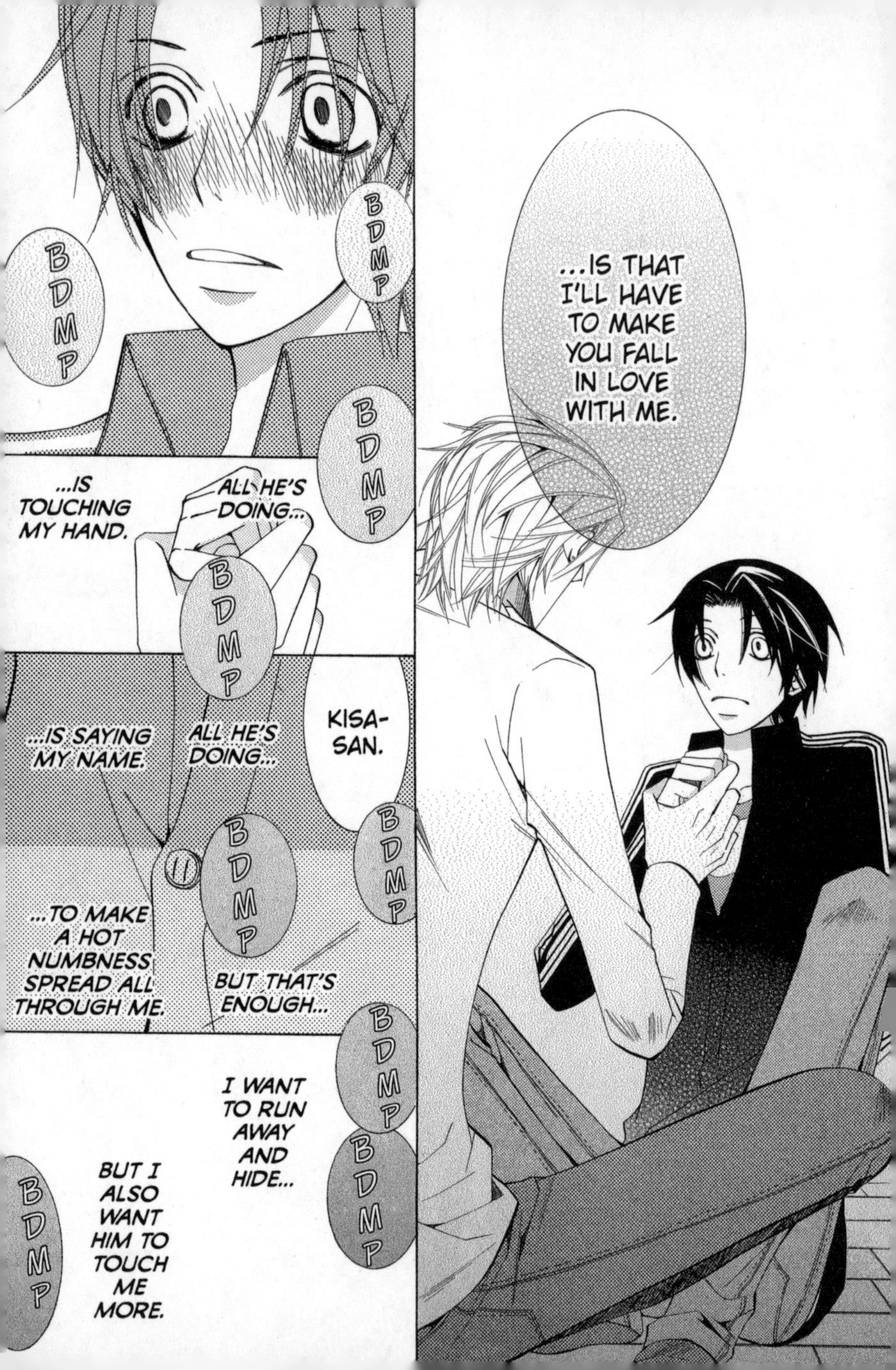
...IS THAT I'LL HAVE TO MAKE YOU FALL IN LOVE WITH ME.
BDMP
BDMP
BDMP
ALL HE'S DOING...
...IS TOUCHING MY HAND.
BDMP
KISA-SAN.
ALL HE'S DOING...
...IS SAYING MY NAME.
BDMP
BDMP
BUT THAT'S ENOUGH...
...TO MAKE A HOT NUMBNESS SPREAD ALL THROUGH ME.
BDMP
I WANT TO RUN AWAY AND HIDE...
BDMP
BUT I ALSO WANT HIM TO TOUCH ME MORE.
BDMP

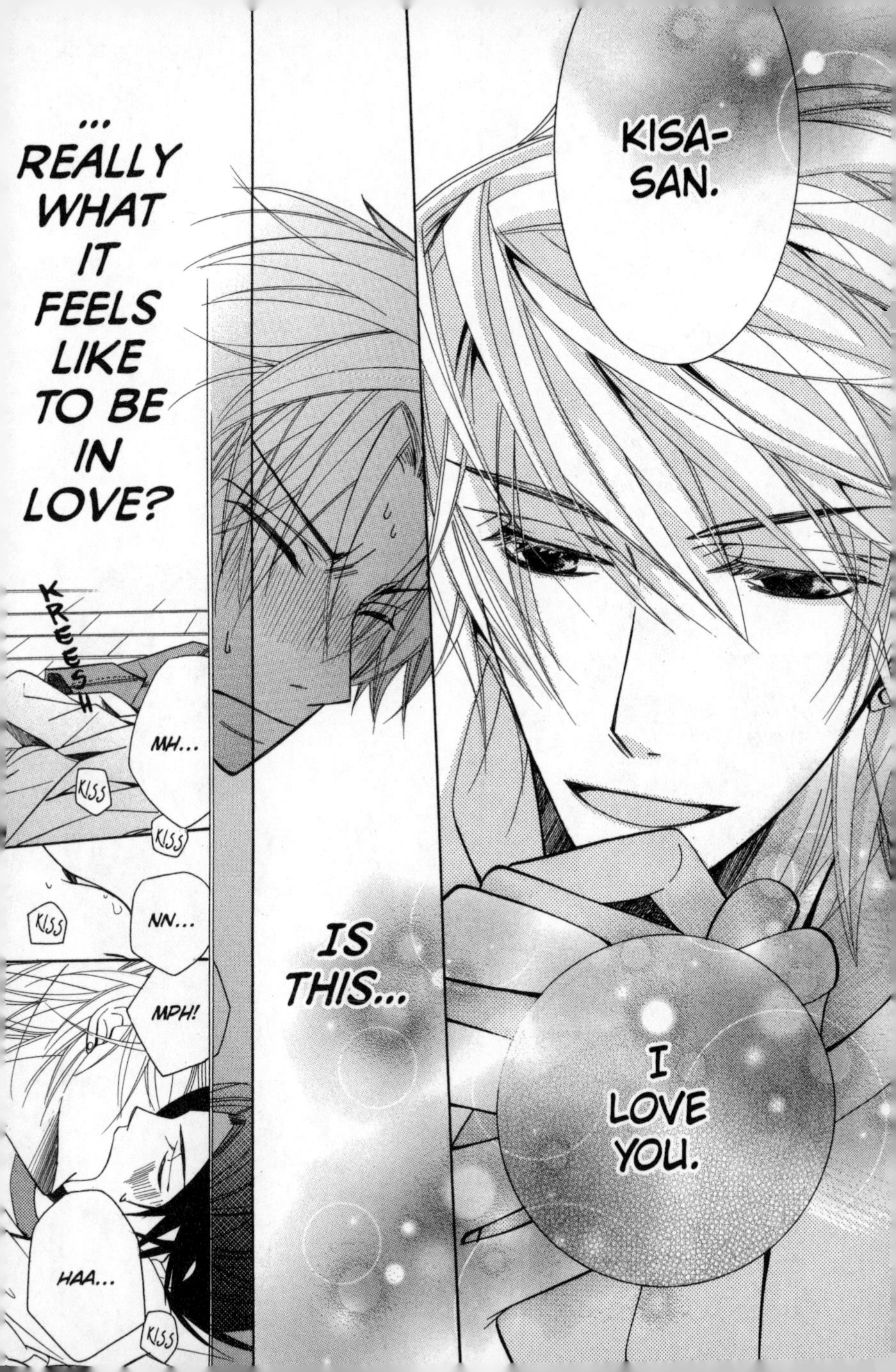
KISA-SAN.
I LOVE YOU.
IS THIS...
...REALLY WHAT IT FEELS LIKE TO BE IN LOVE?
KREESH
MH...
KISS
KISS
NN...
KISS
MPH!
HAA...
KISS

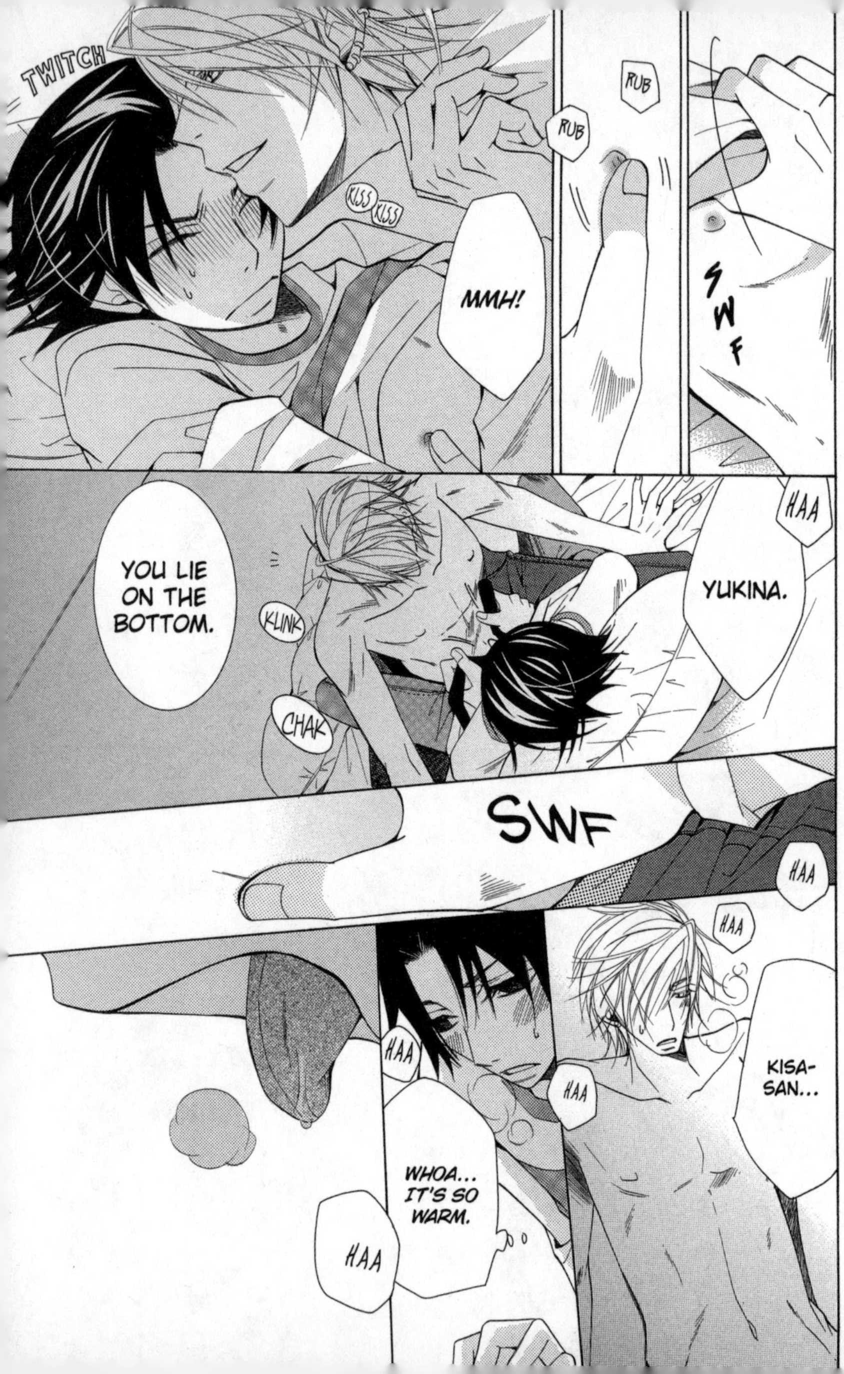
SWF
RUB
RUB
TWITCH
KISS
KISS
MMH!
HAA
YUKINA.
YOU LIE ON THE BOTTOM.
KLINK
CHAK
SWF
HAA
HAA
KISA-SAN...
HAA
HAA
WHOA... IT'S SO WARM.
HAA

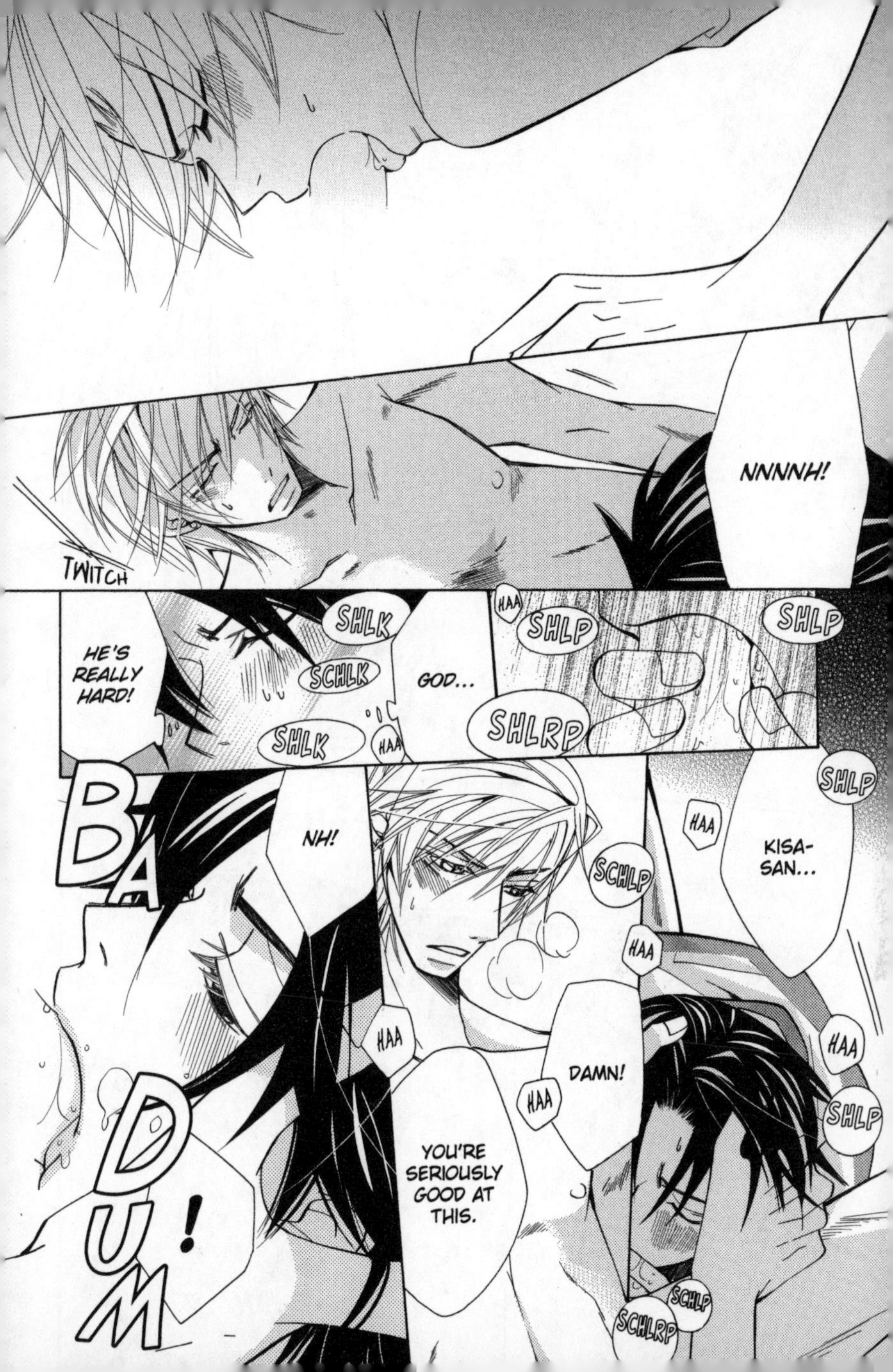
NNNNH!
TWITCH
HAA
SHLP
SHLP
SHLRP
SHLK
GOD...
SCHLK
HE'S REALLY HARD!
HAA
SHLK
SHLP
HAA
KISA-SAN...
SCHLP
NH!
BA
HAA
HAA
SHLP
DAMN!
HAA
HAA
YOU'RE SERIOUSLY GOOD AT THIS.
SCHLP
SCHLRP
DUM!

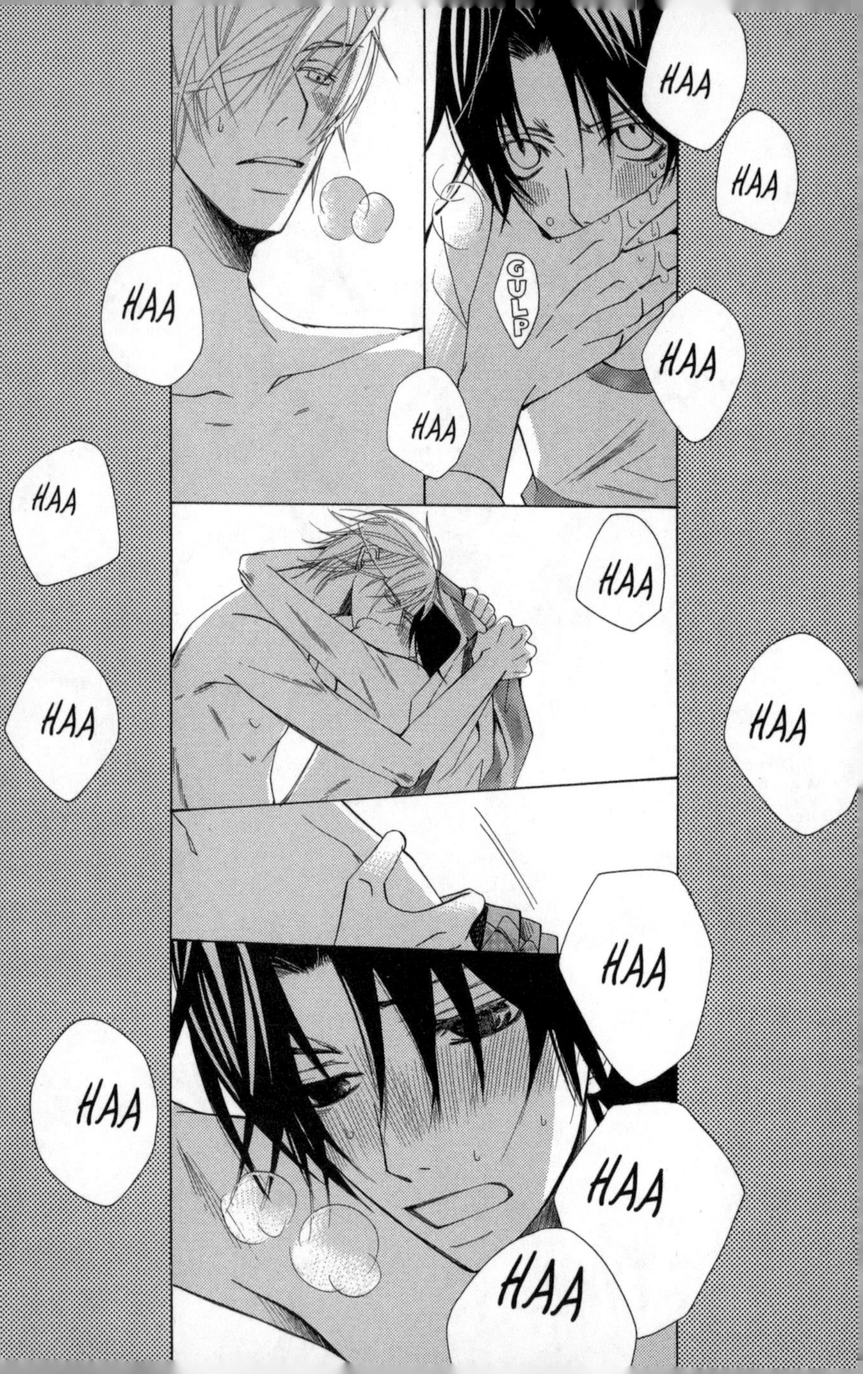
HAA
HAA
GULP
HAA
HAA
HAA
HAA
HAA
HAA
HAA
HAA
HAA
HAA
HAA

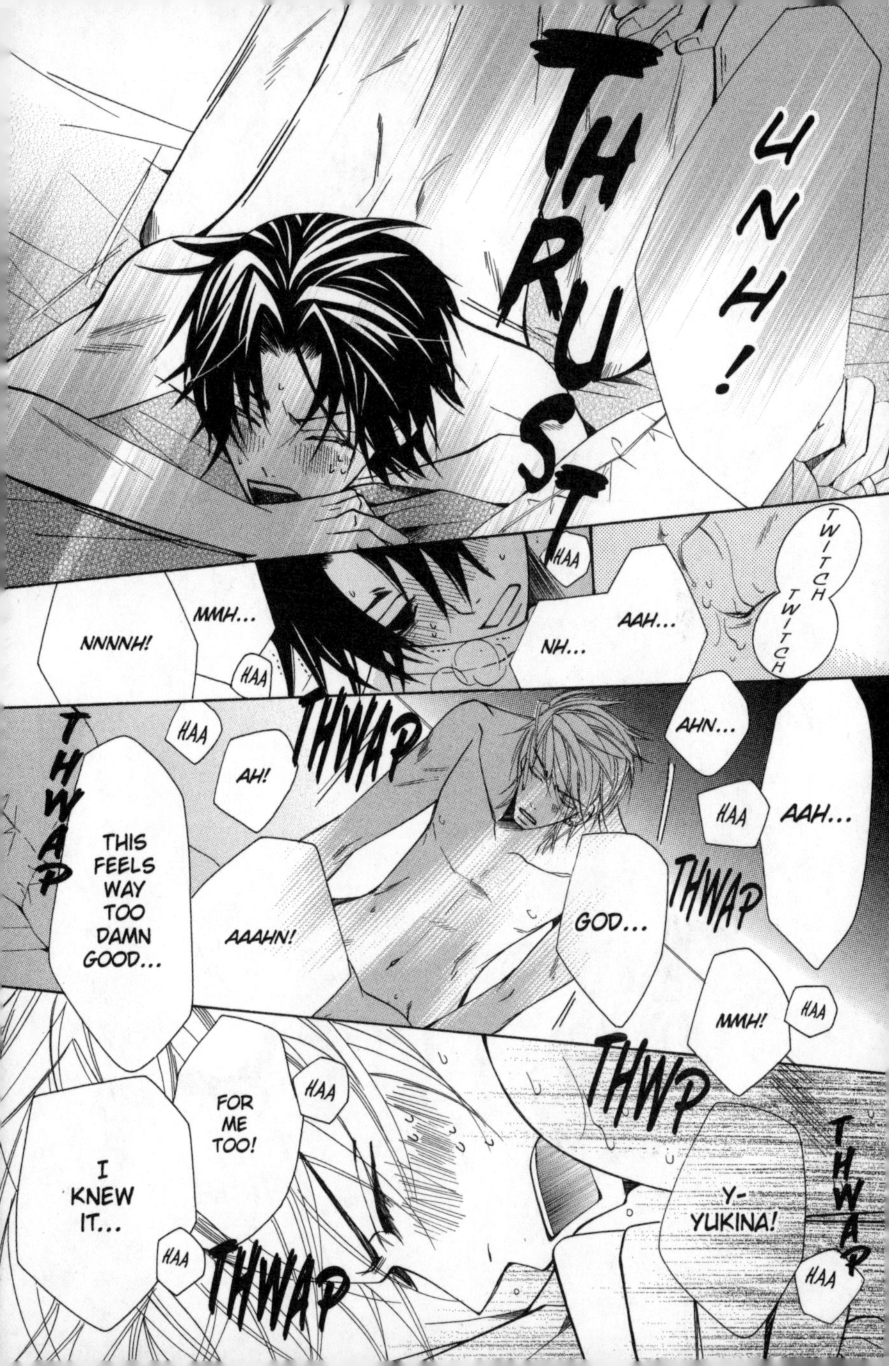
UNNH!
THRUST
TWITCH TWITCH
HAA
AAH...
NH...
MMH...
HAA
NNNNH!
AHN...
AAH...
HAA
THWAP
GOD...
THWAP
HAA
AH!
AAAHN!
THWAP
THIS FEELS WAY TOO DAMN GOOD...
HAA
MMH!
THWP
THWAP
Y-YUKINA!
HAA
HAA
FOR ME TOO!
I KNEW IT...
HAA
THWAP

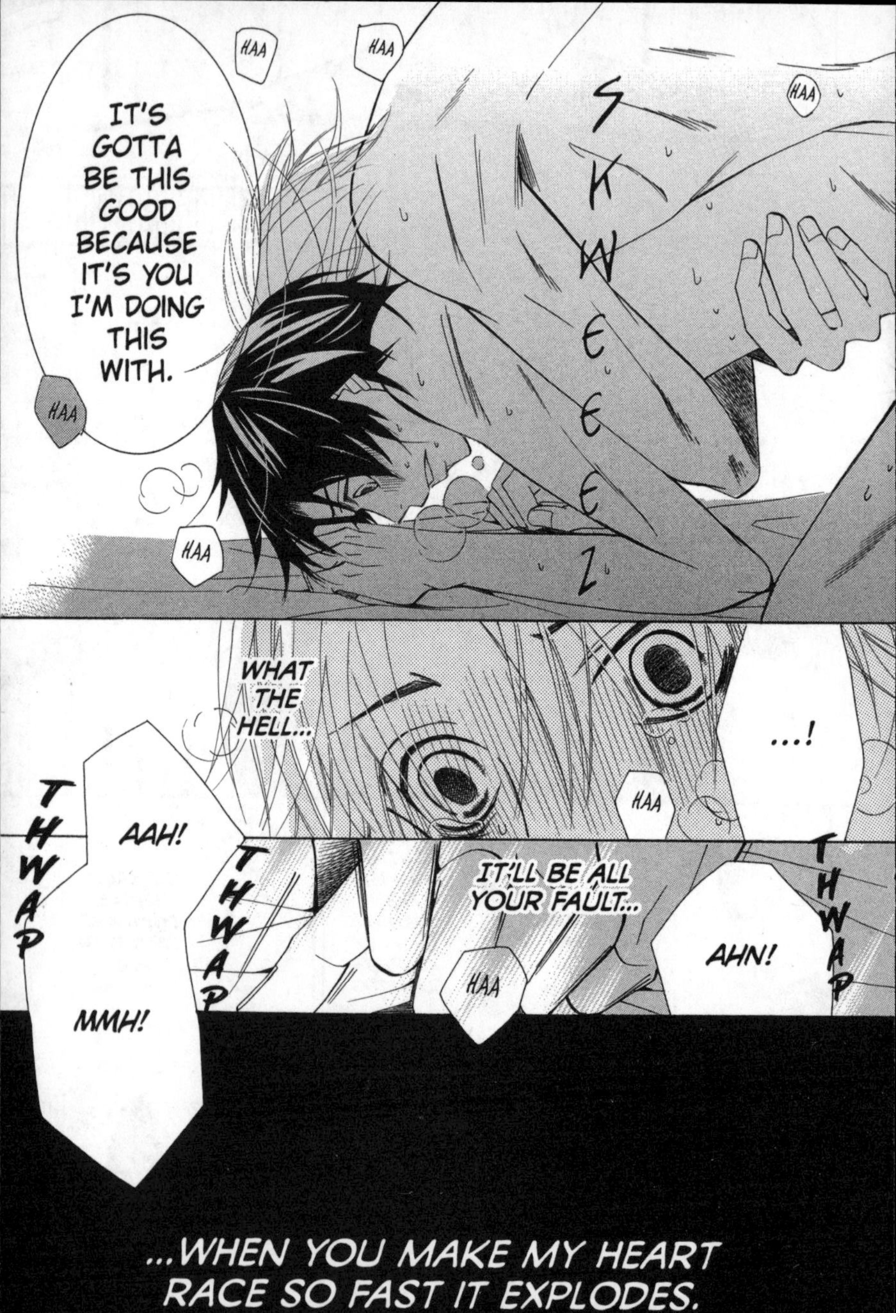
HAA
SKWEEEZ
HAA
HAA
IT'S GOTTA BE THIS GOOD BECAUSE IT'S YOU I'M DOING THIS WITH.
HAA
HAA
...!
HAA
WHAT THE HELL...
THWAP
AHN!
IT'LL BE ALL YOUR FAULT...
HAA
THWAP
AAH!
MMH!
THWAP
...WHEN YOU MAKE MY HEART RACE SO FAST IT EXPLODES.

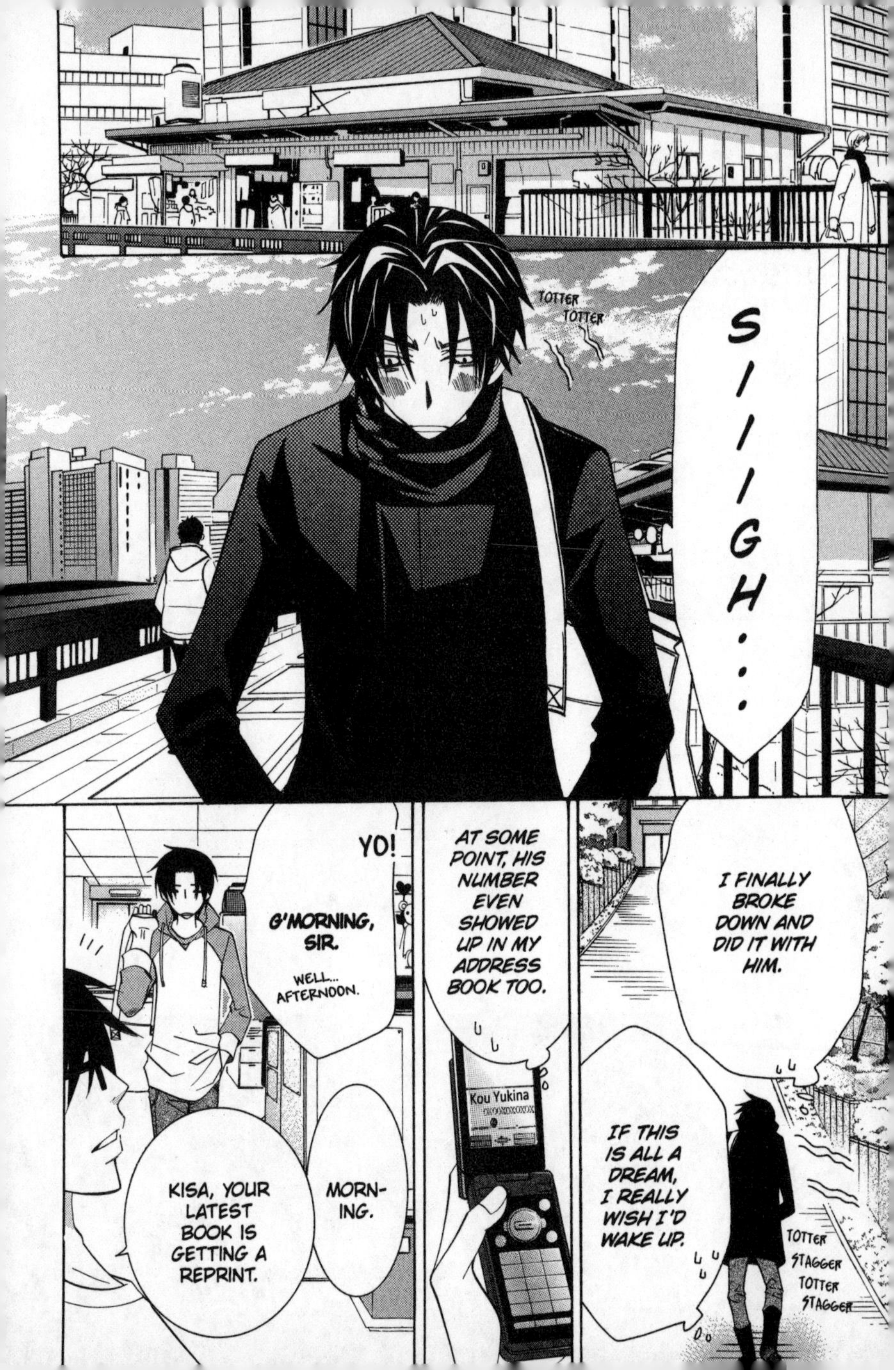
SIIIGH...
TOTTER TOTTER
I FINALLY BROKE DOWN AND DID IT WITH HIM.
IF THIS IS ALL A DREAM, I REALLY WISH I'D WAKE UP.
TOTTER STAGGER TOTTER STAGGER
AT SOME POINT, HIS NUMBER EVEN SHOWED UP IN MY ADDRESS BOOK TOO.
Kou Yukina
YO!
G'MORNING, SIR.
WELL... AFTERNOON.
MORN-ING.
KISA, YOUR LATEST BOOK IS GETTING A REPRINT.

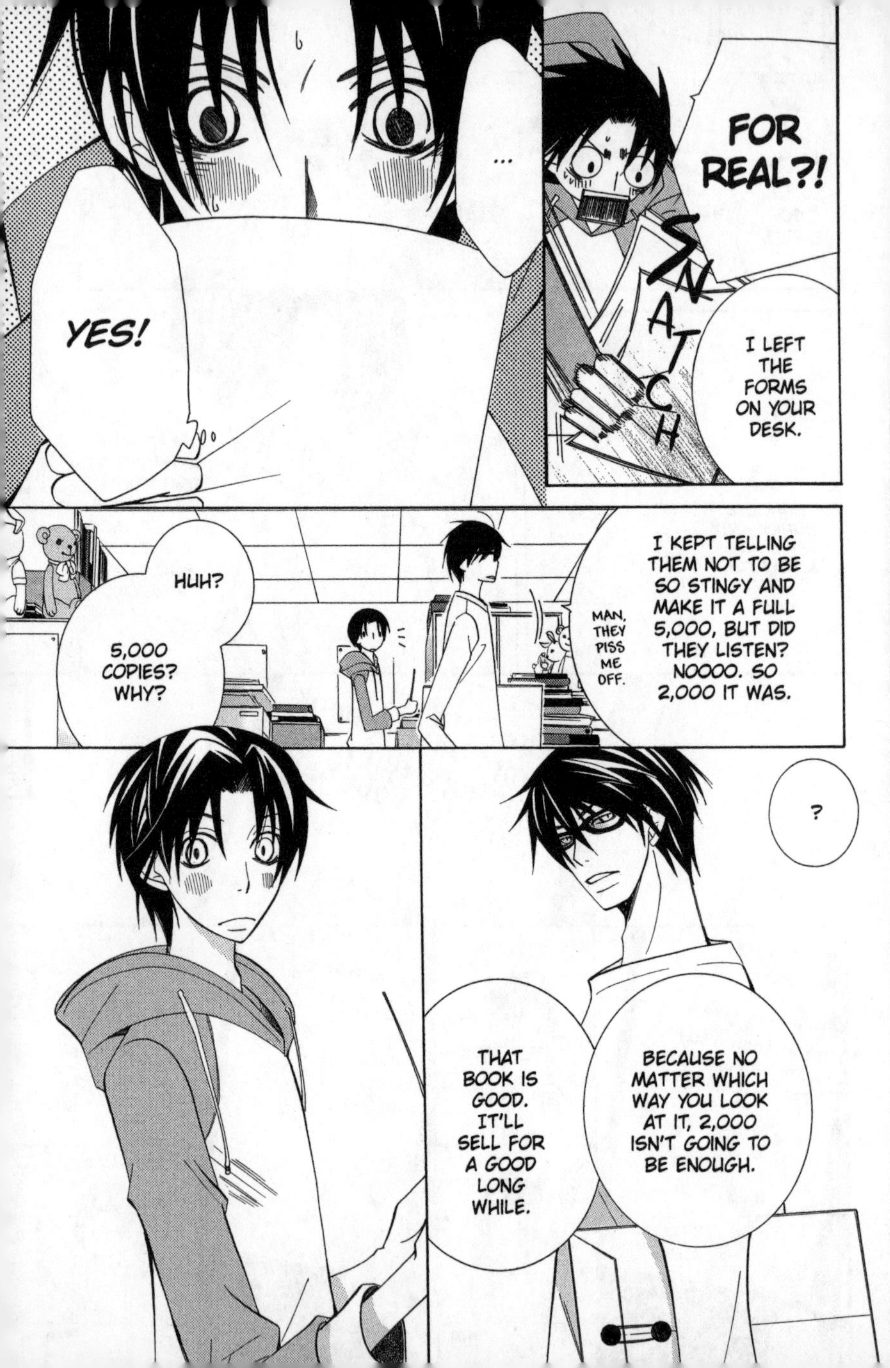
FOR REAL?!
SNATCH
I LEFT THE FORMS ON YOUR DESK.
...
YES!
I KEPT TELLING THEM NOT TO BE SO STINGY AND MAKE IT A FULL 5,000, BUT DID THEY LISTEN? NOOOO. SO 2,000 IT WAS.
MAN, THEY PISS ME OFF.
HUH?
5,000 COPIES? WHY?
?
BECAUSE NO MATTER WHICH WAY YOU LOOK AT IT, 2,000 ISN'T GOING TO BE ENOUGH.
THAT BOOK IS GOOD. IT'LL SELL FOR A GOOD LONG WHILE.

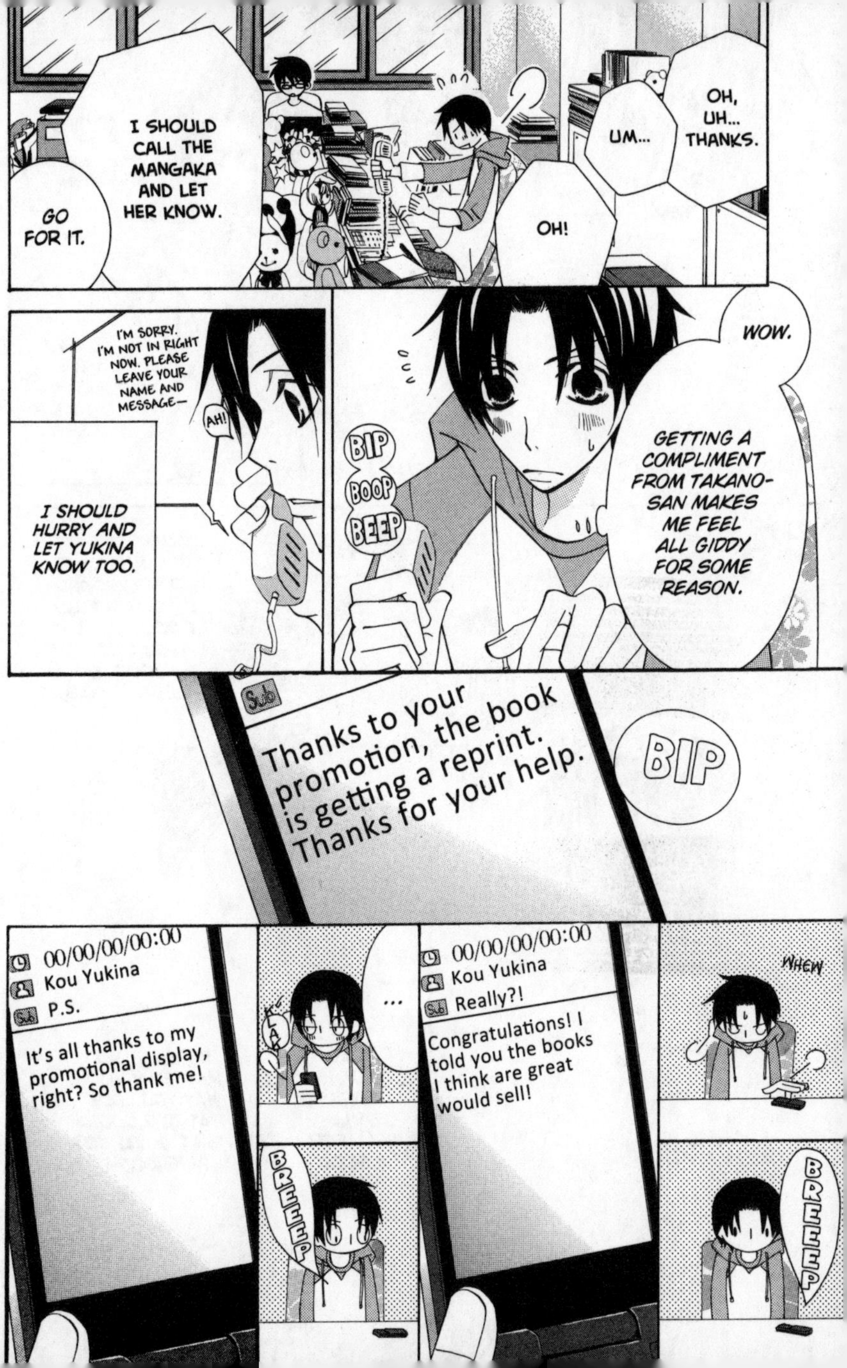
OH, UH... THANKS.
UM...
OH!
I SHOULD CALL THE MANGAKA AND LET HER KNOW.
GO FOR IT.
WOW.
GETTING A COMPLIMENT FROM TAKANO-SAN MAKES ME FEEL ALL GIDDY FOR SOME REASON.
BIP
BOOP
BEEP
I'M SORRY. I'M NOT IN RIGHT NOW. PLEASE LEAVE YOUR NAME AND MESSAGE—
AH!
I SHOULD HURRY AND LET YUKINA KNOW TOO.
BIP
Sub
Thanks to your promotion, the book is getting a reprint. Thanks for your help.
WHEW
BREEEP
00/00/00/00:00
Kou Yukina
Sub Really?!
Congratulations! I told you the books I think are great would sell!
...
KLAK
BREEEP
00/00/00/00:00
Kou Yukina
Sub P.S.
It's all thanks to my promotional display, right? So thank me!

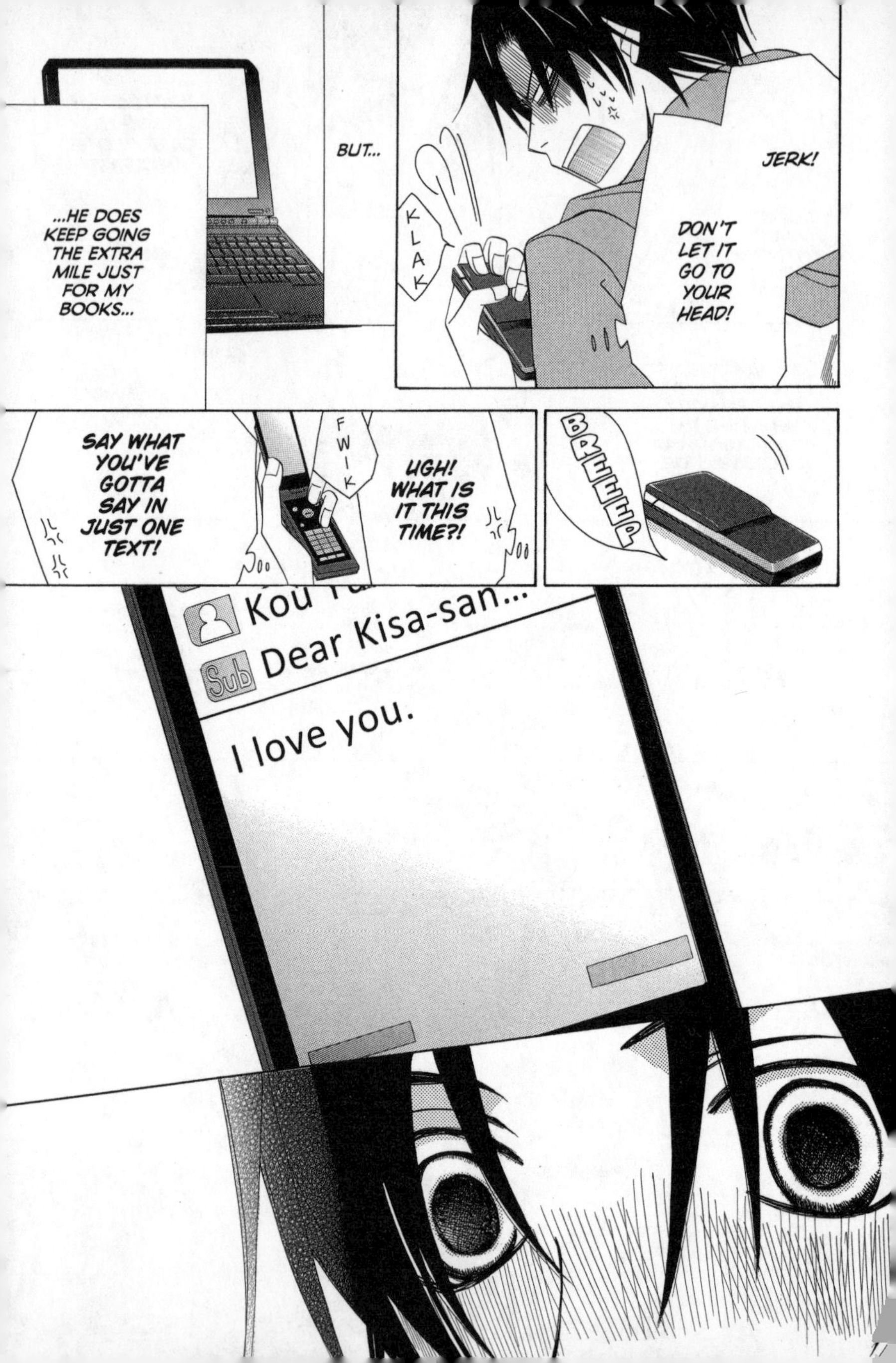
JERK!
DON'T LET IT GO TO YOUR HEAD!
KLAK
BUT...
...HE DOES KEEP GOING THE EXTRA MILE JUST FOR MY BOOKS...
BREEEP
UGH! WHAT IS IT THIS TIME?!
FWIK
SAY WHAT YOU'VE GOTTA SAY IN JUST ONE TEXT!
Sub Dear Kisa-san...
I love you.

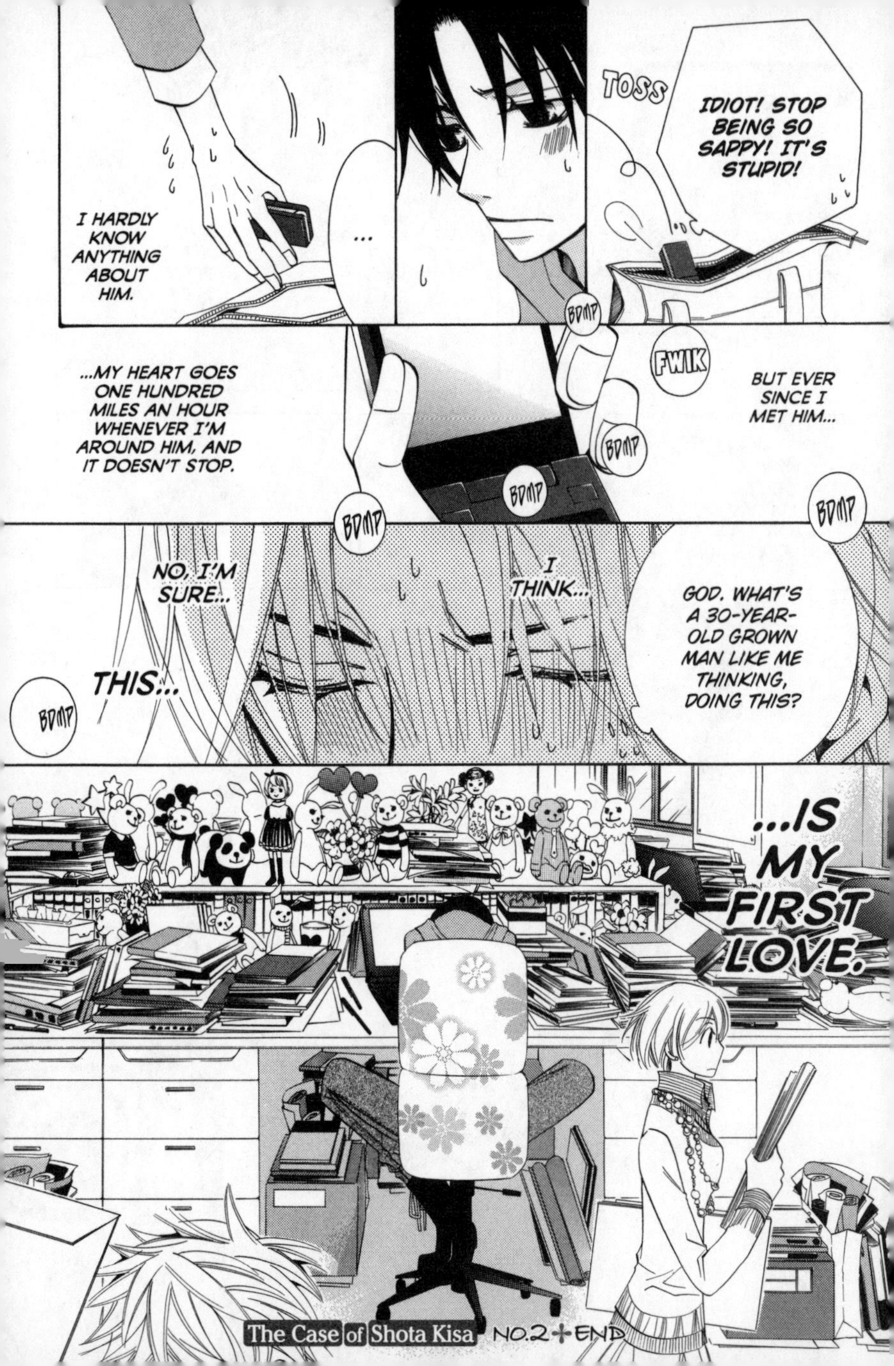
TOSS
IDIOT! STOP BEING SO SAPPY! IT'S STUPID!
...
BDMP
I HARDLY KNOW ANYTHING ABOUT HIM.
BUT EVER SINCE I MET HIM...
FWIK
BDMP
BDMP
...MY HEART GOES ONE HUNDRED MILES AN HOUR WHENEVER I'M AROUND HIM, AND IT DOESN'T STOP.
BDMP
BDMP
GOD. WHAT'S A 30-YEAR-OLD GROWN MAN LIKE ME THINKING, DOING THIS?
I THINK...
NO, I'M SURE...
THIS...
BDMP
...IS MY FIRST LOVE.
The Case of Shota Kisa NO.2 END

Hello. It's good to meet you! My name is Shungiku Nakamura. Thank you for buying Volume 3 of *The World's Greatest First Love ~The Case of Ritsu Onodera~*! Thanks to everyone's kind and generous support, we've made it up to Volume 3. Also, *Ruby Bunko* is releasing *The World's Greatest First Love ~The Case of Chiaki Yoshino~* Volume 3. If you're interested in that, please check it out. I would love to hear your thoughts and comments, so please send them in! This story will be continuing for some time yet. I hope you will continue reading.

See you!
2009
NAKAMURA

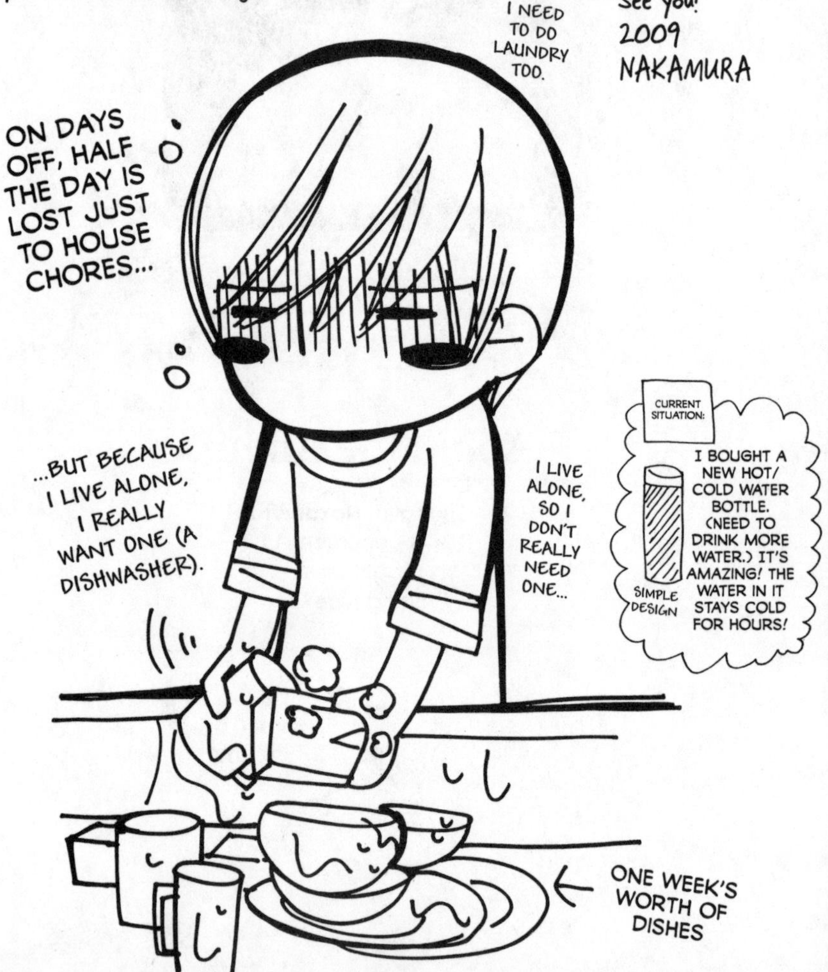
I NEED TO DO LAUNDRY TOO.
ON DAYS OFF, HALF THE DAY IS LOST JUST TO HOUSE CHORES...
CURRENT SITUATION:
I BOUGHT A NEW HOT/COLD WATER BOTTLE. (NEED TO DRINK MORE WATER.) IT'S AMAZING! THE WATER IN IT STAYS COLD FOR HOURS!
SIMPLE DESIGN
I LIVE ALONE, SO I DON'T REALLY NEED ONE...
...BUT BECAUSE I LIVE ALONE, I REALLY WANT ONE (A DISHWASHER).
ONE WEEK'S WORTH OF DISHES

Duck-shaped ice cubes. I took too long trying to take the picture, so they started to melt. Drat.

About the Author

Shungiku Nakamura
DOB December 13
Sagittarius
Blood Type O